The Early Works of John Dewey

1882–1898

John Dewey

The Early Works, 1882–1898

4: 1893–1894

Early Essays
and
The Study of Ethics
A Syllabus

Carbondale and Edwardsville

SOUTHERN ILLINOIS UNIVERSITY PRESS

FEFFER & SIMONS, INC.

London and Amsterdam

The Early Works of John Dewey, 1882–1898, *is the result of a co-operative research project at Southern Illinois University. Jo Ann Boydston is the General Editor, Fredson Bowers is Consulting Textual Editor. The Editorial Advisory Board consists of Lewis E. Hahn, Chairman; Joe R. Burnett; S. Morris Eames; William R. McKenzie; and Francis T. Villemain. Polly Dunn Williams is Staff Assistant.*

The text of this reprinting is a photo-offset reproduction of the original cloth edition which contains the full apparatus for the volume awarded the seal of the Center for Editions of American Authors of the Modern Language Association.

This paperbound edition has been made possible by a special subvention from The John Dewey Foundation.

Contents

Early Essays

The Study of Ethics: A Syllabus

APPENDIXES

Introduction

DEWEY'S PUBLICATIONS during 1893 and 1894 were addressed to students and teachers who were struggling with the scientific and evolutionary points of view against a background of Protestant theology. Whether speaking to Michigan undergraduates or to the readers of professional journals, Dewey seems to have thought of himself as a mediator. He was the exponent of a progressive and broad-minded Idealism, an Idealism that tried to avoid both the iconoclasm of Herbert Spencer and the rigidity of popular theology.

In these early essays and in his *The Study of Ethics: A Syllabus*, the thirty-four-year-old Dewey worked out arguments that were to be used in his pedagogical and logical controversies during the ensuing decade at Chicago. There are even some anticipations of the positions that were to be taken in the Roaring Twenties and the Threadbare Thirties, when Dewey's role as a publicist and social critic was fully developed. But anyone who is inclined to read all of Dewey's later outlook into his 1893 comments will find a corrective in the first and one of the last items in this volume. In those reports of what Dewey said to the Students' Christian Association the reader will not find the completely secular Dewey of the 1920s. By contrast, there is a tactful respect for religious sensitivities and the use of a theological vocabulary that is not characteristic of later writings. Of course, the talks contain some statements which must have jolted the ministerial students at Ann Arbor, such as the suggestion that democracy is the means of "revelation" and the equating of prayer (the "seek and ye shall find") with the inquiry of science. But these quaint remnants serve as a reminder of the climate of opinion and interest within which Dewey was working.

During the 1893–1894 period Dewey was aware of important shifts in his philosophy. The Prefatory Note for *The Study of Ethics* states emphatically that this 1894 syllabus is not a second edition of the *Outlines of a Critical Theory of Ethics* which had been published only three years earlier. The *Syllabus*, clearly the most important work of our two-year period, is called a study in "experimental idealism" (p. 264) and is in-

Introduction

x   *Introduction*

tended to avoid the defects of Kant's excessive rationalism and the hedonists' excessive subjectivism. In this hastily written guide, as in three long essays of the period, Dewey refers repeatedly to William James. James obviously was forcing him to reconsider the German theories of "the self" which had, a few years earlier, seemed so adequate an answer to his yearning for a unifying point of view.

Dewey's references to James are generally favorable and, in a long two-part essay, he tells why he prefers the James-Lange theory of emotion to Darwin's theory. Whereas Darwin surmised that the vestiges of once-useful acts had become expressions of fear and anger, James and Lange held that the bodily actions were responses to the exciting stimuli and that the feelings of fear and anger were peripheral to these "expressions." Dewey suggested that the "expressive" acts were themselves modes of adaptation. But what was of more significance for Dewey's evolving point of view, the James-Lange theory changed his conception of "activity." He comments on the success of James in placing the "feel," the "idea," and the "mode of behavior" in relation to one another. "The reality" is equated with "the co-ordination of these partial activities."[1]

This functional conception of "reality" is in striking contrast to what Dewey had said in his 1888 book on Leibniz. There he had praised Leibniz for asserting that sensations are spiritual activities and had talked about the self-activity of the soul.[2] Other passages in the Leibniz book tell how "activity" has its "reason" in a "substance" (p. 338). Activity is "the manifestation of the ideal unity of substance" (p. 358). Such metaphysical conceptions Dewey now, in 1893, regards as "blank and unmediated." In another paper, "The Ego as Cause," Dewey notes that James, though not entirely consistent, is to be credited with giving the hardest knocks to the theory of "an ego outside and behind."[3]

Dewey's reaction to James is selective and critical, even when he feels most indebted to James for very important insights. Dewey expresses dissatisfaction with James's treatment of "the will," "consciousness," and other topics. He sometimes identifies the trouble as careless phraseology. This is

---

[1]   "The Theory of Emotion," in *The Early Works of John Dewey, 1882–1898*, IV (Carbondale: Southern Illinois University Press, 1971), 176.
[2]   *Leibniz's New Essays Concerning the Human Understanding*, in *Early Works*, I, 319, 324.
[3]   *Early Works*, IV, 95n.

Dewey's retort to readers who had mistaken James as a "materialist." Dewey undertakes to restate what in James had sounded like psycho-physical parallelism; he tries to describe physiological events without seeming to assert that they are the cause of mental events. Nowadays we would perhaps say that Dewey was clearing up a confusion of physical and phenomenal languages. In this effort Dewey shows a dialectical skill that was to startle some of his adversaries in the years ahead.

Dewey's acuity along this line is well illustrated in his review of Lester Ward's *The Psychic Factors of Civilization*. There, in spite of his rather cumbersome vocabulary, Dewey untangles a mixture of psychic and physical descriptions, as follows:

I am not arguing that the "external" motion is the cause of the "internal" state of consciousness. To treat one as *cause* of the other is to suppose one independent of the other, and thus to break the continuity. My point is, that if one chooses to take the standpoint of physical science and describe as far as possible the psychical occurrence, this occurrence is one of the transformation and complication of motion. The fact of feeling and of the existence of ideas must be recognized, but they must be treated from the standpoint of the development of action (p. 205n.).

Dewey was himself seeking a psychological description of the life process that would relate the empirical findings of physiologists and sociologists to man's consciousness of value, but he insisted that a psychological description "cannot involve a different principle" (p. 204). He believed that he had found the "mediating" standpoint in "action" or "activity."

Using *The Study of Ethics* as a benchmark, we can see how far he had progressed toward the "instrumental logic" that he was to champion a decade later,[4] and the "reflective

4   J. H. Tufts in his memorandum to President Harper recommending Dewey's appointment at Chicago states that Dewey had agreed to prepare a volume in the Library of Philosophy series under the title, "Principles of Instrumental Logic." This book was never published. *The Study of Ethics* was, during Dewey's first years at Chicago, his most important systematic statement. Henry W. Stuart, who received his Ph.D. at Chicago in 1900, has written: "In the ever-memorable early Chicago years, this little volume was a scripture—treasured in those years' dearth of systematic writing from Professor Dewey's hand—to be read, pondered, and interpreted. More than one eagerly contested argument was adjourned, to the confusion of a dissenter, with the not wholly humorous recital of the *logion* I here recall." "Dewey's Ethical Theory," in *The Philosophy of John Dewey* (Library of Living Philosophers, I, ed. Paul Arthur Schilpp [Chicago, Evanston: Northwestern University, 1939]), 314n. The reason for the "dearth" mentioned by Stuart was, of course, Dewey's preoccupation with the laboratory school and educational theory.

ethics" for which he was to argue so persuasively fifteen years later. The ethical postulate is now stated in psychological rather than in metaphysical terms:

The conduct required truly to express an agent is, at the same time, the conduct required to maintain the situation in which he is placed; while, conversely, the conduct that truly meets the situation is that which furthers the agent (p. 234).

The moral goal is "the freeing of life . . . through knowledge of its real nature and relations" (p. 226).

In line with his critiques of T. H. Green (discussed in the Introduction to Vol. III, *The Early Works of John Dewey, 1882–1898*), Dewey has moved away from a metaphysical treatment of "will" and is projecting a study of social ethics, a theory of the "sphere of action" to complement his study of the moral agent (pp. 229–34). He is already being influenced by George Herbert Mead, whose critique of physiological psychology was to eventuate in a social behaviorism.[5] Yet, he had not in 1893–1894 generalized his integrating concept (what he was later to call "the problematic situation"). He was still twenty-eight years from a book (*Human Nature and Conduct*) that would get a full treatment of the "agent" and "the sphere of action" in a single work. *The Study of Ethics* breaks off abruptly without an analysis of "the sphere of action."

Dewey is still dependent on the Hegelian notion of "mediation," as he tries to use the Jamesian dynamic psychology and learning theory to correct "pathological and moralistic ethics." He explains how "impulses" are mediated (p. 237), but instead of employing his later "problem-solving" terminology, he talks about the emergence of new ideas as "the emergence of a purpose which expresses the self." Instead of his later "creative intelligence reconstructing the self," Dewey here equates "the troubled conscience" with a "consciousness of division" (p. 295) and the agent's solution of a moral problem as an act that "utters his whole self" (p. 293).

Because he is still a novice in sociological and educational theory, Dewey is unable to make full use of his distinction between customary and reflective moralities (mentioned on p. 224, but not elaborated as in the 1908 *Ethics*). He seems to forget about sociological and physical conditions in many passages, where a too-psychological account of morality might have been corrected (as it was later) by recognizing human

[5]   See the acknowledgement of indebtedness to Mead in his article, "The Theory of Emotion," p. 167n.

history as a succession of periods of relative stability and periods of rapid change. Dewey does talk about "the needs of the situation," "social fact as well as psychical fact," and "the conditions of action" (p. 234). But it was not yet very obvious that he did not need a Hegelian Reality to explain why there should be moral struggles or why any of the struggles should ever come to an end.[6]

Among the reviews of *The Study of Ethics* was one by Josiah Royce. Royce noted that Dewey was trying to get away from judgments concerning the value of conduct based upon a suppositious contrast between appetites and the moral will. Royce labels Dewey's theory "ethical realism," and concludes that it is an "essentially partial doctrine, and not the 'whole' for which Professor Dewey so frequently contends."[7]

At this point in his career Dewey's objection to Hegel, Bradley, Green, and Mackenzie was that they regarded self-realization as "filling in the blank scheme of some undefined, purely general self" (p. 246). Dewey believed that self-realization should be understood as "expressing the concrete capacity of an individual agent." Moral value is the "satisfaction mediated in thought, that is, by reflection upon the nature of an impulse in its relation to the self," but then Dewey adds in parentheses, "or the whole system of impulses." That is the process in which "natural good" is replaced by "a good which is presented to consciousness." It is a process that works out differently for each individual: no two persons can have the same duties as they come out of "the periods of reconstruction in moral progress" (p. 316).

Dewey was here beginning to substitute the conflicting "selves" of William James for the Self of German Idealism, and that is why he insisted that Idealism must be "experimental." He asserts that "the act measures the agent and . . . the act tests the standard as well as the standard the act" (p. 291). But Dewey is still an idealist, resisting "relativity." So he concludes one comment on the individuality of conduct by saying, "The standard and process are absolute, but (and because) individual" (p. 317n.).

The Study of Ethics has an emphasis that is very different

6   His review of books by Ward and Kidd in the *Psychological Review* [*Early Works*, IV, 210] does assert that men go on thinking only because of practical friction or strain somewhere, that thinking is essentially the solution of tension; but *The Study of Ethics* largely omits an inquiry into frictions, strains, and tensions, especially as they appear to a scientific investigator who is not a psychologist.

7   *International Journal of Ethics*, VI (Oct. 1895), 113.

from the 1887 *Psychology* where Dewey asserts that "the essence of self is the self-determining activity of will" and that the "universal nature of will with which the will confronts itself constitutes what we call ideals."[8] He has in the meantime had his attention directed to some natural processes that Hegel did not find morally significant. In 1893 and 1894 Dewey repeatedly expresses his dissatisfaction with Idealists' lack of interest in empirically describable Nature except as Nature is a foil for a self-realizing self.[9] At the same time, he is far from the kind of exposition that he was to present three and four decades later, when he could document contentions that social reconstruction and self-fulfillment were simply two different views of the same situation. I have been unable to find in the early writings detailed statements comparable to his later comments about disease, crime, immorality, and other human pathologies being as much affairs of the "environment" as they are of the "organism."[10]

Dewey's failure to proceed in one jump to an ethical naturalism was not, however, merely because of the limitations of his available information. Dewey had committed himself to a strategy in ethics that called for quarreling with the facts of nature. In 1887 he had opposed Herbert Spencer's reading of ethical goals from the facts as science reported them: "The mere fact that the universe is going to come out so and so in the long run does not constitute any reason why we should act accordingly."[11] Dewey's *Cyclopædia* article on "Moral Philosophy," published in 1894, made a very sharp distinction between "the philosophic" and "the physical" sciences. The philosophic sciences (æsthetics, logic, and ethics) "deal with the investigation of value. They reach their end, not in a description of a given experience, but in an estimate of its worth as a part of the whole system of experience."[12]

The estimate of worth had been thought by Dewey to consist, not in a simple apprehension, but in a dialectical juggling of opposed considerations, gradually approximating the true relation of something finite to the whole universe. He was still under the influence of such an Idealist logic, as witness his 1893 *Monist* article:

---

8   *Early Works*, II, 362.
9   See the review of Bosanquet's *A History of Æsthetic*, in *Early Works*, IV, especially some of the comments on pp. 194–97.
10   See *Individualism Old and New* (New York: Minton, Balch and Co., 1930), p. 164.
11   "Ethics and Physical Science," in *Early Works*, I, 218.
12   *Early Works*, IV, 132.

Consider, then, that tortuous path from reality to reality, *via* a circuit of unreality, which calls the thought of necessity into existence. We first mutilate the actual fact by selecting some portion that appeals to our needs; we falsify, by erecting this fragment into the whole fact.[13]

It had been consistent with this anti-intuitionist epistemology for Dewey to follow the ethical strategy of F. H. Bradley, approaching a more adequate view of the moral life by contrasting the partial insights and failures of less adequate views (*i.e.*, the Kantian and Utilitarian). In 1894 Dewey was in the process of rejecting the Idealist doctrine of an Absolute Self as the end of "the tortuous path"; but he was not abandoning the idea of the tortuous path.

Thus it happened that Dewey's mounting enthusiasm for empirical science did not take the fateful turn that G. E. Moore took nine years later. Both men asserted that ethics is a science.[14] But whereas Moore was to single out precision and consistency as characteristic of science, Dewey identified wideranging curiosity and openness to new evidence as the mark of a scientist.

Of special interest, because it sounds like many much later comments, is the reported speech in Appendix 1 of this volume:

Philosophy as a method means interpretation of experience, or the full life of the race in all times and ages as far as we can get at it. . . . Criticism is testing, investigation, not simple fault-finding. Philosophy is the standpoint of science extended to all life.[15]

In line with their contrasting conceptions of a "scientific ethics," G. E. Moore castigated John Stuart Mill for hopelessly confusing different questions and unwittingly departing from his professed hedonism; Dewey, on the other hand, applauded Mill's deviations as a partial recognition of "an objective standard," a recognition of the importance of the self in moral judgments.[16]

Dewey's direction is further indicated in the conclusion of his short article on "Renan's Loss of Faith in Science":

13   "The Superstition of Necessity," in *Early Works*, IV, 28.
14   Dewey's flat assertion will be found in *The Study of Ethics*, in *Early Works*, IV, 226.
15   "The Relation of Philosophy to Theology," in *Early Works*, IV, 365.
16   *The Study of Ethics*, p. 285.

It is a continual marvel that so many men of science who have abandoned and even attacked all dogmatic authority, should take refuge
for themselves in agnosticism—that they should not see that any
lasting denial of dogmatic authority is impossible save as science itself advances to that comprehensive synthesis which will allow it to
become a guide of conduct, a social motor.[17]

Dewey was disturbed by Renan's abandonment of an earlier
faith in "the larger and social function of science" in enlightening and guiding the entire population (not merely a few
scientists). Dewey had responded warmly to Renan's earlier
vision of social institutions readjusting with every forward
step of science. In order to fulfill that "social mission" science
would have to be synthetic, "universalized in its range by coming to include humanity as its subject-matter." Thus, Dewey's
growing enthusiasm for science assumed that science was, above
all else, a wide-ranging, almost limitless curiosity and eagerness
to learn.

   In contrasting Dewey's conception of science with the
analytic precision that G. E. Moore later tried to emulate I
do not suggest that either Dewey or Moore had in mind the
extremes to which some of their "followers" have sometimes
gone: bumbling juxtapositions of miscellaneous "facts" by windy
Instrumentalists, on the one hand, and minute nit-picking by
analysts forgetful of the issues that called for inquiry, on the
other hand. That Dewey's enthusiasm for "the standpoint of
science extended to all life"[18] was not undisciplined will be borne
out by a review of his comments on the kind of sweeping generalizations that were fashionable in the semi-popular scientific
literature of the nineties. Dewey's reviews of "the latest findings
of science" are cagey. His caginess indicates that he was not
rushing from any *is* to the *ought*.

   Volume IV of *The Early Works* makes accessible a
number of short pieces that do not seem to me to throw much
light on the emergence of the original and distinctive ideas
that Dewey produced at this time. They will, nevertheless, hold
a special interest for those readers who are trying to find the
beginnings of certain of Dewey's later constructions. There are
five items that are representative of his early ventures into
educational theory, the most important of these being "The
Chaos in Moral Training."[19] In saying that Dewey's philosophy

17   *Early Works*, IV, 18.
18   "Relation of Philosophy to Theology," p. 365.
19   "Teaching Ethics in the High School," "Why Study Philosophy?"
"The Psychology of Infant Language," Review of "On Certain Psychological Aspects of Moral Training . . . ," and "The Chaos in Moral
Training."

of education was not well developed in any of his 1893–1894 publications I do not suggest that they are lacking in insight or that his interest in education was not yet intense. There is documentary evidence of Dewey's growing concern with school problems. Indeed, when President Harper invited him to come to the University of Chicago, one of the attractions of the Chicago offer was the fact that the professorship would be in Pedagogy as well as in Philosophy and Psychology.

Five items in the present volume deal specifically with problems of government,[20] but—like his educational writings of this period—they do not contain the pointed criticisms of prevailing practices that were to extend Dewey's influence in later years far beyond the ranks of academic philosophers. His 1893–1894 productions in political and legal philosophy were not noticeably distinguishable from the mild Neo-Hegelianism that was then current in England and the United States.

In the preceding paragraph I may seem to be underestimating what Dewey accomplished in his article on "Austin's Theory of Sovereignty." Dewey there rejects Henry Maine's criticism of Austin (directed against a mistaken paraphrase of Austin rather than against what Austin actually contended). Dewey appears to be offering an *empirical* objection to Austin's theory of law as the command of a sovereign. If it is what it claims to be, I should have to revise what I said about Dewey's plans for a study of social ethics or the theory of the "sphere of action." It would in that case be unfair to call such plans merely programmatic in 1894 and say that they are not yet based upon thorough acquaintance with social science findings.

A careful reading of the article, however, does not disclose any substantial contribution to political theory. As has been pointed out elsewhere,[21] much of Dewey's disagreement with Austin is a disagreement over vocabulary and not over facts. When Dewey gets around to matters of fact, he is quarreling less with Austin's definition than with an application of the definition. And in the application of the definition Dewey thinks Austin guilty of an "insoluble contradiction: sovereignty is not determinate until after it has been exercised—until the vote has been taken." This view of the political process and its

[20] "Christianity and Democracy," "Anthropology and Law," "Austin's Theory of Sovereignty," Review of *The Psychic Factors of Civilization* . . . , and Review of *Philosophy and Political Economy*.
[21] See D. Gerber, "A Note on Woody on Dewey on Austin," *Ethics*, LXXIX (July 1969), 303–8. This dissatisfaction with Dewey's "refutation" does not, of course, prove that Austin had a good theory. There have been other, better informed objections to this part of Austin's legal theory.

tensions is a logician's view of words and is in sharp contrast
to the sophisticated understanding of politics that Dewey later
displays in *The Public and Its Problems* (1927).

The Michigan professor of 1894 is a long way from the
world-famous philosopher-publicist of the 1920s. Some notion
of the distance between the two may be suggested by the contrast
between Dewey's frequent references during the later period to
current political issues and his failure during 1893 and 1894 to
publish any comment on the panic and unemployment of 1893
or Governor Altgeld's controversial pardoning of the Hay-
market Riot anarchists.

Although "the makings" of Dewey's later critiques can be
found in the 1893–1894 writings, it cannot be said that Dewey's
achievement at this time consisted in pointed criticisms of
institutional practices and traditions. He expresses few opinions
that are as challenging as his later objections to philosophizing
about "the" state and "problems in general." Dewey's break-
through during his last years at Michigan was the twist that he
gave to Hegelian logic, a twist that enabled him for the next
fifty years to work out a long series of fecund criticisms of
official thinking and what passed for "the wisdom of the ages."
His insight was partially articulated in *The Study of Ethics*:
"We find ourselves under the necessity of paying equal attention
to the agent and to the conditions with reference to which he
acts" (p. 231). The germinal insight is also evidenced in the
many passages in which he is revising and elaborating his
concept of "action" or "activity."

As Herbert Schneider has elsewhere noted, the 1894 syllabus, *The Study of Ethics*, does not begin with a discussion of
such ethical concepts as "good," "duty," and "freedom."[22] That
had been the way Dewey introduced his 1891 *Outlines of Ethics*.
The 1894 *Study of Ethics* begins with a chapter on the "Nature
of Ethical Theory" and is much concerned with the relations
of ethical theory to practice. As previously implied, Dewey
reaches the conclusion that the judgment of values can be
systematic, critical, and successful in relating practice (action)
to the whole of life (the Hegelian hope). But theory will not,
in that case, be merely a statement of how action does or
does not conform "to some scheme laid down" (p. 226). It
will be a "method for action," "experimental," and ordering "in
sense of setting in order," not in the sense of "commanding"

[22]   "Dewey's Ethics: Part One," in *Guide to the Works of John
Dewey* (Carbondale: Southern Illinois University Press, 1970), p. 106.

(p. 226). And, to qualify as a method for action, theory must be limited to a study of the moral agent. It must also be a study of his sphere of action.

Putting Dewey's program into terms more congenial to the analytic vocabulary of the 1950s and 1960s, it was a proposal to think about human life and its conditions in a language that would find the criterion of action "within, not without, the act" (p. 244n.). Dewey was trying to avoid language that permitted contrasts between objective and subjective, inner and outer, interior and exterior. He needed intellectual tools that would, as he said, "mediate." He believed that he had found the mediating ideas in the psychology of William James.

The Jamesian vocabulary of activity, impulse, attention, etc., provided for Dewey a means of talking about what moralists and sociologists, theologians and biologists, all talked about in different ways that did not permit easy translation. It brought together Royce's worlds of description and appreciation without conceiving of the "physical" world as a "fixed" thing (p. 258).

Here and there in the 1893–1894 publications we catch a glimmering of what Dewey was later to do with this insight. It was going to enable him to challenge the reigning theories in education, economics, government, and art, not so much by quarreling about the evidence for what was being said as by quarreling about the way in which experts stated their problems and questions. He was thus, in 1894, preparing himself for service as a critic of specialists in an age of extreme specialization. He would be able to relate the part to the whole (or at least to the less partial) more effectively than any of the Hegelians and Spencerians could ever do with their languages, hopelessly prejudiced as they were with the point of view of one or another discipline.

Dewey was not proposing a reductionism, a translation from all other languages into the language of action. He was using the language of action as an organizing tool. He outlines what he calls the "phases of action" and is able to say how reports of feelings and reports of consequences are relevant at various stages of action. In *The Study of Ethics* he is mainly concerned with rival theories about moral agents. The power of Dewey's technique would not become fully apparent until he gave more attention to what he then called "the sphere of action."

I believe that it is safe to say that Dewey had put ethics and all other specialized studies into "a larger picture" as the result of his reflections upon James's *Principles of Psychology*.

He was now, in principle, committed to "going beyond conventional right and wrong" as surely as Nietzsche (whom he apparently had not read) had gone "beyond good and evil." But unlike Nietzsche, he did not regard this as a repudiation of morality. "The sense of duty," he contended, is "a phenomenon of moral *progress*, appearing in so far as an intention or ideal demands the transformation of impulse and habit, by adapting them to instruments of its own realization. Without the new ideal, the habit becomes monotonous and dead; sheer routine. Not being in tension with an aim, it falls entirely below consciousness, and thus loses all value and significance. It is the essence of habit to be *instrumental*, a means for accomplishing ends" (p. 313).

In this position Dewey is flatly opposed to F. H. Bradley who regarded the question, "Why be moral?" as either immoral or senseless. But Dewey seems to have thought in 1894 that this subordination of morality to the total life process and the need for "experimentation" were incidental to each individual's unique exploration of a labyrinth. Each had to find his way and a morality of rules (do this, don't do that) was inappropriate. But the labyrinth was not disturbed.

The fact that Dewey had not yet written his projected Social Ethics kept his *program* for a moral revolution from seeming to be dangerous; and his use of phrases like "reflective morality" was reassuring. In view of the climate of opinion in the universities of the nineties (to which we referred in the beginning), it is understandable why Dewey found a responsive audience, whereas Nietzsche had not.

Wayne A. R. Leys

1 February 1970

EARLY ESSAYS

Christianity and Democracy

Looked at from the outside, a religion seems to be a cult and a body of doctrine. It seems to be a cult; that is, a collection of specific acts to be performed, and of special ideas to be cherished in consciousness. The acts, the cult, may be more or less prescribed, more or less detailed, more or less formal, but some special acts there must be. It is these acts which have religious meaning, which are worship, while other acts are outside the pale, are secular, or profane, commercial, or merely moral—they are not communion with God. So, too, the dogmas, the doctrine, may be more or less narrow, more or less rigid, but it seems there must be some special body of ideas set up and apart as belonging to the religious consciousness, while other ideas are scientific, or artistic, or industrial. This is the appearance. Research into the origin and development of religion destroys the appearance. It is shown that every religion has its source in the social and intellectual life of a community or race. Every religion is an expression of the social relations of the community; its rites, its cult, are a recognition of the sacred and divine significance of these relationships. The religion is an expression of the mental attitude and habit of a people; it is its reaction, æsthetic and scientific, upon the world in which the people finds itself. Its ideas, its dogmas and mysteries are recognitions, in symbolic form, of the poetic, social and intellectual value of the surroundings. In time this significance, social and intellectual, is lost sight of; it is so thoroughly condensed in the symbols, the rites, the dogmas, that they seem to be the religion. They become

[*An address delivered at the Sunday Morning Services of the Students' Christian Association, University of Michigan, 27 March 1892. First published in* Religious Thought at the University of Michigan (*Ann Arbor: Register Publishing Co., Inland Press, 1893*), *pp. 60–69. Not previously reprinted.*]

an end in themselves. Thus separated from life they begin to decay; it seems as if religion were disintegrating. In reality, the very life, the very complexus of social and intellectual inter-actions which give birth to these forms, is already and continuously at work finding revelation and expression in more adequate relations and truths.

If there is no religion which is simply a religion, least of all is Christianity simply a religion. Jesus had no cult or rite to impose; no specific forms of worship, no specific acts named religion. He was clear to the other side. He proclaimed this very setting up of special acts and institutions as part of the imperfections of life. "The hour cometh when ye shall neither in this mountain nor yet in Jerusalem worship the Father. . . . The hour cometh and now is when true worshippers shall worship the Father in spirit and in truth"—the hour when worship should be simply the free and truthful expression of man in his action. Jesus had no special doctrine to impose—no special set of truths labeled religious. "If *any* man will *do* his *will*, he shall know of the doctrine." "Ye shall know the truth and the truth shall make you free." The only truth Jesus knew of as religious was Truth. There were no special religious truths which He came to teach; on the contrary, his doctrine was that Truth, however named and however divided by man, is one as God is one; that getting hold of truth and living by it is religion. Dr. Mulford in his *Republic of God*, holds that Christianity is not a religion at all, having no cult and no dogma of its own to mark it off from action and truth in general. The very universality of Christianity precludes its being a religion. Christianity, Dr. Mulford contends, is not a religion but a revelation.

The condition of revelation is that it reveal. Christianity, if universal, if revelation, must be the continuously unfolding, never ceasing discovery of the meaning of life. Revelation is the ascertaining of life. It cannot be more than this; it must be all of this. Christianity then cannot stand or fall with any special theory or mode of action with which men at a given time may choose to identify it. Christianity in its reality knows no such exclusive or sectarian attitude. If it be made to stand or fall with any special theory, historical or ethical, if it be identified with some special act, ecclesiastic or ceremonial, it has denied its basis and its destiny. The one claim that Christianity makes is that God is truth; that as truth He is love and reveals Himself fully to man, keeping back nothing of Himself; that man is so one with the truth thus revealed that it is not so much revealed *to* him as *in* him; he is its incarnation; that by the appropriation of truth, by identification with it, man is free; free negatively, free from sin, free positively, free to live his own life, free to express himself, free to play without let or limitation upon the instrument given him—the environment of natural wants and forces. As revelation, Christianity must reveal. The only tests by which it can be tried are the tests of fact—is their truth constantly ascertained and appropriated by man? Does a life loyal to the truth bring freedom?

It is obvious that in other religions there is no great inconsistency in the claim of certain men to be the special representatives of religion, insisting that there are certain specific ideas to be held, certain special acts to be performed, as religious. No other religion has ever generalized its basis and its motive, apprehending the universality of truth, and its consequent self-revealing power to everyone. But in Christianity the attempt to fix religious truth once for all, to hold it within certain rigid limits, to say this and just this is Christianity, is self-contradictory. The revelation of truth must continue as long as life has new meanings to unfold, new action to propose. An organization may loudly proclaim its loyalty to Christianity and to Christ; but if, in asserting its loyalty, it assumes a certain guardianship of Christian truth, a certain prerogative in laying down what is this truth, a certain exclusiveness in the administration of religious conduct, if in short the organization attempts to preach a fixity in a moving world and to claim a monopoly in a common world—all this is a sign that the real Christianity is now working outside of and beyond the organization, that the revelation is going on in wider and freer channels.

The historic organization called the church has just learned one lesson of this sort. There was a time when the church assumed the finality of its ideas upon the relations of God and the world, and of the relations of nature and man.

For centuries the visible church assumed that it was the guardian and administrator of truth in these matters. It not only strove against the dawning and rising science as false, but it called this science impious and anti-Christian, till science almost learned to call herself by the name so positively and continuously fixed upon her. But it turned out then as ever—truth exists not in word, but in power. As in the parable of the two sons, the one who boasted of his readiness to serve in the vineyard went not, while the younger son who said he would not go, went out into the vineyard of nature and by obedience to the truth revealed the deeper truth of unity of law, the presence of one continuous living force, the conspiring and vital unity of all the world. The revelation was made in what we term science. The revelation could not be interrupted on account of the faithlessness of the church, it pushed out in the new channel.

Again, I repeat, revelation must reveal. It is not simply a question of the reality declared, it is also a question of comprehension by him to whom the reality is declared. A Hindoo religion, a Greek religion, might place its religious truths in mysteries which were not comprehended. A religion of revelation must uncover and discover; it must bring home its truth to the consciousness of the individual. Revelation undertakes, in a word, not only to state that the truth of things is such and such, it undertakes to give the individual organs for the truth, organs by which he can get hold of, can see and feel, the truth.

To overlook this side of revelation is to keep the word but deny the fact. Of late, the theologians, as well as the philosophers, have been turning their guns upon agnosticism, the doctrine that God, and the fundamental realities of life, are hid from man's knowledge. What is true for one must be true for another, and if agnosticism is false, false also is the doctrine that revelation is the process by which an external God declares to man certain fixed statements about Himself and the methods of His working. God is essentially and only the self-revealing, and the revelation is complete only as men come to realize Him.

So much for the first part of my subject. Christianity is revelation, and revelation means effective discovery, the actual ascertaining or guaranteeing to man of the truth of his life and the reality of the Universe.

It is at this point that the significance of democracy appears. The kingdom of God, as Christ said, is within us, or among us. The revelation is, and can be, only in intelligence. It is strange to hear men call themselves Christian teachers, and at the same time condemn the use of reason and of thought in relation to Christian truth. Christianity as revelation is not only to, it is *in* man's thought and reason. Beyond all other means of appropriating truth, beyond all other organs of apprehension, is man's own action. Man interprets the Universe in which he lives in terms of his own action at the given time. Had Jesus Christ made an absolute, detailed and explicit statement upon all the facts of life, that statement would not have had meaning—it would not have been revelation—until men began to realize in their own action the truth he declared—until they themselves began to *live* it. In final analysis, man's own action, his own life movement, is the only organ he has for receiving and appropriating truth. Man's action is found in his social relationships—the way in which he connects with his fellows. It is man's social organization, the state in which he is expressing himself, which always has and always must set the form and sound the key-note to the understanding of Christianity.

Jesus himself taught that the individual is free in his life because the individual is the organ of the absolute Truth of the Universe. I see no reason for believing that Jesus meant this in any but its most general sense; I do not see any reason for supposing that he meant that the individual is free simply in some one special direction or department; I do not see any reason for supposing that his teaching of truth's accessibility to man is to be taken in any unnatural or limited way. Yet the world to which these ideas were taught did not find itself free, and did not find the road to truth so straight and open. Slaveries of all sort abounded; the individual found himself enslaved to nature and to his fellows. He found ignorance instead of knowledge; darkness instead of light. These facts fixed the method of interpretation for that time. It was impossible that the teachings of Jesus should be understood in their direct, natural sense when the whole existing world of action seemed to contradict them. It was inevitable that these teachings should be deflected and distorted through their medium of interpretation—the existing conditions of action.

The significance of democracy as revelation is that it enables us to get truths in a natural, every-day and practical sense which otherwise could be grasped only in a somewhat unnatural or sentimental sense. I assume that democracy is a spiritual fact and not a mere piece of governmental machinery. If there is no God, no law, no truth in the Universe, or if this God is an absentee God, not actually working, then no social organization has any spiritual meaning. If God is, as Christ taught, at the root of life, incarnate in man, then democracy has a spiritual meaning which it behooves us not to pass by. Democracy is freedom. If truth is at the bottom of things, freedom means giving this truth a chance to show itself, a chance to well up from the depths. Democracy, as freedom, means the loosening of bonds, the wearing away of restrictions, the breaking down of barriers, of middle walls, of partitions. Through this doing away with restrictions, whatever truth, whatever reality there is in man's life is freed to express itself. Democracy is, as freedom, the freeing of truth. Truth makes free, but it has been the work of history to free truth—to break down the walls of isolation and of class interest which held it in and under. The idea that man can enact "law" in the social sphere any more than in the so-called "physical" sphere simply shows with how little seriousness, how little faith, men have taken to themselves the conception of God incarnate in humanity. Man can but discover law by uncovering it. He can uncover it only by freeing life, by freeing expression, so that the truth may appear with more conscious and more compelling force.

The spiritual unification of humanity, the realization of the brotherhood of man, all that Christ called the Kingdom of God is but the further expression of this freedom of truth. The truth is not fully freed when it gets into some individual's consciousness, for him to delectate himself with. It is freed only when it moves in and through this favored individual to his fellows; when the truth which comes to consciousness in one, extends and distributes itself to all so that it becomes the Common-wealth, the Republic, the public affair. The walls broken down by the freedom which is democracy, are all the walls preventing the complete movement of truth. It is in the community of truth thus established that the brotherhood, which is democracy, has its being. The supposition that the ties which bind men together, that the forces which unify society, can be other than the very laws of God, can be other than the outworking of God in life, is a part of that same practical unbelief in the presence of God in the world which I have already mentioned. Here then we have democracy! on its negative side, the breaking down of the barriers which hold truth from finding expression, on its positive side, the securing of conditions which give truth its movement, its complete distribution or service. It is no accident that the growing organization of democracy coincides with the rise of science, including the machinery of telegraph and locomotive for distributing truth. There is but one fact—the more complete movement of man to his unity with his fellows through realizing the truth of life.

Democracy thus appears as the means by which the revelation of truth is carried on. It is in democracy, the community of ideas and interest through community of action, that the incarnation of God in man (man, that is to say, as organ of universal truth) becomes a living, present thing, having its ordinary and natural sense. This truth is brought down to life; its segregation removed; it is made a common truth enacted in all departments of action, not in one isolated sphere called religious.

Is the isolated truth about to welcome its completion in the common truth? Is the partial revelation ready to die as partial in order to live in the fuller? This is the practical question which faces us. Can we surrender—not simply the bad *per se*—but the possessed good in order to lay hold of a larger good? Shall we welcome the revelation of truth now going on in democracy as a wider realization of the truth formerly asserted in more or less limited channels and with a more or less unnatural meaning? As democracy comes to consciousness itself, becomes aware of its own spiritual basis and content, this question will confront us more and more.

We are here in the University to think, that is to say, to get hold of the best tools of action. It is our duty not to float with the currents of opinion, but to ask and answer this question for ourselves in order that we may give some answer when others begin to ask it. Will the older formulation, inherited from days when the organization of society was not democratic, when truth was just getting its freedom and its unity through freedom,—will this formulation strive and contend against the larger revelation because it comes from what seems to be outside its own walls, or will it welcome it joyously and loyally, as the fuller expression of its own idea and purpose?

It is your business and mine to answer this question for ourselves. If we answer it for ourselves we shall answer it for more, many more than ourselves; for it is in our hands and in the hands of such as we are, to get this question decided beyond a peradventure. There is no better time than the present for the solution; there is no better place for it than the University of Michigan—an institution based upon inquiry into truth and upon democracy. Can anyone ask for better or more inspiring work? Surely to fuse into one the social and the religious motive, to break down the barriers of Pharisaism and self-assertion which isolate religious thought and conduct from the common life of man, to realize the state as one Commonwealth of truth—surely this is a cause worth battling for.

Remember Lot's wife, who looked back, and who, looking back, was fixed into a motionless pillar.

Renan's Loss of Faith in Science

The fundamental conception of Ernest Renan's work *The Future of Science* is that science is both subjectively and objectively social: that its material, in its most important respects, is to be found in the history of humanity, and that its aim is furthering the organization of humanity. The relation of science to the welfare of man is the true text of the book; and this in no limited definition of welfare, but in a sense so broad as to include his religious attitude, as well as his intellectual and artistic enjoyments. "As for myself," he says at the outset, "I recognize only one result of science: namely the solution of the enigma, the final explanation to mankind of the meaning of things,—the explanation to man of himself,—giving him in the name of the sole legitimate authority (the whole of human nature) the creed which religion gave him ready-made." And if Renan conceives the theoretical outcome of science to be this revelation of man to himself, his conception of its practical resultant is no less broad: "The whole march of Europe for four centuries is summed up in this practical conclusion: to elevate and ennoble the people, and to let all men have a share in the delights of intelligence."

I intend to quote, at some length, a passage from the beginning of the fifth chapter of the *Future of Science*, which sums up his idea both of the nature and the end of science, and afterwards I shall go over some of the main points one by one.

It is not altogether inadvertently that I designate by the name of *science* that which is ordinarily called *philosophy*. To

[*First published in* Open Court, VII (*Jan. 1893*), 3512–15. Reprinted in Characters and Events, *ed. Joseph Ratner (New York: Henry Holt and Co., 1929*), I, 23–30, *with the title "Ernest Renan."*]

philosophize is the word by which I would most willingly sum
up my life; nevertheless, seeing that the popular use of the word
still expresses only a partial form of the inner life, that besides
it only implies the subjective fact of the individual thinker, we
must employ the more objective word; *To know when assuming
the standpoint of humanity.* Yes, the day will come when
humanity shall no longer believe; but when it shall know; the
day when it shall know the metaphysical and moral world as it
now knows the physical; the day when the government of
humanity shall no longer be given to accident and intrigue, but
to the rational discussion of what is best, and to the most
efficacious means of attaining what is best. If such be the aim
of science, if its object be to teach man its final aim and law, to
make him grasp the true sense of life, to make up with art,
poetry, and virtue, the divine ideal which alone lends worth to
human existence, if such be its aim, then is it possible that it
should have its serious detractors? But, it will be asked, will
science accomplish these marvellous destinies? All I know is
that if science does not accomplish them, nothing else will, and
that humanity will forever be ignorant of the significance of
things.

The definition of science, then, is to know from the
standpoint of humanity; its goal is such a sense of life as
will enable man to direct his conduct in relation to his
fellows by intelligence and not by chance. It is to this that I
would direct special attention—Renan's faith in '48 in the
social basis and aim of science.

According to Renan the present era is marked by intelligence coming to consciousness of its social function. Up
to, say, the French Revolution, the function of science had
been analytic—mainly negative and dissolving. All science
is criticism, but criticism in the past has been equivalent to
an analysis of existing conceptions, sentiments, and habits
which resulted in destroying their validity. Reason has thus
appeared to have no positive and constructive function; its
work is to be exhausted in analysis, in disintegration of the
given. But science, having carried its analysis, its tearing
apart, to the end, finally comes upon the underlying unity;
the destruction of the preconceived ideas and institutions
only serves to reveal the basic whole. Thus analytic science
finally came upon humanity as that unity to which all is to

be referred. The work of science is henceforth predominantly synthetic. The unity reveals the law and end; theory must pass over into practice; knowledge into action. This is the final significance of the French Revolution. Humanity finally became conscious of itself as one whole; "after having groped for centuries in the darkness of infancy without consciousness of itself, and by the mere motor force of its organism, the grand moment came when, like the individual, it took possession of itself." The French Revolution is the first conscious attempt to make action, the practical affairs of life, the expression of reason. It presents a scene hitherto unknown in history: "the scene of philosophers radically changing the whole of previously received ideas and carrying out the greatest of all revolutions on deliberate faith in system." That the outward, the apparent, result should have been in many regards unsatisfactory is no cause for wonder. The Revolution interpreted its idea, the control of life by reason, in the light of a narrow conception of reason; it did not recognize the reason already embodied in institutions, simply because that reason had not been inserted by itself; it interpreted reason in a sense which made it opposed to instinct. The inevitable temporary result was the substitution of instability and upheaval for an established order. The outcome was such as to discredit with many the whole attempt. But this is to confuse the application of the principle, at first necessarily imperfect, with the principle itself. In reality, "the principle involved admits of no controversy. Intelligence alone must reign, intelligence alone. Sense is to govern the world." And again Renan says: "The doctrine which is to be maintained at all hazards is that the mission of intellect is the reforming of society according to its own principles." And once more: "Hence by every way open to us we are beginning to proclaim the right of reason to reform society by means of rational science and the theoretical knowledge of existing things."

What, then, is to be the effect of this development of science when it gets to the point of recognizing the unity of humanity, upon art—including poetry—and religion? Upon these points Renan had no more doubt than upon the social mission of science. When science gets to the comprehensive

synthesis of humanity, poetry and science must flow together. Just because science, in its fulness, is the science of
humanity, its highest development must mean, to give the
whole of human nature full play—to give the sympathies
their due place. But, on the other hand, since it is the business of science to reveal in its truth the unity, sympathy
and admiration can have their full (free) chance only as
science does its work, tearing down false idols in order to
make plain the truth. "The pretended poetic natures who
imagined that they could get to the true sense of things without science will then turn out to be so many chimera-
mongers, and the austere savants who shall have neglected
the more delicate gifts . . . will remind us of the ingenious
myth of the daughters of Minyas, who were changed into
bats because unable to get beyond argument in presence
of signs to which a more generous method of explanation
should have been applied." If, indeed, there is no meaning
in the world, then science can only destroy poetry; but only
on this condition. How shall we limit the real universe by
supposing that the paltry dreams which we have been able
up to this time to invent are superior in grandeur and
splendor to the reality which science shall reveal to us? "Has
not the temple of our God been enlarged since science revealed to us the infinity of the worlds? . . . Are we not
similarly justified in supposing that the application of
scientific   method   to   the   metaphysical   and   moral
region . . . will also simply shatter a narrow and paltry
world to open another world of infinite marvels?" The truth
is that either there is no ideal, naught but a deceiving dream,
or else this ideal is embodied in the universe and is to be
found and drawn thence by science. "The ideal is near
every one of us."

     So with religion; whatever science takes away, it is
only because it presents us with deeper truth. This conception is, indeed, the animating spirit of the book; it is so interwoven with the whole treatment that I shall only select one
or two quotations. The man of science is the real "custodian
of the sacred deposit"; "real religion is the culmination of
the discipline and cultivation of the intelligence"; "social
and religious reform will assuredly come . . . but it will

come from enlarged science common to all, and operating in the unrestricted midst of human intelligence"; "hence, science is a religion, it alone will henceforth make the creeds, for science alone can solve for man the eternal problems, the solution of which his nature imperatively demands." In the course of his discussion, Renan brings out at length the point only suggested in the above—that this religious outflowering of science is to be expected when, on one hand, its scope has been extended to take in humanity, and when, on the other, its practical outcome, if not its abstruse results, has been made the possession of all men. "It is not enough for the progress of human intelligence that a few isolated thinkers should reach very advanced posts, and that a few heads shoot up like wild oats above the common level. . . . It is a matter of great urgency to enlarge the whirl of humanity; otherwise a few individuals might reach heaven, while the mass is still dragging along upon the earth. . . . The moment intellectual culture becomes a religion, from that moment it becomes barbarous to deprive a single soul of it."

I may sum up by saying that Renan's faith in '48 was that science was to become universalized—universalized in its *range* by coming to include humanity as its subject-matter; universalized in *application* by being made, as to its salient outcome, the common possession of all men. From this extension, Renan expected further results to flow: he expected that science was to become a "social motor," the basis of ordering the affairs of men; he expected that it was to find expression in a wonderful artistic movement, and that, above all, it was to culminate in a great religious outburst. How was it in 1890?

In one sense Renan stands where he stood forty years before. He still believes that he was right at the outset of his "intellectual career in believing firmly in science and in making it the object of his life." He even says that after all he was right in '48; "save a few disappointments, progress has travelled on the lines laid down in my imagination." And yet when we come to examine Renan's later position in more detail, these few disappointments seem of more importance than the successes attained. Science in the abstract, science as the most worthy end of the few capable ones, Renan un-

doubtedly still believes in as firmly as ever. But the faith in
the social career of science, of a wide distribution of intelligence as the basis of a scientifically controlled democracy,
has all but vanished; the idea of science as lending itself to
art, to a wide idealistic interpretation of the universe, and as
flowering in a religious outburst, the conception of an appropriation of truth by all men has become to him the dream
of a youthful enthusiasm. He has learned through the experience of mature years that "intensive culture constantly adding to the sum total of human knowledge, is not the same
as extensive culture disseminating that knowledge more
and more for the welfare of the countless human beings in
existence. The sheet of water in expanding continues to lose
in depth." Thus it is that "enlightenment, morality, art will
always be represented among mankind by a magistracy, by
a minority, preserving the traditions of the true, the good,
and the beautiful." Instead of science becoming a social
motor and thus giving a basis for social organization at once
free and saturated with law, there is now disbelief in the
power of science to make its own way and realize its truth
in practice: "We have to pay dearly, that is in privileges, the
power that protects us against evil." "While, through the
constant labor of the nineteenth century, the knowledge of
facts has considerably increased, *the destiny of mankind has
become more obscure than ever.*" Could any retraction be
imagined more complete, I had almost said more abject, than
this when compared with his constant proclamation of '48
that *the* business of science is just to reveal to man his
destiny—that any other conception of science makes it but
an elaborate trifling?

As against the faith of '48 that science is to reveal the
meaning incorporate in reality, and that this is the only true
idealism, we have the constant identification, in his later
writings, of the ideal with certain fond dreams which the
cultured man will always cherish for himself, yet without
hope of verification. The ideal is no longer the aim indicated by the universe itself, and to be followed as laid bare
by inquiry; "it is very clear that our doctrine affords no basis
for a *practical* policy; on the contrary, our aim must be carefully dissimulated." As for science and religion, we must

give up all hope of attaining, so far as the mass is concerned at least, any faith and enthusiasm based on knowledge. In his *Intellectual and Moral Reform*, already alluded to,* Renan virtually proposes to the ruling powers a concordat: the ecclesiastic authorities are to allow the savants complete freedom of thought and inquiry, provided the savants, in turn, leave the masses to their existing faith without attempting to extend to them the enlightenment which they themselves have gained. In his Preface of 1890 to the *Future of Science* he seriously doubts whether any consensus of belief is open to mankind at large, except upon condition of return to primitive credulity. "It is possible that the ruin of idealistic beliefs is fated to follow hard upon the ruin of supernatural beliefs; that the real abasement of the morality of humanity is to date from the day when it has seen the reality of things. . . . Candidly, I fail to see how the foundations of a noble and happy life are to be relaid without the ancient dreams."

While a study of the reasons which have induced this apparent loss of faith in the larger and social function of science would be even more interesting than the fact itself, I do not propose here to enter at length upon the discussion. Renan himself indicates one reason when he says that at present science seems to be made for the schools rather than the schools for science. So far as much of its spirit and aim is concerned, science is the legitimate successor of the old scholasticism. The forty years since Renan wrote have not done much to add the human spirit and the human interpretation to the results of science; they have rather gone to increase its technical and remote character. Furthermore, Renan does not seem to have realized sufficiently the dead weight of intrenched class interest which resists all attempt of science to take practical form and become a "social motor." When we remember that every forward step of science has involved a readjustment of institutional life, that even such an apparently distant and indifferent region as the solar system could not be annexed to scientific inquiry with-

---

*   [See *Early Essays and OUTLINES OF A CRITICAL THEORY OF ETHICS* (*The Early Works of John Dewey, 1882–1898*, III [Carbondale: Southern Illinois University Press, 1969]), 178–79.]

out arousing the opposing force of the mightiest political organizations of the day; when we recall such things it is not surprising that the advance of scientific method to the matters closest to man—his social relationships—should have gone on more slowly than was expected. The resistance from the powers whose existence is threatened by such advance has not become less effective in becoming more indirect and subtle. One thing is certain: this decrease of faith cannot be explained as a personal idiosyncrasy of Renan's; it lies deep in the life of the last half century.

I confess to surprise that this partial retraction of Renan's has not been exploited by the reactionaries. It is certainly spoils for those, who, in their assumed concern for the moral and spiritual affairs of humanity, take every opportunity to decry science and proclaim its impotence to deal with serious matters of practice. I cannot but think that the Renan of '48 was wiser than he of '90 in the recognition of the fact that man's interests are finally and prevailingly practical; that if science cannot succeed in satisfying these interests it is hardly more than an episode in the history of humanity; that the ultimate meaning and control will always be with the power that claims this practical region for its own—if not with science, then with the power of the church from which Renan was an early apostate. It is a continual marvel that so many men of science who have abandoned and even attacked all dogmatic authority, should take refuge for themselves in agnosticism—that they should not see that any lasting denial of dogmatic authority is impossible save as science itself advances to that comprehensive synthesis which will allow it to become a guide of conduct, a social motor.

The Superstition of Necessity[1]

Lest my title give such offense as to prejudice unduly my contention, I may say that I use the term in the way indicated by its etymology: as a standing-still on the part of thought; a clinging to old ideas after those ideas have lost their use, and hence, like all superstitions, have become obstructions. For I shall try to show that the doctrine of necessity is a survival; that it holds over from an earlier and undeveloped period of knowledge; that as a means of getting out of and beyond that stage it had a certain value, but, having done its work, loses its significance. Halting judgment may, indeed, at one time have helped itself out of the slough of uncertainty, vagueness, and inadequacy on to ground of more solid and complete fact, by the use of necessity as a crutch; once upon the ground, the crutch makes progress slower and, preventing the full exercise of the natural means of locomotion, tends to paralyze science. The former support has become a burden, almost an intolerable one.

The beginning of wisdom in the matter of necessity is, I conceive, in realizing that it is a term which has bearing or relevancy only with reference to the development of judgment, not with reference to objective things or events. I do not mean by this that necessity refers to the compelling force with which we are driven to make a given affirmation: I mean that it refers to the content of that affirmation, ex-

---

[1]   This article, as the title may indicate, was suggested by Mr. Peirce's article upon "The Doctrine of Necessity Examined." As, however, my thought takes finally a different turn, I have deemed it better to let it run its own course from the start, and so have not referred, except indirectly, to Mr. Peirce's argument. I hope this will not be taken as a desire to slur over my indebtedness to him.

[*First published in* Monist, III (*Apr.* 1893), 362–79. *Not reprinted during the author's lifetime.*]

pressing the degree of coherence between its constituent factors. When we say something or other *must* be so and so, the "must" does not indicate anything in the nature of the fact itself, but a trait in our *judgment* of that fact; it indicates the degree with which we have succeeded in making a whole out of the various elements which have to be taken into account in forming the judgment. More specifically, it indicates a half-way stage. At one extreme we have two separate judgments, which, so far as consciousness is concerned, have nothing to do with each other; and at the other extreme we have one judgment into which the contents of the two former judgments have been so thoroughly organized as to lose all semblance of separateness. Necessity, as the middle term, is the midwife which, from the dying isolation of judgments, delivers the unified judgment just coming into life—it being understood that the separateness of the original judgments is not as yet quite negated, nor the unity of the coming judgment quite attained. The judgment of necessity, in other words, is exactly and solely the transition in our knowledge from unconnected judgments to a more comprehensive synthesis. Its value is just the value of this transition; as negating the old partial and isolated judgments—in its backward look—necessity has meaning; in its forward look—with reference to the resulting completely organized subject-matter—it is itself as false as the isolated judgments which it replaces. Its value is in what it rids judgment of. When it has succeeded, its value is nil. Like any go-between, its service consists in rendering itself uncalled for.

All science can ultimately do is to report or describe, to completely state, the reality. So far as we reach this standpoint regarding any fact or group of facts, we do not say that the fact *must* be such and such, but simply that it *is* such and such. There is no necessity attaching to the fact either as whole or as parts. *Qua* whole, the fact simply is what it is; while the parts, instead of being necessitated either by one another or by the whole, are the analyzed factors constituting, in their complete circuit, the whole. In stating the whole, we, as of course, state all that enters into it; if we speak of the various elements as *making* the whole, it is only in the sense of making it *up*, not of causing it. The fallacy of the necessitarian theory consists in transforming the determinate in the sense of the wholly defined, into the determined in the sense of something externally made to be what it is.

The whole, although first in the order of reality, is last in the order of knowledge. The complete statement of the whole is the goal, not the beginning of wisdom. We begin, therefore, with fragments, which are taken for wholes; and it is only by piecing together these fragments, and by the transformation of them involved in this combination, that we arrive at the real fact. There comes a stage at which the recognition of the unity begins to dawn upon us, and yet, the tradition of the many distinct wholes survives; judgment has to combine these two contradictory conceptions; it does so by the theory that the dawning unity is an effect necessarily produced by the interaction of the former wholes. Only as the consciousness of the unity grows still more is it seen that instead of a group of independent facts, held together by "necessary" ties, there is one reality, of which we have been apprehending various fragments in succession and attributing to them a spurious wholeness and independence. We learn (but only at the end) that instead of discovering and then connecting together a number of separate realities, we have been engaged in the progressive definition of one fact.

There are certain points upon which there is now *practical* agreement among all schools. What one school has got at by a logical analysis of science, another school has arrived at by the road of a psychological analysis of experience. What one school calls the unity of thought and reality, another school calls the relativity of knowledge. The metaphysical interpretation further given to these respective statements may be quite different, but, so far as they go, they come to the same thing: that objects, *as known*, are not independent of the process of knowing, but are the content of our judgments. One school, indeed, may conceive of judgment as a mere associative or habitual grouping of sensations, the other as the correlative diversification and synthesis of the self; but the practical outcome, that the "object" (anyway as known) is a form of judgment, is the same. This point being held in common, both schools must agree that *the progress of judgment is equivalent to a change in the value of objects*—that objects as they are for us, as known, change with the development of our judgments. If this be so, truth, however it be metaphysically defined, must attach to late rather than to early judgments.

I am fortunate in being able to quote from authors, who may be taken as typical of the two schools. Says Professor Caird in his article upon "Metaphysic," (lately reprinted, *Essays in Philosophy and Literature*):

Our first consciousness of things is not an immovable foundation upon which science may build, but rather a hypothetical and self-contradictory starting-point of investigation, which becomes changed and transformed as we advance (*Essays*, II, 398).

On the other hand, Mr. Venn writes (in the first chapter of his *Empirical Logic*):

Select what object we please—the most apparently simple in itself, and the most definitely parted off from others that we can discover—yet we shall find ourselves constrained to admit that a considerable mental process has been passed through before that object could be recognized as being an object, that is, as possessing some degree of unity and as requiring to be distinguished from other such unities.

He goes on to illustrate by such an apparently fixed and given object as the sun, pointing out how its unity as a persistent thing involves a continued synthesis of elements very diverse in time and space, and an analysis, a selection, from other elements in very close physical juxtaposition. He goes on to raise the question whether a dog, for example, may be said to "see" a rainbow at all, because of the complex analysis and synthesis involved in such an object. The "mental whole" (to use Mr. Venn's words, the "ideal unity" as others might term it) is so extensive and intricate that

One might almost as reasonably expect the dog to "see" the progress of democracy in the place where he lives, of which course of events the ultimate sensible constituents are accessible to his observation precisely as they are to ours.

As Mr. Venn is not discussing just the same point which I have raised, he does not refer to the partial and tentative character of our first judgments—our first objects. It is clear enough, however, that there will be all degrees between total failure to analyze and combine (as, say, in the case of the dog and rainbow) and fairly adequate grouping. The difference between the savage whose synthesis is so limited in scope that he sets up a new sun every day and the scientific man whose object is a unity comprehending differences through thousands of years of time and interactions going on through millions of miles of space is a case in point. The distinction between the respective objects is not simply a superimposition of new qualities upon an old object, that old object remaining the same; it is not getting new objects; it is a continual qualitative reconstruction of the object itself. This fact, which is the matter under consideration, is well stated by Mr. Venn, when he goes on to say:

> The act of predication, in its two-fold aspect of affirmation and denial, really is a process by which we are not only enabled to add to our information *about* objects, *but is also the process by the continued performance of which the objects had been originally acquired, or rather produced* (italics are mine).

This statement cannot be admitted at all without recognizing that the first judgments do not make the object once for all, but that the continued process of judging is a continued process of "producing" the object.

Of course the confused and hypothetical character of our first objects does not force itself upon us when we are still engaged in constructing them. On the contrary, it is only when the original subject-matter has been overloaded with various and opposing predicates that we think of doubting the correctness of our first judgments, of putting our first objects under suspicion. At the start, these objects assert themselves as the baldest and solidest of hard facts. The dogmatic and naïve quality of the original judgment is in exact proportion to its crudeness and inadequacy. The objects which are the content of these judgments thus come to be identified with reality *par excellence*; they are *facts*, however doubtful everything else. They hang on obstinately.

New judgments, instead of being regarded as better definitions of the actual fact and hence as displacing the prior object, are tacked on to the old as best they may be. Unless the
contradiction is too flagrant, the new predicates are set side
by side with the old as simply additional information; they
do not react into the former qualities. If the contradiction is
too obvious to be overlooked the new predicate is used, if
possible, to constitute another object, independent of the
former. So the savage, having to deal with the apparently
incompatible predicates of light and darkness, makes two
objects; two suns, for two successive days. Once the
Ptolemaic conception is well rooted, cycles and epicycles, almost without end, are superadded, rather than reconstruct
the original object. Here, then, is our starting point: when
qualities arise so incompatible with the object already
formed that they cannot be referred to that object, it is easier
to form a new object on their basis than it is to doubt the
correctness of the old, involving as that does the surrender
of the *object* (the fact, seemingly) and the formation of
another object.

It is easier, I say, for there is no doubt that the reluctance of the mind to give up an object once made lies deep
in its economies. I shall have occasion hereafter to point out
the teleological character of the notions of necessity and
chance, but I wish here to call attention to the fact that the
forming of a number of distinct objects has its origin in
practical needs of our nature. The analysis and synthesis
which is first made is that of most practical importance;
what is abstracted from the complex net-work of reality is
some net outcome, some result which is of value for life.
As Venn says:

> What the savage mostly wants to do is to produce some-
> thing or to avert something, not to account for a thing which has
> already happened. What interests him is to know how to kill
> somebody, not to know how somebody has been killed (p. 63 of
> *Empirical Logic*).

And again:

> What not only the savage, but also the practical man
> mostly wants, is a *general* result, say the death of his enemy. It

does not matter whether the symptoms, *i.e.*, the qualifying circumstances, are those attendant on poison, or a blow from a club, or on incantation, provided the death is brought about. But they do desire *certainty* in respect of this general result (p. 64).

Now it is this "general result," the net outcome for practical purposes, which is *the* fact, *the* object at first. Anything else is useless subtlety. That the man is dead—that is the fact; anything further is at most external circumstances which happen to accompany the fact. That the death is only a bare fraction of a fact; that the attendant "circumstances" are as much constituent factors of the real fact as the mere "death" itself (probably more so from the scientific point of view)—all this is foreign to conception. We pluck the fruit, and that fruit is the fact. Only when practical experience forces upon us the recognition that we cannot get the fruit without heeding certain other "conditions" do we consent to return upon our assumed object, put it under suspicion and question whether it is really what we took it to be. It is, we may presume, the savage who in order to get his living, has to regulate his conduct for long periods, through changes of seasons, in some continuous mode, who first makes the synthesis of one sun going through a recurring cycle of changes—the year.

As time goes on, the series of independent and isolated objects passes through a gradual change. Just as the recognition of incompatible qualities has led to setting up of separate things, so the growing recognition of similar qualities in these disparate objects begins to pull them together again. Some relation between the two objects is perceived; it is seen that neither object is just what it is in its isolation, but owes some of its meaning to the other objects. While in reality (as I hope later to point out), this "relationship" and mutual dependence means membership in a common whole, contribution to one and the same activity, a midway stage intervenes before this one fact, including as parts of itself the hitherto separate objects, comes to consciousness. The tradition of isolation is too strong to give way at the first suggestion of community. This passage-way from isolation to unity, denying the former but not admitting the latter, is necessity or determinism. The wall of partition between the two separate "objects" cannot be broken at one attack; they have to be worn away by the attrition arising from their slow movement into one another. It is the "necessary" influence which one exerts upon the other that finally rubs away the separateness and leaves them revealed as elements of one unified whole. This done, the determining influence has gone too.

The process may be symbolized as follows: M is the object, the original synthesis of the elements seen to be of practical importance; a, b, c, etc., to h are predicates of constantly growing incompatibility. When the quality i is discovered, it is so manifestly incompatible with a that all attempt to refer it to the same subject M is resisted. Two alternatives are now logically open. The subject-matter M, as the synthesis of the qualities a–h, may be taken up; it may be asked whether the object is really M with these qualities; whether it is not rather Σ, having instead of the predicates a, b, etc., the qualities ρa, $\rho \beta$, with which the new quality i is quite compatible. But this process goes against the practical grain of our knowledge; it means not only that we do not know what we thought we knew; it means that we did not *do* what we thought we did. Such unsettling of action is hardly to be borne. It is easier to erect a new object N, to which the more incompatible predicates are referred. Finally, it is discovered that both M and N have the same predicates r and s; that in virtue of this community of qualities there is a certain like element even in the qualities previously considered disparate. This mutual attraction continues until it becomes so marked a feature of the case that there is no alternative but to suppose that the r and s of one produces these qualities in the other, and thereby influences all the qualities of the other. This drawing together continues until we have the one reconstructed object Σ, with the traits ρa, $\rho \beta \tau$, etc. It is found that there is one somewhat comprehensive synthesis which includes within itself the several separate objects so far produced; and it is found that this inclusion in the larger whole reacts into the meaning of the several constituting parts—as parts of one whole, they lose traits which they seemed to possess in their isolation, and gain new traits, because of their membership in the same whole.

We have now to consider, more in detail, how the intermediate idea of necessity grows up and how it gives away upon the discovery of the one inclusive whole. Let us continue the illustration of the killing. The "general result," the death of the hated enemy, is at first the fact; all else is mere accidental circumstance. Indeed, the other circumstances at first are hardly that; they do not attract attention, having no importance. Not only the savage, but also the common-sense man of to-day, I conceive, would say that any attempt to extend the definition of the "fact" beyond the mere occurrence of the death is metaphysical refinement; that the *fact* is the killing, the death, and that that "fact" remains quite the same, however it is brought about. What has been done, in other words, is to abstract part of the real fact, part of *this* death, and set up the trait or universal thus abstracted as itself *fact*, and not only as fact, but as *the* fact, *par excellence*, with reference to which all the factors which constitute the reality, the concrete fact, of *this* death, are circumstantial and "accidental."[2]

A fragment of the whole reality, of the actual fact individualized and specified with all kind of minute detail, having been thus hypostatized into an object, the idea of necessity is in fair way to arise. These deaths in general do not occur. Although the mere death of the man, his removal from the face of the earth, is the *fact*, none the less all *actual* deaths have a certain amount of detail in them. The savage has to hit his enemy with a club or spear, or perform a magic incantation, before he can attain that all-important

[2]   The reason of this abstraction is in practical nature, as already indicated. For all the savage *cares* about it, the death in general, *is* the real fact. It is all that interests him. It is hardly worth while to attempt to persuade the savage; indeed, if he were not only a savage, but also a philosopher, he might boldly challenge the objector to present *any* definition of object which should not refer objectivity to man's practical activity; although he might, as a shrewd savage, admit that some one activity (or self) to which the object is referred has more content than another. In this case, I, for one, should not care about entering the lists against the savage. But when the common-sense philosopher, who resists all attempts to reconstruct the original object on the ground that a fact is a fact and all beyond that is metaphysics, is also a case-hardened nominalist (as he generally is), it is time to protest. It might be true that the real object is always relative to the value of some action; but to erect this pure universal into the object, and then pride one's self on enlightenment in rejecting the "scholastic figment" of the reality of universals is a little too much.

end of getting rid of him. Moreover, a man with a coat of armor on will not die just the same way as the man who is defenseless. These circumstances have to be taken into account. Now, if the "fact" had not been so rigidly identified with the bare practical outcome, the removal of the hated one, a coherent interpretation of the need for these further incidents would be open. It could be admitted that the original death was a highly complex affair, involving a synthesis of a very large number of different factors; furthermore, the new cases of murder could be employed to reconstruct the original analysis-synthesis; to eliminate supposed factors which were not relevant, and to show the presence of factors at first not suspected. In other words, the real fact would be under constant process of definition, of "production." But the stiff-necked identification of the fragment which happened to have practical importance with the real object, effectually prevents any such reaction and reconstruction. What is to be done, however, with these conditions of spear, of stone, of armor, which so obviously have something *to do* with the real fact, although, as it would seem, they are not the fact? They are considered as circumstances, *accidental*, so far as death in general is concerned; *necessary*, so far as *this* death is concerned. That is, wanting simply to get the net result of the removal of my enemy, so that he will no longer blight the fair face of nature, it is accidental how I do it; but having, after all, to kill a man of certain characteristics and surroundings in life, having to choose time and place, etc., it becomes necessary, *if* I am to succeed, that I kill him in a certain way, say, with poison, or a dynamite bomb. Thus we get our concrete, individual fact again.

Consider, then, that tortuous path from reality to reality, *via* a circuit of unreality, which calls the thought of necessity into existence. We first mutilate the actual fact by selecting some portion that appeals to our needs; we falsify, by erecting this fragment into the whole fact. Having the rest of the fact thus left on our hands for disposal, when we have no need of the concrete fact we consider it accidental, merely circumstantial; but we consider it necessary whenever we have occasion to descend from the outcome which we have abstracted back to the real fact, in all its individuality. Necessity is a device by which we both conceal from ourselves the unreal character of what we have called real, and also get rid of the practical evil consequences of hypostatizing a fragment into an independent whole.

If the purely teleological character of necessity is not yet evident, I think the following considerations will serve to bring it out. The practical value, the fruit from the tree, we pick out and set up for the entire fact so far as our past action is concerned. But so far as our *future* action is concerned, this value is a result *to be* reached; it is an end to be attained. Other factors, in reality all the time bound up in the one concrete fact or individual whole, have now to be brought in as means to get this end. Although after our desire has been met they have been eliminated as accidental, as irrelevant, yet when the experience is again desired their integral membership in the real fact has to be recognized. This is done under the guise of considering them as means which are necessary to bring about the end. Thus the idea of the circumstances as external to the "fact" is retained, while we get all the practical benefit of their being not external but elements of one and the same whole. Contingent and necessary are thus the correlative aspects of one and the same fact; conditions are accidental so far as we have abstracted a fragment and set it up as the whole; they are necessary the moment it is required to pass from this abstraction back to the concrete fact. Both are teleological in character—contingency referring to the separation of means from end, due to the fact that the end having been already reached the means have lost their value for us; necessity being the reference of means to an end *which has still to be got*. Necessary means *needed*; contingency means no longer required—because already enjoyed.

Note that the necessity of the means has reference to an end still to be attained, and in so far itself hypothetical or contingent, while the contingent circumstances are no longer needed precisely because they have resulted in a definite outcome (which, accordingly, is now a fact, and, in that sense, necessary) and we begin to see how completely necessity and chance are bound up with each other.

Their correlation may thus be stated: *If* we are to reach an end we *must* take certain means; while so far as we want an undefined end, an end in general, conditions which accompany it are mere accidents. Whichever way the relationship be stated, the underlying truth is that we are dealing with only partial phases of fact, which, having been unduly separated from each other through their erection into distinct wholes, have now to be brought back into their real unity.

In the first place, then, *if* I am to reach an end, certain means *must* be used. Here the end is obviously postulated; save as it is begged (presupposed), the necessity of the means has no sense. If, when starving, I am to live I must steal a dinner, but, having stolen, the logical but unsympathetic judge may question the relevancy (that is, the necessity) of my end, and thus cut the ground out from under the necessity of my means. My end requires *its* justification, the establishing of its validity, before the necessity of the means is anything more than hypothetical. The proximate end must be referred to a more ultimate and inclusive end to get any solid ground. Here we have our choice: we may deny the existence of any organic whole in life and keep chasing in a never-ending series, the *progressus ad infinitum*, after an end valid in itself. In this case we never get beyond a hypothetical necessity—something is necessary *if* we are to have something else, the necessity being relative to the implied doubt. Or, being convinced that life is a whole and not a series merely, we may say there is one comprehensive end which gives its own validity to the lesser ends in so far as they constitute it. While, on the other alternative, we reach only a hypothetical necessity, on this we reach none at all. The comprehensive end is no end at all in the sense of something by itself to be reached by means external to it. Any such end would be simply one in the infinite series and would be itself hypothetical. Whenever minor ends cease to be in turn means to further ends it is because they have become parts, constituent elements, of the higher end and thus ceased to be steps towards an end and beyond and outside of themselves. Given a final (*i.e.*, inclusive) end, eating and drinking, study and gossip, play and business, cease to be means *towards* an end and become its concrete definition, its analytic content. The minor activities state the supreme activity in its specific factors.

Our dilemma is the choice between an end which itself has no existence save upon presupposition of another end, (is contingent), and an end which as an end in itself simply *is*.

The externality of means to end is merely a symptom of lack of specification or concreteness in the end itself. *If* I am going to invent some improvement in a type-writer, the necessity of going through certain preliminary steps is exactly proportionate to the indefiniteness of my conception of what the improvement is to be; when the end is realized, the operations which enter into the realization cease to be means necessary to an end and become the specific *content* of that end. The improvement is a *fact*, having such and such elements defining it. If I simply want, in general, to get my mail I *must* take this path (there being but one road); but if my end is not thus general, if it is individualized with concrete filling, the walk to the office may become a part of the end, a part of the actual fact. In so far, of course, it loses all aspect of necessitation. It simply *is*. And in general, so far as my end is vague, or abstract, so far as it is not specified as to its details, so far the filling up of its empty schema to give it particularity (and thus make it fact) appears as a means necessary to reach an end outside itself. The growth in concreteness of the end itself is transformed into ways of effecting an end already presupposed. Or, to state it in yet one other way, determination in the sense of definition in consciousness is hypostatized into determination in the sense of a physical making.

The point may come out more clearly if we consider it with the emphasis on chance instead of upon necessity. The usual statement that chance is relative to ignorance seems to me to convey the truth though not in the sense generally intended—viz., that if we knew more about the occurrence we should see it necessitated by its conditions. Chance is relative to ignorance in the sense rather that it refers to an indefiniteness in our conception of what we are doing. In our consciousness of our end (our acts) we are always making impossible abstractions; we break off certain phases of the act which are of chief interest to us, without any regard to whether the concrete conditions of action—that is, the deed in its whole definition—permits any such division. Then, when in our actual doing the circumstances to which we have not attended thrust themselves into consciousness—when, that is to say, the act appears in more of its own specific nature—we dispose of those events, foreign to our conscious purpose, as accidental; we did not want them or intend them—what more proof of their accidental character is needed? The falling of a stone upon a man's head as he walks under a window is "chance," for it has nothing to do with what the man proposed to do, it is no part of his conception of that walk. To an enemy who takes that means of killing him, it is anything but an accident, being involved in *his* conscious purpose. It is "chance" when we throw a two and a six; for the concreteness of the act falls outside of the content of our intention. We intended *a* throw, some throw, and in so far the result is not accidental, but this special result, being irrelevant to our conception of what we were to do, in so far is contingent. The vagueness or lack of determinateness in our end, the irrelevancy of actual end to conscious intent, chance, are all names for the same thing. And if I am asked whether a gambler who has a hundred dollars upon the outcome does not *intend* to throw double sixes, I reply that he has no such intention—unless the dice are loaded. He may *hope* to make that throw, but he cannot intend it save as he can define that act—tell how to do it, tell, that is, just *what* the act is. Or, once more, if I intend to get my mail and there are four paths open to me it is chance which I take, just in proportion to the abstractness of my end. If I have not defined it beyond the mere "general result" of getting mail, anything else is extraneous and in so far contingent. If the end is individualized to the extent, say, of getting the mail in the shortest possible time, or with the maximum of pleasant surroundings, or with the maximum of healthy exercise, the indifference of the "means," and with it their contingency, disappears. This or that path is no longer a mere means which *may* be taken to get a result foreign to its own value; the path is an intrinsic part of the end.

In so far as a man presents to himself an end in general, he sets up an abstraction so far lacking in detail as (taken *per se*) to exclude the possibility of realization. In order to exist as concrete or individual (and of course, nothing can exist except as individual or concrete) it must be defined or particularized. But so far as consciousness is concerned the original vague end is *the* reality; it is all that the man cares about and hence constitutes his act. The further particularization of the end, therefore, instead of appearing as what it really is, viz., the discovery of the actual reality, presents itself as something outside that end. This externality to the end previously realized in consciousness is, taken as mere externality, contingency, or accident; taken as none the less so bound up with the desired end that it must be gone through before reaching that end, it is necessary. Chance, in other words, stands for the irrelevancy as the matter at first presents itself to consciousness; necessity is the required, but partial, negation of this irrelevancy. Let it be complete, instead of partial, and we have the one real activity defined throughout. With reference to this reality, conditions are neither accidental nor necessary, but simply constituting elements—they neither may be nor must be, but just are. What is irrelevant is now not simply indifferent; it is excluded, eliminated. What is relevant is no longer something required in order to get a result beyond itself; it is incorporated into the result, it is integral.

It now remains to connect the two parts of our discussion, the logical and the practical consideration of necessity, and show that, as suggested, logical necessity rests upon teleological—that, indeed, it is the teleological read backwards. The logical process of discovering and stating the reality of some event simply reverses the process which the mind goes through in setting up and realizing an end. Instead of the killing of an enemy as something to be accomplished, we have the fact of a murder to be accounted for. Just as on the practical side, the end, as it first arises in consciousness, is an end in general and thus contrasts with the concrete end which is individualized; so the fact, as at first realized in consciousness, is a *bare* fact, and thus contrasts with the actual event with its complete particularization.

The actual fact, the murder as it really took place, is one thing; the fact as it stands in consciousness, the phases of the actual event which are picked out and put together, is another thing. The fact of knowledge, it is safe to say, is no *fact* at all; that is, if there had been in reality no more particularization, no more of detail, than there is consciousness, the murder would never have happened. But just as, practically, we take the end in general to be the real thing, (since it is the only thing of any direct interest), so in knowledge we take the bare fact as abstracted from the actual whole, as *the* fact. Just as the end of the savage is merely to kill his enemy, so the "fact" is merely the dead body with the weapon sticking in it. The fact, as it stands in consciousness, is indeterminate and partial, but, since it is in consciousness by itself, it is taken as a whole and as the certain thing. But as the abstractness of the "end in general" is confessed in the fact that means are required in order to make it real—to give it existence—so the unreal character of the "fact" is revealed in the statement that the causes which produced it are unknown and have to be discovered. The bare fact thus becomes a result to be accounted for: in this conception the two sides are combined; the "fact" is at once given a certain reality of its own while at the same time the lack of concreteness is recognized in the reference to external causes.

The gradual introduction of further factors, under the guise of causes accounting for the effect, defines the original vague "fact," until, at last, when it is accounted for, we have before us the one and only concrete reality. This done, we no longer have an effect to be accounted for, and causes which produce it, but one fact whose statement or description is such and such. But intermediate between the isolation and the integration is the stage when necessity appears. We have advanced, we will suppose, from the bare fact of the murder to the discovery of a large amount of "circumstantial" evidence regarding that fact. We hear of a man who had a quarrel with the deceased; he cannot account for himself at the time when the murder *must* have been committed; he is found to have had a weapon like that with which the murder *must* have been committed. Finally we conclude he *must* have been the murderer. What do these "musts" (the "must" of the time, weapon, and murderer) mean? Are they not obviously the gradual filling-in of the previously empty judgment, through bringing things at first unconnected into relation with each other? The existence of the man M. N. is wholly isolated from the "fact" of the murder till it is learned that he had a grudge against the murdered man; this third fact, also distinct *per se*, brought into connection with the others (the "fact" of the murder and of the existence of M. N.) compels them to move together; the result is at first the possibility, later, as the points of connection get more and more marked and numerous, the "necessity," that M. N. is the murderer. Further, it is clear that this "must" marks not a greater certainty or actuality than a mere "is" would indicate, but rather a doubt, a surmise or guess gradually gaining in certainty. When the fact is really made out to our satisfaction, we drop the "must" and fall back on the simple *is*. Only so long as there is room for doubt, and thus for argument do we state that the time and weapon must have been such and such. So when we finally conclude that the murderer must have been M. N., it means that we have woven a large number of facts, previously discrete, into such a state of inter-relationship that we do not see how to avoid denying their discreteness and incorporating them all into one concrete whole, or individual fact. That we still say "must" shows, however, that we have not quite succeeded in overcoming the partial and indefinite character of the original "fact." Had we succeeded in getting the whole fact before us the judgment would take this form: The murder *is* a fact of such and such definite nature, having as its content such and such precise elements. In this comprehensive whole all distinction of effect to be accounted for and causes which produce clean disappears. The idea of necessity, in a word, comes in only while we are still engaged in correcting our original error, but have not surrendered it root and branch; this error being that the fragment of reality which we grasp is concrete enough to warrant the appellation "fact."

A great deal of attention has been directed to the category of cause and effect. One striking feature of the ordinary consideration is, that it takes for granted the matter most needing investigation and aims the inquiry at the dependent member of the firm. The effect seems to be so clearly *there*, while the cause is so obviously something to be searched for that the category of effect is assumed, and it is supposed that only the idea of causation is in need of examination. And yet this abstraction of certain phases of fact, the erection of the parts thus abstracted into distinct entities, which, though distinct, are still dependent in their mode of existence, is precisely the point needing examination. It is but another instance of the supreme importance of our practical interests. The effect is the end, the practical outcome, which interests us; the search for causes is but the search for the means which would produce the result. We call it "means and end" when we set up a result to be reached in the future and set ourselves upon finding the causes which put the desired end in our hands; we call it "cause and effect" when the "result" is given, and the search for means is a regressive one. In either case the separation of one side from the other, of cause from effect, of means from end, has the same origin: a partial and vague idea of the whole fact, together with the habit of taking this part (because of its superior practical importance) for a whole, for a fact.

I hope now to have made good my original thesis: that the idea of necessity marks a certain stage in the development of judgment; that it refers to a residuum, in our judgments and thus in our objects, of indeterminateness or vagueness, which it replaces without wholly negating; that it is thus relative to "chance" or contingency; that its value consists wholly in the impulse given judgment towards the *is*, or the concrete reality defined throughout. The analysis has been long; the reader may have found it not only tedious, but seemingly superfluous, since, as he may be saying to himself, no one nowadays regards necessity as anything but a name for fixed uniformities in nature, and of this view of the case nothing has been said. I hope, however, that when we come to a consideration of necessity as equivalent to uniformity, it will be found that the course of this discussion has not been irrelevant, but the sure basis for going further.

Anthropology and Law

Going back in history is like going from the mouths of rivers now far separate, as separate as the Pacific Ocean from the Gulf of Mexico, to a common watershed. We reach a point where mighty streams, now as afar apart in character and use as they are in space, are almost together in place and kind. Indeed, the comparison is not quite adequate; as to the river-streams, we can only say that their sources were almost together, while of the historic streams, we find their rise and spring wholly together. I want to illustrate this general truth by some facts in the development of law; showing how some of the most highly developed legal ideas and practices of to-day can be traced to a beginning in the crude psychological structure of primitive man. On the legal side I shall draw my material almost entirely from a book, of equal interest to the student of law in its professional phases, of history, of anthropology and ethics—I refer to *The Common Law* of O. W. Holmes, Jr. And in passing let me say that this seems to me a book worthy in all respects to be put side by side with anything in the way of historic interpretation produced by Sir Henry Maine, having, in spite of its technical aim, equal comprehensiveness of generalization, while its mastery of detail is, if possible, more complete and accurate.

It is a commonplace of anthropology that the primitive man sees only himself in all his surroundings. I doubt myself if this is any more true of the man of nineteen thousand years before Christ than it is of the man nineteen hundred years after, but the self of the modern man is so much more split up, so much more intricate, that in many of his ideas it

[*First published in* Inlander (*University of Michigan*), III (*Apr. 1893*), 305–8. *Not previously reprinted.*]

seems as if he had got far away from himself. But there is
no such question as to early man. His whole world was himself spread out for inspection. He moved, because he was
alive; rivers and clouds moved for the same reason. When he
struck some one, he struck because he was angry and wished
to hurt; if a tree fell on his hut, there could be no other
reason. In one of the Chippewa Indian legends, it is told of
the "Good Spirit" that after a long and toilsome struggle
with the Evil Spirit (which tale, if we had time to go into
it, would be simply a reflection of the struggle of the Indian
himself for food against the odds of climate and a bad
season), he finally secures an elk for himself. About to eat
it, he hears a creaking in the tree above him, made by the
rubbing of branches together. The Good Spirit, famished
as he is, stops to say: "Ah, you have troubled me enough,
you evil one; but I am not going to hear you croak while I
am eating my dinner." So he climbs the tree and cuts off the
limb! What similarity is there between this frame of mind
(which could be duplicated from any early myth or legend
whatsoever) and the modern law regarding the responsibility of employers for the damage done by their employees,
in the course of their work? None whatever! we should un-
hesitatingly reply—unless we reascended the stream of history to find the watershed where the stream of law began to
part ways with the crude ideas of early man. In this case
we should find, as Holmes found, that the law of indirect
liability for acts of servants, and for animals owned by one,
is a most undeniable offspring of just this attitude of mind.

In an old Athenian cult, there is a story of an ox slain
at the altar of a god who was, so to speak, a strict vegetarian.
Some one must be held responsible for the slight to the god;
as with children still, one passes the blame on to the other,
saying "He did it," until the man who struck the blow fixes
the final responsibility upon the ax. The ax is duly charged,
tried, condemned and punished, and the god is satisfied. In
later days, when this cult was annually gone through with
in Athens, it had become, without doubt, a spectacle, a
dramatic form. That in earlier days, the trial had reality, we
are not left to guess. In the "second-best" state, which Plato
constructs in the *Laws*, we read as follows: "If any lifeless

thing deprive a man of life, except in the case of a thunder-
bolt or other fatal dart sent from the gods, whether a man
is killed by lifeless objects falling upon him or by his falling
upon them, the nearest of kin shall appoint the nearest
neighbor to be a judge, and thereby acquit himself and the
whole family of guilt. And he shall cast forth the guilty
thing beyond the border, as has been said about the
animals" (*Laws*, ix, 873–74). Here the object is recognized
as lifeless, but the story points, like a needle to a pole, to a
time when the object was just as personal and just as personally responsible as any murderer can be. The remark
about the dart from the gods but strengthens the point;
extraordinary moving objects, those upon which people
could not put their hands, were still personified, but attributed to supernal powers. That this proviso was no fancy
sketch of Plato's, but represents the spirit of Athenian life,
is evidenced by the fact that this same provision is found in
the regular Athenian procedure. (See Télfy, *Corpus Juris
Attici*, pp. 590–91.)

That the same principle was applied to animals we find
incidental reference, in the passage quoted from Plato, and
definitely stated in a previous passage. In Exod. (21:28) we
find this: "If an ox gore a man or a woman, that they die:
then the ox shall be surely stoned, and his flesh shall not be
eaten; but the owner of the ox shall be quit." When we
consider that as matter of course slaves would be regarded
in the same way, we begin to get light on the process by
which the modern theory regarding liability for employees
came into existence. The first stage in law is always the immediate reaction against an offender to destroy him; the
next is almost invariably the process of composition, of buying off. It is poor economy all around to destroy so recklessly;
the owner loses his tool, his animal or his slave, and the of-
fended party finds that he is no better off, save for the immediate relief of his feelings. So the owner gradually
secures the privilege of buying off his slave or whatever. It
is in no way regarded as a recognition of liability; it is
simply to save a valuable article from destruction. Gradually
the original principle fades from sight, from memory, and
then it is announced as a fixed principle of right, perhaps as

a part of the unchangeable law of nature, that a principal is responsible for the damage done by his servants.

I shall not go through all the steps, although the interested person will find them in Holmes. One case shows such an interesting survival down almost till to-day that I cannot refrain from specific reference to it. Holmes shows that many peculiarities of modern admiralty law are historically direct consequents of the apparent self-vitality manifested by ships. That a ship is a "thing of life," that it has its own will and wish, that, at times, it follows its own notions, spite of what captain or pilot will do, almost every sailor implicitly believes. By the old maritime law the ship was made both the source and the limit of liability. Not the owner but the ship had to be proceeded against, and the limit of damage to be collected was always the value of the ship. The ship itself came in as personal and responsible being, it might almost be said. As referred to the Middle Ages the doctrine does not strike us as peculiar; it will probably strike the reader strangely to find the notion so deeply imbedded that, so far as form of words is concerned, it has been sanctioned by the Supreme Court of the United States. The following words are those of Marshall, quoted with approval by Story. "This is not a proceeding against the owner; it is a proceeding against the vessel *for all offense committed by the vessel. . . .* The vessel acts and speaks by the master. She reports herself by the master. It is, therefore, not unreasonable that the vessel should be affected by this report."

I do not mean, of course, that these early customs of the savage mind are the causes of our modern law practice. The causes are undoubtedly in the practical value, the working utility, of the rules themselves. But the rules are none the less the historic children of the old customs, preserved and modified through the agency of natural selection. The instances given illustrate, indeed, the law of historical development of all institutional forms. Every new institution is, like the organ of an animal, an old one modified. Continuity is never broken; the old is never annihilated at a stroke, the new never a creation *ab initio*. It is simply a question of morphology. But what controls the modification in the historic continuity is the practical usefulness of the institution or organ in question. It is a psychological law — a law which may be said to underlie all history — that the mind can attend to anything only as that thing enters into some action, only as it is to be put to some use; or more truly stated, the act of attention is the mind getting ready to put the thing to which attention is given to some use. So far then as any law, any institution, loses all practical value, it inevitably drops back out of consciousness; the new use, whatever that is, is read into the affair; interpretation has taken place, and the old institution has changed its form by taking on a new function — and all this without any breach of continuity having occurred in consciousness.

Self-Realization as the Moral Ideal

If one turn to any of the important ethical discussions of hardly a generation ago, he finds the center of interest in the origin of moral judgments. It was assumed, as matter of course, that ethical theory always has been and always will be divided between two schools—the empiricists and the intuitionalists, and that this division exhausts the whole realm. It was assumed that the opposition between utilitarianism and intuitionalism is essentially this question of the origin of our knowledge of moral distinctions. Indeed, I do not know a discussion of that period which even suggests the fact so obvious to us, that the division of ethical theories into these two kinds is a cross-division, one relating to the ethical criterion, the other to the method of arriving at knowledge of it. Three main influences were at work, however, in shifting the center of attention to the question of the nature of the moral end itself. Utilitarianism tended to call attention to the character of the end involved in action; the appearance of intuitive utilitarian systems, like that of Sidgwick, showed the insufficiency of the old disjunction; finally the introduction, from Germany, of a mode of ethical thinking which was neither utilitarian nor intuitive, yet agreeing with the former in holding that the morality of all acts is measured by their efficiency in establishing a certain end, and falling in with the latter in holding that moral ideas are not the result of mere association, but of something in the facts themselves, brought in new problems and new controversies.

In the newer contentions regarding the moral end, the idea of "self-realization" insists upon its claims. The idea

[*First published in* Philosophical Review, II (*Nov. 1893*), 652–64. *Not previously reprinted.*]

seems to me an important one, bringing out two necessary phases of the ethical ideal: namely, that it cannot lie in subordination of self to any law outside itself; and that, starting with the self, the end is to be sought in the active, or volitional, side rather than in the passive, or feeling, side. Yet with those who use the phrase, there is often a tendency, it seems to me, to rest in it as a finality, instead of taking it as a statement of a problem. As warning off from certain defective conceptions, in pointing to an outline of a solution, it is highly serviceable; whether it has any more positive and concrete value depends upon whether the ideas of self and of realization are worked out, or are left as self-explaining assumptions.

As a part of the attempt to give the conception of "self-realization" a somewhat more precise content, I propose in this paper to criticize one idea of the self more or less explicit in much of current discussion. I thus hope to bring out, by way of contrast, what appears to me the important factor of the conception of self as the ethical ideal. The notion which I wish to criticize is that of the self as a presupposed fixed *schema* or outline, while realization consists in the filling up of this *schema*. The notion which I would suggest as substitute is that of the self as always a concrete *specific* activity; and, therefore, (to anticipate) of the identity of self and realization. It is extremely difficult to find an explicit statement of the doctrine of the presupposed or schematic self, and of realization as the filling up of this outline, and I am, accordingly, to some extent, under the difficulty of having to build up the notion criticized through the very process of criticism. One or two considerations, however, will show that the notion is not a figment or man of straw. Such a theory as that of T. H. Green, for example, with its assumption of an "eternally complete consciousness" constituting the moral self to be realized by man, illustrates what I mean by a fixed and presupposed self. Any theory which makes the self something *to be* realized, which makes the process of moral experience a process of gradually attaining this ideal self, illustrates the same conception. Any theory which does not make the self always "there and then," which does not make it a reality as specific and concrete as a growing tree or a moving planet must, in one form or another, set up a rigid self, and conceive of realization as filling up its empty framework. In a previous number of *The Philosophical Review*,[1] I criticized the opposition made by Green between the moral ideal as self-satisfaction in general and all special satisfactions of desire. The present paper may be considered a continuation of that, save that now I desire to discuss the question of realization, rather than the question of the ideal, and to emphasize *the notion of a working or practical self* against that of a fixed or presupposed self.

The idea of realization implies the conception of capacities or possibilities. Upon the basis of a presupposed complete self, the *possibilities* of the present, working or individual self are the *actual* content of this presupposed self.[2] I do not propose to go into the strictly metaphysical difficulties of this conception. The difficulty, however, bound up with the question why a completely realized self should think it worth while to duplicate itself in an unrealized, or relatively empty, self, how it could possibly do this even if it were thought worth while, and why, after the complete self had produced the incomplete self, it should do so under conditions rendering impossible (seemingly eternally so) any adequate approach of the incomplete self to its own completeness—this difficulty, I say, should make us wary of the conception, provided we can find any working theory concerning unrealized powers (capacities) which will avoid the difficulty.

We may accept as a *practical* fact that we do, at a given time, have unrealized powers, or capacities, and that the realization of these powers constitutes, at the time, our

---

[1]   Vol. I, No. 6, "Green's Theory of the Moral Motive" [*Early Works*, III, 155–73].

[2]   *E.g.*, "The one divine mind gradually reproduces itself in the human soul. *In virtue of this principle in him man has definite capacities*, the realization of which, since in it alone he can satisfy himself, forms his true good. They are not realized, however, in any life that can be observed . . . and for this reason we cannot say with any adequacy what the capabilities are" (Green, *Prolegomena*, p. 189). Here we have it definitely implied, the capacities of man are simply the already realized content of the presupposed self. On p. 181 it is even more explicitly stated.

moral goal. The question is as to the interpretation of this "fact." As the first objection to the interpretation which makes the capacities simply the blank form corresponding to a presupposed perfect self, let me point out that the only capacities which demand realization, thus forming our ideal, are *specific* capacities; that, if there is any such thing as capacity in general, it never presents itself to our consciousness, much less imposes an end of action upon us. The capacities of a child, for example, are not simply of *a* child, not of a man, but of *this* child, not of any other. So far as they have to do with the ideal to be realized, it is the precise capabilities existing at that exact moment, capabilities as individualized as that place in space and that portion of time which are concerned. Make the capacities "infinite," or the content of some presupposed self, instead of actually then and there, actually knowable, and they furnish no end to be executed. And if it be objected that the child should be trained to act with reference to some "infinite" capacity, some unlimited and immeasurable power which will keep appearing as he grows older, and that failure to take that into account from the first, means a stunted development for the child, the objection will serve to emphasize the point. If this capacity is anything which may be taken into account, then it is a part of the actual definite situation; it is not infinite in the sense of indefinite, although it may be "infinite" in value—which means, I suppose, that it is the only thing worth specially considering at the time. Suppose, for example, the self which the child is to realize involves some artistic capacity. Let it be said that this end transcends the child's consciousness, and therefore is not an actually present capacity. None the less, the realization of this artistic self can be made the end only if it is present in *some one's* consciousness. The objection means simply that the situation which the parent or the educator sees, the reality upon which he has his eye, is larger than the one which the child sees. It is not a case of contrast between an actuality which is definite, and a presupposed but unknown capacity, but between *a smaller and a larger view* of the actuality. If the child's real end is different from that which would immediately suggest itself to him, it is not because some capacity transcending his specific self (belonging to some presupposed ideal self) has been set up for him, but because the child is not adequately aware of his specific self. Furthermore, the wider range of the educator's knowledge would be useless merely as wider. The mere fact that he saw further ahead, that he foresaw a later development would not avail in determining the self to be realized unless the educator were capable of translating this development back into the present activities of the child. In other words, in no sense does the artistic capacity of the child, *in general*, fix his end; his end is fixed by the fact that even *now* he has a certain quickness, vividness, and plasticity of vision, a certain deftness of hand, and a certain motor co-ordination by which his hand is stimulated to work in harmony with his eye. It is such considerations as these, having absolutely nothing to do with *mere* or with general possibilities, but concerned with existing activities, which determine the end of conduct in the case referred to. Capacity, in any sense in which it requires to be realized for the sake of morality, is not only relative to specific action, *but is itself action*.

If capacity is itself definite activity and not simply possibility of activity, the question arises why we conceive of it as capability, not as complete in itself. If, for example, the artistic capacity of the child is already activity of the eye, hand, and brain, and if the realization of this capacity refer not to some remote attainment, but to the immediate activity of the time, why do we think of it as *capacity* at all?

In answer, we may note that our first conception of our activity is highly vague and indeterminate. We are conscious of the activity of our eye and ear in general, but not of just the way in which they work. We are apt, almost certain, however, to identify this partial and abstract conception of their activity with the real activity. Then, when the more specific factors of the activity force themselves into consciousness, these lie outside of the previous *idea* of the activity, and (the activity having been identified with our consciousness of it) seem, therefore, to be external or indifferent to the activity itself.

One of the many of Professor James's important contributions to psychology is his demonstration of the fact that "the only meaning of essence is teleological, and that classification and conception are purely teleological weapons of the mind."[3] He goes on to state that the essence is that *which is so important for my interests* that, comparatively, other properties may be omitted. Now, in our recognition of our own activity, we are, of course, first conscious (consciousness, as explicit, and immediate interest being one and the same) of that phase of our activity which most interests us. When other parts of the activity force themselves upon consciousness, they seem, to some extent, to be accidental, because lying outside of that which we have conceived as *the* activity. We thus come to divide our activity into parts —one the factor which permanently interests us, the other that in which our interest varies from time to time. The factor of enduring interest comes to be thought of as a sort of fixed permanent core, which is *the* reality, but which may, from time to time, go through more or less external changes, or which may assume new, but more or less transitory operations—these further changes and operations corresponding, of course, to those phases of the activity in which our interest is shifting. In the act of vision, for example, the thing that seems nearest us, that which claims continuously our attention, is the eye itself. We thus come to abstract the eye from all special acts of seeing; we make the eye the *essential* thing in sight, and conceive of the circumstances of vision as indeed *circumstances*; as more or less accidental concomitants of the permanent eye. Of course, there is no such thing as the eye in general; in reality, the actual fact is always an act of seeing, and the "circumstances" are just as "necessary" and "essential" parts of the activity as is the eye itself. Or more truly, there is no such thing as this "eye"; there is only the seeing. Nevertheless, our continuing interest being in the eye, we cannot surrender our abstraction; we only add to it another one— that of certain "conditions of exercise" as also necessary and essential to every act. On this side, too, we carry our abstraction to the utmost possible; we say that light, or vibrations of ether, is the essential condition of the act of vision. *The eye*

---

3   James, *Psychology*, II, 335.

now becomes the capacity of seeing; the vibrations of ether,
conditions required for the exercise of the capacity. That is
to say, instead of frankly recognizing that eye and vibrations
are pure abstractions from the only real thing, the act of
seeing, we try to keep the two in their separateness, while
we restore their unity by thinking of one as capacity, or
possibility to be realized only when the other is present. Instead of the one organic activity we now have an organ on
one side, and environment on the other.

But we cannot stop here. The eye in general and the
vibrations in general do not, even in their unity, constitute
the act of vision. A multitude of other factors are included.
These vary from time to time. Those which continue to attract attention least often are dismissed as merely indifferent; others appear with sufficient frequency so that some
account of them has to be taken. The original core which
was abstracted and identified with the reality, comes to be
conceived as capacity for reaching these things as ends also,
while they are conceived as conditions that help realize it.[4]

With this in mind let us return to our child possessed of
an artistic capacity. I hope the preceding discussion has
made it obvious that the recognition of artistic capacity
means that we are now becoming more aware of what the
concrete reality of the child's activity is. We are not primarily finding out what he *may* be, but what he *is.* But
having already identified his self with what we previously
knew of it, we try to reconcile our two different conceptions
by still keeping our old idea of the child's powers of his
eye, hand, etc., but attributing to them new capacities to be
realized under certain conditions—these conditions, in turn,
being simply the new factors which we have now found in-

---

[4]   In my *Outlines of Ethics*, pp. 97–102 [*Early Works*, III, 301–4],
I have developed this same idea by showing that we may analyze individuality into the two sides of "capacity" and "environment" (this, of
course, being what I have above termed "conditions of action"), and then
destroy the separateness seemingly involved in this analysis by recognizing that either of these, taken in its totality, *is* the other. In an article
entitled "The Superstition of Necessity" in the *Monist,* Vol. III, No. 3
[*Early Works*, IV, 19–36], I have developed at greater length the idea
that necessity and possibility are simply the two correlative abstractions
into which the one reality falls apart during the process of our conscious
apprehension of it.

volved in the activity, though external to it *so far as our previous knowledge was concerned*. We call any activity capacity, in other words, whenever we first take it abstractly, or at less than its full meaning, and then add to it further relations which we afterwards find involved in it. We first transform our partial conception into a rigid fact, and then, discovering that there is more than the bare fact which we have so far taken into account, we call this broken-off fact capacity for the something more.

To realize capacity does not mean, therefore, to act so as to fill up some presupposed ideal self. It means to act at the height of action, to realize its full meaning. The child realizes his artistic capacity whenever he acts with the completeness of his existing powers. To realize capacity means to act concretely, not abstractly; it is primarily a direction to us with reference to knowledge, not with reference to performance. It means: do not act until you have seen the relations, the content, of your act. It means: let there be for you all the meaning in the act that there could be for any intelligence which saw it in its reality and not abstractly. The whole point is expressed when we say that no possible future activities or conditions have anything to do with the present action except as they enable us to take deeper account of the present activity, to get beyond the mere superficies of the act, to see it in its totality. Indeed, if required to go here into the logic of the matter, I think it could be shown that these future acts and conditions *are* simply the present act in its mediated content. But, in any case, to realize capacity means to make the special act which has to be performed an activity of the entire *present* self—so far is it from being one step towards the attainment of a remote ideal self.

One illustration will serve, possibly, to enforce the point practically as well as theoretically. We have to a considerable extent, given up thinking of this life as merely a preparation for another life.[5] Very largely, however, we

---

5   This separation of "this" world and the "other" world serves itself to illustrate the point. The conception of the other world arose with the dawning conception of spiritual meanings beyond those as yet realized in life. But life had been identified with the previous conceptions of it and thus hardened into a rigid fact which resisted change; the new meaning

think of some parts of this life as merely preparatory to other later stages of it. It is so very largely as to the process of education; and if I were asked to name the most needed of all reforms in the spirit of education, I should say: "Cease conceiving of education as mere preparation for later life, and make of it the full meaning of the present life." And to add that only in this case does it become truly a preparation for after life is not the paradox it seems. An activity which does not have worth enough to be carried on for its own sake cannot be very effective as a preparation for something else. By making the present activity the expression of the full meaning of the case, that activity is, indeed, an end in itself, not a mere means to something beyond itself; but, in being a totality, it is also the condition of all future integral action. It forms the habit of requiring that every act be an outlet of the whole self, and it provides the instruments of such complete functioning.

To suppose that an infant cannot take a complete and present interest in learning to babble simple words because this is not the same as rolling off ponderous polysyllables, or that there is any way for him to attain the mastery of the complexities of language save as his attention is *completely* taken up at the proper time with his babbling, is equivalent to that conception of the realization of capacity which makes it a possibility, with reference to some "infinite" ideal in general.

In conceiving of capacity, then, not as mere possibility of an ideal or infinite self, but as the more adequate comprehension and treatment of the present activity, we are enabled to substitute a working conception of the self for a metaphysical definition of it. We are also, I believe, enabled to get rid of a difficulty which everyone has felt, in one way or

---

could not, therefore, be put into life (or this world), and so was dislocated into another life. But the value of the spiritual ideal thus set off was in deepening the insight into the significance of actual life, until it was read back into this actual existence, transforming its meaning. So far as we are yet half way between the complete separation and the complete identification, we consider this world as preparation, or capacity, for the next. We thus attempt to retain the separateness of the two activities while at the same time we recognize the facts which point to their identity. The conception of capacity, when analyzed, will be found in every case to be just this go-between in our understanding of an activity.

another, in the self-realization theory. In the ordinary conception of the presupposed self, that self is already there as a fixed fact, even though it be as an eternal self. The only reason for performing any moral act is then *for* this self. Whatever is done, is done for this fixed self. I do not believe it possible to state this theory in a way which does not make action selfish in the bad sense of selfish.[6] When we condemn an act as bad, because selfish, we always mean, I think, exactly this: the person in question acted from interest in his past or fixed self, instead of holding the self open for instruction;—instead, that is, of finding the self in the activity called for by the situation. I do not see that it is a bit better to act to *get* goodness *for* the self, than it is to get pleasure for the self. The selfishness of saints who are bound to maintain their own saintliness at all hazards, is Pharisaism; and Pharisaism is hardly more lovable, or more practically valuable, than is voluptuarism. *Fiat justitia, ruat coelum*, will serve, if it means: Let the needed thing be done, though the heavens of my past, or fixed, or presupposed self fall. The man who interprets the saying to mean: Let me keep my precious self moral, though the heavens of public action fall, is as despicable personally as he is dangerous socially. He has identified himself with his past notions of himself, and, refusing to allow the fructifying pollen of experience to touch them, refusing to revise his conception of himself in the light of the widest situation in which he finds himself, he begins to disintegrate and becomes a standing menace to his community or group. It is not action *for* the self that is required (thus setting up a fixed self which is simply going to *get* something more, wealth, pleasure, morality, or whatever), but action *as* the self. To find the self in the highest and fullest activity possible at the time, and to perform the act in the consciousness of its complete identification with self (which means, I take it, with complete interest) is morality, and is realization.

The method with which Green meets the difficulty

6   Selfish, of course, in one sense, all action is; but the point here is that if the self is there in some fixed sense already, and action takes place for this self, then, logically, action is selfish in that sense of selfish motive for which we condemn any one.

(though he never, as far as I recall, *specifically* recognizes it) is to split the presupposed self into two parts, one the self so far as realized up to date, the other part the ideal and as yet unrealized self. The realized self then becomes the agent, the ideal self the goal of action. The realized self acts *for* the ideal self. In so acting, its motive is the ideal self, perfection, goodness.[7] We might ask, how, with such a break between the already realized self and the ideal self, the ideal self can possibly become an end at all; we might ask, that is, how this ethical theory is to be reconciled with Green's psychological theory that the object of desire is always the self. With this complete breach of continuity, it is difficult to see how the "ideal self" can interest the agent (the realized self) at all. But this might take us too far from our immediate purpose; and it is enough here to repeat, in changed form, the objection just made. If the particular act is done for the sake of goodness in general, then, and in so far, it is done immorally. For morality consists in not degrading any required act into a mere means towards an end lying outside itself, but in doing it for its own sake, or, again, in doing it *as self*. It is, I think, a simple psychological fact that no act can be completely done save as it absorbs attention.[8] If, then, while doing the act attention must also be directed upon some outside ideal of goodness, the act must suffer, being divided. Not being done for its own sake, or as self, it is only partially done.[9] In other words, acts are to be done *as* good, not for the sake of goodness; for to call an act good means that it is the full activity or self.

It will take us back to our starting-point and round out the argument, if we note the fact that this division of the self into two separate selves (one the realized self, the other the ideal self), is again the fallacy of hypostatizing into separate entities what in reality are simply two stages of

[7]   See, for example, *Prolegomena*, pp. 202–5.
[8]   I cannot refrain from saying that to my own mind this statement is purely tautological. The attention is not something outside the act, and then directed upon it, but absorption of attention and fulness of activity are two ways of naming the same thing.
[9]   We should, then, reverse Kant's statement. Instead of saying that an act is moral only when done from consciousness of duty, we should say that it is immoral (because partial) as long as done *merely* from a sense of duty, and becomes truly moral when done for its own concrete sake.

insight upon our own part. This "realized self" is no reality by itself; it is simply our partial conception of the self erected into an entity. Recognizing its incomplete character, we bring in what we have left out and call it the "ideal self." Then by way of dealing with the fact that we have not two selves here at all, but simply a less and a more adequate insight into the same self, we insert the idea of one of these selves realizing the other. We have an insight which first takes the activity abstractly, and, by cutting off some of its intrinsic relations, arrests it and makes of it a merely realized, or past self; when we perceive these intrinsic relations, instead of using them to correct our previous idea, thus grasping the one continuous activity, we set them off by themselves as ideal—as something *to be* realized. Such is the natural history of the fixed distinction between the realized and the ideal self. It has same source as the process which gives rise to the notion of capacities as possibilities in general.

The more one is convinced that the pressing need of the day, in order to make headway against hedonistic ethics on one side and theological ethics on the other, is an ethics rooted and grounded in the self, the greater is the demand that the self be conceived as a working, practical self, carrying within the rhythm of its own process both "realized" and "ideal" self. The current ethics of the self (falsely named Neo-Hegelian, being in truth Neo-Fichtean) are too apt to stop with a metaphysical definition, which seems to solve problems in general, but at the expense of the practical problems which alone really demand or admit solution. The great need of ethical theory to-day is a conception of the ideal as a working ideal—a conception which shall have the same value and which shall play the same part in ethics that the working hypothesis performs for the natural sciences. The fixed ideal is as distinctly the bane of ethical science to-day as the fixed universe of mediævalism was the bane of the natural science of the Renascence. As natural science found its outlet by admitting no idea, no theory, as fixed by itself, demanding of every idea that it become fruitful in experiment, so must ethical science purge itself of all conceptions, of all ideals, save those which are developed within and for the sake of practice.

Teaching Ethics in the High School

It would be, I am inclined to believe, comparatively easy to bring arguments in support of the conclusion that there has never been such a widespread interest in teaching ethics in the schools as at present; or of the conclusion that there is a general consensus among experts against teaching it. I am not going to try to draw out this antinomy, but I want to run over two or three of the reasons in favor of the latter conclusion. One is the pretty widespread conviction that conscious moralizing in the schoolroom has had its day—if it ever had any; that the mistake has been made of identifying ethical instruction with the conning over and drumming in of ethical precepts; that the most efficient moral teaching is that afforded by the constant bearing in upon the individual of the life-process of the school; that set moral instruction other than grows directly out of occurrences in the school itself, or other than that which calls to the attention of the pupil the meaning of the life of which he is a part, is pretty sure to be formal and perfunctory, and to result rather in hardening the mind of the child with a lot of half-understood precepts than in helpful development. And if moral instruction is conceived not so much as set instruction in regulations for conduct, as cultivation of the child's own conscience, there is the danger of cultivating in some a morbid conscientiousness always prying and spying into the state of feelings, instead of allowing those feelings to develop in their normal intimate connection with action; and in others there is the danger of creating offensive prigs, possibly hypocrites. With all this I agree; indeed, I do not think that the movement against teaching ethics in the schools has gone

[*First published in* Educational Review, VI (*Nov. 1893*), 313–21. *Not reprinted during the author's lifetime.*]

as far as it is likely to go, or as it should go—*provided*, that is, *ethics is conceived in this spirit*. Some of the books which the last year or two have produced, and which are being gradually urged into the schools on account of the great revival of interest in the moral side of school work, seem to me to be based upon an utterly wrong idea of ethics—upon the assumption that if you can only teach a child moral rules and distinctions enough, you have somehow furthered his moral being. Against all this, we cannot too often protest. From the side of ethical theory, we must protest that all this is a caricature of the scientific method of ethics and of its scientific aims. From the standpoint of practical morals, we have to protest that the inculcation of moral rules is no more likely to make character than is that of astronomical formulæ.

If this reaction, however, is simply against all instruction in ethical science in the schools; if it does not rather ask how right instruction in morals may be substituted for wrong, I think we shall not get its full benefit. Rightly read, it is a movement against a false view of morals and a false theory of ethics; the danger is that we are likely to interpret it as meaning that the ethical theory in question may be all right in itself, but is out of place in the schools.[1] At all events, I wish to submit a certain conception of ethical theory upon which that theory seems to me thoroughly teachable in the schoolroom; not only teachable, indeed, but necessary to any well-adjusted curriculum. It is generally admitted, for example, that there has been a talking about number in the school instead of intelligent use of it; that there has been altogether too much attention paid to the examination of the logic of quantity, in the abstract, and altogether too little logic in the attitude of the pupil's mind toward quantity. The one who should, on account of this, urge that mathematical relations, in their reality, had no place in the schools, would be quite on a par with the one who draws a similar conclusion in ethics, because of the similar abuse there. The greater the evil resulting from a

[1]   The most valuable article which I have had the pleasure of reading upon this subject, Professor Palmer's in the *Forum* (XIV, 673), does not seem to me altogether free from this danger.

false conception of the nature of number or of moral action, the greater the demand for introducing instruction based on a right idea.

Ethics, rightly conceived, is the statement of human relationships in action. In any right study of ethics, then, the pupil is not studying hard and fixed rules for conduct; he is studying the ways in which men are bound together in the complex relations of their interactions. He is not studying, in an introspective way, his own sentiments and moral attitudes; he is studying facts as objective as those of hydrostatics or of the action of dynamos. They are subjective, too, but subjective in the sense that since the pupil himself is one who is bound up in the complex of action, the ethical relations have an interest and concern for him which no action of fluid or of dynamo can possibly have. While this subject-matter should be taught from the lowest grade up, I shall choose an illustration of the mode of teaching it better adapted for high schools, or, possibly, the grades just below the high school. In making it, I need hardly say, I suppose, that the method indicated is simply a way; an illustration of the character and spirit of ethical teaching, rather than a method.

Let the teacher, at the outset, ask the pupils how they would decide, if a case of seeming misery were presented to them, *whether* to relieve it and, if so, *how* to relieve. This should be done without any preliminary dwelling upon the question as a "moral" one; rather, it should be pointed out that the question is simply a practical one, and that ready-made moral considerations are to be put one side. Above all, however, it should be made clear that the question is not what to do, *but how to decide what to do.* As this is the rock on which the method is likely to split, let me indicate the force of the distinction. Anyone who is acquainted with the methods in which the well-organized Associated Charities do their work knows that they never discuss giving relief to someone on the basis of abstract principles of charity. They construct, from all available data, an image of the case in question, and decide the particular question upon the basis of the needs and circumstances of that particular case. Now the whole object of the method I am bringing forward is not to get children to arguing about the moral rules which should control the giving of charity—that is a relapse into the method of precepts against which I have protested. The object is to get them into the habit of mentally constructing some actual scene of human interaction, and of consulting that for instruction as to what to do. All the teacher's questions and suggestions, therefore, must be directed toward aiding the pupil in building up in his imagination such a scene. To allow them to discuss *what* to do, save as relative to the development of some case, is to fall back into the very moral abstractions we are trying to avoid. So when children begin to argue (as they are almost sure to do) about the merits of some proposed plan of action, care must be taken not to let them argue it in general, but to introduce their ideas into the case under consideration so as to add new features and phases. The whole point, in a word, is to keep the mental eye constantly upon some actual situation or interaction; to realize in the imagination this or that particular needy person making his demand upon some other particular person. It follows from this, of course, that the line of illustration chosen, that of charity, has no value in itself; it is taken simply as a basis with reference to which to get the child to fix his mind carefully upon the typical aspects of human interaction. The thought which underlies the method is that if instruction in the theory of morals has any practical value it has such value as it aids in forming, in the mind of the person taught, the habit of realizing for himself and in himself the nature of the practical situations in which he will find himself placed. The end of the method, then, is *the formation of a sympathetic imagination for human relations in action*; this is the ideal which is substituted for training in moral rules, or for analysis of one's sentiments and attitude in conduct.

I have tried the method with a class of college students, and a rapid summary of questions which one member of the class or another said he would put in order to decide what to do may give an idea of the character of the ethical material thus placed at the disposal of the teacher. Find out whether the want is real or assumed; investigate its character, *e.g.*, whether immediate, as for food, or remote; whether material or spiritual. Inquire into causes of want: lack of energy, incapacity, accident, sickness, vice as intemperance, loss of work. Search out the past record of individual, his station in life; his family, neighbors, cronies; power of work, any special skill. Find out his character and temperament so as to adjust a method to that. Examine into one's own needs and powers, the demands upon one's own time and money, etc., etc. These are selected from the answers given in the first day; of course, further discussion and question would evolve multitudes more.

We now have our teacher with his ideal and his material more or less definitely before him. How shall he deal with it? The answer in the general is plain. Deal with it so that in and through the special situation chosen the pupil shall have gradually brought home to him some of the *typical features of every human interaction. These typical features are the content of ethical theory*: that is to say, there is no ethical analysis, however advanced and however scientific, which can do more than discover the generic phases of human activity in society. In order to carry out this plan, the teacher should unite, it seems to me, a pretty definite idea of the typical phases which he wishes to bring out, with great freedom in detail. Unless he has the latter, he will fail to take due advantage of the suggestions arising from the pupils' answers; will fail to be alive to their interests and, in general, will be likely to relapse into a formal and rigid mode. But if the freedom is carried so far that the teacher does not have an idea of the goal at which he intends the pupils shall bring up, the work will be so random that its object, the realization by the pupil of human action in its typical features, will be lost.

One of these typical phases is the proper place of the emotions in conduct. In these days, the attacks upon "indiscriminate giving" have permeated a good way, and it is safe to say that some pupil will urge the need of not giving from the mere impulse of the moment. This will open the way for a discussion of the part to be played by sympathy, benevolent impulses, etc. Any teacher who is even moderately acquainted with the literature of charity organizations will have no difficulty in showing the necessity of not giving way to the feelings of the moment. He can show that to do so is not to act for any moral or practical reason, but simply to gratify one's own feelings—and that this is the definition of all selfishness; he can show that, by encouraging idleness and beggary, it does an injustice to society as a whole, while it wrongs the person supposably helped, by robbing him of his independence and freedom. Now all this, I submit, is valuable in itself; treated by a teacher who knows his business (or who is even interested in it, if he does not know it), it can hardly fail to rank in importance with any subject taught in the high school. But it is more than valuable in itself. Any pupil who has worked out these facts day by day for weeks, for a year, who has learned what careful study of conditions and weighing of expedients is necessary to treat many a case of relief, is prepared to understand the true meaning of the term "motive" in ethical discussion better, far better, I submit, than nineteen-twentieths of our college students who have analyzed it at large. The pupil is in position to understand what the relative place and bearing of both impulse and reason in conduct are, and to understand the meaning of those theories which attach such importance to the reasonableness of action.

Another typical phase of all action which the pupil will be in a position to appreciate after carrying on for some weeks a study of this kind, is that of the interrelation of all individuals. When he sees the stress upon the social relations of the person to be helped, upon the dependence of his family upon him, upon the fact that he is out of work, possibly because of a strike, possibly because of speculative movements five hundred miles away, possibly because of some caprice of fashion; when he realizes the pains which must be taken in dealing with him not only not to weaken his own self-respect, but also not to weaken the ties of neighborhood unity—when he sees all this, and a multitude of other details which will develop in the course of the discussion, the interdependence of interests in a single action (though he never hears the phrase) cannot but become a vital fact.

Since, in view of the breakdown of so many of the older motives for morality, the youth of the next generation must more and more draw their inspiration from a realization of the unity of the interest of all in any one and of one in all, there is no need to dwell upon the practical bearing of this.

These two factors of ethical action, namely, the place of impulse and of intelligence, and the multitude of relations to be considered and focused in any human action, may, I think, be taught to all youth as far advanced as the high-school grades. How much further the analysis is carried will have to depend upon the maturity, previous training, and home surroundings of the pupils. In some cases, it might be possible to carry the study of this or some other typical case far enough to indicate the nature of moral law and obliga-tion, and this without detriment to the concreteness of the study. Or, again, it might be possible to introduce a study of the various ideals currently proposed for conduct and test them by application to the problem under consideration. But all this would be a matter of detail. I am concerned only to point out in general in what spirit ethics may and should be taught in the schools, and to suggest an outline of a method for realizing this method in the higher grades. Above and beyond any formal analysis is the result in the way of a new interest in, and a new sense for, human relations in action.

I may be called on to say something of the practicabil-ity of introducing this study into the high school; I may be reminded of the already crowded state of the curriculum, and asked to show the interrelations of this study to others. I should only be expressing what I myself feel, if I were to say that if other studies do not correlate well with this one, so much the worse for them—they are the ones to give way, not it. For it is not the study of ethics I am urging; it is the study of *ethical relationships*, the study, that is, of this com-plex world of which we are members. Where there is one reason for the ordinary student to become acquainted with the intricacies of geometry, of physics, of Latin, or of Greek, there are twenty for him to become acquainted with the nature of those relations upon which his deepest weal and woe depend, and to become interested in, and habituated to, looking at them with sympathetic imagination. And so far as the fetich of discipline, or the culture-value of studies, or anything of that sort, is concerned, one need have no fear that the world of ethical activities will not afford scope for all the powers of analysis, of interpretation, and of observation, of which any pupil may be possessed. The subject here is so important, the mental power brought into play in dealing with it is of such quality and kept at such pitch, that, ultimately, the subject-matter of ethics must furnish the measure for other studies and not *vice versa*. But it is not necessary to carry the argument to this extreme. Except through a study of ethical material from the standpoint here outlined, and with the ideal here suggested (though not, of course, necessarily with just the material I have employed), it is impossible for the pupil to get the full meaning either of literature or of history—the two studies of whose future we may be certain, happen what may to the others now entering into our curricula. Such a study of ethics as I am pleading for will play at once into the study and appreciation of both literature and history, while the latter will constantly introduce new material, new problems, new methods for the ethical imagination—the imagination that is occupied with making real for the individual the world of action in which he lives.

No one can be more conscious than I am myself of the apparent gap between the meager outline of the study I have presented and the claims made for it. There is, however, in my own mind no fear that I have exaggerated the importance of a study of ethics conceived in the spirit I have indicated, and I am glad to *seem* to exaggerate if the seeming will lead any to question for even a moment the highly formal character of high-school instruction as at present administered; and to entertain, if but for a moment, the possibility of a time when the central study shall be human life itself; a time when science shall be less a quantity constant in itself and more a method for approaching and dealing with this human life; a time when language and literature, as well as history, shall be less realms of thought and emotion by themselves and more the record and the instruments of this human life.

Why Study Philosophy?

It was Bishop Berkeley who remarked that philosophers threw dust into their own eyes, and then complained because they could not see. Well, philosophers have been pursuing their industry for the last twenty-five hundred years, and have by this time raised considerable clouds which have got not only into their own eyes, but into those of others. Our intellectual atmosphere is pretty well permeated by this dust; we breathe it whether we will or no—even when we are congratulating ourselves that we are assimilating the purest truth, freshly blown to us from the newly discovered peaks of science. And the only way of getting immunity against this dust, to see straight and clear, is to know enough of its origin and antecedents, its methods of traveling, to recognize its presence, and to make allowance for the disturbance which it introduces. Or, to drop the figure, the reason for studying philosophy, (to put it at its lowest) is that there have been philosophers before us, and the only way to avoid being imposed upon by them is to turn philosophers ourselves. If it takes a thief to catch a thief, it may fairly be presumed that it takes a philosopher to catch a philosopher.

If our wise ancestors, instructed in the lore of Rousseau concerning the uselessness and harmfulness of the philosopher, had isolated him as soon as he showed himself, all might still be well. But the philosopher was allowed to be at large, and succeeded in infecting his time. By giving others his trouble, his problem and his solution, he got rid of it himself, and went on to new fields. The philosopher's ideas have never remained his own technical possession. The phi-

[*First published in* Inlander (*University of Michigan*), IV (*Dec.* 1893), 106–9. *Not previously reprinted.*]

losopher, even he, is a social being, and works out his ideas by expressing them, by trying them on others, by making them influence the actions of others. By the time he has freed himself of them, they have become embodied in the educational systems and methods, in the theological codes and dogmas, in the legal attitude and practice, in the turns and terms of language. In dying as philosophy the ideas come to live as a part of the common and unconscious intellectual life of men in general. They become the presupposed background, the unexpressed premises, the working (and therefore controlling) tools of thought and action. Filtered to us through the media of education, law, language, religion and science itself they take possession of us. Unless we are to be mastered by them, we must master them. And this involves a continual dragging of them out of their unconscious hiding places; a deliberate and reflective overhauling of them—that is to say, the study of philosophy.

In the history of philosophy, we turn around and demand the origin of these our present instruments; we inquire into the circumstances in which they foisted themselves upon us; we learn to see how they cohere, how one drags another along with it. As we draw them into the light of day, we free ourselves from them. In logic, or in metaphysic, if one prefer that name, we compel them to present their credentials; we ask after their origin, not historical now, but the logical need which brought them into existence and gave them their efficacy; we ask how far they answer this need, and how far under pretense of meeting it they have extended their claims to fields to which they have no title. In psychology, we inquire into the mechanism through which these ideas and habits come into existence and get their hold. In all these ways, we make conscious objects out of what are otherwise our ruling prepossessions or prejudices, whether personal in their origin, or inherited from our intellectual ancestry. We get them out before us and are able to judge them, instead of having them move us passively here and there. We use our tools instead of having them use us.

The philosophy of the passing century has been above all things a critical philosophy, a philosophy of reflective examination into origins, into values, into instruments. It is,

historically, but a continuation of that clearing-up of the
intellectual store-house, that season of house cleaning, which
began in the eighteenth century. It is true that the last
century looked upon this store-house as a rubbish heap to
be swept away, while we look through it, sympathetically
and eagerly, hoping to come across some neglected tool, or
hoping to remake to new use some older instrument. But it
is the same continued taking of stock; an intellectual inventory which is to tell us where we stand; what our resources
are and what our liabilities; an inventory which has for its
object to enable us to master our past instead of being
mastered by it; that we may walk forward more freely and
boldly, less hampered by shadows coming from behind, forgetting after these many centuries of dependence upon the
past, the things that are behind and stretching forward to
the things that are before.

Nor need any one think that is a purely negative work
on the part of philosophy. The dust after all is not mere
blinding dust. It is true, I believe, that without refraction
and reflection there is pure light, but no play of color; certain it is that without obstructions, without interfering media there are no shades, and hence no values in light. If the
chief use of philosophy at present is to enable us to get a
conscious mastery which will change them from assumptions which control us into tools of inquiry and action, yet it
is by passing through this criticism that our intellectual
world gets its tones, its lights and shades, its softened and
its deepened meaning. I am not here to magnify my calling
unduly, but I feel that one who has done what is termed
"completing his education" without an insight on his own
behalf into the processes historical, logical, psychological,
by which the present structure of ideas and of emotional and
volitional attitudes, has been brought into existence has an
outlook, at once narrow and rigid, upon a field monotonous,
of hard and fast perspective, of fixed horizon, while he
might, relatively at least, be looking with wide and flexible
vision upon a scene of melting hues, of playing lights, shifting limits.

It is implied in what has been said that philosophy
while it lets us into the secret of the ideas and attitudes

which have been created in the past, also constructs, or at least reconstructs, intellectual tools for present use. In so far as this is so, we find a further motive for philosophic study. This motive is still largely in the region of the "ought to be"; criticism has hardly done her perfect work as yet. But that only shifts the emphasis; it does not remove the motive. If we cannot undertake the study of psychology and ethics as yet with the full confidence that in them we shall find direct aid in the attack of practical questions, we can go at their study with the aim of hastening the time when they shall afford such weapons. 'Tis certain that a time is to come when the practice of medicine will as closely depend on psychology as upon that of physiology; when a lawyer of repute will need a knowledge of the ethics of the social structure as much as of common law pleading. It would be absurd to claim that that time is now here, but every advance step that brings psychology more within the reach of laboratory methods, of statement in terms of the organism, every reconstruction that enables us to use the categories of philosophy as instruments of inquiry and statement as to social organization, hastens that day.

I began with an apparent slur upon philosophy quoted from one of the greatest philosophers of modern times. I may conclude with another apparent slur upon it by one of the acutest, at least, of present day philosophers. "Metaphysics," says Mr. Bradley, "is the finding of bad reasons for what we believe upon instinct, but to find these reasons is no less an instinct." The final "why" for studying philosophy is that there are some who need no "why"; who study upon instinct. The pressure, the momentum, of a mind bent in a given direction, a momentum set free whenever opportunities and facilities present themselves, is a thing not easily to be resisted. As one of old said: "Wonder is the feeling of a philosopher, and philosophy begins in wonder." So long as the wondering mind and the wonderful universe confront each other there will always remain to some the best of reasons for studying philosophy — necessity.

The Psychology of Infant Language

In his interesting and valuable article on "The Language of Childhood,"[1] Mr. Tracy undertakes, upon a basis of 5400 words used by at least twenty different children, to determine the relative frequency of the various parts of speech. Before making some remarks, I wish first to submit my own mite for the further use of students. A refers to a boy; B to a girl, 20 months younger.[2]

A at 19 mos. old

Parts of Speech		Per cent
Nouns	68	60
Verbs	24	21
Adjectives	13	11
Adverbs	4	3
Interjections	6	5
Total	115	100

Pronouns, prepositions, conjunctions, none.

B at 18 mos. old[3]

Parts of Speech		Per cent
Nouns	76	53
Verbs	40	28
Adjectives	2	1
Adverbs	9	6
Interjections	7	5
Pronouns	8	6
Conjunctions	2	1
Total	144	100

Prepositions, none.

[1] *American Journal of Psychology*, Vol. VI, No. 1, reprinted in *The Psychology of Childhood*, Boston: D. C. Heath and Co., 1893.
[2] The presence of other children in the family should always, I think, form part of the data with reference to a child's vocabulary. At least, it is one of the old wives' saws on this matter that the presence of other children both hastens and extends a vocabulary.
[3] A's vocabulary was kept continuously; B's vocabulary was taken from words actually used within a period of five or six days; a number of words contained in her vocabulary four months previously do not appear at all.

[*First published in* Psychological Review, I (*Jan. 1894*), 63–66. *Not reprinted during the author's lifetime.*]

For purposes of comparison, I append the per cents reached by Mr. Tracy by averaging all his results:

Nouns	60
Verbs	20
Adjectives	9
Adverbs	5
Pronouns	2
Prepositions	2
Interjections	1.7
Conjunctions	0.3
	100.0

I wish to remark (1) concerning the relative frequency of verbs, and (2) concerning the different rates of distribution in different children:

1. Mr. Tracy notes that since the relative frequency of verbs in the language is but 11 per cent, the child, *comparatively* speaking, uses verbs with 1.81 the ease with which he uses nouns, and makes some judicious remarks concerning the prevalence of concepts of activity in the child mind. I think he could make his case much stronger. Mr. Tracy, I take it, has classified his words according to the sense which they have to an adult, and I have followed that principle in my own table.[4] In a sense, however, this is as artificial as Mr. Tracy notes that it is to put knife under *k* instead of under *n*, because *we spell* it with a *k*. The psychological classification is to class the word according to what it means to a child, not to an adult with his grammatical forms all differentiated.

Such a classification would in all probability increase immensely the percentage of verbs. It is true that such a method demands much more care in observation, and opens the way to the very variable error of interpretation; but the greater certainty of the method followed above is after all only seeming—it does not express the *child's* vocabulary,

---

[4]   Phrases like "all light," "all dark," "all gone," "out" (for "go out"), etc., I have treated as verbs. It is obvious that they might be considered either as interjections or as adjectives. The relatively larger per cent of verbs in my table may be due to this classification.

but our interpretation of it according to a fixed but highly conventional standard. It is out of the question to redistribute the language of A and B, given above; but I subjoin the vocabulary of a child in his twelfth month where contemporaneous observation makes me reasonably sure of what the child means:

See there; bye-bye; bottle; papa; mamma; grandma; Freddy; burn; fall; water; down; door; no, no; stop; thank you; boo (peek-a-boo); daw (used when he sees anything which he wants given to him) — 17 in all.

Of the above, only the four proper nouns are, psychologically speaking, names of objects. Water is a verb as well as a noun; door is *always* accompanied by gestures of reaching, and an attempt to swing the door back and fro; "daw" is apparently a request, an expression of expectation of something good to eat and the name of a thing all together; bottle certainly has adjectival and verbal implications as well as nominal. At present I should regard it as a complex, "nominal-adjectival-verbal," the emphasis being on the noun, while six weeks previously it was, say, "verbal-adjectival-nominal." "Stop"; "no, no"; "burn"; "see there," etc., are equally interjections and verbs. "Thank you" is at times a request for something, and is almost invariably said when giving an article to any one else. We have then a graded and continuous series, so far as *sense* is concerned, the proper names (23 per cent) at one end, and the interjectional forms "no, no," "peek-a-boo," at the other. These have a verbal coloring, however. Between these classes are a nominal-adjectival-verbal-interjectional complex, the verbal-interjectional meaning prevailing on the whole, the adjectival in all cases subordinate.[5] The tendency to apply the same term to a large number of objects ("ball" to ball,

---

[5]   The fact that interjections fail so late, as a rule, in aphasia, taken with the highly immediate and emotional character of child-life, indicates the defective character of a method of classification which reduces the percentage of interjections to 1.7. The philologist's objections to making interjections a primitive form of speech, however sound grammatically, seem to me to rest upon attaching a limited, technical sense to the concept *interjection*, which is without ground psychologically. In the infant mind (whether race or child) the emotional state and the tendency to react aroused by an object *must*, I should say, be fused, and both precede any clear recognition of the "object" as such, or of any objective quality.

orange, moon, lamp-globe, etc.) can be understood, I think, only if we keep in mind the extent to which the formal noun, "ball," has really an active sense. "Ball" is "to throw" just as much as it is the round thing. I do not believe that the child either confuses the moon with his ball, or abstracts the roundness of it; the roundness suggests to him something which he has thrown, so that the moon is something to throw—if he could only get hold of it.

What I would suggest, then, along the line of a study of the distribution of vocabulary into parts of speech is such observation and record as would note carefully the original sense to the child of his words, and the gradual *differentiation* of the original protoplasmic verbal-nominal-interjectional form (as it seems to me), until words assume their present rigidity.

2. No one can examine the statistics given without being struck by the great differences in different children. F, in Mr. Tracy's tables, has 15 per cent interjections; while K, with a vocabulary of 250 words, has none at all. F has 11 per cent adverbs; while K has but 2 per cent; in my own table, A has 4, while B has 9 per cent. So in my two, A has 11 per cent adjectives; B, 1 per cent; while Mr. Tracy's vary from a maximum of 13 to a minimum of 3 per cent. I believe the tendency in all psychological investigation, at present, is to attempt to get a *uniform* mathematical statement, eliminating individual differences; for pedagogical and ethical purposes, at least, it is these differences which are, finally, most important. And on strictly psychological grounds the varying ratio of adverbs and pronouns on one side and nouns and adjectives on the other must denote a very different psychological attitude—different methods of attaching interest and distributing attention. Observation of different mental traits as connected with these linguistic differences would not only add to the *terra incognita*, individual psychology (and it would seem that all psychology must be finally individual), but throw great light upon the psychology of language. How vague and formal at present our answers, for example, when we are asked to what psychological state and need an adverb corresponds!

Austin's Theory of Sovereignty

I.

A careful study of Austin's *Lectures on Jurisprudence* has convinced me that the theory which is ordinarily put forward under his name is not his at all. If it belongs to any one, Hobbes and Cornewall Lewis deserve that it be accredited to them. So far as I can trace the origin of the statement which is usually put forward as Austin's, it came from Sir Henry Maine. From his *Early History of Institutions* I take the following, which will serve as a sufficient statement of the ordinary misconception, whether originating with Maine or not:

> There is in every independent political community some single person or combination of persons which has the *power of compelling the other members of the community to do exactly as it pleases.* . . . This sovereign . . . has in all such communities one characteristic, common to all the shapes sovereignty may take, the *possession of irresistible force.* . . . That which all the forms of sovereignty have in common is the power (the power, but not necessarily the will) to *put compulsion without limit on subjects or fellow-subjects* [pp. 349, 350].

The phrases which I have italicized give the gist of the misconception—the perversion, it may be called—of Austin's theory. The work of misstatement which Maine commenced on the historical side, T. H. Green completed on the philosophical side. According to him, Austin's doctrine "considers the essence of sovereignty to lie in the power . . . to put compulsion without limit on subjects, to make them do ex-

[*First published in* Political Science Quarterly, IX (*Mar. 1894*), 31–52. Not previously reprinted.]

actly as it pleases."[1] These statements give what I may without disrespect call the Austinian myth as it has gradually developed. Cornewall Lewis regarded himself as a disciple of Austin, and undoubtedly thought he was representing his master's doctrine correctly when he said: "As long as a government exists, the power of the person or persons in whom the sovereignty resides over the whole community, is absolute and unlimited."[2] But as a matter of fact, no such conception of sovereignty as consisting in absolute force is to be found anywhere in Austin. Before coming to a positive discussion of Austin's doctrine, it therefore seems necessary to get the false conception of his theory out of the way.

The following statement by Austin is typical:

> If perfect or complete independence be of the essence of sovereign power, there is not in fact the human power to which it will apply. Every government, let it be ever so powerful, renders occasional obedience to the commands of other governments. . . . And every government *defers* habitually to the opinions and sentiments of its own subjects.[3]

Again he writes:

> To an indefinite though limited extent the monarch is superior to the governed, his power being commonly sufficient to secure compliance with his will. But the governed, collectively or in mass, are also the superior of the monarch, who is checked in the abuse of his might by fear of exciting their anger, and of arousing to active resistance the might which slumbers in the multitude.[4]

If it be said that Lewis, too, recognizes a distinction between legal and moral force, and speaks of a use of the term sovereignty "to signify the moral influence of a whole or a part of the community upon the acts of the sovereign,"[5]

---

1   *Works*, II, 401.
2   *Use and Abuse of Political Terms*, p. 33.
3   *Jurisprudence*, I, 242, ed. of 1869.
4   *Jurisprudence*, I, 99. Compare the following from Maine, who seems to think he is urging something *contrary* to Austin: "The vast mass of influences, which we call for shortness moral, perpetually shapes, limits or forbids actual direction of the forces of society by its sovereign" (*Early History of Institutions*, p. 359).
5   *Use and Abuse*, p. 40.

the reply is that Lewis has absolutely no criterion by which to distinguish between moral and legal, while the characteristic thing in Austin is (as we shall see presently) the careful way in which he endeavors to fix a basis for such a distinction. So far as Lewis's theory is concerned, whatever actually exercises control must be sovereign; if the "sovereign" is influenced by the wishes of his subjects, so as to "defer habitually" to them, they are really sovereign and he is the subject. "If a sovereign has not power to enforce his commands . . . he is not sovereign."[6] Indeed, Lewis is essentially a legalist, Austin a moralist. Lewis is simply after a definition which will hold water legally; Austin, in spite of the legal form which his main work took, was, like Bentham, preëminently interested in social reform and progress. Law, as such, was to him a means to realize this reform. To be convinced of this, one has only to read his chapters on "Utility," introduced at the outset of his *Lectures*, and note especially what he has to say upon the importance of diffusing correct ethical knowledge among the masses of the people (1, 129–43).

If Lewis thus completely inverts Austin's conception, it is perhaps not surprising to find that the necessity of basing force upon some common interest and purpose, which Green urges against Austin, is not only recognized, but stated by Austin at considerable length.[7] He defines the proper end of a sovereign political government—"the purpose or end for which it ought to exist"—to be "the greatest possible advancement of human happiness."[8] He thus recognizes as distinctly as Green a moral end back of and controlling the political institution. Not only this, but he recognizes that the motive which induces men to obey government is, even under existing conditions, very largely an ethical one, and not mere fear of force,[9] while under proper conditions it would be completely ethical. "Supposing," he says, "that a

---

[6]   *Use and Abuse*, p. 15.
[7]   It is true that Green and Austin do not use the language of the same philosophical school; Green uses the language of action, Austin that of feeling. But Austin's "general happiness" is *practically* one with Green's "general will."
[8]   *Jurisprudence*, I, 298.
[9]   How far this is consistent with another phase of his teaching, viz., his definition of law, we shall have to consider hereafter.

given society were adequately instructed or enlightened, the habitual obedience to its government which was rendered by the bulk of the community would exclusively arise from reasons bottomed in the principle of utility" (1, 301). And even as things are now, the recognition of the utility of government is "the only cause of the habitual obedience in question, which is *common* to all societies, or nearly all societies" (1, 303), utility being definitely Austin's moral standard.

It would be worth while, I think, to reopen the question of Austin's theory of sovereignty, were it only for the purpose of bringing to light this current misapprehension; but that is not my main motive at present. Austin's real theory raises questions as important as does that of Lewis which so far has done duty for Austin's—questions which are completely kept out of sight, however, in the ordinary way of stating it. It is these questions which I propose to raise in this article.

II.

I wish to point out that at the bottom of Austin's conception (and influential in much of the existing discussion) there is a confusion of sovereignty with the organs of its exercise,[10] and that this confusion has for its result a radical error concerning the mode in which sovereignty is exercised —an error which, so far as acted upon, is likely to result in harm.

I have already indicated that Austin has a specific criterion for distinguishing moral from legal order and influence. As it happens, the consideration of this criterion will also suffice to reveal Austin's theory of the residence of sovereignty, and thus to prepare the way for showing his confusion of sovereignty with an organ of its exercise. Austin begins by distinguishing between positive law and moral law. As he does not admit that anything but a command can

[10] This confusion, in its nature and in the evil results flowing from it, is parallel with that between the state and government, so clearly brought out by Professor Burgess; *cf. Political Science and Comparative Constitutional Law*, I, 68.

properly be called a law, one *differentia* commonly employed for distinguishing between the two is not open to him: I refer to that which makes the moral law a law of the "ought to be," while positive law is a law which actually obtains. Every law implies to Austin a person (or persons) who issues a command, the command being the signification of a wish, together with the power and purpose of inflicting an evil in case the wish is not complied with. "Being liable to evil from you in case I do not comply with a wish which you signify, I am bound or *obliged* by your command, or I lie under a *duty* to obey it" (1, 91). The positive law equally with the moral sets up duty; the moral law equally with the positive implies an actual force and a sanction. Both involve actual authority, an actual law-giver and an actual law-subject, and therefore, on Austin's theory, an evil to which the latter is liable from the former in case of disobedience. The distinction between the legal and the moral, accordingly, cannot be the presence or absence of a personal authority imposing the command and enforcing obedience through sanctions. It can only be in some trait or characteristic of the authority imposing the command. What is the defining peculiarity of this authority?

Positive law, according to Austin, is that set by a political superior to an inferior. Moral law must be distinguished into two classes. Moral law, properly so-called, is a command proceeding from a determinate source and having a sanction and an obligation, yet not positive law, because not proceeding from a sovereign. Moral law, improperly so-called, is that set by the opinions and sentiments of an indeterminate public. The difference between positive law and moral law properly so-called depends then simply upon whether or not the rules are set by a sovereign. But how is this to be ascertained? A sovereign is a power *not* in the habit of obedience to a determinate superior. The commands of such a power are positive law, while the commands of a power which *is* in the habit of obedience to a determinate superior are moral law. That is, the commands which a master issues to a slave, or a parent to his child, are truly laws; yet they are moral, not positive, because the superior power is, in turn, in the habit of obeying a power still above him.

The distinction between moral law, improperly so-called, and positive law is not so clear on the surface. We have to remember that Austin admits that, in one sense, the opinions and sentiments of the mass are supreme in power; the sovereign "habitually defers" to them. From this point of view, then, moral law improperly so-called is above positive law: it controls, in ultimate analysis, the latter. Why not say that it, the general or controlling opinion, is sovereign? Here we finally come upon the distinguishing factor, disregard of which leads Lewis, Maine and Green all astray. Laws proper must proceed from a *determinate* source, and the public at large is indeterminate. Sovereignty is defined by the following traits:

1. The bulk of the given society are in the habit of obedience to a *determinate* and common superior. . . . 2. That superior is *not* in the habit of obedience to a determinate common superior [I, 226].

It is the determinateness of the authority which issues the commands, then, which is the sole essential *differentia* of sovereignty from the force exerted by public opinion. Austin admits as definitely as Maine that obedience is rendered to other authorities than the sovereign; he admits as definitely as Green that a moral reason (a reason based on social welfare) underlies the bare fact of obedience to the government, and that the society whose welfare is in question is always, as matter of fact, in possession of the supreme or controlling power. But it is not sovereign, because it is an indeterminate or vague body, while law proper can proceed only from a numerically determinate body.[11] So far does Austin go in this direction that he holds that the whole political society is only figuratively called sovereign: "The party truly independent is not the society, but the sovereign *portion* of the society." The following will sum up that part of Austin's definition of sovereignty which alone is of further interest to us:

An independent political society is divisible into two portions: namely, the portion of its members which is sovereign or supreme, and the portion of its members which is merely

[11]   See *Jurisprudence*, I, 89 and 174–90.

subject. . . . In most actual societies, the sovereign powers
are engrossed by a single member of the whole, or are shared
exclusively by a very few of its members; and even in the actual
societies whose governments are esteemed popular, the sovereign
number is a slender portion of the entire political community[12]
[1, 243].

III.

The question raised, then, by Austin's conception of
sovereignty is precisely whether it resides in a specific nu-
merical portion of the body politic. The question is of
special interest in this country; for if Austin's theory is
correct, the theory of popular sovereignty is obviously
wrong, not only in the crude form in which it is ordinarily
stated, but in any possible development of it.

The first thing that strikes one is the slenderness of the
reason given by Austin for limiting sovereignty to a part.
Substantially his argument is, that every law must be a command, and that a command, in the proper sense, can proceed
only from a person or persons capable of specific enumera-
tion. Hence the rules set by public opinion are not truly laws,
and hence the body holding the opinion cannot be said to
be sovereign.

For, since it is not a body precisely determined or certain,
it cannot, as a body, express or intimate a wish. As a body, it
cannot signify a wish by oral or written words, or by positive or
negative deportment. The so-called law or rule which its
opinion is said to impose, is merely the sentiment which it feels,
or is merely the opinion which it holds, in regard to a kind of
conduct [1, 188].

To Austin the statement that a body uncertain as to
number cannot act as a body, and cannot, therefore, issue
commands, seems so self-evident as to need no further argument. To one surrounded with institutions of a "popular"

[12]   Austin's theory is thus the complete antithesis of Rousseau's. According to Rousseau, it is of the essence of sovereignty to belong to the
whole as a whole, *i.e.*, to the general will. According to Austin, it is of its
essence to be partial. Green, in the criticism already referred to, opposes
Austin and Rousseau as types of the theories which make sovereignty
consist in force and will respectively. I hope it is now obvious that both
find it equally in will, but that one conceives of this will as necessarily
inhering in a part, the other as inhering in the whole of society.

character, and accustomed, almost every day, to see government affected and controlled by various agencies of clamor,
mass meeting, petition and newspaper writing, this inability
of a body numerically uncertain to express itself, as a body,
in ways having the force of command, will, I think, seem less
axiomatic. Austin himself admits that it is "not the style in
which the desire is signified" that makes it a command.
Willingness to inflict harm in case of disobedience, is the
essence of the command. "*Preces erant, sed quibus contradici
non posset*,"—these were commands, though taking the form
of a humble request.[13] He distinctly states that one who does
not comply with the wishes of the indeterminate body
which sets the rule of public opinion, will probably suffer,
by reason of not complying, some inconvenience or evil from
some party or other; and that by this prospect of evil the acts
of persons obnoxious to it are influenced to take a specified
form, and from this fact exhibit a steadiness and uniformity
which they would otherwise probably lack.[14] Against all this
likeness to true laws and to real sovereignty, the only point
of distinction which marks off what Austin calls moral law,
improperly so-called, is that "the person who will enforce
the so-called law against any future offender is never determinate and assignable,"—a somewhat slight support, I submit, upon which to base the whole difference between law
and moral sentiment, between real sovereignty and mere
opinion. Indeed, it seems as if Austin were here reasoning
simply in a circle. First the law is defined as a command set
by the sovereign; then, having the benefit of the idea of
sovereignty to help differentiate political from moral law, the
sovereign is defined as the power which sets law—the idea of
determinateness being slipped in so incidentally as almost
to conceal its fundamental importance.

Let us, however, grant Austin his assumption and see
how it stands the test of facts. Austin's idea of the residence
of sovereignty in the United States is familiar to students of
constitutional law. His theory is that neither the federal
government as such, nor the separate state governments as
such, nor yet a combination of the two is sovereign; going

13   *Jurisprudence*, I, 91.
14   *Jurisprudence*, I, 190.

back to the clause of the constitution which indicates how
amendments are to be made, he finds there the key to the
problem. The sovereign is the electorate appointing the
legislatures of the respective states, the electorate being
taken as an aggregate body.[15]

What is this electorate, either as a class, or as to the
particular members which compose it? Suppose a generation
has passed away since any amendment has been passed, or
since any legislature has acted upon any amendment proposed by Congress; where is the portion or class constituting
the sovereign to be found? Those who actually determined
the constitution may no longer be living; if it be said that
those who would vote in case a new question were submitted
are the class sought for, this would base sovereignty not on
the actual expression of wishes and the observance of these
wishes by others under sanctions, but on a mere capacity or
potentiality. Admit, however, that sovereignty can be thus
latent; then is every individual who composes this possible
electorate a sharer in sovereignty? He must be, if the class
is to be determinate (capable of having its constituents
specified); yet, *per contra*, it is evident that, prior to any
given vote, there is no way of telling in respect to any
given individual whether he will be in the majority or in   .
the minority. If it turns out that he is one of the defeated
party, we are in a hopeless dilemma. If we say he did share
in sovereignty because he had a right to vote, we say
sovereignty may be exercised apart from the utterance of
commands, indeed, even in opposing the fundamental command. But if we say that, since not participating in the
expression of the supreme command, he is not sovereign, the
question arises by what right he voted at all. Why is he not
disfranchised from this time on? Take, again, the citizens of
a state which is one of the number constituting less than one-
fourth of the whole. Suppose this state votes against an

[15]   Judge Jameson, in an article upon "National Sovereignty," *Political Science Quarterly*, v (June, 1890), 193, has criticized the correctness
of this definition as an account of the actual facts, and has also brought
out the important fact that the electorate (always of course a mere majority, not a whole) makes its decisions, not as a separate whole, but
within the processes of the nation itself, and controlled in a multitude of
ways by this larger whole, of which it is in reality simply an organ. But
I wish here to admit Austin's own definition and show that, by his own
definition, this sovereign is *not* determinate.

amendment which is adopted; are the citizens in this state participants in sovereignty or not? We come here, as before, to an insoluble contradiction; sovereignty is not determinate until after it has been exercised—until the vote has been taken. I fail to see how any definition whatever of sovereignty in the United States could be given which would not make it indeterminate, in the sense in which Austin uses that word.

Again, consider the dispute as to the residence of sovereignty in Great Britain. Is it in the crown alone, since whatever the courts and the legislature do, is done, according to legal theory, by the crown through them? Is the sovereign the crown, the lords and the commons acting conjointly? Is it the electorate of the House of Commons? Or is it the majority of such electorate? In the first case, the crown can be identified with a person only by a great stretch of the imagination; it means a legal institution and hence cannot be determinate. In the second case, we have an approach to determinateness, although the problem about majority and minority is sure to arise. In the third case, we get again into difficulty in trying to decide when and by what part of the electorate sovereignty is exercised. Moreover, all these different views of the residence of sovereignty have been maintained by competent judges within the last fifty years. Austin himself holds one; his disciple, Holland, another. When careful students of constitutional law cannot agree as to the body of persons in whom sovereignty resides, what becomes of determinateness as the essential feature of sovereignty? If Austin were correct in supposing a numerically definite body essential to sovereignty, such uncertainty as this would mean that Great Britain is in a state of anarchy, having no such determinate body capable of detection even by a body of experts. Were Austin correct, Great Britain would long ago have been engaged in a practical struggle to decide the uncertainty as to the possessors of sovereignty, since the anarchy could be settled only by having it clear that just this set of persons and no other were those from whom all laws proceed.

The ultimate weakness of Austin's theory is that, in identifying sovereignty with a part only of the body politic, he gives (and allows) no reason why this limited body of persons have the authority which they possess. The conception of sovereignty as the possession of power by a numerically determinate body of persons, supplies no criterion for determining what body of persons shall thus be set off, or how many of them there shall be. Such a conception, applied to any existing government as such (to say nothing of the ultimate sovereignty), would only state the bare fact that, at the given time, just such and such persons, so many in number, happened to make up the government. Let the government be already recognized as a certain definite body of persons, and, on Austin's theory, you could say that that body is the government: let there be any dispute as to who is the real government, and, on Austin's theory, you would have to wait till the dispute was settled and a certain set of men were, past all controversy, in possession of the ground. Number, without a principle of measurement or rule of distribution, is about as vague a defining principle as may be imagined. As it happens, in every existing civilized state governmental power is in the hands of a certain body of persons, capable of more or less accurate assignment (very rarely, however, of such complete assignment as Austin's theory would require), and thus Austin's conception seems to agree fairly with facts. But that there are such determinate governments, is a matter lying quite outside the range of Austin's theory; they exist precisely because large social forces, working through extensive periods of time, have fixed upon these governments as organs of expression. It is these forces, gradually crystallizing, which have determined governments and given them all the specific (determinate) character which they now possess. Take away the forces which are behind governments—which have made them what they are, and the existence and character of these governments is an accident, likely to be changed at any moment. Admit these forces, and, since they determine the government, *they* are sovereign.

IV.

This brings us explicitly to the question of the relation of government to sovereignty. Can government be identified with sovereignty? My contention thus far has been that there is no ground for holding that the residence of sovereignty can be found in a certain definitely limited portion of political society. Broadening the field I shall now attempt to show that the most important operations of sovereignty, namely, the institution and development of law, are incompatible with an identification of sovereignty with government.

My thesis is, that the institution and development of law as an operation of sovereignty is consistent only with the theory that government is an organ of sovereignty, not sovereignty itself. A natural cleavage of the discussion appears in the fact that law falls easily into two classes, one of which, constitutional law, is bound up with the very existence of government, while the other, municipal law in the broad sense, presupposes the government already established and already at work.

Dealing first with constitutional law, we are struck by the apparent fact that law determines government. As Austin says:

> Constitutional law is that which determines the character of the person or persons in whom, for the time being, the sovereignty shall reside: and, supposing the government in question an aristocracy, or government of a number, determines the mode in which the sovereign powers shall be shared by the constituent members [1, 274].

If this definition is to be objected to, it is on the ground of narrowness rather than of breadth: certainly modern constitutional law is as definite in its statements of the manner in which the various constituent factors of government shall exercise their powers (in their large features), as it is in regard to the character and number of the persons concerned. But taking the minimum of determination allowed by Austin, we find that constitutional law implies a determining force back of the government and giving it character, both as to persons and as to the distribution of power among them. Surely *this* force, then, is sovereign, and the formation of constitutional law is the primary and radical exercise of sovereignty. But such a conception is inconsistent with Austin's whole theory. How does he avoid the conclusion? By holding that constitutional law is not properly law at all, but is positive morality,—the statement of a certain line of conduct which will meet the approval of an indefinite mass. "Constitutional law and international law are nearly in the same predicament. Each is positive morality, rather than positive law." Against the government, constitutional law is enforced and protected from infringement by merely moral sanctions.[16]

Now personally I should agree with Austin in thinking that the ultimate basis of order in the state, constitutional as well as all other, is moral. But Austin goes to the point of holding that it is *merely* moral—which is quite another matter. It may indeed be said that the moral (or social) forces get definition and crystallized form in determinate political institutions, and that constitutional law is one of the ways in which the moral forces, otherwise relatively inchoate, assume shape. This is only to say that sovereignty, the working will of society, is indefinite, or a more or less shapeless wish, except as it finds expression in organized institutions, of which government is one. It is to say, in other words, that all institutions, government included, are sovereignty, the moral or social force, *organized*. But Austin makes a complete gap between the social forces which determine government and that government itself. The former cannot state law, the latter can; the former is a mere aggregate, the latter is sovereign; the former is *merely* moral, the latter *merely* legal. The conception that constitutional law is not law will, I believe, commend itself as little to the lawyer, as the conception that laws issued by government are not ethical will commend itself to the moralist.

The stress here is so great that Austin actually contradicts himself in words—a thing which he very rarely does. On page 196 of the first volume, he points out that, unless there is to be continuous anarchy, the mode of acquiring government must be prescribed as to its generic modes— that the question, how far a society has attained political stability and tranquillity, is precisely the question of pre-

16   *Jurisprudence*, I, 277.

determining who shall assume government and how they shall assume it. Speaking of the anarchy in the Roman Empire, he goes on to say that "there was no mode of acquiring office which could be called constitutional; which was susceptible of generic description and which had been predetermined by *positive law* or morality." Here the very orderliness of political society is supposed to be due to the fact that government, as to its *personnel* and chief methods, is determined by law. But on page 271 and the following he returns to his only consistent position and holds that all attempts to regulate the line and mode of succession are advisory only and possessed of only moral value.

I suppose every one would agree that one of the greatest political advances yet made is precisely in substituting regular and definite modes of assuming governmental powers for irregular and chaotic methods; that it is the change from political anarchy to order. Yet this entire advance, according to Austin, cannot be conceived as an advance in law, but only in morality; and in morality, be it remembered, in a sense which shuts all definite organization out of the moral region, leaving it simply the mere expression of wishes on the part of individuals as individuals.

Coming, now, to the question of constitutional progress, of changes in the form of government, we find that Austin's theory does not provide any way of treating them. All constitutional changes whatever, according to him, are directed against sovereignty; they are not its further expression. They affect it; they do not issue from it. That is to say, they are revolutionary. Take the question of the formation of the North German Confederation. Upon Austin's theory, the governments existing prior to that Confederation were themselves sovereign. Grant this, and the Calhoun theory follows at once. The only alternative is that the change is completely revolutionary. Revolutionary, in one sense, of course it is. New ends are set up; new means are used in making the changes; new agencies for future action are created. But a revolutionary act by a permanent and continuous sovereign is one thing; a revolution in the sense of a complete submergence of sovereignty, a period of interregnum in which there is no sovereign, and then an utterly new sovereign with no point of continuity with the old, is another thing. Yet there is no alternative between this view and that which would make the new government simply a creature dependent upon previously existing sovereigns and, therefore, dissoluble at their will.

As matter of fact, the erection of the new governmental structure was led up to by a series of orderly changes all pointing the same way. There was the tendency towards a common military system, towards a common customs system and towards a common jurisprudence, besides a large number of minor social changes. The overt acts by which the new government was brought into being were *through* existing agencies in every respect.[17] What conclusion is it possible to draw, save that the immediate governmental agencies which set up the new government were not themselves sovereign, but were the organs of a sovereignty acting through them; a sovereignty which, by modifying these very agencies, created a new, more adequate agency, partially displacing the old? There was no more an interruption of sovereignty than there is an interruption of organic life when an organ of an animal is morphologically changed.

The case against Austin's theory becomes even stronger when we take into consideration the minor modifications which government is always undergoing. What is the authority for this change in government? What validity does it have? Here again, upon Austin's theory, there is no alternative between saying that it is not a modification of government at all, or else that, politically speaking, it is purely revolutionary. To say that it is not a modification of government, is to say that if it is a change produced *by* government, it cannot possibly be a change *in* government. Government, according to Austin, cannot be a subject or recipient of law: it cannot have duties. Whatever changes it undergoes, are in respect to merely moral considerations and may be retracted at any moment. Take, for example, the change which government, both national and state, has undergone in this country since 1820. All our ordinary views of con-

---

17   *Cf.* Hudson, "The North German Confederation," *Political Science Quarterly*, VI (Sept. 1891), 424.

stitutional law would make us say that the sovereignty, the effective social force, had been making over the form and operation of government so as to make it express more adequately the aims and methods of the sovereign. Upon Austin's theory we must either say that the government is just what it was in 1820, that the government existing then is still the sovereign, and could retract the changes which have occurred, since they are wholly its creatures, or else that there have been a succession of interruptions of sovereignty, of revolutions, so that the sovereign itself has changed as many times as the government has been modified.

v.

If it stands this way with the adoption and development of constitutional law, how is it with municipal laws? In the first place, common, as distinct from statute law, evidently presents difficulties—difficulties which, taken in connection with his own preferences, led Bentham to denounce all "judge-made law" as essentially usurpation. Austin, as against this view, has no great difficulty in showing that judicial legislation, when overt, may be regarded as proceeding from the sovereign; that the judge as much as the legislator acts as authorized by the sovereign—as a part of the sovereign. The problem recurs, however, with renewed stress when we come to the part played by custom in the development of law. Austin himself contends that custom is not law until expressly so declared by the judiciary. He holds that custom may be the occasion, but is never the source of law.[18] This position is so untenable, however, even from a strictly legal standpoint, that Holland, on the whole Austin's disciple, admits that the courts act retrospectively as well as prospectively upon customs, making decisions which declare what the law *was*, based upon the fact that the custom was such and such at the time. Holland would evade the difficulty by holding that this recognition of custom as law is due to an express or tacit law, giving to such customs the effect of laws.[19] Now in the first place, this

18 *Jurisprudence*, I, 103–5 and 204.
19 Holland, *Jurisprudence*, p. 48.

may be doubted as a fact. Two cases, which I borrow from
Wharton, will show the nature of the doubt. One case is the
abolition, in the American colonies, of English law, both
common and statute, by mere disuse,—an abolition which
has been noted by American courts as having occurred prior
to any action whatever of courts or legislature. The other
is the recognition given by the United States to some of
the customs of the Indian tribes relating to marriage and
inheritance. But give Holland the benefit of the doubt. To
say that customs are regarded as laws by virtue of a *tacit*
law to that effect, is simply to beg the whole question. It is
to say that custom is law in virtue of custom. And even if
the law is statutory, it is always declaratory of what has
previously been the case, rather than constructive of future
practice. It simply takes note of the fact in such a way as
to remove from it the doubt that might attach to it in complicated cases, or that might be thrown upon it by captious
persons.

Another fact is equally fatal to the theory that sovereignty operates through the commands of a certain determinate portion of society. Not only is "ancient and reasonable
custom" law, but the development of law is kept up by the
fiction that any principle which is found by the courts to-day
to be involved in past decisions of the court, not only is now
law, but always has been law.

A principle newly applied is not supposed to be a new principle;
on the contrary, it is assumed that from time immemorial it has
constituted a part of the common law of the land, and that it
has not been applied before only because no occasion has arisen
for its application.[20]

It is hardly necessary to add that this assumption is
made, not only in cases where the principle thus declared
always to have been law was not in the consciousness of
earlier judges, in whose decisions it is found by presumption,
but in cases where it would have been strongly repudiated
by them if consciously presented. I confess I should like to
see how a consistent Austinian would deal with law thus

[20]   Cooley, *Torts*, pp. 13–14.

formed; unless he can deal successfully with it, the theory that law, as the operation of sovereignty, is always the command issued by a determinate part of society, has no standing whatever.

Turn from the formation of explicit law to those laws whose authority is actually felt by the individual, and which are constantly enforced as against his own whims or caprice. As matter of fact the regulations which control most effectively the lives of most men who are not criminals, are not the laws formally declared by the state in its capacity as government, but the minor laws of subordinate institutions—institutions like the family, the school, the business partnership, the trade-union or fraternal organization. A large part of legislative activity consists in sketching in outline the sphere of these various institutions, giving to each institution within its own circumference almost plenary power. It is by and through the activities of these institutions, infinitely more than through the direct action of government, that the order of society is maintained. The question I raise is concerning the disposition to be made of the authority exercised in and by such institutions. What are we to say of the continued exercise of regulating authority involved in the operation of a family, a factory and a church? Does the sovereign command these things? Does the sovereign command a father, under sanction of punishment, to exercise just such and such control over his children? Holland indicates rather than solves the problem when he says:

All authority is, of course, exercised by permission of the state; *e.g.*, of a father over his family, but it is better to see here only a relation of private life sanctioned by the sovereign, not a delegation of the sovereign power.[21]

Why better? Better for the theory, undoubtedly; but on Austin's principles it is absurd to talk of sanction save where there is command, and, therefore, threatened penalty. Sir Henry Maine has called attention to the difficulty in thinking that the local customs of the Jews under their vassalage to Persia were maintained at the command of the monarch at Susa. But do we have to go so far afield for the

21   Holland, *Jurisprudence*, p. 77.

difficulty? Surely it is paralleled in the case of the authority exercised in any social institution.

But, it may be objected, you have already admitted that the government lays down the lines of these various institutions, and, in that sense, it does command whatever special deeds are involved in the carrying out of the authority thus entrusted. Is not the authority *delegated* by sovereignty? In any case, may we not say that whatsoever the sovereign does not forbid, it enjoins? These questions seem to me to point to an undoubted truth, which, however, they express in somewhat mechanical form. It is not that there is already a sovereign *and* institutions, and that the former then delegates to the latter authority to act. The institution exists only as it has this effective authority, and sovereignty is only a metaphysical substratum, save as it is embodied in positive institutions. Surely a government apart from all special institutions is a pure abstraction. The truth pointed to by the phrases is the fact that sovereignty exists as a definite actuality only as it is realized in institutions which act as its effective organs. The difficulty with the idea that "whatever the sovereign does not forbid, it enjoins" is, that it proves altogether too much for the doctrine of Austin. The result is that the whole social activity, the entire play of social life, has to be conceived as carried on in obedience to the commands of a certain particular group of persons, and in fear of penalties to be imposed by this group in case of disobedience. Surely this differs little, if at all, from a *reductio ad absurdum* of the doctrine.

I mentioned in an earlier part of this paper that attention would be directed further on to Austin's statement that the ultimate reason for obedience is recognition of the utility of the government. We have now arrived at the point where the contradiction is apparent between this idea and the notion that sovereignty, as a definite part of society, operates through the imposition of commands with their correlative sanctions. Command and obedience are correlative terms. They must exist on the same plane; if a command is a statement of a wish with a threat of evil attached in case of disobedience, then obedience is deference to this wish for fear of the evil. How, then, can it rest upon a perception of utility

(unless, indeed, this simply means a perception of the usefulness of not getting punished)? Persons may act just as
the one commanding would wish them to act; but, upon
Austin's definition, such conduct is not "obedience"; it is
not response to command unless it occurs from fear of penalty. We have seen that we must extend the idea of the
operation of sovereignty and of recognition of its authority
clear through from constitutional law to the working of institutions like the family—wherever there is authorized control on one side, and subjection on the other. If this complex
of organizations exists for the sake of what Austin calls
utility, then the operation of sovereignty cannot be reduced
to the imposition of commands by a certain portion of society upon another portion, the part which imposes being
itself exempt. And, conversely, if sovereignty is what Austin
says it is, then we must not stick at saying that the whole
organization of society is based upon fear of the commands
of a certain part of society.

VI.

In concluding, I wish again to refer to the general
bearings of this discussion. I should hardly think it worth
while to spend so much time criticizing Austin if he did not
represent a type, and an important type, of political theory.
I do not believe that any theory whatsoever that places sovereignty in some one part of the social organization can logically avoid the other positions of Austin. If sovereignty
resides in a part, it is necessary that this part be numerically
determinate; otherwise sovereignty is doubtful and anarchy
supervenes. It is also necessary that one portion should be
wholly and only sovereign while another portion is wholly
and only subject. Given this radical split, sovereignty must
be exercised by way of commands merely. There is no common interest which holds together the two sides; there being
two separate parts, one can act upon the other only by way
of command, while this other can react only by more or less
complete obedience from fear of punishment. Although not
all thinkers who have rejected Rousseau's idea of sovereignty as resident in the common will have come to these

conclusions, I cannot resist the feeling that it is because they are less logical than Austin, rather than because they have presented any theory essentially superior to his. At all events, I would raise the question whether there is any alternative between a theory like Austin's, which, placing sovereignty in a part of society, makes government an entity *per se*, whose operations are all commands, and a theory which finds the residence of sovereignty in the whole complex of social activities, thus making government an organ — an organ the more efficient, we may add, just in proportion as it is not an entity *per se*, but is flexible and responsive to the social whole, or true sovereign.

But Austin not only serves us by presenting in a typical form one theory of sovereignty, with its logical consequences worked out; he also, as it seems to me, points in the right direction in his emphasis upon determinateness. I cannot, indeed, retract what I have said already about the uselessness, as matter of theory, and the unverifiableness, as matter of fact, of the claim that sovereignty inheres in a certain specific number of persons. But "determinate" suggests another idea, that of definite organs. Except as sovereignty secures for itself definite and definable modes of expression, sovereignty is unrealized and inchoate. Constitutional development has consisted precisely in creating definite ways in which sovereignty should exercise its powers. The great weakness in Rousseau's theory that the general will is sovereign, is that he makes its generality exclude all special modes of operation. While, then, Austin's identification of the determinate factor with a specified group of individuals seems indefensible, yet in insisting that sovereignty requires determinate forms of exercise he is guarding us against the error which would make generality equivalent to vagueness. The practical, as well as the theoretical problem of sovereignty, may fairly be said to be this: To unite the three elements isolated by Lewis, Rousseau and Austin respectively: force, or effectiveness; universality, or reference to interests and activities of society as a whole; and determinateness, or specific modes of operation — definite organs of expression.

The Ego as Cause

Pretty much all libertarians nowadays insist that their doctrine of freedom of will is quite distinct from the older theory of indifferent choice. They suggest that their opponents are quite out of date in devoting their attention to the latter doctrine, which, under present conditions, is wholly a man of straw; they profess themselves quite as devoted adherents of the doctrine of causation as are the determinists, holding that the sole difference is as to the nature of the cause involved in volition.[1] Now, in one sense, I believe this latter contention to be quite correct; only I should go a step further and say the idea of "causation" as implying a productive agency or determining force has no standing whatever in science—that it is a superstition, and accordingly the libertarian is the *only* believer in causation. Much of the opposition to determinism is due, I believe, to the fact that the determinist either is understood to, or actually does, carry over into his use of the term "cause" this sense of efficient agency, instead of using it in its sole justifiable scientific meaning—the analysis of a vague and unrelated fact into definite and cohering conditions.[2] For my own part, I wish by "causation" to mean nothing more nor less than the possibility of analyzing the vague undefined datum of a volition into a group of specific and concrete conditions, that is, factors.

Admitting then, for sake of argument, the libertarian's

[1]   See, for example, the discussion by Dr. Gulliver in the January 1894 number of this *Review*.
[2]   With reference to this point I may be permitted to refer to an article in the *Monist* for April 1893, on "The Superstition of Necessity" [*Early Works*, IV, 19–36].

[*First published in* Philosophical Review, III (*May 1894*), 337–41. *Not reprinted during the author's lifetime.*]

position that the ego is an efficient cause of volition, I wish to make a confession of ignorance and a request for information. My confession is that I cannot frame to myself any conception of freedom of will (in the libertarian sense) which does not come in the end to the old-fashioned doctrine of a freedom of indifference. My request is that some libertarian who sees the distinction clearly will point it out to me.

Let me indicate the special point where I need light. For the sake of argument, it is conceded that the ego is the cause of volition in general; that, then, is not the problem. The libertarian, however, puts great stress upon choice between alternatives; as I understand (or *if* I understand) him, the possibility of such choice is the essence of freedom. Now, in order to avoid pure undeterminism (or the freedom of indifference), it becomes necessary to find a cause for this preference of one alternative over the other. What is the cause of the choice of one *rather* than the other? The ego simply as ego in general *may* be (*ex hypothesi*) the cause of the volition; but exactly the same ego cannot be the cause of two different and even quite opposing effects; there must be some difference in the cause when it operates to bring about one effect from that which would be operative in case the other is effected. I say, "cannot be" and "must be"; the reader will please understand this not in a dogmatic sense, but as expressing my difficulty; I do not see how identically the same cause, with no additional qualification whatever, can be regarded as a sufficient explanation of the choice of *a* rather than of *b*, *except upon the basis of indifferentism*. A stroke at billiards may be given so as to make a ball move either to the right or the left; if the ball is so struck that it moves to the left, it is because some further qualification has entered in other than that involved in case it moves to the right. Is the case the same or otherwise with the choice between alternatives? Does identically the same ego, without any further modification or qualification, choose to steal a loaf of bread that would also have chosen to go hungry? If yes, then how does the neo-libertarian differ from the old-fashioned indifferentist? If no, how does he differ from a determinist—from a determinist that is, who sees that the introduction of this further modification is simply a further step in the concrete analysis of the act?

Be it remembered, it is not a cause for volition in general which is wanted; it is a cause for *this* volition rather than *that*: for choosing hunger rather than dishonesty. The old-fashioned indifferentist has an answer before which I stand rebuked. He, I imagine, would exclaim: "What, do you think to catch me in this easy way? When I tell you that the essence of freedom is the ability to choose either *a* or *b* without any further cause, am I supposed to be so simple as at once to contradict myself by attempting to assign a cause?" I should not know what the indifferentist means, but his meaning (if there be any meaning) would at least be self-consistent. But when I am told both that freedom consists in the ability of an independent ego to choose between alternatives, and that the reference to the *ego* meets the scientific demand with reference to the principle of causation, I feel as if I were being gratuitously fooled with. My libertarian informant must know as well as myself that the question is concerning motivation as to choice; if there is adequate statement for the choice of *a rather* than *b*, surely there is determinism; if there is not, surely there is freedom of indifference. The power of attention is now the favorite philosopher's resort. Putting the question in terms of attention: is there any reason in the conditions of the case, any specific or assignable reason, why attention gives its little boost to this side rather than to that? any assignable condition on the basis of which it gives a jog in this direction rather than in that? As I understand the matter, the whole question lies here: In considering the relation of attention to a given choice, can we (or if foiled in a given instance are we still to try) carry back our analysis to scientific conditions, or must we stop at a given point because we have come upon a force of entirely a different order—an independent ego as entity in itself? If the action of the latter in swaying mental emphasis this way or that is one of the conditions, can we analyze *this* condition any further, or is it an ultimate fact? If the former, it seems to me an awkward determinism; if the latter, a frank indifferentism.[3]

***

[3]   It is somewhat aside from the point in discussion, but when Professor James says that views like the one quoted from Mr. John Fiske, on p. 577, Vol. II, of his *Psychology* are caricatures, arising from "not distinguishing between the possibles which really tempt a man and those

The same point may be briefly repeated from the ethical side. When one man says to another, "You did that, and I shall hold you responsible for it," he means by his "you," not a metaphysical ego, but a definite individual— John Smith. Every step away from the concrete individual, John Smith, with his special aptitudes, habits, desires, ideas, and ignorances, every step towards an ego in general, means a weakening of the connection between the man and the act, and a release of the man from responsibility for the act. Determinism means that the individual and his act are one. What does libertarianism mean? Will not some libertarian explain to me the causal agency of the ego in volition in terms of some concrete self, instead of in terms of a metaphysical ego?

One point more. Why does the libertarian change his standpoint so completely when considering the act *before* and *after* its performance? When considering the process of volition prior to the overt act, the presence in *consciousness* of two alternatives, the presence there of two attracting, yet incompatible ends, he treats as a fact in itself outside the freedom of will; it is capable of being accounted for on the ordinary principles of habit, association of ideas and desire. It is, he insists, an occasion for the exercise of freedom, but in itself lies outside of will proper. If he admitted the presence of the two alternatives to be an adequate basis for

---

which tempt him not at all," and that "free-will, like psychology, deals with the former possibles exclusively," this seems partly only a mitigation of the scientific havoc wrought by the idea of free-will; and partly to be entering on the deterministic path—and a mitigation *only* so far as the deterministic path is entered upon. From the anti-libertarian standpoint there is no break in the process; the fact of temptation and the fact of choice are related as the more undefined and the more definite establishing of relations within the self, or "between our Self and our own state of mind" (II, 568). Surely the determinist as well as the libertarian may recognize facts of uncertainty, of hesitation, of tentative action, of first trying on this and then that. And it is difficult to see why uncertainty will not do everything in giving zest and sting to life, that James thinks can be given only by sheer liberty (*Psychology*, I, 453). Our feeling that matters are "really being decided" looks to the future, not to the past; consequences *do* depend upon whether we act this way or that—*and this fact is one of the determining factors*. When Mr. James puts as the alternative to libertarianism "the rattling off of a chain that was forged innumerable ages ago," he must have in mind, not logical determinism, but theological *pre*determinism. And the theological view harks back to an independent entity or ego as Cause—to the "free-will" doctrine—not to the determinism of knowledge.

freedom, there would, of course, be no need whatever to call upon the outside entity, the ego. But if this consciousness of different ends, of competing interests, with the process of reflection upon them to ascertain their respective values, does not prove freedom, why use the *memory* of such consciousness—the conviction that we might have acted otherwise—to prove freedom? No determinist (that I know of) denies the facts of conflict of desire, denies that different ends with competing interests attaching to them come to consciousness, or denies the existence of deliberation or a tentative rehearsal of the different acts. He simply urges that choice, when it appears, is the normal psychological conclusion of this same process; that it no more requires the intervention of an outside faculty or entity as efficient cause, than the drawing of a conclusion from theoretical data requires more than recognition of the full meaning of the data.[4] In any case, we should have one interpretation or the other; not a mixture of two contradictory conceptions. Let us say, if we please, that our consciousness of ability to have acted otherwise does prove freedom, because the presence in consciousness of alternative ends with the reflection which that calls out, *is* freedom; or, let us say that since this consciousness cannot prove freedom, no subsequent revival of it in memory can prove freedom. In either case, the role of ego as separate efficient agent in causation seems to be excluded.

[4]   It is strange that Professor James, who recognizes so far as knowledge is concerned the entire uselessness of an ego outside and behind, who indeed has given that theory the hardest knocks it has yet received from the psychological side (*Psychology*, I, 360–70), should feel bound to set up its correlate when he comes to deal with will. If the stream of thought can run itself in one case, the stream of conduct may administer itself in the other. Why should he deny to the transcendentalist ego in knowing a power which he claims for attention in acting? Historically, I think the independent Ego in knowledge is a survival and transference from the action of an entity of Will in choice.

Reconstruction

It does not need any special acuteness of observation to note that the present is a time of unusual ferment in the development of theology and in the religious life of the churches. Signs of change and of agitation present themselves to even the dull eye. We are somewhat apt, however, to occupy ourselves over much with the signs of change and to overlook the deeper forces which are at work in bringing about the change. We pick up a newspaper and it tells us of Dr. Briggs and of the trial of Dr. Smith, or of some other phase of the so-called higher criticism—a change in the view of the Scriptures. We pick up another newspaper and we find in it some discussion regarding church union or regarding the assumption by the church of new philanthropic activities—the development of an "institutional" church. Or, again, it is a question of the revision of the creed of a church —making it over either in whole or in part—or else a question of its relation in general to church work. Getting our information regarding these things in such a haphazard, disconnected way, we are apt to think of the changes themselves as if they were likewise disconnected. We do not see their bearings upon each other, nor their dependence upon certain large tendencies which have been at work for centuries. The result is that much of the discussion regarding these and similar points is futile. We think we are settling problems and establishing principles when we are only dealing in a superficial way with superficial symptoms. It is, perhaps, better for those who are immediately engaged in the agitation, whether pro or con, to have attention absorbed in the details of the matter. But for us who stand outside, it

[*An address before the Students' Christian Association of the University of Michigan, 27 May 1894. First published in the* Monthly Bulletin, xv (*June 1894*), 149–56. *Not previously reprinted.*]

is certainly better, upon occasion, to take stock of the whole affair. Accordingly, I shall this morning inquire first what is the meaning in general of a critical change in life, of the reconstruction of activities; secondly, I shall ask for the special causes of the reconstruction now going on in religious life; and thirdly, endeavor to make one or two practical applications to our own duties.

Reconstruction is a periodic need of life. It represents, in history, the conflict between ideas and the institutions which embody those ideas. In animal life, it stands for the conflict between function and the structure which exercises the function; in the life of the individual, it is the conflict between habits and ideals; in general, it is the conflict between ends or aims and the means or machinery through which these ends are realized. Neither of these sides is anything without the other. Ideas, functions, aims are all helpless and inert unless there is a system of objective powers through which they are exercised. The machinery, the structure, the institution or the habit is mere routine, is dead bones, unless animated by a purpose. Spite of this necessary interdependence of idea and machinery, of thought and institution, there come times when one side conflicts with the other. At such a period reconstruction is necessary. We are apt to assume that it is always the ideal which outruns the means of its execution; that the objective form is always behind the animating idea. But this overlooks the fact that ideas finally become embodied in outward life, that aims become realized as habits. To suppose anything else is to suppose that our ideals and our aims are without hands and feet, that they never succeed. Such is not the case. Any aim worth striving for is always at some definite period or other realized; if not wholly, at least sufficiently realized to demand a further development of the idea. The execution of our purposes creates a new purpose. It makes necessary the transmuting of the accomplished institution or habit into a means, an instrument for the outworking of the new idea. This is the period of reconstruction. The very success of the former ideal demands that we no longer go on striving for that ideal, but that we form for ourselves a new principle of action. A student who has set his mind on preparing for law, or medicine, or theology, may spend a period of years in preparation, but when that period is complete it is incumbent upon him to see that he does not go on idly repeating the same acts, attempting to do over again a thing which is now done. A time of reconstruction has come, a time in which he must square up what he has already accomplished and turn it over so as to make it face the future, so that it becomes a means for a higher idea. All history is full of just such crises. The Greek people succeeds in Socrates, and that very success demands such a facing about of the older civilization as to involve the practical destruction of its outward form. The outward form must go when it has served its purpose, in order that the purpose may live on in new forms.

Is Christianity an exception to this law of all life? Have none of the ideas and aims which were set up in the earlier centuries of our era been realized? Have they not succeeded to such an extent that their very success now demands reconstruction, an advance in the ideas themselves? Unless the ideals with which Christianity started were immobile and inert, or unless they were so far away as to be out of relation to actual life, they must by this time have embodied themselves in the institutions and habits of practical life; they must have converted themselves into structure, into institutions, into a system of working means. If such is the case, it is idle for us to go on repeating the old ideals and cherishing the old aims. That which is prophetic, and therefore inspiring, at its outset becomes stale and meaningless in reiteration after its prophecy has fulfilled itself. It is as if persons were still agitating the emancipation of the Negroes in the South, and were calling upon everyone to arouse himself in great excitement to deeds of heroism—in a cause already won.

Turning from the general to the more specific, what are some of these successes of the early Christian ideas, and what reconstruction does their accomplishment require from us?

One of the great thoughts of early Christianity was that of the value, the inalienable worth, of the individual soul. When the question was asked, "What shall it profit a man if he gain the whole world and lose his own self?" it was assumed that the soul is worth more to itself than all outer acquisitions whatsoever—that the possession of the universe does not equal in weight the meaning of the individual to himself. We do not need to relate how this thought of the absolute immeasurable value of the self permeated all forms of Christian thought. It formed the very heart of the Christian consciousness. But the thought was propounded in a world which seemed to give it the lie. The more this infinite value of the individual was asserted, the more apparent was the slavery in which the individual was actually held. Politically, industrially, almost physically, the individual was, as matter of fact, in bonds. There existed no such all-embracing value as the thought ascribed to him. He was everywhere, in large part, a mere means to things outside himself, not a free self-possessed end in himself. As a result, the thought was turned into an ideal. Because it was not true in act, it was held to be true only in emotion, or at some remote time, or by some supernal means. But the inspiration which the ideal gave, the moving power which the emotion offered, went to transform the thought into reality. Through this very thought, in co-operation with a multitude of other forces, Greek science and Roman law, democracy as a social fact was born. Through the growth of democracy, through assured rights and freedom, the individual has now become to a considerable extent, in fact, what at the outset he was only in name; a being who is self-possessed, an end in himself, and whose life permits no law which does not spring out of its own basis and destiny.

Is there not necessary a reconstruction of the religious life resulting from this passage of idea into habit, of thought into realized deed? It seems to me that this change calls for a reconstruction, even wider than we can imagine, of what is termed personal religion. It becomes meaningless to assert, simply by itself in general terms, the infinite value of the self when that self becomes free to realize this infinite value in act. It becomes artificial, unreal, to attempt in special ways and by special forms and peculiar acts, to work up a set of emotions corresponding to this conception when the individual is free to enjoy the feeling of his freedom in his common every-day acts. It becomes wearisome to keep reiterating, in technical forms, simply as ideals and sentiments, what has come to belong to man in the very makeup of life and the habits of daily action. Much of what is termed devotion and religious service, in the way of praise and prayer and exhortation, much of the experience which the individual is called upon to pass through in order to get the name of being religious, needs honest and thorough overhauling in the face of these changed facts of life.

Another great ideal of Christianity was expressed in the Kingdom of God. This was a conception of the common incarnate Life, the purpose and interest animating all men and binding them together into one harmonious whole of sympathy and action. This ideal suffered also from its discrepancy with the outward historical facts of life. The idea lost its original, normal significance, the true relationship between man and man in all forms whatsoever, and assumed the form of the special organization called the church. In the church, that unity and brotherhood which seemed impossible beyond its walls, whose very idea, indeed, seemed contradicted by the principles upon which existing life was organized – in the church, this sought-for unity of life might be found. This ideal also went on realizing itself. The church could not realize this idea within itself alone. It could realize the idea only as it permeated the mass of life. "Ye are the salt of the earth," but it is a self-contradiction to suppose that to be the salt represents a privilege, or that it can be performed by mere existence. It represents a function, a duty, and can be performed only in action. But the idea was also working outside the church. The very organization and structure of the Roman Empire, the scientific and geographic discoveries, the growth of commerce – all represent tremendous agencies in the practical furthering of the unity of life and interest among men. In and through a co-operation of all these agencies, that which two thousand years ago was an ideal, almost a dream, has now become a practical fact of life.

This idea, too, has succeeded, and in its success demands a new idea. A distinguished lecturer has recently been urging that the church ought to sacrifice itself to the world; that it ought to surrender whatever monopoly of truth and spiritual life it seems to possess, and make itself an humble instrument in the service of man. Would that Dr. Herron, and all others who think with him, might realize the extent to which this sacrifice is already accomplished. If they could but see that the church long ago ceased to have this monopoly, that the organs of grace, the means for lifting up the individual and binding men together in harmony are now found working in all forms of life; if they could but see how political, domestic and industrial institutions have become in fact an organized Kingdom of God on earth, making for the welfare of the individual and the unity of the whole. The sacrifice which is now demanded of the church is not one in general, but one of detail. It is not a sacrifice to some great mission in the future; it is rather a willingness to recognize accomplished facts and readjust itself accordingly. It simply needs to see that it can claim no longer to be the sole, or even the preëminent representative in the cause of righteousness and good-will on earth; that partly through, and partly without, its own past activities, the ideal which at the outset it represented has now become a common fact of life; so that its present duty is to take its place as one among the various forces of social life, and to coöperate with them on an equal basis for the furtherance of the common end.

Another great thought of Christianity was that of the revelation of absolute truth to man — absolute, that is, in the sense of being sufficient and supreme for the guidance of life. Christianity brought to consciousness the great thought that living and controlling truth is not a far away thing, but is living incarnate in the individual himself; that the individual, therefore, has open access to its inexhaustible stores. But this idea, too, fell, to all appearance, on stony ground. It came into a world where all historic conditions did not square with the principle proclaimed. In the form of life two thousand years ago, the access of the individual to truth, the methods for realizing and testing it were feeble and inadequate. As a result, this idea, too, was conceived in a narrow and technical, and often unnatural sense. It was not thought that the individual in and through the very process of living had access to truth as such, but rather that by cer-

tain unusual and external agencies truth of a certain practical kind, called religious truth, might be poured into the
individual.

But since this word was first proclaimed, science has
had a tremendous development. In the centuries, since the
Middle Ages, those centuries in which there was the most
efficient organization of the church as a special institution,
science both as a method and as a body of results, has made
over intellectual life. The old world of human conception
was an unmoving world, fixed and at rest. It was a world
definitely bounded. The earth was its center and it had a
limited circumference. Since it was a dead unmoving world,
it was a world of parts and pieces, there was no living unity
to hold it together. Now we see the universe as one all-
comprehensive, interrelated scene of limitless life and motion. No bound can be put to it in imagination or in thought.
No detail is so small that it is not a necessary part of the
whole; no speck is apparently so fixed that it is not in reality
a scene of energy. But great as is the change in outlook upon
the world, the changed attitude in method is greater still.
Science as a method of inquiry, as an organized, comprehensive, progressive, self-verifying system of investigation has
come into existence. The result has been an almost bound-
less confidence in the possibility of the human mind to reach
truth. We feel that our instruments are so ample and so
mighty that, given time, nothing can resist them. It is true
that many of our men of science still call themselves
agnostics, and proclaim the impossibility of reaching any
supreme controlling truth. But if we look below the surface
we find that it is always implied that the inaccessible truths
are really not truths, or are at least not worth finding out.
It is assumed, however unconsciously, that all truth which
is worth while, all truth which promises to be of practical
avail in the direction of man's life, may be gotten at by scientific method. Men do not throw away their belief in the most
valuable things of life unless they feel themselves possessed
of a sure way to regain the lost treasure and more. Along
with this confidence in general is gained a spirit of doubt in
particular. Nor are the two things so contradictory as at
first sight they seem. The more one believes in truth and

in the possibility of discovering it, the more he is bound at all hazards to test whatever proclaims itself to be truth. It is a mere make-believe, self-deceived love of truth which does not insist that its pretended truth be really truth. Faith in truth does not reveal itself in loud, profuse exclamations concerning the importance of truth and its defense, but in the patient unwearied search for what the truth really is.

Now all this, if I mistake not, means a reconstruction. The discussion regarding the Scriptures, regarding the nature and authority of creeds, does not come simply from the growth of this or that science; it is not simply a question of reconciling history and astronomy with Genesis, or of reconciling historical and philological research with Chronicles and Isaiah; it is a question far deeper. It is indeed astounding that large bodies of men should think themselves at liberty to ignore or to defy the established results of physical and historical science; but it is a matter of even deeper import that we should fail to recognize how completely science has changed the conception of the concrete relation of truth to human action. It is because science represents a method of truth to which, so far as we can discover, no limits whatsoever can be put, that it is necessary for the church to reconstruct its doctrines of revelation and inspiration, and for the individual to reconstruct, within his own religious life, his concepton of what spiritual truth is and the nature of its authority over him. Science has made real to us, and is bound to make still more real, the actual incarnation of truth in human experience and the necessity for giving heed to it.

Now as to one or two practical conclusions for ourselves. The question of conservatism versus radicalism comes home to every thinking man, whether he consciously puts the question to himself in that way or not. Let us recognize to the full that the only honest and efficient conservatism is one which remains true to the spirit of the past and not to its mere outward forms. No one can moor himself in the past. The present is the true past. It is the past in its fuller expression, in the revelation of its deeper meaning. The only way to be genuinely loyal to the past, to be honestly conservative, is to accept without carping its onward movement. I am astonished at the impertinence with which many so-called Conservatives attribute the violence and causes of the French Revolution to the liberal element. It is a useful moral to call to mind that the French Revolution was the work of the conservative party; that it was because the conservatives attempted to dam up the stream of life, that that stream burst forth in such irregular and abnormal fashion. The attempt to arrest the onward flow of thought will succeed no more than the effort to stop the movement of political and industrial life. The only conservative who can respect himself as a conservative, is the man who puts to himself this question: What is the meaning, the idea which has animated the past, and what attitude, what change of outward form does that spirit demand of me in order that I may remain true to it?

On the other hand, the radical, the one who is for progress, cannot gain his end if he shuts himself off from established facts of life. If he turn to the future before he has taken home to himself the meaning of the past, his efforts will in so far be futile. The progress for which he seeks will not come. The only force, the only instruments with which he may carry out his projects of progress are the traditions, the institutions of the past in their readjustment and reconstruction. It is folly, it is worse than folly, it is intellectual dishonesty, to shut our eyes to the facts of life and proclaim that spiritual truth is just as it was in method and content nineteen hundred years ago, or one hundred years ago, or ten years ago; it is folly, it is worse than folly, it is mere individual conceit, for one to set out to reform the world, either at l.rge or in detail, until he has learned what the existing world which he wishes to reform has for him to learn. The only final conservative force in life is the most radical idea absorbed into the character which has thus learned the lesson of the past. The most progressive force in life is the idea of the past set free from its local and partial bonds and moving on to the fuller expression of its own destiny. Intellectual honesty, a spirit which will not deceive itself with words or with half-formed ideas and sentiments, because these symbols and sentiments have meant power and influence in the past; seriousness of purpose, a seriousness which identifies intellect with character and which is cautious about allowing its intellectual notions prematurely to run ahead of its acquired habits; and a charity which is the outgrowth of this honesty and this seriousness—these are the duties which the present period demands of us.

I certainly cannot give, and I do not see how any one can give, a patent or a ready made solution for this problem of readjustment which I know faces so many a student of life today. But I think any man or woman who exacts of himself sincerity and honesty, who recalls that the reconstruction now needed is needed because the earlier ideals have so far accomplished themselves, is in a fair way to solve on the best possible terms this conflict between loyalty to the past and faithfulness to new truth.

It is a greater, not a less, responsibility as to belief which faces us. The responsibility now upon us is to form our faith in the light of the most searching methods and known facts; it is to form that faith so that it shall be an efficient and present help to us in action, in the co-operative union with all men who are sincerely striving to help on the Kingdom of God on earth.

The Chaos in Moral Training

In teaching undergraduates in the subject of ethics, I have been impressed with the need of getting the discussion as near as possible to what is going on in the minds of students themselves. Although ethics is the most practical of the philosophic studies, none lends itself more readily to merely technical statement and formal discussion. It is easy to forget that we are discussing the actual behavior, motives, and conduct of men, and substitute for that a discussion of Kant's or Mill's or Spencer's theory of ethics. It seems to me especially advisable to get in some contact with the practical, and accordingly largely unconscious, theory of moral ends and motives which actually controls thinking upon moral subjects. One is, however, considerably embarrassed in attempting this. As any one knows who has much to do with the young, their conscious thoughts in these matters, or at least their statements, are not fresher, but more conventional, than those of their elders. They are apt to desire to say the edifying thing, and the thing which they feel is expected of them, rather than express their own inner feelings. Moreover, some points have been so much discussed that any direct questioning upon them is apt to bring forth remnants of controversies that have been heard or read, secondhand opinions, an argumentative taking of sides, rather than to evoke the spontaneous and native attitude. Among other devices for eliminating or at least reducing these disturbing factors the following method was hit upon: To ask each student to state some typical early moral experience of his own, relating, say, to obedience, honesty, and truthfulness, and the impression left by the outcome upon his own mind, especially the impression as to

[*First published in* Popular Science Monthly, xlv (*Aug. 1894*), 433–43. *Not previously reprinted.*]

the reason for the virtue in question. The answers brought out a considerable mass of material, incidentally as well as directly. Some of this seems to me to have value beyond the immediate pedagogical occasion which called it forth, as furnishing a fairly representative sample[1] of the motives instilled by existing methods of moral training, and the impressions which these methods leave behind.

Nine-tenths of the answers may be classified under one of the following heads: The impression left by the mode of treatment was that the motive for right doing is (1) found in the consequences of the act; (2) fear of being punished; (3) simply because it is right; (4) because right doing pleases the parent, while wrongdoing displeases; (5) the religious motive. In number the religious motive predominates; next to that comes fear of punishment. In many cases, of course, several of these reasons were inculcated.

1. The regard for consequences as a reason for morality takes the form of regard either for external consequences or for intrinsic reactions—that is to say, upon the character of the agent or upon those about him. A number seem to have learned the value of obedience by observation of disagreeable results proceeding from its opposite. For example, one child was told not to take off her shoes and stockings; she disobeyed, and had croup in the night—whence, she remarks, she derived the idea that others knew more than she, and that disobedience was dangerous. Another girl was told not to wear a lawn dress to a picnic; she disobeyed, but a rain storm came up and faded it out. "From this and other similar experiences I deduced the idea that obedience was wise. Yet this was with the reservation that obedience was to be tempered with discretion, as I observed that in some instances acting upon my own judgment was justified by the outcome."

When we come to the moral motive as determined by the intrinsic results of the act, we are obviously approaching the question, so mooted upon its theoretical side, of intui-

[1] The class numbered over one hundred. About ninety replied. About twenty of the answers were put aside, as indulging in general statements, or as bearing the stamp of artificiality. The remaining answers represent Central Western States, particularly the States of Michigan, Illinois, and Indiana. Pretty much all grades of homes are represented, and at least three lines of descent beside native American.

tionalism *versus* empiricism. Nothing was said upon this point in giving out the questions; the students may fairly be presumed to have been unconscious of any such bearing in their answers, and so these may be taken as fairly free from any bias. No one reply indicates any distinct recognition of right or wrong prior to the commission of some particular act.[2] After acting, a number of persons note the fact that they became so uncomfortable that they either owned up or resolved not to do that sort of thing again. This experience, however, is noted only in the case of a lie told or acted. Several expressly state that obedience and honesty (as a regard for the property of others) appeared quite artificial, their need being seen only after considerable instruction and some rather crucial experiences. Obedience, in many cases, seemed quite arbitrary—"necessary for children," as one puts it, "but not for grown people"; or, as another notes, "till he got big enough so he wouldn't have to mind"; while a third states that obedience, as such, was always accompanied with a certain resentment and a desire to have the positions reversed, so that he could do the commanding. As for honesty, one says that it always seemed to him that anything he wanted to use belonged to him; another, that any pretty thing which she admired was her own. One child notes that she saved up the pennies her father had given her to take to Sunday school, and bought a valentine with them, which she gave to him, to surprise him. The father threw this into the fire first, and then punished her, taking it for granted that she knew she was doing wrong.[3] Not even after that, however, did she feel it was wrong, but rather felt indignant and humiliated that her father had treated her gift in such a way. Another child could see no wrong in taking the pennies from a bank which she and her sister had in com-

---

[2]   This *may* be due, of course, to the way in which the question was put.

[3]   A sense of injustice seems to have been the first distinctly moral feeling aroused in many. This, not on account of the wrong which the child did others, but of wrong suffered in being punished for something which seemed perfectly innocent to the child. One of the distinct painful impressions left on my own mind by the papers is the comparative frequency with which parents assume that an act is consciously wrong and punish it as such, when in the child's mind the act is simply psychological —based, I mean, upon ideas and emotions which, under the circumstances, are natural.

mon. The following instance is worth quoting in full: "Before I was four, I remember several instances in which I saw moral delinquencies in others, which I wished to punish or did punish, but none in myself. As to honesty, I claimed all the eggs laid in the neighborhood as coming from my own pullet. After being convinced of the physical impossibility of this, it was a long time before I would believe that everything I laid hands on was not mine. I was once driven off from a field where I was picking berries; this made a great impression upon me, and led to questions regarding the rights of others to be so exclusive. The effectual appeal always lay in being led to put myself in the place of others." A number note that there was great difficulty in appreciating that a fence could institute a moral barrier between mine and thine. But as regards lying, a few report having been made thoroughly uncomfortable by its after effects in their own emotions. The following story, trivial in itself, is not trivial in meaning: "Once, when I had two apples, I wished to give one to my playmate; I knew she would expect the best one, which I also wished for myself, so I held out the best side of the poorer one and made her think that was the better of the two. Her belief that I had really given her the best took away all the sweetness from my own apple, and I decided that straightforwardness was better." This instance, as well as others pointing in the same direction, so far as they would justify any conclusion, fall in line with the case reported by Professor James relative to the experience of a deaf-mute. This boy had stolen ten dollars, thinking it a smaller sum, having previously stolen many small amounts with no compunctions of conscience. In this case, the reaction into himself was, so to speak, so massive and bulky that he became thoroughly uncomfortable and ashamed; was brought spontaneously to recognizing its badness, and kept from stealing money in the future. This genuine meaning of the innate theory of conscience seems accordingly, to Professor James, to mean that any act, if it can be experienced with adequate detail and fullness, "with all that it comports," will manifest its intrinsic quality.[4]

---

[4]   *Philosophical Review*, I, 624. I can but think, however, that Professor James is very charitable in ascribing to the ordinary intuitionalist any such reasonable view.

2. An astonishingly large number record that they got their first distinct moral impressions through punishment, and of these a considerable fraction got the idea that the chief reason for doing right was to avoid punishment in the future. This division runs into that dealing with the religious motive, as sometimes the fear was of punishment from parent, sometimes from God; it also runs into the fourth head to be considered, practically if not logically, for a number record that the motive appealed to by their father was fear of punishment, while that of their mother was love of her, and grief caused by wrongdoing.

A few samples tell, in different language, the almost uniform tale of the outcome of the appeal to force. "I rebelled with feelings of hatred and of desire for revenge. It seemed to me unjust, imposed by sheer force, not reason." One tells the story of being coaxed by older boys to steal some tobacco from his father. "I was caught and given a whipping, no questions being asked and no explanation given. The result was certainly a fear of punishment in the future, but no moral impression. I thought my father whipped me because he wanted the tobacco himself, and so objected to my having any of it." Another reports that the impression left by punishment was a mixture of a feeling of personal indignity suffered—a feeling so strong as to blot out the original offense—and a belief that she was punished for being detected. Another thought she was punished because her father was the stronger of the two; another, that fear of harm to self induced people to do right things; another tells that he longed for the age of independence to arrive so that he might retaliate. One upon whom fear of punishment from God was freely impressed formed the idea that if he could put off death long enough, lying was the best way out of some things. One child (five years old) went in the front part of the house after she had been forbidden, and, falling, hurt herself. She was told that this was a punishment from God; whence she drew the not illogical conclusion that God was a tyrant, but that it was possible to outwit him by being more careful next time, and not falling down. One peculiarity of the method of inducing morality by creating fear is that some parents, in order to prevent lying, deem it advisable to lie themselves; *e.g.*, talk about cutting off the end of the boy's tongue or making him leave home, etc. But there is hardly any need of multiplying incidents; all the reports re-enforce the lesson which moralists of pretty much all schools have agreed in teaching—that the appeal to fear as such is morally harmful. Of course, there are a number of cases where good results are said to have come from punishment, but in such cases the punishment was incidental, not the one important thing; it was the emphasis added to an explanation.

3. Some report that they were instructed to do right "because it is right," either as the sole reason or in connection with other motives, such as harm to one's character, or displeasing God or parents. A little more than one-tenth of the persons report this as a leading motive instilled. Most simply mention the fact, with no comment as to the impression made upon them. One remembers displeasing her mother (after she had been told that she must do right because it was right) by asking why she must do what was right rather than what was wrong. On the whole, she was confused, and the basis of morality seemed to be arbitrary authority.

4. Such answers as the following are exceedingly common: "I saw by mother's face that I had grieved her"; "was made to feel that I had shocked and pained my parents"; "the motive appealed to was giving pain to my parents, who loved me"; "I felt ashamed when I found I had grieved my father"; "was made to feel sorry when my parents were made unhappy by what I did," etc. There is a paucity of information about the attitude toward morality left by this mode of treatment. The following, indeed, is the only comment made in any of the reports: "Upon disobeying my mother, I was told that I was naughty and bad, and that she would not love me unless I was sorry and promised not to disobey again. This impressed me with the *necessity* of obeying, but I did not see then, and can not now, any *reason* for it."

5. We come now to the religious motive as the ground for right doing. There are different kinds of answers here— appeals to fear and love, to Bible teachings and Bible warn-

ings, to terror of an avenging God, and to the wounded
affection of a personal friend and Saviour; sometimes one,
and sometimes a mixture of all. Certain of the practical ones
among the parents used, indeed, not only all these appeals,
but pretty much all the foregoing mentioned as well, evidently on the principle that it is not possible to use too many
inducements toward morality, and that if one fails, another
may hold. I shall give one or two typical quotations
illustrating each method. First, of fear: "My mother told
me, 'You must tell the truth, for God knows all about it, for
he is continually watching you, and I certainly shall find out
all about it.' This caused great fear; we thought of God as a
powerful avenger, and also believed that he communicated
with our parents about our faults." Three or four mention
that the story of Ananias and Sapphira was used with considerable effect. Second, of Biblical authority: "I was taught
that the Bible said that these things were right and wrong,
and that it must be so. I can not remember a time when I
did not think that it was wrong to break any of the ten com-
mandments, because they had been given by God in the
Bible." "When I asked the reason why I should not do certain things, I was told that it was because they were forbidden in the Bible." Third, of love: "I was taught that
Jesus looked upon me, just as my parents did; that he was
pleased when I did right, and grieved when I did wrong, and
that he had done so much for me that I ought to be sorry to
grieve him." "I was taught that wrong acts grieved our
Lord, and that he knew about them even if no one else did;
also that he was pleased when I did any little act of kindness
to any one." Fourth, mixed cases: "I was brought up in a
distinctly Christian home. I was made to feel that certain
things were right and their opposites wrong; was taught that
there is a God who sees and knows everything that I do;
that he looked upon disobedience with an eye of displeasure;
the Bible was taught from early infancy as a text-book of
morals; was made to feel that not only would punishment
result from wrongdoing, but that both God and my parents
were hurt by my wrongdoing. The impression left on my
mind was that certain things were right and that God was
the standard; at first fear, awe, and reverence were induced,

with occasional feelings of rebellion; the general effect was to awaken respect for the right qualities, and to make me consider the right and wrong of things in my own consciousness." "After the first lie which I remember, I was not punished, but was given a lecture on the words in the Revelation, 'Without are . . . whosoever loveth and maketh a lie.' I was made to see that the habit would grow and dishonor me in the sight of God and man, and left with the promise of a good whipping if I ever told another. In general, I remember that I was taught that my faults had the peculiarity of increasing at an astonishing rate; that I was a very naughty child, and that every wrong act grieved a heavenly Father who loved me and who was ever present to see both the good and the bad." "After lying I was told that I got no good from it; that teachers and friends disliked such persons; that my honest playmates would look down on me; that God was grieved with me. The room was filled with the splendor of the setting sun, and it seemed to me that God must be up there looking at me and seeing what a naughty girl I was. Then I was told that God would forgive me if only I confessed, and that in the future he would help me to be good if only I tried."

I am not afraid that any one will despise these incidents as trivial. It is easy, indeed, to recall our own childhood, to look out at what is now around us, and say that there is nothing new here; that all this is commonplace and just what any one would expect. Precisely; and in that consists its value. It all simply brings out the most familiar kind of facts, but still facts to which we shut our eyes, or else ordinarily dismiss as of no particular importance, while in reality they present considerations which are of deeper import than any other one thing which can engage attention. Every one will admit without dispute that the question of the moral attitude and tendencies induced in youth by the motives for conduct habitually brought to bear is the ultimate question in all education whatever—will admit it with a readiness and cheerfulness which imply that any one who even raises the question has a taste for moral truisms. Yet, as matter of fact, moral education is the most haphazard of all things; it is assumed that the knowledge of the right reasons to be in-

stilled and knowledge of the methods to be used in instilling
these reasons "come by nature," as reading and writing came
to Dogberry. There is, if I mistake not, a disposition to re-
sent as intrusion any discussion of the subject which goes
beyond general platitudes into the wisdom of the motives
and methods actually used. Yet I do not see how any successful training of children as to their conduct is possible
unless the parents are first educated themselves as to what
right conduct is, and what methods are fit for bringing it
about. I do not see how that is to be accomplished without a
free treatment of present aims and methods.

The first thing which strikes one's attention in these
answers is the great gap existing at present between theory
and practice. Either prevailing theory is egregiously wrong,
or else much of present practice, measured by that theory,
may be fairly termed barbarous in its complete disregard of
scientific principle. If there is one thing in theory upon
which all schools are agreed, it is that conduct is not moral
except as its motive is pure—except, that is, as free from
reference to personal fear of punishment and hope of reward.
The intuitionalist insists that duty must be done for duty's
sake; the empiricist, that while consequences make the
moral criterion, yet the agent is truly moralized only in so
far as his motive is regard for the consequences which follow
intrinsically from the act itself. And yet the main motive
actually appealed to is the desire to avoid either actual punishment, whether from God or from one's parent, or else the
reflex into one's self of their displeasure in the way of being
grieved or hurt. The last motive appealed to, it would seem,
is that connected with the act itself. Enlightenment as to the
true nature of the act performed, irrespective of the source
of its imposition, irrespective of the favor or disfavor which
the act will arouse from others (save, of course, in so far as
that disfavor or favor is, through the social structure, one of
the *intrinsic constituents* of the act) and the development of
interest in that act for its own sake, seem to be the last things
aimed at.[5] It is commonly said, I know, that a child can not

[5]   I hope I shall not be understood here as arguing for the principle of
doing right because it is right. In the first place, the phrase is very ambig-
uous, meaning either doing the act for the sake of something right, in

understand the moral bearing of his acts, and that therefore rather arbitrary and external motives must be appealed to. Of this, I would say two things: First, it is true that the child can not see in the act all that an adult sees in it. There is not the slightest reason why he should. If he did, it would be an entirely different act, an act having different conditions, a different aim, and a different value. The question is whether the child can be made to see the reason why *he* should perform the act, not why some other older person should perform it. Limiting the question in this way, it loses, I think, a large part of its force. As for what remains, it may still be said that the ideal is to appeal to the child's own intelligence and interest *as much as possible*. One of the strongest impressions made upon me by the papers is the natural strong interest of children in moral questions—not, indeed, as consciously moral, but as questions of what to do and what not to do. We do not have to take any position regarding the intuitive character of moral distinctions or the *a priori* character of moral laws to be sure that a child is intensely interested in everything that concerns himself, and that what he does and how other people react to it is a very intimate part of himself. To decline to show the child the meaning of his acts, to hold that his desire to know their reasons (that is, their meaning) is a sign of depravity, is to insult his intelligence and deaden his spontaneous interest in the whys and wherefores of life—an interest which is the parent's strongest *natural* ally in moral training.

Secondly, in and so far as the child can not see the meaning and value of his acts and value them for himself, it becomes absurd to insist upon questions of morality in connection with them. Make the widest possible allowance for the necessity that a child perform acts, the bearing of which he can not realize for himself, and the contradiction in the

---

the abstract or at large, a right whose connection with the particular act is not seen; or else doing the act for its own sake, for the meaning which the act itself has for the agent—a principle which is the extreme opposite of the other sense. But, in the second place, I am desirous to state the matter in terms upon which all schools are agreed; and I understand that (however differently they may phrase it) all schools are agreed that an act has really moral worth only when the agent does it because of what *he* sees and feels in it.

present method is only emphasized as long as parents impress upon the children strictly moral considerations in connection with such acts. Surely, if morality means (as all moralists are agreed) not simply doing certain acts, but doing them with certain motives and disposition, rational training would emphasize the moral features of acts only when it is possible for the child to appreciate something of their meaning, and in other cases simply manage somehow to get the acts done without saying anything about questions of right and wrong. To continue the present method of holding, on one side, that a child is so irrational that he can not see for himself the significance of his conduct, while, on the other, with regard to these self-same acts, the child is punished as a *moral* delinquent, and has urged upon him, on *moral* grounds, the necessity for doing them, is the height of theoretical absurdity and of practical confusion. Present methods seem to take both the intuitive and utilitarian positions in their extreme forms, and then attempt the combination of both. It is virtually assumed that prior to instruction the child knows well enough what he should and should not do; that his acts have a conscious moral quality from the first; it is also assumed, to a large extent, that only by appeal to external punishments and rewards can the child be got to see any reason for doing the right and avoiding the wrong. Now these two propositions are so related that they can not possibly both be true, while both may be false—and *are* both false unless all contemporaneous tendencies in ethics are in a wrong direction.[6]

The gap between theory and practice comes out also in the great reliance placed upon religious motives in the moral life. It is not necessary to enter into controversial questions here. The fact is enough that contemporary moralists, almost without exception and including all schools, hold that the reasons and duties of the moral life either lie within itself, or at least may be stated by themselves without direct reference to supernatural considerations. In running over

---

[6]   There is one basis upon which both views may be logically held—total depravity. It may then be assumed that the child knows the right in advance, but can be got to *do* it only through punishment.

the names of moral theorists of the present day, of all schools, I can think of but two exceptions to this statement. Sidgwick holds that it *may* be impossible to get a *final* statement of morals without postulating a supreme moral Being and Ruler, while Martineau holds that obligation is derived from such a Being. But even Martineau holds that the *facts* of obligation may be found directly in human nature; that it is only when we demand a philosophical explanation of its *nature* that we bring in the reference to God. Either, then, theory is working in a very unpractical direction, or else much of practice is going on in very anti-scientific fashion. A readjustment is demanded.

This brings me to my final point. An influential movement of the present times (I refer to the ethical culture movement) holds, as I understand it, that it is possible to separate the whole matter of the moral education of children and adults from theoretical considerations. With their contention that education can be (must be, I should say) separated from dogmatic theories I am heartily at one; but as, after all, a dogmatic theory is a contradiction in terms, the question is, whether such an emancipation can be effected without a positive theory of the moral life. It is a critical and practical question with every teacher and parent: What reasons shall I present to my child for doing this right act? What motives in him shall I appeal to in order that he may realize for himself that it is right? What interests in him shall I endeavor to evoke in order to create an habitual disposition in this right direction? I fail utterly to see how these questions can be even approximately answered without some sort of a working theory. To give a reason to a child, to suggest to him a motive—I care not what—for doing the right thing, is to have and use a moral theory. To point out its consequences to himself in the ways of pains and pleasures; to point out its reaction into his own habits and character; to show him how it affects the welfare of others; to point out what strained and abnormal relations it sets up between him and others, and the reaction of these relations upon his own happiness and future actions—to point to any of these things with a view to instilling moral judgment and disposition is to appeal to a theory of the moral life. To suppose that the appeal to do a thing simply because it is right does *not* involve such a theory; to suppose that the practical value of this appeal must not itself be submitted to investigation and statement—to theory—strikes me as decidedly naïve.

Here as elsewhere our greatest need is to make our theories submit to the test of practice, to experimental verification, and, at the same time, make our practice scientific —make it the embodiment of the most reasonable ideas we can reach. The ultimate test of the efficacy of any movement or method is the equal and continuous hold which it keeps upon both sides of this truth.

Fred Newton Scott

As the various periphrastic modes of saying that the subject's biography could be better written if the subject himself were only dead have been about exhausted by previous writers of sketches, I will simply begin at the beginning. Fred Newton Scott was born at Terre Haute, Indiana, in 1860. He was fortunate enough to combine, in his early years, town and country life. His father was a lawyer in the city who, by reason of somewhat poor health, bought a farm near town. Mr. Scott's tendency as a teacher to keep literature and æsthetics in connection with the concrete may have been favored somewhat by the concreteness of his early surroundings. At any rate, he has never forgotten in later life the lesson taught in early years—that real life is made of things like ploughs, and mud turtles and fields of growing grain. He has never allowed himself to be so caught in the machinery of science as to forget that the grist ground for life is, after all, the main thing.

Mr. Scott got his education in the public schools of Terre Haute. His early tastes were in the direction of physical inquiry. A closet in the Terre Haute Normal School is even now full of electrical apparatus, originating from Mr. Scott's fertile brain and ingenious hand. His *chef d'œuvre* was perhaps an electric battery of forty Leyden jars, which would—and did—kill a cat. Mr. Scott also became an expert telegrapher, and could now earn his living by receiving associate press dispatches, if need were.

But Mr. Scott was switched off from the opening career of electrical engineer by a German tutor, a Mr. Boyesen, afterwards an instructor in Boston University. He it is who

[*First published in the* Oracle (*University of Michigan*), *1894. 4 pp. Not previously reprinted.*]

persuaded the youth that salvation was found along the line
of Greek, who awakened in him a desire for a University
education, and who tutored him in his preparation. The
young man was ready for college at eighteen, but not finding
himself in robust health decided to wait a year or two. He
was already master of shorthand, having done more or less
newspaper work, and so he became private secretary of
Dr. Kellogg, of the Battle Creek Sanitarium. For two years
he traveled with this gentleman, going at one time to the
Pacific Coast, and residing in Washington, D.C., for a
while. He returned to Battle Creek in the spring of '80 to
graduate at the High School, and bring his diploma to the
University of Michigan in the fall. Here he graduated in '84,
having made his record as a clever writer as well as a thorough student. He was managing editor of the *Oracle*, a
reminiscence of which he has embodied in recent years in
this journal. He was also one of the founders of the *Argo-
naut*, and, as its exchange editor, created what may be
termed a sensation in that usually perfunctory department,
by the brightness and humor of his touch. In the second se-
mester of his Junior Year he also did newspaper work in
Detroit. Mr. Scott has always retained a friendly interest in
newspaperdom, as successive editors of college journals and
annuals will gratefully testify.

The experience thus gained during his college years
was extended during the years '85–'87, which were spent on
a Cleveland newspaper. When appointed in the autumn of
'89 to an instructorship in English in the University this
experience was at once utilized in the more efficient and
practical organization of the essay work in the traditional
grind of "Freshman English." Students were surprised to
find the work not only useful, but actually interesting. And,
indeed, one of the characteristic features of Mr. Scott's work
in theoretical as well as practical rhetoric, has been his sense
—a sense which he has imparted to his classes—that writing
is not a pyrotechnic exhibition of fine phrases, or an orna-
mental addition to the bare truth of things, but the direct,
natural reporting of what one has one's self seen and
thought. On the side of the theory of style and literature this
original germ of practice is now evolving into a comprehen-

sive theory of the social character of literary expression which 'livens up the dry bones of formal theories. A theory which sees in the style and matter of literature phases of the movement of intelligence toward complete social expression is significant as theory and inspiring and effective on the practical side.

In 1890 Dr. Scott was made assistant professor of rhetoric. He had other qualifications for the position beside personal skill and taste in verse and prose, and practical contacts in life. During his undergraduate years he had been a diligent student along the line of languages and literatures taught in the University. The years spent in the University Library and in working for his doctor's degree ('84, '85 and '87–'89), were bent largely in the same direction; so that to-day Mr. Scott is equipped with a working control of Sanskrit, Greek, Italian, Spanish, Danish and Russian, as well as a pretty complete outfit in the general theory and method of philology. Meantime, he had become interested in psychology and philosophy, considered as helps to literary interpretation, and has a knowledge of these subjects which professed teachers of these branches would not sneeze at— knowledge turned to good account in his lecture and seminary courses in Æsthetics, and in his discussions of the "Principles of Style." The reader may judge for himself as to Dr. Scott's industry. The success of his work is recorded chiefly where it should be, in the lives and thoughts of students quickened and deepened through contact with the good sense, the ease, the learning and practical bent of Mr. Scott. He has been assiduous and successful in contributions to the general world of letters. Aside from frequent occasional productions in prose and verse to current journals, Dr. Scott is the author of the following: *Paragraph-Writing*, a help to correct writing (in connection with Mr. J. V. Denney), *A Guide to the Literature of Æsthetics* (a bibliography in connection with Professor Gayley), and Monographs on *Æsthetics: Its Problems and Literature*, and *Principles of Style*, models of suggestion and direction in their respective lines. Mention should also be made of an article published in *Modern Language Notes*, showing the indebtedness of Sidney in his theory of poetry to Boccaccio,

part of Mr. Scott's broader doctorate thesis on the relations
of early English criticism to Italian criticism. Certainly not
least in students' eyes of Dr. Scott's literary work, is the part
he played in the composition of the *Yellow and Blue*, a po-
tent factor in the recent development of college spirit, as
well as among the cleverest volumes of college verse yet issued from any American University.

Mr. Scott is still young enough to have his best work
before him. I do not know just what direction it will take,
but I am not afraid to prophesy that it will be marked by
command of the resources available, by poise and facility of
mind, by adaptation to the real currents of modern life, and,
not least, by a style delicate enough to reflect the tints and
shades, and broad enough to depict the leading features, of
his subject-matter.

Intuitionalism

INTUITIONALISM [from Lat. *intu'itus*, partic. of *intue'ri*, look on]: the theory, in its broader sense, that fundamental principles of being are known directly without the intervention of either sense-experience or discursive logical processes; in its narrower sense, the theory that moral distinctions are known in this direct fashion. The common use of the word in philosophical discussion seems to date mainly from Price, but the idea is at least as old as the philosophy of Aristotle. Complication arises in defining the word from the fact that most modern intuitionalists have modified the theory, and use the term to denote the existence of *a priori* principles native to the structure of the mind and regulative of its operations, but not necessarily brought before consciousness save through experience and reflection. In this sense "intuitionalism" is often used to designate any theory which holds that there are universal and necessary principles either of knowledge or of being, the mode in which these principles come to consciousness being held *sub judice*.

Theory in the Greek Period.—A history of the development of the conception will show the transformations through which the idea has gone in the history of thought. As the development of the ethical concept of intuitionalism has, upon the whole, determined the metaphysical concept, attention will be paid mainly to the former. The concept takes its birth from the discussions carried on by the Sophists as to whether law is by nature or by institution and convention. If the former, then there must be some power of mind which shall deal with moral distinctions. The efforts of

[*First published in* Johnson's Universal Cyclopædia, *ed. Charles Kendall Adams* (*New York: A. J. Johnson Co., 1894*), IV, 657–59. *Reprinted only in* Johnson's Universal Cyclopædia, *1895, 1896, 1897, 1899, 1900.*]

Socrates, Plato, and Aristotle to solve the problem in the direction of the independence of law from arbitrary institution did not, however, at once give birth to a full-fledged intuitionalism. Emphasis was indeed put upon reason as the power which alone could insure the intrinsic validity of the moral life, but reason was not conceived as a faculty of immediate instruction. On the contrary, with Socrates, in whom the emphasis upon knowledge is at its height, the attaining of rational moral ideas is regarded as the most difficult of problems, the end of philosophy, and their adequate attainment conceived as the solution of the whole moral problem, since the man who knows the good will certainly follow it. Plato retains the conception of the good as the object of all philosophic endeavor, and brings it into relation with the philosophy of nature, thus extending its range and making its adequate discovery still more difficult; at the same time he adds the idea that its discovery by the philosophers can be made available to the mass of men only by a complete social reconstruction—so far is he from the idea of fundamental moral distinctions known directly by the reason of every man. Aristotle, while attaching much less importance to a theoretical knowledge of the good as such, still holds that with practical knowledge of it all other virtues are given; hence it is to be regarded as the *terminus ad quem* of the moral life, and not with the intuitionalist as the *terminus ab quo*. In his logical theory, however, Aristotle insisted upon the need of certain fundamental and indemonstrable principles, called, generally, common axioms, as the basis of all demonstration. Since Aristotle himself conceived moral distinctions to be known through the judgment of the man who has already made ethical attainments, it never occurred to him to apply this theory of axioms known *per se* to morals. With the disintegration of the moral codes of local communities the need of a scientific basis for morality was more and more keenly felt, and thus there was a constant tendency to assimilate the methods of ethics to the principles laid down by Aristotle for the purely theoretical sciences. In this sense he may be regarded as the founder of intuitionalism.

Roman Development—The later development of the theory took two directions. The Neo-Platonic movement carried to its extreme the postulate underlying all Greek theories of knowing—that like is known by like—and gave rise to the mystical theory of intuitionalism, holding full knowledge to involve a complete absorption of both subject and object into one underived and undifferentiated state of being. This idea leaves its impress upon the whole mystical side of the Catholic faith in the idea of the "beatific vision." The counterpart of mysticism was scholasticism, and the scholastic theory of direct knowledge is derived (aside from dependence upon Aristotle already referred to) from a fusion of Stoic theories with the philosophy of Roman jurisprudence. In the pantheism of the Stoics the two ideas of nature and law were identified, and both meant the one vital, all-comprehensive, and orderly force expressing itself in both the world without and the mind within. The required transformation of this idea was made by Cicero, who is the real, as Aristotle is the putative, father of intuitionalism. The practical development of the Roman people had made necessary an ethical conception of law which should effect two things: First, allow a qualitative reconstruction of earlier codes and practices to meet present needs; and, secondly, permit a quantitative extension of it to the tribes and peoples now brought under Roman jurisdiction. Cicero found the needed instrument in the Law of Nature. This law is objective—that is, existent in the very structure of the universe; it is precedent of, and the norm for, any civil institution whatever; it is universal, binding upon gods and men; it is unqualified in its authority, and is eternal and unchangeable. As the Stoics had already conceived of reason in man as an offshoot of the reason or logos present in nature, the way was prepared for Cicero (without accepting the whole Stoic metaphysic) to give a popular account of the subjective faculty needed in order to make the law of nature available for the practical purposes of life. The law, at least in germ, is *innate* in the human mind, and its main features are known directly to the conscience of man. *Ratio naturalis* comes to mean both the objective structure of law and the mental power by which it is immediately descried. The following description taken from Cicero's oration, *Pro Mil.*, 4, 10, shows the main points: "Non scripta, sed nata lex, quam non

didicimus, accepimus, legimus, verum ex natura ipsa arri-
puimus, hausimus, expressimus; ad quam non docti, sed
facti, non instituti sed imbuti sumus."

Influence of Practical Jurisprudence—That the later
development of this idea was under the influence of practical
jurisprudence rather than of reflective philosophy, and that
it was full of inconsistencies, only the better prepared it for
its large historic *rôle*. One of these inconsistencies was in the
wider and in the narrower sense given to the term natural
law. In the wider sense it was coextensive with instinct, comprehending all activity not the result of acquired experience;
in the narrower it was the moral law made known through
reason. Another confusion was from the association of natural law with *jus gentium* on one side and with *æquitas* on the
other. So far as the law of reason was identified with the law
common to all peoples under Roman jurisdiction, the scope
of intuition was confined to the fundamental principles of all
social morality—to the relations belonging to *societas hu-
mana* as such. The tendency to identify the law of reason
(or nature) with equity tended to bring about a differentiation of conscience as subjective authority from all social relations and authority whatever, the former being supreme over
the latter.

The Mediæval Contribution—The result of this confusion is most completely found in the moral philosophy of the
Catholic Church in the scholastic period. On one hand the
power of moral intuition was located completely in the individual, wholly independent of any society (the sense of
æquitas); while on the other, the strictly jural connotations
appropriate to the idea of the law of human society (*jus
gentium*) were carried over into the entire structure of moral
ideas. The result was the conception of moral law as command given by God to his human subjects after the analogy
of laws imposed by a political king on his subjects. These
laws were made known through three organs: conscience,
the divine command speaking directly to the individual and
aiming at natural virtue; civil law, commands expressed
with reference to determinate outward acts, and aiming at
the coercion of evil characters; and revealed law, or the will
of God as made known through the channels of the Church
and aiming at man's eternal and supernatural happiness.

With the fall of scholasticism, the channel for the direct knowledge of the moral law became the instrument through which moral science recovered its independence of theology. The argument ran: Since the moral law is rational, God himself follows reason in imposing it. Hence this law may be considered, on the ground of reason, free from any theological consideration whatever. It would still be true and binding even if there were no God. As at an earlier period the intuitional theory was a means by which moral science was freed from the limits of the customs current in particular places, at this period it was one of the main influences permitting an independent growth of moral science.

Moral Reason versus Civil Law — With Hobbes (1588–1679) the controversy shifted, and intuitionalism had henceforth to contend with new foes. Two factors in Hobbes's theory control all later discussion. Hobbes held that fixed moral obligations were wholly the creation of the sovereign political power; he also held that men are naturally selfish, and aim at the maximum of happiness each for himself. The first of these views elicited the primary reaction. Against the idea that moral distinctions are the creatures of the civil authority, a number of voices protested; the most convenient weapon of attack was the assertion that they are inherent in "nature" or "reason," and are made known directly. Differing among themselves in many particulars, Cudworth (1617–88), in his *Eternal and Immutable Morality*, Henry More (1614–87), in his *Enchiridion Ethicum*, and Clarke (1675–1729), in his *Demonstration of the Being and Attributes of God* (Vol. II), all agree in holding that moral distinctions are not arbitrarily decreed by positive authority, but have objective existence and are known through an intellectual power appropriate to them. All would now be termed "intellectual intuitionalists," holding that distinctions are made known through reason rather than through a sense or mode of feeling, but differ as to the character of this rational power, Cudworth and More holding to the immanence in the individual of the divine reason, Clarke assimilating the process of moral knowledge to that of geometry.

Influence of Psychological Analysis — Meantime Hobbes's assertion of the purely egoistic character of man's impulses had necessitated a more careful psychological investigation of action. As this became the center of interest, the antithesis between moral distinctions as based respectively upon positive law and upon reason, fell into the background. Hobbes's opponents, in upholding the existence of primary social impulses in man's makeup, tended to resolve man into a system of impulses, some of which aim at self-interest, others at the good either of humanity or of particular individuals. While the three chief representatives of this tendency—Shaftesbury (1671–1713), Butler (1692–1752), and Hutcheson (1694–1746)—all agree that these two classes of impulses tend to coincide, there is still felt the need of some power which shall decide between them in cases of conflict and maintain their due proportion when they agree. All three (in spite of many differences in method and mode of statement) find this in a power called either "moral sense" (Shaftesbury and Hutcheson), or "conscience" (Butler). Intuition now means not the rational knowledge of objective moral law, but the immediate consciousness of the value of our respective impulses expressed in approbation and disapprobation. This tendency to identify moral intuition with a direct feeling of worth is at its height in Hutcheson, who expressly makes moral sense a feeling of the relations of harmony or the reverse among sensations and impulses, and thus tends to identify it with a feeling of beauty or ugliness. This emphasis upon feeling called out an emphatic protest within the intuitional school from Price (1723–91), *Principal Questions and Difficulties of Morals*, who makes right and wrong distinct qualities, incapable of definition or analysis, and holds that moral knowledge is simply a special case of the immediate discernment of truth by the understanding.

Influence of Utilitarian Theory—It is an example of the irony of history that the next foe which intuitionalism had to meet was a product of its own arguments against Hobbes as to the existence in man of disinterested impulses for the welfare of others. The rising UTILITARIANISM (*q.v.*) carried the argument a step further, asserting that if man's nature may be resolved into a system of impulses aiming at personal and social happiness, the tendency of an act to produce such happiness is a sufficient test of its morality, and there is no need of any intuitive faculty. This tendency was

intensified by the baldness with which Price held that rightness and wrongness are unanalyzable qualities of acts themselves. This seemed, on one side, to reduce moral science to
sheer dogmatism, and, on the other, it came in conflict with
the regnant psychological theory which was analyzing all
ideas into complexes of sense-qualities and associated experiences. Intuitionalism thus assumed the form which it
still retains to-day—the assertion that moral distinctions flow
from, and are reached by an inspection of, acts themselves
and not from a consideration of results.

Influence of Kant—Kant (1724–1804) added another
signification to the kaleidoscope of meanings now attaching
to the word. He shifted the center of interest, both in metaphysics and ethics, from the question of the psychological
origin of knowledge to the question of its *validity* when attained. In coming to the conclusion that its validity could be
maintained only in case it is not the result of experience, he
substituted the idea of an *a priori* determination of experience for the concept of an immediate knowledge of truth,
and thus gave a new argument for intuitionalism (in a
widened sense of the term) and a new confusion to its definition. The confusion was intensified from the fact that the
Scotch school, reacting like Kant from the empiricism of
Hume, asserted the *a priori* partly in its old psychological
sense, and partly as the practical doctrine of "common-
sense." The only essentially new factor the nineteenth century has added to the discussion is the contention of Spencer
that by the doctrine of biological evolution and heredity he
is enabled to reconcile empiricism and intuitionalism, fundamental moral distinctions being now intuitive for the individual, but the product of experience for the whole race.

Present Position and Criticism—It should now be obvious that intuitionalism has no fixed meaning, but has gone
through a series of changes during its history, according to
the center of ethical interest at the time, and the foes with
which it has had to contend. At present its meaning in popular discussion (and to a considerable extent even in its philosophic representatives) is a fusion of all its various historic
meanings. The sense which is uppermost is undoubtedly
that which it derives from its opposition to utilitarianism—

the idea that knowledge of moral distinctions is derived
from an inspection of the moral act itself, and not from a
calculus of results. But reminiscences of Kant's metaphysical *a priorism*, of Butler's conscience, of the Roman natural law, and of the Platonic and Aristotelian *Nous* are in-
extricably interwoven. Just what form the doctrine would
take if purified from this historic fusion it is impossible to
say. It is altogether probable, however, that intuitionalism,
as a system, derives much of its force from its confusion, on
one side, of intuition with the theory of the objective and
determining character of moral law, and, on the other side,
with the psychological doctrine of unreflective knowledge
or immediate tact. It is probable that the mass of men decide most cases of action without a process of conscious reflection upon past experience, or calculation of probable
consequences; but this is a psychological, not a metaphysical or moral fact; it affords no presumption as to the validity
of the conclusion reached, since this process depends, in
the main, not upon abstract reason, but upon the habits or
established disposition of the agent. On the other hand, it is
quite possible that moral distinctions may have objective
validity and yet not be made known by intuition. The law
of gravitation is none the less true of bodies possessing mass
because it has been arrived at by a laborious process of
inquiry, and the same may hold of moral truths.

    A history of intuitionalism is a desideratum. Refer-
ences to the subject will be found in all the standard histories of ethics. (See MORAL PHILOSOPHY [*Early Works*,
IV, 132–51] and the works mentioned in the body of this
article.) For natural law and its relation to intuitionalism see
Voigt, *Die Lehre vom jus naturale der Römer* (Leipzig,
1856); Hildenbrand, *Geschichte und System der Rechts- und
Staatsphilosophie* (Leipzig, 1860), Part Two; Sir Henry
Maine, *Ancient Law* (New York, 1864), Chs. 3 and 4; Stahl,
Geschichte der Rechtsphilosophie (Tübingen, 1878). For
the influence of Cicero upon the official ethics of the Roman
Catholic Church see Ewald, *Der Einfluss der Stoisch-
Ciceronianischen Moral auf die Darstellung der Ethik bei
Ambrosius* (Leipzig, 1881). The modern representatives of
the intuitional school are found mainly among the members

of the Scottish school. Prominent names here are McCosh, *The Intuitions of the Human Mind* (New York, 1866), and Calderwood, *Handbook of Moral Philosophy* (14th ed., London, 1888). Most of the text-books current in U.S. colleges during the past generation are written from this standpoint. Among these it may not be invidious to single out as representing a modified intuitionalism Porter, *Elements of Moral Science* (New York, 1885). The chief philosophical upholders of intuitionalism at present are Sidgwick, *Methods of Ethics* (3d ed., London, 1884), and Martineau, *Types of Ethical Theory* (Oxford, 1885). Green, *Prolegomena to Ethics* (Oxford, 1883), is often classed among the intuitionalists, but this involves an extension of the term to include *a priorism* of the Kantian type.

Moral Philosophy

MORAL PHILOSOPHY [*moral* is from Lat. *mora'lis*, relating to morals or manners, deriv. of *mos*, *mo'ris*, manner, custom, conduct, way of life]: the theory of the *value* of human conduct. Moral philosophy, or ethics, is a branch of the philosophic as distinct from the physical sciences. The latter investigate facts and relations in their objective character. They fulfill their end, therefore, when the facts are adequately described and their relations stated. The philosophical sciences—namely, æsthetics, logic, and ethics —deal with the investigation of value. They reach their end, not in a description of a given experience, but in an estimate of its worth as a part of the whole system of experience. The philosophical sciences are sometimes termed normative, in that they all recognize a norm or standard, as duty, truth, and the good. This, however, is a derivative mark, not the primary differentia. The norm is simply the basis employed in estimating value.

The Origin of Ethical Theory—In primitive societies morality is identified with the customs of the community; and these customs, receiving religious sanction, are thus binding religiously as well as morally. This fact tends to retard the growth of any theory of conduct. Custom when consecrated by religion is the essence of conservatism. Free inquiry would imply both lack of loyalty to the community and disrespect to the gods. The chief offset to this extreme conservatism is found in the existence of the councils of the community, in which certain questions are discussed and decided on their own merits; but among every folk, except

[*First published in* Johnson's Universal Cyclopædia, *ed.* Charles Kendall Adams (*New York: A. J. Johnson Co.*, 1894), v, 880–85. *Reprinted only in* Johnson's Universal Cyclopædia, *1895, 1896, 1897, 1899, 1900.*]

the Greek, this germ of free inquiry was checked by the assumption that the decision simply declared existing custom, or else (when the council was a priesthood) made known the immediate will of the gods. In Greece, the discussion of the means and ends relating to the welfare of the community took at an early period a wide range, and was freed from any slavish subserviency to the fixed habits of the past or to the divine will. A divine sanction was supposed to attach to the *themistes* (or judicial decisions), but this was rather in virtue of the wisdom displayed in them than because they were regarded as authoritative expressions of will. We find the early proverbs and maxims—the so-called gnomic morality—different from those of other peoples in putting importance upon certain habits of mind and states of character rather than upon the performance of certain outward acts. Such maxims as "Know thyself" and "In nothing excess" already contain in themselves the principle of a free as distinct from a customary morality. The development of democracy, with its popular judicial tribunals and its assemblies for the general discussion of political matters, was a further influence in promoting the growth of moral reflection. A premium was put on power to persuade and to move the citizens of a community in all matters of public policy. At the same time the Greek, with his strong community feeling, always referred the measures under discussion to the welfare of the state as a decisive criterion. Along with this development of a reflective standard and method of judgment went a continual increase in the exchange of culture between Greece proper and the Greek colonies in Asia Minor and Italy. The effect of this was to abstract the consideration of moral questions from their identification with local customs. If we add the vast expansion in art and science found in Athens, consequent upon the Persian wars, we have all the material for a growth of conscious ethical theory. The immediate stimulus to this came from the Greek dramatists on one side and from the teachings of the Sophists on the other. Amid the decay of older religious beliefs and customs, attending the expansion of life, the dramatists tried to uphold a morality based upon a purification of the older mythology. This tendency culminated in the assertion that the fundamental ethical relations are absolute, eternal, and controlling in all the affairs of life; meantime the Sophists were moving in quite a different direction.

The Influence of the Sophists—In connection with the rise of democracy and the increase of intellectual intercourse, already mentioned, there grew up a well-defined class of persons who made it their business to instruct ambitious citizens in the community in whatever was best calculated to make the latter capable of securing political influence. Protagoras, for example, affirmed that he was able to give his pupils skill in both private and public affairs; that his pupils learned to order their own houses in the best manner, and became able to speak and act for the best in affairs of the state (Plato, *Protagoras*, 319). The Sophists, in other words, professed to abstract questions of social welfare from the traditions and habits of any particular community, and to discuss them with reference to the welfare of the state at large. This generalization of the idea of the state and its welfare or good formed the basis at once of the art of politics and of the science of ethics. More than this, many of the Sophists made use of concepts derived from the philosophic theories of the time to attack all traditional morality and, at least indirectly, morality itself. There was, for example, a general agreement among them that, so far as the subjects or citizens of the community are concerned, moral rules are simply the expressed will of the stronger; that duty is simply the necessity of submitting to superior force; while, on the part of the rulers, or stronger, moral rules are simply expedients for securing personal advantage.

Influence of Socrates—The work of Socrates may be described as an effort to use the positive side of the Sophistic teaching against the negative side, and in the interest of an intrinsic morality like that taught by the dramatists, but freed from its religious dependence. The question raised by the Sophists was whether morality exists by nature (φύσει) or by institution—that is, by sheer enactment (θέσει). Socrates endeavored to show that it exists by the very nature of man and the state; that there is a single and supreme good or end for the individual and the community, reference to this end fixing the value of all particular acts and habits. The basis of morality is therefore knowledge of this good. Except in so far as the agent knows the good and acts with reference to it, his conduct is purely haphazard. Socrates is therefore in agreement with the Sophists in attacking all morality that is merely customary. So far as morality is merely traditional, it may be regarded as based upon either arbitrary authority or considerations of private expediency. All such conduct therefore is more than non-moral; it is immoral. Socrates, at the same time that he founds reflective theory, is the creator of a new type of morality. He introduces, as the precondition of all other virtues, the virtue of insight into the good and the doing of acts because of their value with reference to this good. He differs from the Sophists, not in the emphasis put on the discussion of moral questions—in that respect he is himself a Sophist—but in his insistence upon the necessity of a standard and method for the discussion—a standard and method to be derived from an examination of the essential end and laws of conduct itself. Hence his generalization of the Delphic Γνωθισεαυτόν as the fundamental principle of morals.

The Limits of the Socratic Ethics—In contrast with both the customary and the Sophistic moral teaching, Socrates points to the practice of the artists and artisans. The latter know the ends at which they aim; they proceed from a definite model or pattern, and follow a method every step of which has definite reference to the end to be reached; moreover, in the use of their method, they observe continually rules of measure and proportion. In decided contrast with this is the practice, not only of the ordinary citizen, but of the politician, the poet who sets up as a moral teacher, and the Sophist as a professed teacher of virtue. No one of these has a fixed or universal aim, pattern, or rule of measurement. Socrates himself does not claim to have himself any knowledge of what this supreme controlling good is; he represents simply a demand that men do not claim to be moral, much less teachers of morals, until they can base their conduct upon assured insight into the good. His own attitude toward knowledge of the good is thus finally de-

cidedly ironical. Meantime Socrates urged, not only by
precept, but still more by his own practice, loyalty to the
spirit of the community of which one is a member. The
relation between loyalty to the community and insight into
the good is nowhere developed by Socrates. We may assume
that he *felt* the identity of the good as known by scientific
insight, and the good as expressed in the laws of the community, but he nowhere affords any justification for the
identification. These limitations fix the problem for his
successors.

Influence of Plato—Speaking roughly, we may say that
Plato, following the fundamental Socratic principle of the
identity of knowledge and virtue, had to accomplish two
things—to work out more positively the content of the good,
and to establish more in detail its connection with social
organization. The first of these tasks he attempted to perform by bringing the problem of the nature of the good into
closer connection with the problem of the objective structure
of the universe. He united, that is to say, the ethical
analysis of the end of man with the philosophical analysis
of the nature of reality. Nature itself was interpreted teleologically; the good or end is the supreme law and unity of
both being and knowing. The second problem he met by
admitting that most men can never of themselves attain to
insight into the good or to true moral action. It is necessary, therefore, to reconstruct the whole social fabric so that
the knowledge of the good obtained by the philosophers or
the wise shall be mediated to the rest of the community
through the very structure of the social organization. His
scheme of virtues and his idea of social organization stand,
therefore, in direct relation to each other. The supreme or
controlling class in a state must, by the moral necessity of
the case, be those who comprehend the supreme good, and
who can estimate the value of particular acts by reference
to the supreme good as a standard. This class follows the
good simply because they appreciate it; their virtue is wisdom. Of them it is true that knowledge and virtue are
identical. The next class in the state is composed of those
who, without ability in themselves to comprehend the good,
can appreciate it sufficiently when made known by the

ruling class to defend and maintain it at all hazards. Their virtue is courage, or knowledge of the good at one remove. The lowest class in the state is composed of those who neither know nor can *positively* assert, under the direction of others, the good, but who can, when restrained, devote their energies to supplying the material making possible its realization by others. This is the industrial class, whose virtue is control or temperance; that is, knowledge at two removes. Justice is the whole made one by wisdom. Plato further began the psychological analysis of conduct by transferring the constitution of the state over into the structure of the individual soul. The appetites and desires, on their more passive side, correspond to the industrial class, the impulses and active desires to the loyal citizen class; reason to the ruling class, and the balance of the powers to the just state.

Influence of Aristotle—Aristotle tended to separate ethics from its close connection both with metaphysics and with political organization. Plato himself had been obliged to admit that his idea of the universal and absolute good was but a bare outline; that it represented an ideal to be filled up rather than an accomplished fact. Aristotle added that in any case the ethical problem must relate to a good practically realizable by man, and not to some transcendent good. In place, therefore, of a metaphysical analysis of the good, Aristotle substitutes a description of the moral excellence found in the best type of the citizen gentleman, a type which Athens, with its centuries of disciplinary and refining influences, had reared up. His account of goodness and of the chief virtues describes the ideals and habits of the typical Athenian gentleman; his principle of the golden mean is the generalization of the artistic principle upon which the Athenian character, in its best estate, had formed itself. Aristotle thus put at the disposal of all later peoples the net product of Greek life on its strictly moral side. As regards the method of attaining virtuous character, Aristotle substituted for the Platonic ideal of direction through social organization (now no longer possible, even as a dream, because of the loss of Athenian independence) the ideal of habits formed through careful discipline and training.

Personal education tends to become the instrument for doing what previously social life as a whole had done. This emphasis upon the personal training of the individual made necessary more attention to the nature of the individual agent. Aristotle's ethics are thus as decidedly psychological as Plato's are political. It must not be thought, however, that Aristotle completely severs ethics from politics. Education is still conceived as carried on by the state; the community is thus the chief ethical instrument, indirectly if not directly. Moreover, since the individual is by nature social, he can realize his full good only in relation to others; his good includes a life in a community. In this way the state is also one form of the ethical end, but Aristotle distinctly separates the practical and social virtues from the contemplative virtues, making the latter higher in type, and thus prepares the way for the later isolation of the individual, and the divorce of ethics from politics.

Further Greek Development—The so-called one-sided Socratic schools, namely, the Cynic and the Cyrenaic, had already entered upon the individualistic development. With the growth of the Macedonian and Roman supremacies, the welfare and customs of the local community came to mean less and less to the individual. He was thrown back upon himself for moral strength and consolation. It is customary to put the two later schools, the Stoic and Epicurean, corresponding to the two one-sided schools already spoken of, in marked opposition to each other, and even to regard the Stoic school as the embodiment of all that was manly and truly virtuous in the life of the times, while the Epicurean is regarded as given over to lax and selfish pleasure-seeking; but considered in relation to the place which they occupy in the development of ethical problems and methods, the agreement between these two schools is much more important than the differences. Both are concerned with the question of how the individual, in an environment which is becoming more and more indifferent to him, can realize satisfaction; both answer in terms of a personal detachment from all outward concern, and of an attainment of internal self-sufficiency; both make wisdom the chief means in reaching this end: both, in a word, deal with the problem of the true satisfaction of desire in a world where good is no longer mediated through social organization, but has to be attained through the individual himself. Both schools therefore continue the psychological analysis, working out, indeed, the whole problem of will in its relation to desire, reason, and pleasure. In both schools there is an equilibrium reached through a remarkable compromise between self-satisfaction and self-sacrifice. While the Stoic school represents, upon the whole, asceticism, it has strongly hedonistic factors in it. The wise man was freed from everything merely customary, and this gave rise, in extreme cases at least, to a shameless disregard of the ordinary conventions of life in the satisfaction of passions. Moreover, the very contempt which the Stoic displayed for pleasure was in itself largely hedonistic; he felt that the pleasures which he despised were of little account compared with the pleasure of knowing that he was independent of them. On the other hand, there is a marked ascetic factor in Epicurus. He emphasizes the necessity, in order to secure stable pleasures, of moderating and even surrendering the urgency of desire. On the social side, the Stoics introduced an abstract cosmopolitanism by the side of their self-sufficient individualism. They conceived of the whole universe—"nature," in their phrase—as a vast city of which gods and men are the citizens, and for which the immanent reason, the Logos, gives laws. They thus generalize the ethical analysis which Plato and Aristotle had made with reference to the Athenian community. To live according to nature was to assume the same kind of relation to the whole world that Plato had required of the citizen with reference to his own community. The Epicurean school was even more definitely hostile in its moral aims to actual political life than the Stoic; but it set up the ideal of a brotherhood of like-minded men whose bond was not formal law, but personal friendship and voluntary sympathies.

Influence of Christianity—The introduction of Christianity tended rather to deepen the existing antithesis than wholly to shift the center of interest. Within Christianity itself there were two contending strains. One, in its emphasis upon individual salvation and the freedom of the will, tended to reduce to the lowest terms possible the social side of conduct. It regarded social life, from the family to the state, as having primary relation to man's appetites, in themselves evil; social institutions therefore were either to be got rid of or, since that was impossible for most men, to be endured as necessary evils. On the other hand, the conception of love as the supreme law of life, and of a kingdom of heaven as a supreme social institution having complete community of interests—harmony of man with man—made the social aspect of conduct more prominent than it ever had been before. In the early centuries these two factors exist side by side with almost no consciousness of their contradiction. The chief immediate result in ethical theory was to center all moral questions in the will, and to conceive of will as power of personal choice rather than as expression of either desire or wisdom. God's will was the source and sanction of all moral law; man's will the free source of either goodness or badness; and the eternal destiny of man was fixed by the relation assumed between the divine will on one side and the human on the other.

Roman Influence—The Roman Empire formed at once the scene upon which all the contending ideas and tendencies met, and the framework which held them together and gave them objective consistency. The Latin influence furnished no new ethical analysis. It supplied neither a new idea of the supreme good, nor a further demand for personal righteousness. What it did afford was a vast and coherent system of practical means for realizing the ideal elsewhere developed. The system of private rights which civilization owes to Roman genius made the individualism of the Greek morals and Christian religion more than a speculation of the philosopher and an inner state of the saint; it gave this individualism objective body. In the same way the unified system of law and executive power necessary to the centralization of the Roman Empire afforded at once a symbol and an objective support for the otherwise vague aspirations toward a unified humanity current in Greek and Christian thought. The first five centuries of our era are an epoch of fusion and assimilation. The Greek ideas furnish the theoretical analysis of conduct;

Christianity insists upon the infinite meaning of life, and both are interpreted, on the practical or working side, by means of the legal and administrative concepts of Rome.

Mediæval Ethical Theory—The result of this fusion is the Catholic Church of the Middle Ages with its well-defined structure both as a political institution and the maintainer of a dogmatic system of truth. Ethical theory as free examination of conduct ceased; but none the less the Catholic Church gathered up into itself the net product of previous culture, and made it a tremendous influence in the practical discipline of men, both in their inner consciousness and in their community life. The official ethics was dominated by the legal ideas inherited from the Roman Empire. God was the absolute lawgiver and judge. Moral laws and the laws of physical nature were the expression of his will, almost his arbitrary commands. The moral life was a process of conforming to legal rules; moral discipline a scheme for paying, either directly or vicariously, the penalties incident to infraction of law. The idea of government was everywhere supreme. The complete subordination of science, art, and ordinary social life to the demands imposed by the transcendent God, resulted in making an organized dualism out of conduct. The supernatural is the all-important, but the present and actual is the natural, which therefore can not be ignored. Thus there are two organs of moral knowledge, wisdom, making known the natural law, and revelation, declaring the supernatural; two types of virtue, the natural and the theological; two instruments for realizing the law, the state, the secular expression of the divine will, the kingdom of nature, and the Church its sacred expression, the kingdom of grace.

The Beginnings of Modern Moral Philosophy—The Renaissance, here as elsewhere, marks a body of thought working free from constriction and subordination, and beginning to assert itself on its own account. After two or three centuries of conflict we find free theory finally able to maintain itself. Moral philosophy is severed from its theological subjection. From, say, 1625 to 1785 there are two main currents of ethical thought, the continental and the English, flowing on in relative independence of each other.

The continental is from the *De Jure Belli et Pacis* (1625) of
Grotius to the ethical writings of Kant; the English from
the *Leviathan* of Hobbes to the death of Adam Smith. The
continental school grew up under the traditions of Roman
law and administration. It was interested mainly in an
analysis of law; its source, sanction and content, jurally
considered. English thought grew in connection with the
struggle for political and industrial freedom. Hence it took
the individual agent as its focus of interest and discussed
moral questions as they bore upon the individual's life.

*Agreement and Difference of the English and the Con-
tinental Movements* — It is customary to contrast the English
and the continental phases of moral philosophy, regarding
the former as empirical and the latter as rationalistic; yet
their identity in principle was far more important than
their difference in method. The problem of both was fixed
by their attitude to the dogmatic character of mediæval
theory; both were seeking a free basis for morality; in
finding this, both start from the nature of the individual
in himself, carrying out the same tendency in ethics which
the Protestant Reformation introduced into religion and
Descartes into metaphysics. Both neglected the positive
and historical element — a neglect lasting until after the
French Revolution. Both had the same fundamental question to deal with, the relation of the individual to society.
The chief difference was that the English movement conceives of this relation as the adjustment of self-interest and
benevolence, while the continental deals with it as the relation between the inner morality of the individual and the outward order of the state; moreover, English thought deals
with the individual as a feeling and desiring being, while
continental thought derives its conclusions from his rational
nature.

The Continental Development — Grotius (1583–1645)
initiated ethical science on the Continent. With the break-up
of the feudal system and of the political authority of the
Catholic Church, together with the emergence of independent nationalities, it became necessary to find a new source
for authority and law. Grotius was particularly concerned
with the problem of the relations between the various Eu-

ropean states. Obviously there was no political sovereignty to impose law, and yet if there was no law anarchy was a sure result. Grotius fell back upon the idea of a law of nature antecedent to and controlling positive law. This natural law might be defined both as the law of reason and as a fundamental social law. It sprang from the rational impulse in the nature of man to seek for permanent union with his fellows, and to identify his good with theirs. The law of nature or right is to do whatever tends to execute this impulse. To Leibnitz (1646–1716) we owe the idea of a distinct philosophy of morals. Puffendorf (1632–94) had distinguished between a *forum internum* and a *forum externum*. The former was the region of religion in which all moral duties were included, the latter the region of jurisprudence. Leibnitz pointed out that moral duties must have a sphere of their own, separate from theology on one side and from jurisprudence on the other. Thomasius (1655–1728) tried to find a common principle underlying the sciences of morals and of civil law. The fundamental nature of man is toward rational happiness; the primary law of nature is therefore to seek both inner and outer peace. Morals deal with the former law; jurisprudence with the latter. The duties of the latter are expressed negatively: do not injure others. Its law is the law of justice; its defining mark the coercive character of such duties. The moral law is positive: do unto others as one would be done by; its law the law of benevolence, and its defining trait the impossibility of using coercive force. Thomasius thus afforded a philosophical basis for the growing tendency toward confessional religious freedom. Wolff (1679–1754) contributed no materially new elements, but carried out the idea of the rational character of morality on the formal side, working out the scheme of duties and virtues into a regular system on the basis of the principles of logic.

The English Development—Hobbes (1588–1679) did for English thought what Grotius did for continental. The characteristic of his moral philosophy is the peculiar union of a thoroughly egoistic psychology, with an assertion that the basis of all moral obligation is positive law issued by a sovereign. The individual left to himself aims always and

only at his own pleasure, so much so as to bring every individual into conflict with every other. The institution of
the state is necessary to set limits to this self-seeking; by
its enactments, which bring order out of anarchy, it sets up
the moral ideal and definite moral duties. This theory of
the positive origin of moral law called out the first reaction
—an assertion of the intrinsic character of ethical distinctions. (See INTUITIONALISM [*Early Works*, IV, 123–31].)
The intuitionalists asserted that one law directly made
known was that of benevolence, or the duty of considering
the common good as one's own, but neither More (1614–87),
Cumberland (1632–1718), nor Clarke (1675–1729) showed
how this principle of benevolence appealed to the individual.
Indeed, so far as they dealt with the question of how
benevolence could become a working motive for the
individual, they tended to fall back on external rewards and
punishment. In so far they not only left the psychological
egoism of Hobbes unrefuted, but also implicitly asserted it.
This deficiency Shaftesbury (1671–1713) attempted to make
good by a new analysis of the individual's make-up, with
a view to showing the active presence within him of disinterested impulses or social affections on the same level as
his self-seeking tendencies. Butler (1692–1752) went a
step further and denied that even the self-regarding impulses, so called, aim at pleasure, claiming that each is
directed to its own appropriate object. Self-love he held
to be a general principle arising from reflection, and subject therefore to reason, as determining in what it really
consists and how it may truly be obtained. Hutcheson (1694–
1746) applied the same idea to the analysis of the social
impulses, distinguishing between the natural and turbulent
impulses on one side, whether personal or social, and calm
self-love and calm benevolence on the other. He thus attempts to give the ultimate moral value to the balance of
the impulses as affected by reason, claiming that a reasonable
self-love and a reasonable benevolence coincide. He also laid
great stress on the disinterested character of the social
affections. Since no one of these writers assumed that the
moral good coincides absolutely with the benevolent impulses, the question of the object of approbation, or the good,

came to be a distinct problem. Hutcheson intensified this problem by recognizing the opposition between the disposition or character from which acts proceed and the nature of the acts themselves. He distinguished between the formally good, whose criterion is in the character, and the materially good, whose criterion is in the results of acts, holding that the test of the goodness of an act is its tendency to promote the greatest happiness of the greatest number. He thus prepared the way for the later utilitarianism. Hume (1711–76) attempts to unite Hutcheson's account of the object of approbation with a psychological account of approbation considered as a state of mind. According to him, approbation is the state of pleasurable consciousness, arising through sympathy, when we contemplate any traits or acts which are agreeable or useful to others. Hume thus carries to its extreme the emphasis upon feeling latent in the earlier writers; that which is approved and the act of approbation are both states of feeling. Reason comes in only as enlightening the feelings. Adam Smith (1723–90) carries out still further the idea of sympathy. Hume had not attempted to differentiate moral approbation from the sympathetic pleasure arising at the contemplation of any enjoyment whatever. Smith undertook to supply this lack by holding that our moral sympathy is not with the mere experiences of others, but with the active impulses from which the experiences arise. Moreover, he substituted for the more or less haphazard sympathies of Hume's moral agent the sympathies which would arise in a spectator who was both impartial and enlightened. Our own conscience or self-judgment is simply the reflex of such an imaginary spectator. Hartley (1705–57) completed this psychological analysis by the fuller use of the idea of association. He practically eliminated the "reason" of the older moral writers by accounting for all complex facts as associations of pleasure and pain with simple sensations and appetites.

Transition to the Moral Philosophy of the Nineteenth Century—The common tendency of more recent ethical thought, underlying all differences between the various schools, is fixed by the effort to deal more adequately with the social factors of morality. Kant (1724–1804), in Ger-

many, and Bentham (1748–1832), in England, represent the
transition from their respective sides. In Kant the contradiction in previous rationalistic ethics almost comes to consciousness. This contradiction lay in deriving the moral
laws from reason, which is assumed to be universal and
necessary, and yet in beginning with the individual and
considering the state simply as a compact between individuals. Kant became aware of the necessity of explicitly asserting the universal character of the individual as to his
rational nature, and he set it over against the particular
side found in his appetites and feelings. Morality thus becomes the struggle of the rational universal will to give the
law to conduct, as against the inducements of the sensuous
appetite. These two selves, moreover, he tends to identify
with the results of Rousseau's political analysis, according
to which the individual is to be considered both as sovereign or legislator and as subject, or recipient, of law. The
universal character of the law to be realized forces Kant to
the verge of realizing the social nature of morality. Having,
however, excluded all historical content as empirical, he can
get no further than asserting that the moral law, since universal, demands equal regard to all personalities, and
requires of each that he act so as to make possible the
harmony of all—the kingdom of ends. Instead, therefore, of
continuing the parallelism between the inner and the outer
(that is, the moral motive and political structure) erected
by Thomasius, he asserts the necessity of having the
outward conditions of action so regulated as to enable the
internal moral motive to be really executed. Thus the structure of the state and law, though not in themselves moral,
must be made of such sort as will permit the realization of
morality. It was, of course, impossible that this unstable
equilibrium of the individual and society could be continued. Meanwhile Bentham, on his side, had been effecting
a similar transformation in English ethics. On one side he
asserted that the sole criterion of morality is found not in
the disposition of the agent, but in the tendency of acts to
affect the happiness and misery of all sentient creatures; he
condemned all other standards as capricious and subjective.
On the other hand, he demanded that the whole legal

structure and machinery, both legislative and judicial, be transformed so as, in the first place, to have equal regard to the welfare of all, and, in the second place, to induce the individual really to identify his own happiness with that of others. Thus the contradiction latent in the earlier English thought comes to consciousness. The more (from Shaftesbury down) the writers had insisted upon the benevolent character of the individual the more it was open to cynical observers like Mandeville to point out the discrepancy between the theory and the actual facts of political and economic life in England, where self-seeking seemed the rule. Bentham's utilitarianism may thus be considered an assertion that the previous utilitarian theory of the identity of private and public happiness can become a fact only when the legislative and judicial agencies of the state are brought into play to equalize conditions and furnish motives. Utilitarianism thus became the intellectual instrument of reform in the interest of the rising democratic spirit. Ethical theory was forced from the attitude of mere psychological analysis into a theory of the nature and methods of social well-being.

Recent Ethical Theory—The movement in Germany subsequent to Kant consists in translating the abstract universal will of his theory into concrete social terms. The unified life of society was substituted for formal reason. The particular or sensuous self was transformed into a given individual within the social whole. The categorical imperative, that is, the consciousness of the legislative character of the rational self, was translated into the consciousness on the part of the individual of his place in the social organism, and of the duties devolving upon him because of this place. In Hegel (1770–1831) this tendency reached its culmination. In his philosophy the moral consciousness of the individual is but a phase in the process of social organization. In England Bentham was followed by James Mill (1773–1836), who, uniting the psychology of Hartley with the reforming utilitarian spirit of Bentham, became the center of the philosophical liberal school—a school which had an influence quite out of proportion to its actual numbers. The son of James Mill, John Stuart Mill (1806–73), came early in life under the influence of the disciples of Coleridge, who was introducing German transcendental philosophy into England according to his understanding of it. While the younger Mill remained at bottom a Benthamite, he modified utilitarianism in such ways as to meet the intuitionalism of the other school at least half-way. He introduced the conception that the quality of pleasure is more important than its quantity, and that the highest quality is found in the satisfied conscience of the wise and virtuous man. He admitted an independent moral consciousness in the sense which the individual has of himself as a member of a community. He thus added to the external sanctions of Bentham a strictly internal sanction. He further deepened the social factor of morality, introduced by Bentham, by laying less emphasis upon the direct activity of political administration, and more upon the organic and continuous national life with its moral bent and religious attitude. This, as an educative force, he came to regard as the finally determining element in morals.

Recent Scientific Influence in Ethics – As we have already seen, the democratic tendencies in social and industrial life resulted in attaching greater importance to the objective and social content of morality. This practical tendency has been re-enforced in the last half of the nineteenth century by the development of science. The historical method, worked out in Germany and applied first to law and language, became the ruling instrument of scientific investigation. The effect was to put in clear and definite light the dependence of the individual upon his social environment. This idea was generalized by Comte (1798–1857), who made it the basis of a religious doctrine as well as of a moral theory. The theory of evolution broadened and deepened the historical method by applying it to the entire past history of the world. The result in ethical theory has been the introduction of biological concepts, and the attaching of new importance to anthropological researches into the early customs of humanity. The last decades have witnessed an effort to rethink the previous results of ethical speculation in the light of the new scientific methods, and by the incorporation of the anthropological and sociological data thus attained. The result, curiously enough, has been that the moral philosophy of Germany has been rendered more empirical, while that of England has become more meta-physical. German ethics had reached by its rational analysis the necessity of building up ethics on a social basis. The groundwork was thus provided for the ready assimilation of the historical data. On the other hand, English thought, having been led by its psychological analysis of the individual to the necessity of recognizing the social relations of the individual, felt the need of philosophical concepts, which would enable it to emerge from its individualism, and assert the organic place of the individual in the social whole. These organic ideas it found prepared in the philosophical systems of Germany.

Bibliography—There is one excellent brief history of moral philosophy in English—Sidgwick, *History of Ethics* (3d ed., London and New York, 1892). The earlier writings by Mackintosh, *On the Progress of Ethical Philosophy during the Seventeenth and Eighteenth Centuries* (Edinburgh, 1872), Whewell, *History of Moral Philosophy* (Cambridge, 1862), and Maurice, *Moral and Metaphysical Philosophy* (London, 1861), are by no means antiquated, although their "tendency" has to be allowed for. Leslie Stephen, *English Thought in the Eighteenth Century* (London, 1876), should be consulted for that period. Martineau's and Bain's (see below) ethical writings have historical sketches. Bonar, *Philosophy and Political Economy in their Historical Relations* (London and New York, 1893), contains much valuable historical material. Lecky's *History of European Morals* (2 vols., New York, 1870), is a history of customs rather than theories, but should be consulted.

In German the historical literature is much more abundant. Among earlier writings Schleiermacher, *Grundlinien einer Kritik der bisherigen Sittenlehre* (Berlin, 1834); Stahl, *Philosophie des Rechts* (Vol. 1, 5th ed., Tübingen, 1878); Raumer, *Die geschichtliche Entwickelung der Begriffe von Recht, Staat und Politik* (3d ed., Leipzig, 1861); Mohl, *Geschichte und Literatur der Staatswissenschaften* (Erlangen, 1855–58). Among the best of the recent histories is Jodl, *Geschichte der Ethik* (Stuttgart, 1889), dealing, however, only briefly with earlier thought and colored by a distinct tendency. In addition, we have Ziegler, *Geschichte der Ethik* (2 vols., Strassburg, 1881–86; a third still to appear); Köstlin, *Geschichte der Ethik* (Tübingen, 1887; as yet incomplete). In French we have Janet, *Histoire de la philosophie morale et politique* (2 vols., Paris, 1858).

Limits of space compel us to keep detailed references to the ethical thought of the nineteenth century. The most important literature is Bentham, *Principles of Morals and Legislation* (Vol. i of *Works*, Edinburgh, 1838; also a separate ed., London, 1879); Austin, *Jurisprudence* (2 vols., London, 1869); Mill, *Utilitarianism, Dissertations and Discussions*, Vol. iii (Boston, 1865; also separate ed., Boston, 1887); Bain, *Moral Science* (New York, 1869) and *Emotions and Will* (3d ed., London, 1888); Sidgwick, *Methods of Ethics* (4th ed., London and New York, 1890); Wilson and Fowler, *Principles of Morals* (2 vols., Oxford, 1886–87). The foregoing are all utilitarian, though the last two in particular attempt a reconciliation with intuitional factors. The chief English writers who have made use of the evolutionary idea are Darwin, *Descent of Man* (New York, 1871), Chs. 5 and 6; Spencer, *Data of Ethics* (New York, 1882; embodied also in *Principles of Ethics*, 2 vols., New York, 1893); Stephen, *Science of Ethics* (London, 1882). Accounts and criticisms will be found in Sorley, *Ethics of Naturalism* (Edinburgh, 1885); Schurman, *Ethical Import of Darwinism* (New York, 1887) and *Kantian Ethics and the Ethics of Evolution* (London, 1881); Williams, *Evolutional Ethics* (New York, 1893). Martineau, *Types of Ethical Theory* (2 vols., Oxford, 1885), continues more than any other one writer the English ethical traditions of the eighteenth century. In Germany, Kant, *Werke* (Vol. v, Leipzig, 1867, ed. Hartenstein; trans. by Abbott as *Kant's Theory of Ethics*, London, 1883); Hegel, *Philosophie des Rechts, Werke*, Vol. viii (Berlin, 1833); account of it in Morris, *Hegel's Philosophy of State* (Chicago, 1887); and trans. of selected portions in Sterrett's *Ethics of Hegel* (Boston, 1893). Among recent writers Steinthal, *Allgemeine Ethik* (Berlin, 1885; Herbartian, upon the whole), von Ihering, *Der Zweck im Recht* (Leipzig, 1877), Wundt, *Ethik* (2d ed., Stuttgart, 1892), Paulsen, *System der Ethik*

(3d ed., Berlin, 1894), should be mentioned. Höffding, *Ethik* (German trans., Leipzig, 1888), gives what is probably the best existent statement of a social utilitarianism. The introduction of German philosophic concepts into English ethics is represented by Bradley, *Ethical Studies* (London, 1876); Green, *Prolegomena to Ethics* (Oxford, 1883; and Vol. ii of *Works*, London, 1890); Caird, *Social Philosophy of Comte* (2d ed., New York, 1893) and *Critical Philosophy of Kant* (2 vols., Glasgow and New York, 1889). Alexander, *Moral Order and Progress* (London, 1889), and Ritchie, *Darwin and Hegel* (London, 1893), are attempts to unite this mode of thinking with evolutionary concepts.

The Theory of Emotion

1. Emotional Attitudes

In the following pages I propose, assuming Darwin's principles as to the explanation of emotional attitudes, and the James-Lange theory of the nature of emotion, to bring these two into some organic connection with each other, indicating the modifications of statement demanded by such connection. This close dependence upon results already reached, together with the impossibility of an adequate discussion of all details in the given limits (to say nothing of the immediate availability of most of the details in every one's experience), must be my justification for the generic, and even schematic, quality of the discussion. This may be regarded either as a sketch-map of a field previously surveyed, or as a possible outline for future filling in, not as a proved and finished account.

The necessity of bringing the two theories together may be seen from the fact that the very phrase "expression of emotion," as well as Darwin's method of stating the matter, begs the question of the relation of emotion to organic peripheral action, in that it assumes the former as prior and the latter as secondary.

1. Now this assumption, upon the basis of the discharge theory (as I shall call the James-Lange theory), is false. If one accept the latter theory, it is incumbent upon him to find the proper method of restating Darwin's principles, since there is no doubt of their substantial significance, however erroneous may be their underlying assumption

[*First published in* Psychological Review, I (*Nov. 1894*), 553–69; II (*Jan. 1895*), 13–32. *Not reprinted during the author's lifetime.*]

as to the relation of emotion and peripheral disturbance.[1]

Professor James himself does not seem to me to have adequately realized the inconsistency of Darwin's principles, as the latter states them, with his own theory; or the needed restatement would already have been performed by a much more competent hand than my own. At least he quotes, with apparent approval, explanations from Darwin which assume the priority of an emotion of distress to the contraction of the brows; and even suggests that Darwin does not go far enough in recognizing the principle of reacting similarly to analogous feeling stimuli.[2] Surely if James's conception of the origin of emotion is true, the statement that we react similarly to stimuli which feel alike must be translated into the statement that activities which involve, in like fashion, the same peripheral structures feel alike.[3]

2. One does not, however, need to be committed to James's theory to feel the need of a different way of stating the particular undoubted facts discovered by Darwin. Physiologists agree that there are no muscles intended primarily for purposes of expression. A psychological trans-

[1]   While Darwin's language is that of the dependence of "expression" upon emotion, it is interesting to note that so careful an observer has, in one place, anticipated and definitely stated the discharge theory, *Expression of Emotions*, p. 239. (My references are to the American edition.) "Most of our emotions are so closely connected with their expression that they hardly exist if the body remains passive—the nature of the expression depending in chief part on the nature of the actions which have been habitually performed under this particular state of mind." (Note in this latter phrase the assumption of the priority of emotion; but the continuation is unambiguous in the other sense.) "A man, for instance, may know that his life is in extremest peril, and may strongly desire to save it; yet as Louis XVI said when surrounded by a fierce mob, 'Am I afraid? Feel my pulse.' So a man may intensely hate another, *but until his bodily frame is affected* he cannot be said to be enraged" (italics mine).

[2]   *Psychology*, II, 480–81. The exactness of the latter statement may be doubted, as Darwin recognizes the facts, but includes them under the principle of serviceable associated habits (*Expression*, p. 256), as he certainly has a right to; for Mr. James himself recognizes (*Psychology*, II, 481, footnote) that the "analogous feeling" principle goes back to the teleology of the movements concerned.

[3]   The *facts* conveyed in this principle seem to me of themselves a strong argument for the discharge theory. Left as Darwin and Wundt state it, all mediating machinery, physiological and psychological, is absent, and we cannot even start a hypothesis as to *how* a feeling (recognizing that it feels *like* another feeling!) sets out along the same afferent paths. Upon the discharge theory the mystery vanishes and we have the practical tautology: like affections of like structures give like feeling, the interest lying in the genetic tracing of the details.

lation of this would be that there is no such thing (from the standpoint of the one having the experience) as expression. We call it expression when looking at it from the standpoint of an observer—whether a spectator or the person himself as scientifically reflecting upon his movements, or æsthetically enjoying them. The very word "expression" names the facts not as they are, but in their second intention.[4] To an onlooker my angry movements are expressions—signs, indications; but surely not to me. To rate such movements as primarily expressive is to fall into the psychologist's fallacy: it is to confuse the standpoint of the observer and explainer with that of the fact observed. Movements *are*, as matter of fact, expressive, but they are also a great many other things. In themselves they are movements, acts, and must be treated as such if psychology is to take hold of them right end up.

3. I shall attempt to show, hereafter, that this standpoint of expression of pre-existent emotion complicates and aborts the explanation of the relevant facts in the cases of "antithesis" and "direct nervous discharge." At this stage I wish to point out that in the case of "serviceable associated habits," the principle of explanation *actually* used, whatever the form of words employed, is that of survival, in the form of attitudes, of acts originally useful not *qua* expressing emotion, but *qua* acts—as serving life. In the discussion of movements in animals (*Expression*, pp. 42–48) the reference to emotion is not even nominal. It is a matter of "satisfaction of desire" and "relieving disagreeable sensations"— practical ends. The expressions of grief and of anxiety (Chs. 6 and 7) are explained, in their detail, whatever the general phraseology employed, by reference to acts useful in themselves. It would take up too much space to follow all cases in particular, but the book is open and the reader may easily discover whether in every case the idea of expression of emotion does not enter in only to confuse. *The reference to*

---

[4]   This, of course, is in no way inconsistent with the development of certain movements to serve as expressive. On the contrary, since movements take place in a social medium, and their recognition and interpretation by others is a fact of positive import in the struggle for existence, we might expect the development of gesture and signs through selection.

emotion in explaining the attitude is wholly irrelevant; the attitude of emotion is explained positively by reference to useful movements.

An examination of one apparent exception may serve to clear up the principle. Of laughter, Mr. Darwin says, "We can see in a vague manner how the utterance of sounds of some sort would naturally become associated with a pleasurable state of mind" (*Expression*, p. 207). But Darwin does not use this idea, even in a "vague" way. With his inevitable candor he goes on, "But why the sounds which man utters when he is pleased have the peculiar reiterated character of laughter we do not know."

Now I am not so rash as to attempt to deal in detail with laughter and its concomitant features, but I think something at least a little less vague than Mr. Darwin's account may be given. I cannot see, even in the vaguest way, why pleasure *qua* feeling (emotion?) should express itself in uttering sounds. As matter of fact it does not, nor even in smiles;[5] it is pleasure of a certain qualitative excitement or vivacity which breaks out in laughter, and what we can see, in a "vague way," is why excitement affecting the entire organism should discharge in the vocal apparatus. The problem is the discovery of that special form of excited action which differentiates the laugh from other excitations. Observe a crowd of amateurs just from a game. Note how, irrespective of what they say, you can judge whether they have won or lost. In one case postures are erect, lungs frequently expanded, movements quick, abrupt, and determined; there is much gesturing, talking, and laughing in high keys,—a scene which, looking at it "ejectively," we term one of liveliness, exhilaration, etc. In the other case there is little speaking, and that subdued; all movements tend to be slow, or, if rapid, indicate a desire to escape or expel something; meditative postures are frequently observed, etc.,—a scene of depression. It is the contrast between spontaneous overflow and lowering of overt activity.

5   The "pleasures" of eating have their characteristic attitude— smacking lips, rolling tongue; the pleasures of sex theirs, etc. Many pleasures are accompanied by holding the breath to maintain the excitation at its maximum, not at all by the expiration found in laughter.

What is the difference? In either case the energy, muscular, nervous and visceral, aroused in the game, persists to some extent. What determines the antithetical lines of discharge of this surplus energy (that antithesis of "dejection" and "elation" running through all our terms)? In one case, I answer, there are frictionless lines of action, harmonized activity; or, in more psychological language, all existing kinæsthetic images reinforce and expand one another; in the other case there are two more or less opposed lines of activity going on—the images of the present situation and those of the past game cannot be co-ordinated. The energy is largely directed "inwards"; that is, it is used up in rethinking the game, in making hypothetical changes, in recalling blunders (that is, images which one wants to expel), etc. The movements appropriate to the present activity cannot be identified with the nervous and motor energies which image the game. In the case of exhilaration, etc., there is identification of the thoughts (the nerve and muscular activities relative to the past game) and the present motor discharges.

The connection between *il penseroso* and melancholy more or less mild, and between *l'allegro* and joy, is thus organic and literal, not one of chance or analogy—as if analogy were somehow a force! When one can put up with his defeat, it ceases to bother him, he does not consider it longer. That is, the "downcast" emotion and the intellectual reflection vanish together—the moment there is identification of images. The essential identity of the attitudes of thought and of regret is because of the condition of divided activity; there is still a struggle. Means and end are apart. The identity of attitudes of joy and of activity, of life (alert, wide awake, brisk, animated, vivacious, cheerful, gay— showy, lively, sprightly) is because of the unification of activity. Meditation and regret are both activities of arrest, of conflict; joy and "lively" movement, of stimulation—expansion. No wonder, then, they have the same signs.

Thinking, to be sure, in certain professions, though not for the ordinary man, is an end in itself. In so far as thinking is an end in itself, the activity is unified and has its own joys. It ceases to be occupied with merely instrumental, and (therefore) more or less burdensome, movements. Yet the pangs, the travail of thought, the arduousness of reflection, the loneliness of meditation, the heaviness of deliberation, are all proverbial. Only in rare cases is the whole system involved or unified, and the joy voluminous. Its ordinary form is the "thrill" of identification or the satisfaction of "good taste" in a clear, neat discrimination. When a long and comprehensive process is concluding and approaching its final successful or unified discharge, then, indeed, the hand of a Newton may tremble and joy become intoxicating. But I cannot admit, even in a half-hearted way, the idea that the sense of abundance and ease in thought (James, *Psychology*, II, 477) may be purely cerebral.[6] It appears to me that it is in a literal sense that the object "sets trains going" —these are revivals of motor discharge and organic reinforcement. Upon such occasions thinking becomes really whole-hearted; it takes possession of us altogether, and passes over into the æsthetic.

This, however, is only preparatory to the question of the specific "sign" of joy, the laugh. How is that to be brought under this principle of being an actual portion of a useful activity? Why should the excitation, admitting that it affects the vocal organs, manifest itself in this form? While I feel pretty sure of the following explanation, I cannot hope that it will convince many. Though the result of considerable observation, it can be briefly summed up. The laugh is by no means to be viewed from the standpoint of humor; its connection with humor is secondary. It marks the ending (that is, the attainment of a unity) of a period of suspense, or expectation, an ending which is sharp and sudden. Rhythmical activities, as peek-a-boo, call out a laugh at every culmination of the transition, in an infant. A child of from one and a half to two years uses the laugh as a sign of assent; it is his emphatic "I do" or "yes" to any suggested idea to which he agrees or which suddenly meets his expectations.

6   Such distinctions as James makes here—in reality purely verbally—between spiritual and physiological, instead of between cerebral and viscero-motor, are what give the opponent the sole reason for labelling the theory materialistic—as if the bowels were really more material than the brain!

A very moderate degree of observation of adults will convince one that a large amount of laughter is wholly irrelevant to any joke or witticism whatever. It is a constant and repeated "sign" of attaining suddenly to a point. Now all expectancy, waiting, suspended effort, etc., is accompanied, for obvious teleological reasons, with taking in and holding a full breath, and the maintenance of the whole muscular system in a state of considerable tension. It is a divided activity, part of the kinæsthetic images being fixed upon the immediately present conditions, part upon the expected end. Now let the end suddenly "break," "dawn," let one see the "point" and this energy discharges—the getting the point is the unity, the discharge. This sudden relaxation of strain, so far as occurring through the medium of the breathing and vocal apparatus, is laughter. Its rhythmical character seems to be simply a phase of the general teleological principle that all well-arranged or economical action is rhythmical.[7] The laugh is thus a phenomenon of the same general kind as the sigh of relief. The difference is that the latter occurs when the interest is in the *process*, and when the idea of labor, slow and continuous, is at its height; while the laugh occurs when the interest is all in the outcome, the result—the sudden, abrupt appearance of the "point." In one case the effort is continued until it accomplishes something; in the other case the effort is arrested, and then the energy accumulated is set free from a seemingly outside source. The connection of humor with the laugh, and the ideas of relative superiority—triviality, and of incongruity, involved in humor, etc., seem to be simply more complex, and more intellectually loaded, differentiations of this general principle.

Not only are joy and grief practically in a peculiar qualitative antithesis, seeming to imply a common principle of which they are the extremes, but the "signs" of joy and grief, especially when these become violent, are identical. This fact, otherwise so meaningless, becomes natural if we adopt the above explanation. Both crying and laughing fall under the same principle of action—the termination of a

[7]   Acute crying, etc., is non-rhythmical; when it does take the form of rhythmical sobbing, one experiences a sensation of relief—grief has "moderated."

period of effort. If we fix our attention upon the conventional and literary conceptions of grief, this will seem far-fetched; if we take children and simple cases, it seems to stare us in the eyes. Crying is either a part of an effort to expel an intruder,[8] an effort so general as to engage spasmodically the lungs and vocal organs (a sort of general gripe); or, as we see so often in children, an explosion of energy, accumulated in preparation for some act, suddenly discharged *in vacuo* upon the missing of the essential part, the finishing factor of the act.[9]

Beginning with the simpler case, the phenomena of matured grief become easily explainable. They are phenomena of *loss*. Reactions surge forth to some stimulus, or phase of a situation; the object appropriate to most of these, the factor necessary to co-ordinate all the rising discharges, is gone; and hence they interfere with one another—the expectation, or kinæsthetic image, is thrown back upon itself.

4. In dealing with grief we have unconsciously entered upon a new field. The point of our third head is that the principle which Darwin calls that of "movements useful in expressing an emotion" explains the relevant facts only when changed to read "useful as parts of an act which is useful as movement." In dealing with grief we have passed over into the phenomena of the breakdown of a given teleological co-ordination, and the performance of acts which, therefore, objectively viewed, are not only useless but may be harmful. My proposition at this point is that the phenomena referred to the principle of direct nervous discharge (the response to an idiopathic stimulus) are cases of the failure of habitual teleological machinery, through some disturbance in one or more of the adjusted members of the habit.

---

[8]   While Darwin's explanation of shutting the eyes—to protect blood-vessels from gorging on account of the violent screaming—undoubtedly accounts for the selection of this attitude, it can hardly account for its origin. I think originally it had the same end as screaming—to shut out or off some threatening object, as the ostrich, etc., or as one shuts his eyes on firing a gun the first time.

[9]   I suppose every one has seen a young child go into a rage of screams and violent movements upon being handed, say, a broken cooky. The thing explains itself on the above principle. The concluding factor in a co-ordination of energy does not appear, and the child goes literally to pieces. I should like to see any explanation upon the anti-James theory, save that offered by Saint Augustine for similar phenomena of his infancy —total depravity.

In order to avoid misconception, let me point out a great ambiguity in the use of the term idiopathic. In one sense even the "associated useful" movements are idiopathic, provided, that is, they originally were useful in reaching an end, and not simply in expressing an emotion. They are the reactions to their appropriate stimuli, and the sole difference between them and the liver changes, nausea, palpitation of heart, etc., usually classed as idiopathic, is that in them stimuli and reaction are more definitely limited to certain particular channels than in the latter cases; there is a defined, as against a vague and diffuse, direct nervous discharge. The fact that this defined discharge happens to be useful may state the kind of idiopathic response we have, but cannot make it other than a response. Furthermore, upon evolutionary principles, the limited, adjusted, and useful discharge must be a differentiation, selected and perpetuated because of its utility in the struggle for life, out of an original more diffuse and irradiating wave of discharge.

Admitting, then, that all emotional attitudes whatever are idiopathic in the broad sense, the sole difference being in the definiteness or limitation of the stimulus and its response, what are we to do with the cases now disposed of as "idiopathic" in the narrower sense?—such phenomena as Mr. James briefly but excellently sums up on p. 482 (*Psychology*, II). My proposition, I repeat, is that all such idiopathic discharges, possessing emotional quality, are in reality disturbances, defects, or alienations of the *adjusted* movements. While not immediately teleological in the sense that they themselves are useful, they are teleologically conditioned. They are cases of the disintegration of associations (co-ordinations) which are serviceable, or are the use of means under circumstances in which they are totally inappropriate.

Idiopathic discharges which are not themselves adjusted movements or the disturbances of such adjusted movements do not appear to me to have any *emotional* quality at all. The trembling with cold or sheer fatigue is certainly qualitatively different from the tremble of rage or fear. The sensations of weakness in the bowels and of nausea, which are idiopathic to their appropriate stimuli, can be called emotional only by such a stretch of the term as renders all sensations and impulses emotions. Professor James seems to me wholly successful in dealing with the charge brought that, upon his theory, all laughing ought to give the mirthful emotion, all vomiting that of disgust, etc.[10] The diffusive wave in one case is incomplete; but is there no reason or meaning in this difference? There is no doubt, in my own mind, that, *under existing conditions*, the supplying of the missing organic excitations will change the laugh and the nausea into mirth and disgust as emotions— this without any change in the "object." But whence and why these "existing conditions"? The change from mere cachinnation to mirthful emotion is a distinct change in psychical quality, and this change of quality does not seem to be adequately *accounted* for by mere addition of more discharges—though, I repeat, simply adding on more discharges will undoubtedly *make* this difference. If these supplementary factors report the meaning or value of past co-ordinations, this change of quality is reasonable and inevitable; if not, if they are simply some more accidental discharges, the peculiar qualitative "feel" is miraculous—it admits of no explanation.

This is but to say, from the psychological side, that all normal emotion of terror has an *object*, and involves an attitude *towards* that object; this attitude, under the given circumstances, perhaps not being useful, nay, being harmful, but yet the reproduction of an attitude or, rather, a mixture of attitudes which have been useful in the past. The uselessness of the attitude is due to the fact that some feature in the stimulus (the situation or object) awakens its appropriate reactions, but these do not co-ordinate with the reactions aroused by other features of the situation. The pathological emotion is, as Mr. James calls it, the *objectless* emotion, but its content is controlled by the active attitudes previously assumed towards objects, and, *from its own standpoint*, it is not objectless; it goes on at once to supply itself with an object, with a rational excuse for being.[11] This im-

---

10   *Psychological Review*, I, 522.
11   The pathological emotion is to the normal as hallucination is to perception. An unusual stimulus takes advantage of and controls the lines of co-ordination and discharge which have been built up with reference to the usual or normal stimulus. Psychologically the process is quite regular; it is only in its teleology that it is "off."

mediate correlation of the emotion with an "object," and its immediate tendency to assume the "object" when it is not there, seem to me mere tautology for saying that the emotional attitude is normally rational in content (*i.e.*, adjusted to some end), and, even in pathological cases, sufficiently teleological in form to subsume an object for itself.

In any case, upon James's theory, the admission of any idiopathic cases which cannot be reduced to abnormal use of teleological adjustments is more or less intolerable. Their permanent resistance to such reduction would be a strong objection to the theory. Hope, fear, delight, sorrow, terror, love, are too important and too relevant in our lives to be in the main[12] the "feel" of bodily attitudes which have themselves no meaning. If the attitude is wholly accidental, then the emotion itself is brute and insignificant, upon a theory which holds that the emotion is the "feel" of such an attitude.

One more word of general explanation. The antithesis here is between the merely accidental and the adjusted excitation—not between the mechanical and the teleological. I add this because of the following sentence in James: "It seems as if even the changes of blood-pressure and heartbeat during emotional excitement might, instead of being teleologically determined, prove to be purely mechanical or physiological outpourings through the easiest drainage-channels" (*Psychology*, II, 482). Certainly, if these are the alternatives, I should go a step farther and say that even the clenching of the fist and the retraction of the lips in anger are simply mechanical outpourings through the easiest available channel. But these are not the alternatives. The real question is simply how this particular channel came to be the easiest possible, whether purely accidentally or because of the performance of movements having some value for life preservation. The ground taken here is that the easiest path is determined by habits which, upon the whole, were evolved as useful.[13]

---

[12]   In the main, I say; for doubtless it is pedantry to hold that every slight feature of the attitude is conditioned by an activity directed towards an object.

[13]   It is admitted, of course, as Mr. James puts it, that there are "reactions incidental to others evolved for utility's sake, but which would

Coming a little more to details, it is obvious that the teleological principle carries within itself a certain limitation. Normal and usual are identical; the habit is based upon the customary features of the situation. The very meaning of habit is limitation to a certain average range of fluctuation. Now if an entirely strange (forgive the contradiction in terms) stimulus occurs, there will be no disturbance of function, though the organism may be destroyed by the impact of the foreign force. But let some of the features of a situation habitually associated in the past with other features be present while these others fail, or let the ordinary proportion or relative strength of stimuli be changed, or let their mode of connection be reversed, and there is bound to be a disturbance and a resulting activity which, *objectively viewed*, is non-teleological. We thus get an *a priori* canon, as it were, for determining when, in a given emotion, we shall get symptoms falling under the "serviceable associated habit" principle and when under the idiopathic. Whenever the various factors of the act, muscular movement, nutritive, respiratory, and circulatory changes, are co-ordinated and reinforce each other, it is the former; whenever they interfere (the "idiopathic"), the "feel" of this interference *is* (applying the general principle of James) the pathological rage, or terror, or expectation.

Once more, we work in a wrong, a hopeless direction when we start from the emotion and attempt to derive the movements as its expression; while the situation clears itself up when we start from the character of the movement, as a completed or disturbed co-ordination, and then derive the corresponding types of normal and pathological emotion. We can understand why the so-called idiopathic principle comes into play in all cases of extreme emotion, the maximum limit seeming to be the passage into spasm when it

---

never have been evolved independently" (*Psychology*, II, 484). Indeed, in one sense of the term "incidental" this is a necessary part of my proposition. The only question is whether "incidental" means purposeless, or means having their purpose not in themselves, but as relative to, as facilitating or reinforcing, some other useful act. The fact, once more, that upon Darwin's method of statement no such relative or incidental movements can be admitted is an undoubted objection to Darwin's mode of statement of the principle of useful habit.

assumes a rigid type, of hysteria when it involves complete
breakdown of co-ordination.

The attitude of normal fear may be accounted for upon
direct teleological principles; the holding of breath marks
the effort; the opening of mouth, the act arrested half-way;
the opening of eyes, the strained attention; the shiver, of
retraction; the crouching down, the beginning of escape;
the rapid beating of heart, the working up of energy for
escape, etc. Now if these activities go on to complete themselves, if, that is, they suggest the further reaction which will
co-ordinate into a definite response, we get judicious fear—
that is, caution. Now if these do not suggest a further movement which completes the act, some or all of these factors
begin to assert themselves in consciousness, isolatedly or in
alternation—there is confusion. Moreover, each particular
phase of the act which is normal in co-ordination, as the more
rapid beating of the heart, being now uncontrolled by lack of
its relevant motor associates, is exaggerated and becomes
more and more violent. The response to the normal demand
for more nutrition finds no regular outlet in supplying the
motor-energy for the useful act, and the disturbances of
viscera and associated organs propagate themselves. The
trembling marks, so far as I can see, simply this same disco-
ordination on the side of the muscular system. It is the
extreme of vacillating indecision; we start to do this, and
the other thing, but each act falls athwart its predecessor.

Speaking roughly, there is exaggeration of the entire
vegetative functions of the activity, and defect of the motor
side—the unstriped muscles being included, on a functional
basis, with the vegetative system. Now this is just what we
might expect when there is a great stirring up of energy
preparatory to activity, but no defined channel of discharge.
Thus the agent becomes entirely taken up with its own
state and is unable to attend to the object.

The pathological emotion is, then, simply a case of
morbid self-consciousness. Those factors of the organism
which relate most immediately to the welfare of the organism, the vegetative functions, absorb consciousness, instead
of being, as they normally are, subsidiary to the direction
of muscular activity with reference to the "object." This is

equally true in extreme terror, and in being "beside one's self" with anger. The cases in which sanguine excitement and apprehension affect the bladder will be found, I believe, to be almost uniformly cases where it is not possible to do anything at once with the aroused activities; they cannot be controlled by being directed towards the putting forth of effort upon the "object," that being too remote or uncertain.

Certainly, the principle for attitudes commonly called those of morbid self-consciousness is precisely the one just laid down. In these cases muscular (not vegetative) functions normally useful in the attainment of an end are first aroused in response to stimuli, and then, not being completely co-ordinated into action, are *not* used with reference to the end, and so stand out in consciousness on their own account. I shall not attempt any detailed statement here, but leave it to the reader to answer if the above does not give a precise generic description of the sensations of awkwardness, of bashfulness, of being ridiculous (as when one starts an appropriate movement, but is made conscious of it in itself apart from its end) on one side, and of affected grace, mincing ease, pomposity and conceit on the other.

All these facts taken cumulatively seem to me to render it fairly certain that the "idiopathic" cases, as a rule, are to be conceived of as the starting of activities formerly useful for a given end, but which now, for some reason, fail to function, and therefore stand out in consciousness apart from the needed end.

5. I come now to the principle of antithesis. According to Mr. Darwin, when certain movements have been habitually of service in connection with certain emotions, there is a tendency, when a directly opposite state of mind is induced, to the performance of movements of a directly opposite nature, "*though these have never been of any use*" (*Expression*, p. 50, italics mine). Here we have a crucial case; if the antithesis of the emotion determines the antithesis of expression, James's theory is, in so far, overthrown; if, on the other hand, the antithesis of "expression" goes back to activities having their own ends, the ground is at least cleared for the discharge theory.

Beginning with animals, Mr. Darwin illustrates his

principle of antithesis from the cat and dog. No one can read his account or examine the pictures without being convinced that the movements *are* antithetical. But there is something intolerable to the psychologist in the supposition that an opposite emotion can somehow select for itself channels of discharge not already used for some specific end, and those channels such as give rise to directly opposed movements. Antithesis is made a causal force. Such an idea is not conceivable without some presiding genius who opens valves and pulls strings. The absence of mediating machinery, of inter-linking phenomena, is even more striking in this case than in that of "analogous feeling."

If, again, the matter be treated as a case of the connection of movements with reference to certain acts, the mystery vanishes. Mr. Darwin's cases are taken from domestic animals. Now wild animals have, speaking roughly, just two fundamental characteristic attitudes—those connected with getting food, including attack upon enemies, and those of defense, including flight, etc. A domestic animal, by the very fact that it is domestic, has another characteristic attitude, that of reception—the attitude of complete adaptation to something outside itself. This attitude is constituted, of course, by a certain co-ordination of movements; and these are antithetical to those movements involved in the contrary attitude, that of resistance or opposition. A study of the dogs upon pp. 52–55 will show that the attitude of opposition is naturally self-centred and braced, the best position from which to fall, on one side, into an attitude of overt attack, and, upon the other side, into that of resistance to attack. The attitude of "humility" and "affection" consists, as Mr. Darwin well says, in continuous, flexuous movements. These movements are precisely those of response and adaptation. The centre of gravity is, as it were, in the master, and the lithe and sinuous movement is the solution of the problem of maintaining balance with respect to every change in this external centre of gravity. It is the attitude of receiving favor and food from another. The dependence is actual, not symbolic. Unless Mr. Darwin were prepared to equip the animal with a full-fledged moral consciousness, the "humble" attitude of the dog can hardly be other than the habitual attitude of reception, or the "affectionate" attitude other than the recurrence of movements associated with the food-getting. The same general principle will apply to the antithetical cat expressions, save that the dependence in the case of the cat assumes more the form of passive contact and less that of active adjustment. The reminiscence of sexual attitude is possibly also more marked.[14]

The other cases of antithesis given by Mr. Darwin are the shrug of impotence, and the raising of the hands in great astonishment. I feel certain that the rational hypothesis is to suppose that these are survivals of certain acts, and not symbolic indications of certain emotions. As a contribution to such a working hypothesis, I suggest the possibility that the throwing up of the arms in attention is partly the survival of a movement of warding off the approaching hostile object, and partly a reinforcement of the holding of the chest full of air characteristic of expectancy and of astonishment—a movement whose analogue is found in the raising and drawing back of the arms in yawning.[15] The shrug of impotence seems to be complex; the union of survivals of three or four distinct acts. The raising of the brows is the act of retrospect, of surveying the ground to see if anything else could have been done; the pursing of the lips, the element of tentative rejection (doubt); the raising of the shoulders, the act of throwing a burden off (*cf.* "he shouldered it off on some one else"); the holding out of the hand, palm up, the attitude of asking or taking. To my introspection the *quale* of the emotion agrees entirely; it is a feeling of "I don't see how I could possibly have done anything else, so far as I am concerned, but I'm willing to hear what you have to offer"

---

[14]   Being unable to do anything with these cases, I called them to the notice of my friend and colleague, Mr. G. H. Mead. The explanation given, which seems to me indubitable, is his. The relation between the vegetative and the motor functions, given above in discussion of pathological emotion and to be used again below, I also owe to him. While I have employed the point only incidentally, Mr. Mead rightly makes it essential to the explanation of emotion and its attitudes, as distinct from the identification and description which alone I have attempted. I hope, therefore, that his whole theory may soon appear in print.

[15]   Since writing the text, I have repeatedly noticed this attitude of the arms, without the rigidity, assumed by a child of two years while watching the preparation of his food.

—of "I don't know; you tell." It thus has the distinctly expressive or social element in it, and marks the passing over of emotional attitude into gesture.

Summing up, we may say that all so-called expressions of emotions are, in reality, the reduction of movements and stimulations originally useful into attitudes. But we note a difference in the form and nature of the reduction, and in the resulting attitudes, which explain the apparent diversity of the four principles of "serviceable associated habits," of "analogous stimuli," of "antithesis," and of "direct nervous discharge." A given movement or set of movements may be useful either as preparatory to, as leading up to, another set of acts, or in themselves as accomplished ends. Movements of effort, of bracing, of reaching, etc., evidently come under the former head. Here we have the case of useful associated movements in its strict sense. The culmination of all these preparatory adjustments is the attainment of food or of the sexual embrace. In so far as we have attitudes which reflect these acts, satisfying in themselves, we get cases of so-called analogous stimuli. The antithetical attitudes of joy and grief, and all that is differentiated from them, mark the further development of actual attainment of an end (or failure to get it), occurring when the activity specially appropriate to the particular end reached (or missed) is reinforced and expanded by a wide range of contributory muscular and visceral changes. The cases of failure bring us to the breakdown of co-ordinations habitually useful, to their alienation, or to reciprocal disturbance of their various factors, and thus to the facts usually subsumed under the idiopathic principle. In this progression we have a continually changing ratio of the vegetative to the motor functions. In the preparatory adjustments the latter has the highest exponent, and the strictly emotional *quale* of feeling is at its minimum. In joy and grief, as in less degree with "sweetness," disgust, etc., the organic resonance is at its height, but strictly subservient to the motor performances. In the idiopathic these vegetative functions break loose and run away, and thus, instead of reinforcing the efficiency of behavior, interfere by their absorption of consciousness.

In the following article I shall take up the discharge

theory of the nature of emotion, and discuss it in the light of the conclusions now reached.

II.   The Significance of Emotions

In a preceding article[16] I endeavored to show that all the so-called expressions of emotion are to be accounted for not by reference to emotion, but by reference to movements having some use, either as direct survivals or as disturbances of teleological co-ordinations. I tried to show that, upon this basis, the various principles for explaining emotional attitudes may be reduced to certain obvious and typical *differentiæ* within the teleological movements. In the present paper I wish to reconsider the James-Lange, or discharge, theory of the nature of emotion from the standpoint thus gained; for if all emotions (considered as "emotional seizures," *Affect*[17] or "feel," as I may term it) are constituted by the reflexion of the teleological attitude, the motor and organic discharges, into consciousness, the same principle which explains the attitude must serve to analyze the emotion.

The fact, if it be a fact, that all "emotional expression" is a phase of movements teleologically determined, and not a result of pre-existent emotion, is itself a strong argument for the discharge theory. I had occasion to point out in my previous article that the facts brought under the head of "antithesis" and "analogous stimuli" are absolutely unaccountable upon the central theory, and are matters of course upon the James theory. But this statement may be further generalized. If every emotional attitude is referred to useful acts, and if the emotion is *not* the reflex of such an act, where does it come in, and what is its relation to the attitude? The first half of the hypothesis prevents its being the antecedent of the attitude; the latter half of the hypothesis precludes its being the consequent. If it is said that the emotion is a mere side issue of that central excitation (corresponding to the purpose) which issues in the muscular and organic changes,

---

[16]   *Psychological Review*, Nov. 1894 [*Early Works*, IV, 152–69].
[17]   See "The Physical Basis of Emotion," this *Review*, Sept. 1894, p. 523.

then we are entitled to ask, *a priori*, for some explanation of its unique appearance at this point, some sort of mechanical or teleological *causa essendi*; and, *a posteriori*, to point out that, as matter of fact, every one now supposes that his emotion, say of anger, does have *some* kind of direct relation to his movements — in fact, common usage compels us to speak of them as movements of anger. I think, then, that logic fairly demands either the surrender of the "central" theory of emotion or else a refutation of the argument of the preceding paper, and a proof that emotional attitudes are to be explained by reference to emotion, and not by reference to acts.

More positively, this reference to serviceable movement in explanation of emotional attitudes, taken in connection with the hypothesis that the emotional "feel" is always due to the return wave of this attitude, supplies a positive tool for the analysis of emotion in general and of particular emotions in especial. As indicating the need of a further consideration, it may be pointed out that Mr. James himself lays the main emphasis of his theory upon its ability to account for the *origin* of emotions, and as supplying emotion with a "physical basis," not upon the psychological analysis which it might yield of the nature of emotional experience. Indeed, James definitely relegates to the background the question of classification,[18] saying that the question of genesis becomes all-important. But every theory of genesis must become a method of analysis and classification. The discharge theory does, indeed, give the *coup de grâce* to the fixed pigeon-hole method of classification, but it opens the door for the genetic classification. In other words, it does for the emotions precisely what the theory of evolution does in biology; it destroys the arbitrary and subjective schemes, based on mere possession of likenesses and differences, and points to an objective and dynamic classification based on descent from a given functional activity, gradually differentiated according to the demands of the situation. The general conclusion indicated regarding the nature of emotion is that:

Emotion in its entirety is a mode of behavior which is

18   *Psychology*, II, 454 and 485.

purposive, or has an intellectual content, and which also reflects itself into feeling or Affects, as the subjective valuation of that which is objectively expressed in the idea or purpose.[19]

This formula, however, is no more than a putting together of James's theory with the revision of Darwin's principles attempted in the last number. If an attitude (of emotion) is the recurrence, in modified form, of some teleological movement, and if the specific differentia of emotional consciousness is the resonance of such attitude, then emotional excitation is the felt process of realization of ideas. The chief interest lies in making this formula more specific.

In the first place, this mode of getting at it relieves Mr. James's statement of the admittedly paradoxical air which has surrounded it. I can but think that Mr. James's critics have largely made their own difficulties, even on the basis of his "slap-dash" statement that "we feel sorry because we cry, angry because we strike, afraid because we tremble." The very statement brings out the idea of *feeling* sorry, not of *being* sorry. On p. 452 (*Psychology*, ii) he expressly refers to his task as "subtracting certain *elements of feeling* from an emotional state supposed to exist *in its fulness*" (italics mine). And in his article in this *Review* (Sept. 1894), he definitely states that he is speaking of an *Affect*, or emotional seizure. By this I understand him to mean that he is not dealing with emotion as a concrete whole of experience, but with an abstraction from the actual emotion of that element which gives it its differentia—its feeling *quale*, its "feel." As I understand it, he did not conceive himself as dealing with that state which we term "being angry," but rather with the peculiar "feel" which any one has when he is

---

[19]   In my *Psychology*, *e.g.*, p. 19 and pp. 246–49 [Early Works, ii, 21–22 and 215–17], it is laid down, quite schematically, that feeling is the internalizing of activity or will. There is nothing novel in the doctrine; in a way it goes back to Plato and Aristotle. But what first fixed my especial attention, I believe, upon James's doctrine of emotion was that it furnishes this old idealistic conception of feeling, hitherto blank and unmediated, with a medium of translation into the terms of concrete phenomena. I mention this bit of personal history simply as an offset to those writers who have found Mr. James's conception so tainted with materialism. On the historical side, it may be worth noting that a crude anticipation of James's theory is found in Hegel's *Philosophie des Geistes*, §401.

angry, an element which may be intellectually abstracted, but certainly has no existence by itself, or as full-fledged emotion-experience.

What misled Mr. James's critics, I think, was not so much his language, as it was the absence of all attempts on his part to connect the emotional seizure with the other phases of the concrete emotion-experience. What the whole condition of *being* angry, or hopeful or sorry may be, Mr. James nowhere says, nor does he indicate why or how the "feel" of anger is related to them. Hence the inference either that he is considering the whole emotion-experience in an inadequate way, or else—as Mr. Irons took it—that he is denying the very existence of emotion, reducing it to mere consciousness of bodily change as such. Certainly, even when we have admitted that the emotional differentia, or "feel," is the reverberation of organic changes following upon the motor response to stimulus, we have still to *place* this "feel" with reference to the other phases of the concrete emotion-experience. "Common-sense" and psychological sense revolt at the supposed implication that the emotional "feel" which constitutes so much of the meaning of our lives is a chance arrival, or a chance super-imposition from certain organic changes which happen to be going on. It is this apparently arbitrary isolation which offends.

If, preparatory to attempting such a placing, we put before us the whole concrete emotional experience, we find, I think, that it has two phases beside that of *Affect*, or seizure. (1) It is a disposition, a mode of conduct, a way of behaving. Indeed, it is this practical aspect of emotion which common speech mainly means to refer to in its emotional terms. When we say that John Smith is very resentful at the treatment he has received, or is hopeful of success in business, or regrets that he accepted a nomination for office, we do not simply, or even chiefly, mean that he has a certain "feel" occupying his consciousness. We mean he is in a certain practical attitude, has assumed a readiness to act in certain ways. I should not fear a man who had simply the "feel" of anger, nor should I sympathize with one having simply the "feel" of grief.[20] Grief means *unwillingness* to

[20]   I take it that this separation of "feel" from practical attitude is precisely what makes the difference between an emotional and a senti-

resume the normal occupation, practical discouragement, breaking-up of the normal reactions, etc., etc. Just as anger means a tendency to explode in a sudden attack, not a mere state of feeling. We certainly do not deny nor overlook the "feel" phase, but in ordinary speech the behavior side of emotion is, I think, always uppermost in consciousness. The connotation of emotion is primarily ethical, only secondarily psychical. Hence our insulted feeling when told (as we hastily read it—our interpretation is "slap-dash" rather than the sentence itself) that we are not angry until we strike, for the sudden readiness to injure another is precisely what we mean by anger. Let the statement read that we do not have the emotional seizure, the "feel" of anger, till we strike, or clench our fist, or have our blood boil, etc., and the statement not only loses its insultingly paradoxical quality, but (unless my introspection meets a different scene from that of others) is verified by every passing emotion. (2) But the full emotional experience also always has its "object" or intellectual content. The emotion is always "about" or "toward" something; it is "at" or "on account of" something, and this prepositional reference is an integral phase of the single pulse of emotion; for emotion, as well as the idea, comes as a whole carrying its distinctions of value within it. The child who ceases to be angry *at* something—were it only the floor at last—but who keeps up his kicking and screaming, has passed over into sheer spasm. It is then no more an emotion of anger than it is one of æsthetic appreciation. Disgust, terror, gratitude, sulkiness, curiosity—take all the emotions seriatim and see what they would be without the intrinsic reference to idea or object. Even the pathological or objectless emotion is so only to the rational spectator. To the experiencer (if I may venture the term) it subsumes at once its own object as source or aim. This feeling of depression must have its reason; the world is dark and gloomy; no one understands me; I have a dread disease; I have com-

---

mental experience. The fact that the "feel" may be largely, though never wholly, simulated, by arousing certain organic excitations apart from the normal practical readiness to behave in a certain way, has played a sufficiently large part in our "evangelical" religions. The depth, in a way, and the hollowness, in another way, of the subjectively induced religious sentiments seems to me, in itself, a most admirable illustration of the truth of James's main contention.

mitted the unpardonable sin. This feeling of buoyancy must
have its ideal reference; I am a delightful person, or one of
the elect or have had a million dollars left me.[21]

It is perhaps at this point that the need of some reconstruction which will enable us to place the phases of an entire
emotional experience becomes most urgent. In Mr. James's
statement the experience is apparently (apparently, I say; I
do not know how much is due to the exigency of discussion
which necessitates a seeming isolation) split up into three
separate parts: First comes the object or idea which operates
only as stimulus; secondly, the mode of behavior taken as
discharge of this stimulus; third, the *Affect*, or emotional
excitation, as the repercussion of this discharge. No such
seriality or separation attaches to the emotion as an experience. Nor does reflective analysis seem to establish this order
as the best expression of the emotion as an object of psychological abstraction. We might almost infer from the way Mr.
James leaves it that he is here a believer in that atomic or
mosaic composition of consciousness which he has so effectively dealt with in the case of intellectual consciousness.
However this may be, Mr. James certainly supplies us, in
the underlying *motif* of this "chapter" on emotion, with an
adequate instrument of reconstruction. This is the thought
that the organic discharge is an *instinctive* reaction, not a response to an idea as such.

Following the lead of this idea, we are easily brought
to the conclusion that *the mode of behavior is the primary
thing, and that the idea and the emotional excitation are
constituted at one and the same time; that, indeed, they
represent the tension of stimulus and response within the co-
ordination which makes up the mode of behavior.*

It is sheer reflective interpretation to say that the
activity in anger is set up by the object, if we by object
mean something consciously apprehended as object. This
interpretation, if we force it beyond a mere way of speaking
into the facts themselves, becomes a case of the psychological fallacy. If my bodily changes of beating heart, trem-

---

[21]   I do not mean, of course, that every "pathological" emotion creates
an intellectual delusion; but it does carry with it a changed intellectual
coloring, a different direction of attention.

bling and running legs, sinking in stomach, looseness of bowels, etc., follow from and grow out of the conscious recognition, *qua conscious recognition*, of a bear, then I see no way for it but that the bear is already a bear of which we are afraid—our idea must be of the bear as a fearful object. But if (as Mr. James's fundamental idea would imply, however his language may read at times) this reaction is not to the bear as *object*, nor to the *idea* of bear, but simply expresses an instinctive co-ordination of two organic tendencies, then the case is quite different. It is not the idea of the bear, or the bear as object, but a certain *act of seeing*, which by habit, whether inherited or acquired, sets up other acts. It is the kind of *co-ordination of acts* which, brought to sensational consciousness, constitutes the bear a fearful or a laughable or an indifferent object. The following sentence, for example, from James (this *Review*, I, 518) seems to involve a mixture of his own theory with the one which he is engaged in combatting: "Whatever be our reaction on the situation, in the last resort it is an *instinctive reaction* on that one of its elements which strikes us for the time being *as most vitally important*." The conception of an instinctive reaction is the relevant idea; that of reaction upon an element "which strikes us as important" the incongruous idea. Does it strike us, *prior* to the reaction, as important? Then, most certainly, it already has emotional worth; the situation is already delightful and to be perpetuated, or terrible and to be fled, or whatever. What does recognition of importance mean aside from the ascription of worth, value—that is, aside from the projection of emotional experience?[22] But I do not think James's expression in this and other similar passages is to be taken literally. The reaction is not made on the basis of the apprehension of some quality in the object; it is made on the basis of an organized habit, of an organized co-ordination of activities, one of which instinctively stimu-

[22]   It seems to me that the application of James's theory of emotion to his theory of attention would give some very interesting results. As it now stands, the theory "in attention" of preferential selection on the *basis* of interest seems to contradict the theory of emotional value as the *outcome* of preferential selection (that is, specific reaction). But the contradiction is most flagrant in the case of effort, considered, first, as emotion and then as an operation of will.

lates the other. The outcome of this co-ordination of activities constitutes, for the first time, the object with such
and such an import—terrible, delightful, etc.—or constitutes
an emotion referring to such and such an object. For, we
must insist once more, the frightful object and the emotion
of fear are two names for the same experience.

Here, then, is our point of departure in placing the
"feel," the "idea," and the "mode of behavior" in relation to
one another. The idea or object which precedes and stimulates the bodily discharge is in no sense the idea or object
(the intellectual content, the "at" or "on account of") of the
emotion itself. The particular idea, the specific quality or
object to which the seizure attaches, is just as much due to
the discharge as is the seizure itself. More accurately and
definitely, the idea or the object is an abstraction from the
activity just as much as is the "feel" or seizure. We have
certain organic activities initiated, say in the eye, stimulating, through organized paths of association in the brain,
certain activities of hands, legs, etc., and (through the
co-ordination of these motor activities with the vegetative
functions necessary to maintain them) of lungs, heart, vaso-
motor system, digestive organs, etc. The "bear" is, psychologically, just as much a discrimination of certain values,
within this total pulse or co-ordination of action, as is the
feeling of "fear." The "bear" is constituted by the excitations of eye and co-ordinated touch centres, just as the
"terror" is by the disturbances of muscular and glandular
systems. The reality, the co-ordination of these partial activities, is that whole activity which may be described equally
well as "that terrible bear," or "Oh, how frightened I am." It
is precisely and identically the same actual concrete experience; and the "bear," considered as one experience, and the
"fright," considered as another, are distinctions introduced
in reflection upon this experience, not separate experience.
It is the psychological fallacy again if the differences which
result from the reflection are carried over into the experience itself. If the fright comes, then the bear is not the bear
of that particular experience, is not the object to which the
feeling attaches, *except* as the fright comes. Any other supposition is to confuse the abstract bear of science with the
concrete (*just this*) bear of experience.

The point may be further illustrated by the objection which Mr. Irons has brought against the James theory (*Mind*, 1894, p. 85). "How can one perceptive process of itself suffuse with emotional warmth the cold intellectuality of another?" Note here the assumption of two distinct "processes," apparently recognizing themselves as distinct, or anyhow somehow marked out as different in themselves. The continued point of Mr. Irons's objection is that Mr. James makes intellectual and emotional "states," (values) the knowledge of an object and the emotion referred to it, both due to currents from the periphery, and the same kind of current cannot be supposed to induce such radically different things as an intellectual and an emotional process. The objection entirely overlooks the fact that we have but the one organic pulse, the frightful bear, the frightened man, whose reality is the whole concrete co-ordination of eye—leg—heart, etc., activity, and that the distinction of cold intellectuality and warm emotionality is simply a *functional* distinction within this one whole of action. We take a certain phase which *serves a certain end*, namely, giving us information, and call that intellectual; we take another phase, having another end or value, that of excitement, and call that emotional. But does any one suppose that, *apart from our interpretation of values*, there is one process in itself intellectual, and another process in itself emotional? I cannot even frame an idea of what is meant. I can see that the eye-touch process gives us information mainly, and so we call that intellectual; and that the heart-bowels process gives us the valuation of this information in terms of our own inner welfare,—but aside from this distinction of *values* within a concrete whole, through reflection upon it, I can see nothing.

If, then, I may paraphrase Mr. James's phraseology, the statement would read as follows: Our customary analysis, reading over into the experience itself what we find by interpreting it,[23] says we have an idea of the bear as some-

23   This is simply circumlocution for "common-sense." Common-sense is practical, and when we are practical it is the value of our experience, what we can get out of it or think we can, that appeals to us. The last thing that concerns us is the actual process of experiencing, *qua* process. It might almost be said that the sole difficulty in psychology, upon the introspective side, is to avoid this substitution of a practical interpretation of an experience for the experience itself.

thing to be escaped, and so run away. The hypothesis here propounded is that the factors of a co-ordination (whether due to inherited instinct or to individually acquired habit) begin to operate and we run away; running away, we get the idea of "running-away-from-bear," or of "bear-as-thing-to-be-run-from." I suppose every one would admit that the complete, mature idea came only in and through the act of running, but might hold that an embryonic suggestion of running came before the running. I cannot disprove this position, but everything seems to point the other way. It is more natural to suppose that as the full idea of running away comes in from the full execution, so the vague suggestion comes through the vague starting-up-of the system, mediated by discharge from the centres.

The idea of running away must certainly involve, as part of its content, an excitation of the "motor-centres" actually concerned in running; it would seem as if this excitation must involve some, however slight, innervation of the peripheral apparatus involved in the act.[24] What ground is there for supposing that the idea comes to consciousness save through the sensorial return of this peripheral excitation? Is there any conceivable statement, either in terms of introspection or of nervous structure, of an idea of movement coming to consciousness absolutely unmediated peripherally? Sensorial consciousness, mediated by the incoming current, is an undoubted fact; it is *vera causa*. Putting the two hypotheses side by side simply as hypotheses, surely the logical advantage of economy and of appeal to *vera causa* is on the side of the theory which conceives the idea of movement in terms of a return of discharge wave, and against that which would make it a purely central affair.[25]

---

[24]   I do not mean that this innervation comes to consciousness as such; on the contrary.

[25]   There are further logical grounds for expecting acquiescence from those who accept the general standpoint of Mr. James. To say nothing of the insistence upon consciousness as essentially reactive or motor, "idea" and emotional seizure hang together. Fear-of-bear, bear-as-fearful-object cannot be separated. Besides, when I introspect for my "fringe" in the stream of thought I always find its particular sensorial basis in shiftings of directions and quantity of breath, and other slight adjustments, just as certainly as I always can pick out the sensorial basis for my emotional

But this is far from being all. I suppose one is fairly entitled now to start from the assumption of a sensory-continuum, the "big, buzzing, blooming confusion," out of which particular sensory quales are differentiated. Discrimination, not integration, is the real problem. In a general way we all admit that it is through attention that the distinctions arise, through selective emphasis. Now we may not only rely upon the growing feeling that attention is somehow bound up with motor adjustment and reaction, but we can point to the specific facts of sensorial discrimination which show, that, as a matter of fact, the range and fineness of discrimination run parallel to the apparatus for motor adjustments. We can also show that, in the only case in which there has, as yet, been a serious attempt to work out the details of discrimination, namely, space distinctions, all hands agree that they come through motor adjustments—the question whether "muscular" or joint surface sensations are primary, having here no importance. Such being the case, how can the particular stimulus which excites the discharge be defined as *this* or *that* object apart from our reaction to it? I do not care to go into the metaphysics of objective qualities, but dealing simply with the psychological recognition of such qualities, what basis or standard for qualitative definiteness can we have, save the consciousness of differences in our own organic response? The bear may be a thousand times an individual entity or distinct object metaphysically, if you please; you may even suppose, if you will, that the particular wave-lengths which deflect from the bear, somehow sort themselves out from the wave-lengths coming from all the rest of the environment, and come to the brain as a distinct bundle or package by themselves—but the recognition of just *this* object out of the multitude of possible objects, of just this bundle of vibrations out of all the other bundles, still remains to be accounted for. The predominating motor response supplies the conditions for its objectification, or selection. There is no competing hypothesis of any other machinery even in the field.

---

seizures. *A priori*, it is difficult to see what the "fringe" can be save the feeling of the running accompaniment of aborted acts, having their value now only as signs or cues, but originally complete in themselves.

We return, then, confirmed, to our belief that the mode of behavior, or co-ordination of activities, constitutes the ideal content of emotion just as much as it does the *Affect* or "feel," and that the distinction of these two is not given in the experience itself, but simply in reflection upon the experience. The mode of action constituted by the organic co-ordination of certain sensori-motor (or ideo-motor) activities, on one side, and of certain vegetative-motor activities on the other, is the reality, and this reality has a value, which, when interpreted, we call intellectual, and a value which, when interpreted we call Affect, or "feel." In the terms of our illustration, the mode of behavior carried with it the concept of the bear as a thing to be acted towards in a certain way, and of the "feel" of our reaction. It is brown and chained—a "beautiful" object to be looked at. It is soft and fluffy—an "æsthetic" object to be felt of. It is tame and clumsy—an "amusing" object to while away time with. It is hungry and angry—and is a "ferocious" object to be fled. The consciousness of our mode of behavior as affording data for other possible actions constitutes the bear an objective or ideal content. The consciousness of the mode of behavior as something in itself—the looking, petting, running, etc.—constitutes the emotional seizure. In all concrete experience of emotion these two phases are organically united in a single pulse of consciousness.

It follows from this that all emotion, as excitation, involves inhibition. This is not absolute inhibition; it is not suppression or displacement. It is incidental to the co-ordination. The two factors of the co-ordination, the "exciting stimulus" and the excited response, have to be adjusted, and the period of adjustment required to affect the co-ordination, marks the inhibition of each required to effect its reconstruction as an integral part of the whole act. Or, since we have recognized that the exciting stimulus does not exist as fact, or object, until constituted such by the co-ordination in the final act, let us say that the activities needing adjustment, and so partial inhibition, are the kinæsthetic (sensori-motor or ideo-motor) activities which translate themselves into the "object," and the vegetative-motor activities which constitute the "reaction" or "response" to the "object."

But here, again, in order to avoid getting on the wrong track it must be noted that this distinction of "object" and "response" is one of interpretation, or value, and not a plain matter of course difference in the experiencing. I have already tried to show that the "object" itself is an organic excitation on the sensori-motor, or, mediately, ideo-motor side, and that it is not *the* peculiar object *of* the emotion until the mode of behavior sets in, and the diffusive wave repercussates in consciousness. But it is equally necessary to recognize that the very distinction between exciting or stimulating sensori-motor activity and excited or responding vegetative-motor activity is teleological and not merely factual. It is because these two activities have to be co-ordinated in a single act, to accomplish a single end, and have therefore to be so adjusted as to co-operate with each other, that they present themselves as stimulus and response. When we consider one activity, say the sensori-ideo-motor activity, which constructs or constitutes the bear as an "object," not in itself, but from the standpoint of the final act into which it merges—the stopping to look at the bear and study it scientifically, or enjoy its clumsy movements—that activity takes the form of stimulus. So the vegetative-motor activity, which is, in itself as direct experience, simply the intrinsic organic continuation of the sensori-motor activity, being interpreted again as a reduced factor of, or contribution to, the final outcome, assumes the form of response. But, I repeat, this distinction of stimulus and response is one of interpretation, and of interpretation from the standpoint of the value of some act considered as an accomplished end.

The positive truth is that the prior and the succeeding parts of an activity are in operation together; that the prior activity beside passing over into the succeeding also persists by itself, and yet that the necessary act cannot be performed until these two activities reinforce each other, or become contributing factors to a unified deed. The period of maximum emotional seizure corresponds to this period of adjustment. If we look at the deflection or reconstruction which either side undergoes during this adjustment, we shall call it inhibition—it is arrest of discharge which the activity would perform, if existing by itself. If we look at the final outcome, the completed adjustment, we have co-ordination.

I think it must be obvious that this account in no way
runs athwart Mr. James's denial of inhibition as a necessary
phase of the *Affect* (*Psychology*, ii, 476, note). He there
speaks of inhibition as if it could mean only complete suppression—which is no inhibition at all, psychologically, since
with suppression or displacement, all tension vanishes. It is,
indeed, a question of primary impulsive tendencies, but of
these tendencies as conflicting with one another and therefore mutually checking, at least temporarily, one another.
Acts, which in past times, have been *complete* activities, now
present themselves as contemporaneous phases of one activity. In so far as they were once each complete in itself,
there is struggle of each to absorb or negate the other. This
must either occur or else there is a readjustment and a new
whole, or co-ordination, appears, they now being contributory factors. The inhibition once worked out, whether by displacement of one or by reconstruction of both contending
factors, the *Affect* dies out.

This sort of inhibition the James theory not only permits, but demands—otherwise the whole relation between
the exciting stimulus and the instinctive response, which is
the nerve of the theory, disappears. If the exciting stimulus
does not persist over into the excited response, we get simply
a case of habit. The familiar fact that emotion as excitement
disappears with definiteness of habit simply means that in so
far as one activity serves *simply* as means, or cue, to another
and gives way at once to it, there is no basis for conflict and
for inhibition. But if the stimulating and the induced activities need to be co-ordinated together, if they are both means
contributing to one and the same end, then the conditions
for mere habit are denied, and some struggle, with incidental
inhibitory deflection of the immediate activity, sets in. In
psychological terms, this tension is always between the
activity which constitutes, when interpreted, the object as
an intellectual content, and that which constitutes the response or mode of dealing with it. There is the one phase
of organic activity which constitutes the bear as object;
there is the other which would attack it, or run away from
it, or stand one's ground before it. If these two co-ordinate
without friction, or if one immediately displaces the other,

there is no emotional seizure. If they co-exist, both pulling apart as complete in themselves and pulling together as parts of a new whole, there is great emotional excitement.[26] It is this tension which makes it impossible to describe any emotion whatever without using dual terms—one for the *Affect* itself, the other for the object "at," "towards," or "on account of," which it is.

We may now connect this analysis with the result of the consideration of the emotional attitudes. The attitude is precisely that which was a complete activity once, but is no longer so. The activity of seizing prey or attacking an enemy, a movement having its meaning in itself, is now reduced or aborted; it is an attitude simply. As an instinctive reaction it is thoroughly ingrained in the system; it represents the actual co-ordinations of thousands and thousands of ancestors; it tends to start into action, therefore, whenever its associated stimulus occurs. But the very fact that it is now reduced to an attitude or tendency, the very fact that it is now *relatively* easy to learn to control the instinctive blind reaction when we are stimulated in a certain way, shows that the primary activity is inhibited; it no longer exists as a whole by itself, but simply as a co-ordinated phase, or a contributory means, in a larger activity. There is no reason to suppose that the original activity of attack or seizure was emotional, or had any *quale* attached to it such as we now term "anger." The animal of our ancestor so far as it was given up without restraint to the full activity undoubtedly had a feeling of activity; but just because the activity was undivided, it was not "emotion"; it was not "at," or "towards" an object held in tension against itself. This division could come in only when there was a need of co-ordinating the activity which corresponded to the perception and that

---

[26]   See James, *Psychology*, II, 496–97. But more particularly I should apply to the difference between relatively indifferent and emotionally excited consciousness precisely what James says of the difference between habitual and reasoned thinking (II, 366). "In the former, an entire system of cells vibrating at any one moment discharges in its totality into another system, the order of the discharges tends to be a constant one in time; whilst in the latter a part of the prior system still keeps vibrating in the midst of the subsequent system, and the order . . . has little tendency to fixedness in time." Add to this that it is necessary to perform a unified act—or reconstitute a single, comprehensive system, and the reality (though strictly incidental character) of inhibition appears.

which corresponded to the fighting, as means to an activity which was neither perceiving nor fighting. The animal growling and lashing its tail as it *waits* to fight may have an emotional consciousness, but even here, there may be, for all we know, simply a unified consciousness, a complete concentration on the act of maintaining that posture, the act of waiting being the *adequate* response to the given stimulus. Certainly,[27] so far as I can trust my own introspection, whenever my anger or any strong emotion has gained complete possession of me, the peculiar *Affect quale* has disappeared. I remember well a youthful fight, with the emotions of irritation and anger before, and of partial fear and partial pride afterwards, but as to the intervening period of the fight nothing but a strangely vivid perception of the other boy's face as the hypnotizing focus of all my muscular activities. On the other side, my most intense and vengeful feelings of anger are associated with cases where my whole body was so sat on as to prevent the normal reaction. Every one knows how the smart and burn of the feeling of injustice increases with the feeling of impotency; it is, for example, when strikes are beginning to fail that violence from anger or revenge, as distinct from sheer criminality, sets in. It is a common-place that the busy philanthropist has no occasion to feel the extreme emotion of pathos which the spectator or reader of literature feels. Cases might be multiplied ad libitum.

It is then in the reduction of activities once performed

[27]   I have no intention here of constructing, *a priori*, the animal consciousness. I use this merely as hypothetical illustration; *if* unification of activity, then no emotion; *if* emotion, then tension of intellectual recognition on one side and consideration of how to behave towards object recognized on the other. I must add, however, that such interpretations as Darwin's umbrella case (in his *Descent of Man*), as illustrating a rude sense of the supernatural, seem to me most unwarrantably anthropomorphic. Surely, the only straightforward interpretation is, there was interruption of a reaction which had started to discharge, and that such a change in stimulus suddenly set up another discharge totally at crosspurposes with the first, thus disintegrating the animal's co-ordinations for a moment. Unless the animal recognizes or objectifies the familiar reaction, and recognizes also the unexpected reaction in such a way that there tension arises between the two, there can be no *emotion* in the animal, but simply a shock of interrupted activity—the sort of fit which James speaks of, *Psychology*, II, 420. It may well be that the feeling of the supernatural in man, however, *is* precisely the feeling of such tension —instead of there being an idea of the supernatural, and then an associated feeling of terror towards it.

for their own sake, to attitudes now useful simply as supplying a contributory, a reinforcing or checking factor, in some
more comprehensive activity, that we have all the conditions for high emotional disturbance. The tendency to large
diffusive waves of discharge is present, and the inhibition of
this outgoing activity through some perception or idea is also
present. The need of somehow reaching an adjustment of
these two sides is urgent. The attitude stands for a recapitu-
lation of thousands of acts formerly done, ends formerly
reached; the perception or idea stands for multitudes of acts
which may be done, ends which may be acted upon. But the
immediate and present need is to get this attitude of anger
which reflects the former act of seizing into some connection
with the act of getting-even or of moral control, or whatever
the idea may be. The conflict and competition, with incidental inhibition and deflection, is the disturbance of the
emotional seizure.

Upon this basis, the apparent strangeness or absurdity
in the fact that a mere organic repercussation should have
such tremendous values in consciousness disappears. This
organic return of the discharge wave stands for the entire effort of the organism to adjust its formed habits or co-
ordinations of the past to present necessities as made known
in perception or idea. The emotion is, *psychologically, the
adjustment or tension of habit and ideal*, and the organic
changes in the body are the literal working out, in concrete
terms, of the struggle of adjustment. We may recall once
more the three main phases presented in this adjustment as
now giving us the basis of the classification of the emotions.
There may be a failure to adjust the vegetative-motor function, the habit, to the sensori-(or ideo-)motor; there may
be the effort, or there may be the success. The effort, moreover, also has a double form according as the attempt is in
the main so to use the formed reactions as to avoid or exclude the idea or object, setting up another in its place, or to
incorporate and assimilate it—*e.g.*, terror and anger, dread
and hope, regret and complacency, etc.[28]

[28]   Because of the tension, however, these cannot be set over against
each other absolutely. All terror, till it passes into pathological fright,
involves anger, and anger some fear, etc. All moral experience is only

I shall not carry out this classification; but further suggest that, in my judgment, we now have the means for discriminating emotion as *Gefühlston*, as emotional disturbance, or *Affect* (with which we have been dealing so far) and as interest.

Interest is the feeling which arises with the completed co-ordination. Let the tension solve itself by successive displacements in time, *i.e.*, means assuming a purely serial form in which one stimulates the next, and we get the indifference of routine. But let the various means succeed in organizing themselves into a simultaneous comprehensive whole of action, and we have interest. All interest, *qua* interest, it would follow from this, is qualitatively alike, being differentiated simply by the idea to which it attaches. And experience seems to verify this inference. Interest is undisturbed action, absorbing action, unified action, and all interests, *as interests*, are equally interesting. The collection of postage stamps is as absorbing, if it *is* absorbing or an interest, as the discovery of double-stars; and the figuring of indefinite columns of statistics as the discovery of the nature of sympathy. Nor is this a pathological principle, as it might seem to be were we to instance merely fads or hobbies. The multiplicity of deeds which demand doing in this world is too great to be numbered; that principle which secures that if only full or organic activity go into each end, each act shall equally satisfy in its time and place, is the highest ethical principle; it is the statement of the only religious emotional experience which really seems worth while —the sense of the validity of all necessary doing. I cannot dwell upon this matter of interest, but I suggest the case of purely scientific interest as crucial. On one side, it seems wholly unemotional, so free from all disturbance or excita-

---

too full of the subtle and deceiving ways in which regret (condemnation) and complacency (self-approbation) run into each other. There is the Pharisee who can maintain his sense of his own goodness only by tension with his thought of evil; or who can make his depth of remorse material for self-gratulation. And there is the sentimental selfish character which disguises its own disgrace from itself by emotional recognitions of the beauty of goodness, and of its own misfortunes in not being able, in the past, to satisfy this ideal. I have never known other such touching tributes to goodness as can proceed from the sentimental egoist, when he gets into "trouble," as he euphemistically terms it.

tion may it become; on the other, it represents a culmination of absorption, of concentrated attention. How this apparent paradox is to be dealt with save on the supposition that emotion (as *Affect*) is the feeling of tension in action, while interest is the feeling of a complex of relevant activity unified in a single channel of discharge, I do not see.

As for the *Gefühlston*, I shall only state the conclusion that would seem to follow from a thorough-going application of the principle already laid down. I do not know that this complete application is advisable, much less necessary, but I share somewhat in the feeling of Mr. Baldwin as expressed in the November number (p. 617) of this *Review*, that there is a presumption that a unitary principle holds all the way through.[29] At all events, those who have followed me so far may like to see how the hypothesis already propounded might conceivably apply to the case of, say, delight in certain tones, colors or tastes, while those who do not accept the hypothesis will hardly be shocked at one absurdity the more.

The suggestion, then, is that the *Gefühlston* represents the complete consolidation of a large number of achieved ends into the organic habit or co-ordination. It is interest read backwards. That represents the complete identification of the habits with a certain end or aim. The tone of sense-feeling represents the reaction, the incorporate identification, of the successful ends into the working habit. It is not, as I have hitherto indicated, habit as habit which becomes feelingless; it is only the habit which serves as mere means, or serial stimulus. That a given co-ordination should assume into itself the value of all associated co-ordinations is a fact of every day experience. Our eye-consciousness takes up into itself the value of countless motor and touch experiences; our ear takes up the value of motor and visual experiences, etc. There is no apparent reason why this vicarious assumption should not become so organically registered—

---

[29] It hardly seems fair, though, to charge Mr. James with inconsistency because he declines to force his theory beyond the limits of the facts upon which he feels himself to have a sure hold. Surely we may admire this reserve, even if we cannot imitate it, instead of virtually accusing him of giving away his whole case by admitting, hypothetically, the existence of facts whose explanation would require an opposite principle.

pace Weismann—as to become hereditary; and become more and more functionally incorporated into structure.

To sum up:—Certain movements, formerly useful in themselves, become reduced to tendencies to action, to attitudes. As such they serve, when instinctively aroused into action, as means for realizing ends. But so far as there is difficulty in adjusting the organic activity represented by the attitude with that which stands for the idea or end, there is temporary struggle and partial inhibition. This is reported as *Affect*, or emotional seizure. Let the co-ordination be effected in one act, instead of in a successive series of mutually exclusive stimuli, and we have interest. Let such co-ordinations become thoroughly habitual and hereditary, and we have *Gefühlston*.

Reviews

A History of Æsthetic, by Bernard Bosanquet, formerly
    Fellow of University College, Oxford. London:
    Swan Sonnenschein and Co.; New York: Mac-
    millan Co., 1892.

The third volume of the important international
Library of Philosophy, under the editorship of Mr. J. H.
Muirhead, should, for many reasons, be of a character to
command attention. It is the first volume in the series by an
Englishman; it represents a branch of philosophy within
which English philosophical literature is most deficient, and
it comes at a time when reflection is awakening to the profound importance of art as a subject-matter for philosophy
— when, indeed, it seems likely to divide with psychology
the interest of the immediate future. We may congratulate
ourselves upon having a volume so nearly adequate to its
occasion. Mr. Bosanquet has written neither a history of
æsthetic speculation in its most technical sense, nor has he
fallen into the opposite mistake and given us a history of
the details of the concrete arts. The plan of writing the
history of "the æsthetic *consciousness* in its intellectual
form of æsthetic theory, but never forgetting that the central matter to be elucidated is the value of beauty for human life, no less as implied in practice than as explicitly
recognized in reflection," Mr. Bosanquet has carried out in
such a way that his volume unites a philosophic continuity of
thought with something of the wealth of actual art. I mention this point at the outset, for the characteristic trait of the
work before us seems to me the successful way in which

[*First published in* Philosophical Review, II (*Jan. 1893*), 63–69.
Not previously reprinted.]

Mr. Bosanquet has combined the use of certain philosophic
ideas as tools to bring unity and orderly development into
the discrete and tangled mass of æsthetic speculation with a
certain maturity of judgment about concrete facts. The book
carries with itself as its atmosphere ripeness and soundness
of incidental remark. Although, for example, Mr. Bosanquet
in his Preface especially denies any large firsthand acquaintance with mediæval thought, I cannot but think that the
student of general history as well as of æsthetic theory, will
find what is said upon this subject lingering fruitfully in
memory.

Mr. Bosanquet's definition of art is so important as
controlling his whole treatment of the historic development
of æsthetics that it must be fully reported. He gets his definition by comparing the Greek conception of beauty with that
most characteristic of modern thought. Among the ancients
the emphasis was laid upon the formal or logical traits:
upon rhythm, symmetry, harmony, in short, upon the
general formula of unity in variety. The modern way of
looking at it thinks rather of meaning, of expressiveness,
"the utterance of all that life contains." The contrast gives
not only the conditions for a complete definition, but suggests the lines for the historical discussion. The resulting
definition is that beauty is characteristic or individual expressiveness for the imagination, subject to the conditions of
expressiveness within the same medium. The historical
record evidently consists in tracing the steps by which the
more formal conception of the ancients was broadened to
include, under the notion of characteristic, material which
both the ancient theory and practice would have excluded as
beyond the range of the beautiful. Because of this method
Mr. Bosanquet devotes much attention to the æsthetics of
the ugly and the sublime, as they gradually emerge in
historic reflection, since the consideration of these topics
marks a widening horizon in conceiving of beauty. The important problem of the relation of beauty to the feeling of
pleasure Mr. Bosanquet disposes of, by saying that we must
have some generic conception of what beauty is before we
have any differentia for marking off æsthetic pleasure from
any other kind of pleasure; as such differentia he suggests

"pleasure in the nature of a feeling or presentation, as distinct from pleasure in its momentary stimulation of the organism." The equally important question of the limitation of beauty to art to the exclusion of nature is disposed of by showing that the beauty of art does not exclude that of nature; any natural product in so far as it is viewed as beautiful becomes, for the time being at least, artistic. "Nature for æsthetic theory means that province of art in which every man is his own artist."

Mr. Bosanquet, as it seems to me, shows good judgment in making his discussion of ancient theory turn about the fact which has perplexed every student of ancient thought,—the seeming paradox that the Hellenic nation, the most artistic in the world in its practice, should in its theory, as seen in Plato and Aristotle, either have taken a hostile attitude to art or adopted a theory—that of imitation—which reduces the meaning of art to a minimum.[1] According to Mr. Bosanquet this attitude is due to a subordination, among the Greeks, of strictly æsthetic considerations to metaphysical and moralistic assumptions. The metaphysical assumption, almost inevitable to the period of transition from artistic production to that of reflection upon the products of art, was that artistic representation is no more than a kind of commonplace reality, related to the purposes of man precisely as everyday objects are related, except that the existence of the work of art is less complete and solid. Hence the essence of art was conceived, not as symbolic of an unseen reality behind the common object, but as merely imitative of the common object. This being premised, the moralistic assumption at once follows: to represent an immoral content is just to duplicate the instances of immorality and the temptations to it. In the region of *specific* æsthetic criticism the Greeks contributed, and Aristotle in particular worked out into some detail the idea already referred to—that of unity in variety, or the relation of the part to the whole. The

[1]   It may be noted here that Mr. Bosanquet makes no reference to that interpretation of Aristotle according to which "limitation" is not of any given product, but rather of the process by which the thing is originally brought into existence. Upon such a theory, imitation becomes re-creation (or reproduction), and the apparent discrepancy is very largely covered.

metaphysics of art has a value partly negative and partly positive; positively, Plato and Aristotle contributed the necessary basis of all æsthetics in the conception that art deals with images and not with realities. Negatively they furnished a *reductio ad absurdum* of the imitation theory. Plato's discussion might be summarized, "*So far* as this is the true explanation of art, art has not the value popularly assigned to it."

I must omit all that is said of the details of Plato and Aristotle as well as of the Græco-Roman period (although this latter well illustrates what I have said regarding Mr. Bosanquet's cultured judgment) and come to Plotinus, in whom Mr. Bosanquet finds the first important theoretical reconstruction of the Platonic conception. While Plotinus still retains the conception of a spiritual or immaterial beauty, he admits a true natural beauty produced by participation of the material thing in the reason which emanates from the divine. Thus he defines art as following not visible things directly, but rather the reasons from which visible things proceed. This same theory, by carrying beauty back of merely formal and surface traits, also broke the tradition which limited beauty to symmetry, and gave a chance for theories which made something more vital of it.

The development of Christian thought with relation to æsthetics connects itself naturally, and perhaps historically, with the ideas of Plotinus. Corporeal objects were conceived as signs or even as counterparts of spiritual realities. Such a theory may be turned in either of two ways, according as either the likeness or the unlikeness involved in the idea of symbolism is emphasized. In the early church there was a profound sense of the unity of man with the world, of spirit with nature. The result was an increasing sense of the beauty of nature. But even at the first, there was a tendency to accompany this with a depreciation of the worth of man and his products. As time went on and the sense of the infinite value of the spiritual world deepened, this tendency grew into a belief in the impossibility of any adequate conveyance of spiritual things through sense symbols, and Christianity assumed a hostile attitude to the whole region of pictorial art. Erigena sums up the outcome in his theory, that man has no right to take delight in the visible creation, save as one has already learned of the perfections of God and then goes to nature as showing forth his praises. An interesting comparison of Dante and Shakespeare makes the transition from the mediæval to the modern consciousness. Dante with his subordination of this world to the next, with his allegorical element resting upon the subordination of perceptible forms to a hierarchy of ethical interpretations, completes the mediæval position. Shakespeare gives us the net result of the immense spiritual value added to life through Christianity, but without the supernatural machinery so superbly manipulated by Dante.

The origins of modern æsthetic Mr. Bosanquet finds in the mingling of two streams—criticism and metaphysic. Criticism from Sidney and Scaliger to Lessing and Winckelmann, furnished æsthetic philosophy with its *data*: metaphysic from Descartes to Kant with postulate and *problem*. At first each of these streams worked in entire independence, therefore, during this time, there is no true æsthetic. Each side had both to adjust itself to theories and problems bequeathed from antiquity, and to absorb the great practical wealth of the immediate past. Since, as Mr. Bosanquet remarks, pre-Kantian æsthetic is not the generating cause of later æsthetic theory, but only an external attribute of the movement which was such cause, I omit his discussion of the metaphysic. In the chapter upon the data of modern æsthetic, we have a pretty full statement of the influence of the growth of philology and archæology upon æsthetic, as well as something concerning the distinctively critical writers. Although Corneille, Voltaire, Burke, and Gottsched, besides minor critics, as well as Lessing and Winckelmann, are taken up, I cannot but feel that, upon the whole, this chapter is the most deficient of any in the book. Nothing is said of the early Italian writers, although they were not only the first to reintroduce Aristotelian canons and methods, but to write specific critical treatises. It is now well enough established that the true source of the Elizabethan criticism is in Italy. Diderot has hardly more than a passing remark, while of Rousseau the saying of Amiel that "nobody has had more influence on the nineteenth century" is quoted, but the extended discussion such a statement calls for, is conspicuously absent. The proper notice of the Italian writers would, I feel sure, have supplied the thread of continuity which seems to be snapped at this point; while Rousseau, here as in his social speculation, is *the* connecting link between the popular and practical tendencies of the eighteenth century, and the distinctly reflective treatment of the nineteenth. Only an academic superstition seems to me to account for giving to Lessing a more important place than belongs to Rousseau.

In Kant, Schiller, and Goethe, or rather *through* them, the data of æsthetic were brought face to face with the metaphysical problem, and the union of Kant's abstract æsthetic with the appreciation of art as an expression of the human spirit, sharing its development, gave rise to modern concrete theory. This highly abstract summary introduces us to that portion of Mr. Bosanquet's work which by its very familiarity and present interest is most difficult to reproduce in a review. I can only call attention to a few of its salient features. In the first place the general method of treatment cannot be too highly commended. After an excellent account of the *Critique of Judgment* in its æsthetic part, Mr. Bosanquet goes on to Schiller and Goethe. He shows how Schiller being interested in the same problem from æsthetic reasons that appealed to Kant from metaphysical reasons, went on to remove the essential limitation of Kant, and thus opened the way for a further development in metaphysics as well as in æsthetic and concrete criticism. Certainly one of our greatest needs at present is a closer connection between what is now relegated on one side to technical histories of philosophy, and on the other to histories of literature and general "culture." The need is equally pressing in order to save the human and practical interest of the history of philosophy, now tending under the influence of floods of monographs to degenerate into purely "scientific" material divorced from human life, and to save histories of literature from a sentimental character, because of their divorce from the main current of the intellectual development of humanity. It is not too much to say that Mr. Bosanquet in his alignment of Kant, Schiller, Goethe, and Hegel, has done more than any

English writer to put these matters on their right footing. Were it not for the inexplicable omission of Herder's name, this statement could be broadened still further. In the second place, I wish to call particular attention to Mr. Bosanquet's conception of idealism, since the detail of his treatment is obviously controlled by his general agreement with the positions of objective idealism. "The central principle of idealism is that nothing can be made into what it is not capable of being. Therefore when certain syntheses and developments are actual, it is idle to deny that they are objective or immanent in the nature of the parts developed." Or, if I may venture to enlarge upon the definition, when it is shown that beauty or morality are products of a purely "natural" development, their reality is in nowise impugned; the reality is neither in the first state merely as such, nor in the latter in its isolation, but in the law or movement which holds all in one unity. Finally the terms with which the specific problem common to both metaphysic and æsthetic may be expressed, are how to reconcile feeling and reason; how sense material may be pregnant with meaning—this problem being first a practical one and only afterwards a theoretical one.

Mr. Bosanquet treats the æsthetic of the nineteenth century under three rubrics: first there is a chapter devoted to "exact æsthetic," understanding by this an attempt to get at the formal features which constitute any object beautiful. This chapter includes writers seemingly as diverse as Schopenhauer and Stumpf, Herbart and Fechner. Then comes a chapter dealing, under the caption of "Methodical Completion of Objective Idealism," with such authors as Rosenkranz, Schasler (to whom an amount of space is given seemingly disproportionate to his real importance), and Hartmann. The concluding chapter is upon recent English æsthetic, and is occupied largely with Ruskin and Morris. The general significance of this movement is found to be in an attempt to get a better conception of how in the work of art the content and expression are united, in a return to life as the real medium, for German æsthetic has in its later days fallen into scholasticism, over-refinement, and formalism through the touch of life. The signs of this return to life are found in Mr. Ruskin's study of the details of the beautiful in nature as against the more general formulations of the Germans, and in both Ruskin's and Morris's insistence upon the place of the individual workman in all art, the necessity that art be a genuine expression of the joy of the worker in his work, and the consequent greater attention to the minor arts, so-called.

It is significant that Mr. Bosanquet expects the next fruitful movement to come from England rather than from Germany. "As the true value of German idealism in general philosophy was never understood till the genius of English naturalists had revolutionized our conception of the organic world, so the spirit of German æsthetic will not be appreciated until the work of its founders shall have been renewed by the direct appreciative sense of English art and criticism."

There are a number of points in the implied or expressed philosophy of the book which I should like to see developed by themselves. The entire conception, for example, of a fixed distinction between the realm of art and that of commonplace reality seems to me to need a good deal of explanation. That there is such a distinction there can be of course no doubt, but Mr. Bosanquet makes something positive and rigid of the distinction; he makes it a datum which can be used in marking off regions of experience and deciding questions. I should have thought, on the contrary, that the distinction was a problem and a problem lying at the very heart of æsthetic. Instead of accounting for Plato's treatment of art by saying that he failed to distinguish between common reality and the artistic image, it seems to me more philosophical as well as more historical to say that man was then becoming conscious of ideas (principles of action) wider than those expressed in previous civilization; ideas demanding therefore new forms of embodiment and calling for new art, ideas which since they had not found embodiment for themselves appeared at the time to be hostile to all embodiment and thus to all art. The growing up of this distinction between commonplace reality and art seems to be due to just those historical periods when man has become aware of new principles of action just enough to condemn old action, but not sufficiently to secure expression for them. Commonplace reality, in other words, is simply the material which art has not yet conquered, which has not yet become a plastic medium of expression. Such a conception, indeed, is in line with Mr. Bosanquet's remarks about the future of art, when he says that in spite of the present apparent interruption of the art tradition, in spite of the fact that the discord of life has now cut deeper than ever before, we may feel sure that the human mind will find a way to resolve this discord and "the way to satisfy its imperious need for beauty." Two conceptions of art, finally, seem to be struggling with each other throughout Mr. Bosanquet's history: one of art as essentially a form of symbolism, the other of art as the expression of life in its entire range. The former can be reconciled with Mr. Bosanquet's fundamental philosophy only by a great stretch of the idea of symbolism; it agrees, however, with the fixed distinction between commonplace reality and artistic reality, and at once lends itself to a conception of art which marks it off into a little realm by itself. The conception of art as expression of life leaves no room for any such division. Art becomes one with fulness of life. As Emerson says, "There is higher work for Art than the arts. . . . No less than the creation of man and nature is its end."

"On Certain Psychological Aspects of Moral Training," by Josiah Royce, *International Journal of Ethics*, III (July 1893), 413–36; "Moral Deficiencies as Determining Intellectual Functions," by Georg Simmel, *International Journal of Ethics*, III (July 1893), 490–507; "The Knowledge of Good and Evil," by Josiah Royce, *International Journal of Ethics*, IV (Oct. 1893), 48–80.

The problem proposed by Dr. Royce is to discover the mental factors, or the psychological side, of the fact ethically called conscience; to show, so far as psychology is concerned, why we have a sense that conscience is immutable and au-

[*First published in* Psychological Review, I (*Jan. 1894*), *109–11.*
Not previously reprinted.]

thoritative, while, at the same time, it is historically fallible and variable. The judgments of conscience reduce themselves to two types: one advises sympathy, devotion to a will beyond one's own; the other, justice, reasonableness, the regulation of life according to a consistent plan. Morality is the complete union of these two principles, and comes into play when these motives conflict either with opposing forces or with one another. Conscience, as thus defined, is our awareness of certain fundamental psychological tendencies —the tendency to imitate, leading to sympathy, and the tendency to form fixed habits, leading to regularity and consistency of conduct. The authoritative nature of conscience, its innate character, is due to the radical nature of these instincts. Its fallibility, its origin in experience, is due to conflict between these tendencies. Our imitativeness, our social suggestibility, act immediately, giving us generous impulses, but always tend to confuse our general plans. Our fixed habits, on the contrary, lend themselves to generality, but tend to become so fixed as to make us unmindful of the calls of sympathy.

The moral bearings of the discussion lie, of course, outside our scope. The psychological identification of imitation with immediacy of action, and of habits with reasonableness of action, seems to me, however, very questionable. Habit, as such, (apart from a need of changing it) is, upon the whole, opposed to conscious reflection; and one could make out a very fair case for the hypothesis that imitation is one form of the law of habit, instead of a principle opposed to it. Dr. Royce, to be sure, makes much of the element of conflict, but only as affecting the ethical value, not as having an intrinsic psychological significance.

Simmel's extremely acute essay falls within our range so far only as it deals with the psychological and anthropological relation existing between knowledge and intellectual acuteness on one side, and activity denominated moral on the other. It is noteworthy for maintaining the anti-Socratic paradox that immorality is important to intellectual development in certain directions. It is a fundamental principle of modern psychology that an idea of an act is the first inclination to its execution; that, indeed, there is an organic psycho-physical connection between a conception of an act and its performance. This granted, it follows that complete recognition of the act can be had only by following the idea to its consummation—that the act *is* the idea consummated. Hence immoral acts are the condition of our comprehension of immorality; the reproduction of the evil passion the only way to know it. This general principle is reinforced by considerations from criminal anthropology—the immoral man swims against the stream, and, hence, requires more strength, acuteness, etc., to succeed. Through lying, the mind grows wary, comprehensive, delicate and strong, acquires a good memory, quickness of invention, power of imagination, etc. A third psychological connection is found in the relation of the emotions to knowledge. Morality requires interest, sympathy with subject-matter; science requires indifference, approaching hard-heartedness—*e.g.*, vivisection. Development of æsthetic power, regard for the picturesque, etc., requires also quiescence of altruistic emotions.

Dr. Royce's second article (considering the same problem as the foregoing, and, in part, a reply to it) attempts to reduce the apparent conflict between the demands of morality and those of intellectual progress to one special case of a more general law, psychological and even biological in character. This law is that every organic process is the combination in harmony of opposing tendencies: living tissue involves, as part of its own activity, phenomena which by themselves would mean death; every voluntary movement, action on the part of antagonist muscles; every nervous stimulation a corresponding inhibition; every virtuous act a known tendency to evil. In each case, the organic activity involves the reduction of an opposing tendency to a contributing factor in the activity itself. Applying this to the paradox of Simmel, it follows (1) that knowledge of evil does not require the actual evil-doing, but simply the presence of an evil tendency; and (2) that there is deep insight into the nature of the evil deed only so far as it is transcended; this being, apparently, a special case of the general law that we do not truly know any activity as long as we remain in it, but only when, by getting beyond it, we are able to turn back on it as an "object" of reflection.[1] The same principle is involved in the fact that the attainment of virtue involves a constant approach to a condition where evil motives have no force and are ignored. Here the question is as to the relation of habit and consciousness. We are completely conscious only when the function concerned is learning, only when it is novel; mastered, or become habitual, it passes into unconsciousness. We cannot affirm from this, however, that consciousness is aiming at its own absolute extinction, for this unconscious function is the instrument for mastering wider situations and thus subserves a wider consciousness.

Dr. Royce would have made his case still stronger, psychologically, it seems to me, if he had not admitted that the evil tendency is evil *per se*. It is difficult to see how any organic process can be bad in and of itself. It is *in* entering into a larger activity, of which, therefore, it must become an inhibited factor, that it becomes bad as it would be in itself. Instead, then, of saying with Simmel that only the bad man can know evil, it is a psychological necessity to say that only the good man can know it—know it, that is, as evil.

The Psychic Factors of Civilization, by Lester F. Ward. Boston: Ginn and Co., 1893; *Social Evolution*, by Benjamin Kidd. New York and London: Macmillan Co., 1894; *Civilization during the Middle Ages*, by George B. Adams. New York: Charles Scribner's Sons, 1894; and *History of the Philosophy of History*, by Robert Flint. New York: Charles Scribner's Sons, 1894.

An attempt to state the foundations of a sociology definitely based upon psychological methods and data has an interest for psychologists quite independent of its worth

---

[1]   I say apparently, because, while this is implied, I do not quite know whether Dr. Royce expressly means it.

[*First published in* Psychological Review, 1 (*July 1894*), 400–411. *Not previously reprinted.*]

for students in the social field. This interest is a double one: it is worth while to see what sort of psychological ideas are used to lay the basis of another science, and it is worth while to note the reaction of their social application upon the ideas themselves—to note, that is, how psychological ideas look when handled by one whose chief interest is in their efficiency to explain the development of social life. Accordingly I shall consider Mr. Ward's work on both sides: how in his essay psychology contributes to sociology, and how sociology in his hands supplies valuable data to the psychologist. And if I am led to the conclusion that Mr. Ward gives back considerably more to the psychologist than he succeeds in borrowing from him, the conclusion only adds to the psychologist's interest in the work, however it may square with Mr. Ward's intention.

There are two questions of paramount interest in sociology: one, the question of the nature of the social forces; the other, the question of their control. As it happens, both of these questions are psychical questions. The force which keeps society moving is a psychical one, the "soul," using the term *soul* not in a theological or even technical philosophical sense, but in its popular meaning—the feelings taken collectively. The power which gives direction to these forces is also psychical—the intellect. Now, on one hand, according to Mr. Ward, these considerations suffice to overthrow the reigning *biological* method in sociology, as represented by Spencer, in its theory, and still more as to the practical conclusions (*laissez-faire*) drawn from it. As to this—save to suggest that possibly Mr. Ward takes Spencer somewhat more seriously than a psychologist would take him, and to regret that the somewhat irritating self-consciousness of Spencer's style should occasionally have infected Mr. Ward's way of putting things—we have nothing to do. We are concerned with his subjective psychology, or account of feeling as psychical motor, and his objective psychology, or intellect as psychical director.

Mr. Ward's psychology of feeling and action is a compound (not a happy one, as I shall try to show) of the old-fashioned psychology of sensation, dating from Locke, and Schopenhauer's theory of will. The crudeness of his account of sensation and idea may best be gathered from his own words: "When the end of the finger is placed against any material object two results follow. There is produced a *sensation* depending upon the nature of the object, and there is conveyed to the mind a *notion* of the nature of the object" (p. 16). If the sensation is indifferent as to pleasure and pain, attention will be fixed upon the notion conveyed, and abstracted from the sensation. In this case perception occurs. What sort of thing the percept of an object will be independent of the qualitative character of the sensation, Mr. Ward does not try to say: he only tells us that "the sensation and the notion are not one and the same, but two distinct things." This complete dualism (he tells us of the "dual" nature of mind, p. 12) lies at the basis of his conception of feeling as psychical and social force, and intellect as directing power.

While indifferent sensations are neglected for the notion which they convey, the intensive sensations meet a different fate. Pleasure and pain are connected with them, and this fact occasions movement: movement which is definite and purposeful[1]—away from object when there is pain, towards it when pleasure. These acts are the simple impulsive movements. But besides this sensori-motor apparatus, there is an ideo-motor apparatus, which gives rise to rational acts. These acts, Mr. Ward asserts (p. 33), come as clearly as the sensori-motor within the generic definition of being the result of sensations and away from pain and towards pleasure. This may be true; but how it can be true without a complete reconstruction of his original dualism between the "subjective" sensation and the "objective" idea, I fail to see, the "idea" having been defined as wholly without pleasurable or painful quality.

Desire is the next stage of development, and is "the recorded and remembered pain and pleasure." Since the representative states are much more important in our life than presentative sensations, our whole being becomes a theatre of desires seeking satisfaction, but checked in many ways, so that there results a perpetual striving to obtain

[1]   If this be true in the unqualified way in which Mr. Ward states it, it is difficult to see why the intellect should ever be needed to "direct."

the objects of satisfaction. From this time on the psychology of will completely supersedes that of sensation: the appetites of hunger and thirst, love, æsthetic and moral cravings, all springs to action, are included under desire, and language is strained to exhibit "all animated nature burning and seething with intensified desires" (pp. 52–53). We are next told that all desire is a form of pain, while effort aroused by desire is simply to satisfy it, that is, allay the pain. "All the enormous exertions of life are made for the sole purpose of getting rid of the swarm of desires that goad and pursue every living being from birth to death" (p. 55). That a remembered pleasure as well as a remembered pain should be of itself desire, that it should be pain (not simply painful), and that of itself it should know how to terminate itself, and that this termination should be pleasure—all this will probably strike the psychologist as curious enough; but the end is not yet. The satisfaction of desire terminates it, and the subject returns, psychologically, to its previous condition. But this of itself leads to the pessimistic conclusion: the sole spring to action is desire, desire is pain, and the satisfaction of desire is simply the cessation of pain. Yes, replies Mr. Ward, all this would be true if the act of gratifying a desire were absolutely instantaneous (p. 65). But the sensation of gratification is continuous; it takes time; in the higher form of love, indefinite time. "So long as the object is present the pleasure abides" (p. 68). Now I do not intend to question this as a fact; but, again, I do not see how the statement can be true if Mr. Ward's previous psychology be true. All gratification of desire implies the presence of desire; a non-existent desire can hardly be gratified, and all desire is pain. *Ergo*, as long as there is gratification there is pain—at most a mixed state of pleasure-pain. This is Mr. Ward's only logical conclusion. The *object* whose permanence gives permanent satisfaction is a visitor from another sphere than that of sheer feeling which forms, with memory, the whole of Mr. Ward's data. The contradiction becomes oppressive when we are further told (p. 74) "that, provided the means of supplying wants can be secured, the greater the number and the higher the rank of such wants, the higher the state of happiness attainable."

While feeling (pleasure) is the result of desire *psy-*

chologically (or for the individual), *function* is the result so far as nature is concerned. The satisfaction of the desire to eat builds up the whole system's further structure, and that develops organic function. There is still another result, *totally* (p. 79) different from either feeling or function. In satisfying desire the individual puts forth *action*, and this is a condition of building up structure. It is the connecting link between pleasure and function—the consequence of the former, the condition of the latter. The transformations thus wrought constitute material utilities, material civilization. Of these neither the individual nor nature is the beneficiary, but society. Thus there are three distinct ends—function for nature, pleasure for the individual, and action, with its products, for society.

I mention these points for their negative rather than their positive value. All these separations, with the contradictions previously indicated, result logically from the original premises. Let the fundamental thing be conceived as impression resulting from contact with an object, and thought, perception, must be another sort of thing; desire and action can be brought in from passive feeling only by a virtual contradiction, while nature, the individual, and society have independent ends.

For, to begin with the last point, it is simply the insertion of a passive impression between the "object" and the feeling and idea that makes such a break in the respective ends of nature, individual, and society as Mr. Ward introduces. Let once the standpoint of *action* be taken and there is a continuous process: the sensory ending is a place, not for receiving sensations and starting notions on their road to the mind, but a place (viewed from the standpoint of nature) for transforming the character of motion; the brain represents simply a further development and modification of action, and the final motor discharge (the act proper) the completion of this transformation of action. Whether the discharge is sensori-motor or ideo-motor depends simply upon the intermediate transformation which the original motion undergoes. Now while the psychological description of the process may employ different terms, it cannot involve a different principle. To suppose that feeling starts off action attributes a causal power to a bare state of consciousness at which many of the "metaphysicians," before whom Mr. Ward so shudders, would long hesitate. What feeling adds is consciousness of value of action in terms of the individual acting. While this appreciation of value marks a tremendous factor in the development of life, it is altogether too much to suppose that its introduction means the introduction of a new agency: the abdication of "natural" energy (motion) and the substitution for it of a new power-feeling.[2]

Furthermore, there is no reason to make function the "end" of nature: its "end" (like its beginning) is activity, or motion; the structural organization (and the corresponding functioning which goes along with it) being simply the objective manifestation of the transformation of motion. Even from the standpoint of "nature," function (or rather structure, which I take Mr. Ward to mean, since function always *is* action) is instrumental, not final. Only because Mr. Ward tries to get action out of passive states of feeling (pleasures and pains) does he have to reverse this natural order, and make action the intermediate term between feeling (the individual's end) and function (nature's end). Once adopt the united and continuous standpoint of action, and our three different ends resolve themselves into one—an end which may be termed valuable (felt) functional activity.

It probably is hardly necessary to deal at length with the weakness of Mr. Ward's treatment of original and representative action. The ignoring of impulse, save as representative, or the memory of previous pain and pleasure; the reduction of both ideo-motor and sensori-motor action to response to feelings of pain and pleasure, leaving out of account both the qualitative side of sensation and ideas, and also the connection of sensation (directly) and ideas (indirectly) with impulse; the account of desire as representa-

[2]   It may avoid misapprehension here if I remark that I am not arguing that the "external" motion is the cause of the "internal" state of consciousness. To treat one as *cause* of the other is to suppose one independent of the other, and thus to break the continuity. My point is, that if one chooses to take the standpoint of physical science and describe as far as possible the psychical occurrence, this occurrence is one of the transformation and complication of motion. The fact of feeling and of the existence of ideas must be recognized, but they must be treated from the standpoint of the development of action.

tive pleasures, which are suddenly asserted to be a state of pain; the abrupt appearance of permanent objects of satisfaction—all this is its own sufficient commentary.

When, however, we remember that Mr. Ward's original text is the need of relatively less attention to the intellect and more to the motive side of mind, and that his object is to get a basis for social dynamics on the side of its motor powers, we have an instructive object-lesson. All this unsatisfactory and self-contradictory analysis results from the fact that Mr. Ward is so under the spell of an old psychology of sensation that he fails to recognize the radical psychical fact, although just the fact needed to give firm support to his main contentions—I mean *impulse*, the primary fact, back of which, psychically, we cannot go. Starting with impulsive action, Mr. Ward would have, I think, no difficulty in showing the secondary or mediate position occupied by intellect. In order to secure this, his main purpose, he could well afford to sacrifice both the theory of feelings of pleasure-pain as stimulus to all action, and the old myth of sensation somehow walking from the object over into the mind. He would secure both a consistent psychology and a unification of the ends now attributed to three different existences by a psychology which states the mental life in active terms, those of impulse and its development, instead of in passive terms, mere feelings of pleasure and pain.

It is a pleasure to turn from these somewhat negative results to the other field—the light which Mr. Ward throws upon psychology from the standpoint of sociological evolution. I must omit more than bare reference to Mr. Ward's account of the reaction upon environment resulting from the introduction of specialized psychical phenomena. The points he makes (pp. 84–89) regarding the effects upon vegetable life in the way of the evolution of flowers and fruit, of the appearance of mind (in insect and bird organisms), and concerning the effect upon physical characters, including the brain, of the male animal of the development of sexual appetite in the female, are well worth attention.

But Mr. Ward's main contribution in this direction is in the theory which he propounds regarding the growth of intelligence, and the differentiation of the male and female types. It would perhaps hardly be safe to say that there is anything absolutely original in the points urged by Mr. Ward, but I do not know any writer who has made them in so striking and effective a way.

The key-word to the whole evolution of mind is *advantage*. Gain consists in increased ability to satisfy desire; hence the arousing of direct effort, of that striving which we call brute force. But many desires cannot possibly be satisfied by the primary method of direct effort. When a desire having a certain amount of active vigor at command meets obstacles, the result is that the animal is no longer simply checked; while external motion is arrested internal motility is increased. In this way the animal may continually change its position or point of attack, and thus by an indirect or flank movement finally reach its goal. This advantageous method would be selected and perpetuated until, finally, the power of mental exploration is developed. This incipient power leads up to "intuition," defined as the "power of looking into a complicated set of circumstances, and perceiving that movements which are not in obedience to the primary psychic force are those which promise success."

Intelligence is thus indirection—checking the natural, direct action, and taking a circuitous course. This accounts for the touch of moral obliquity attaching to all words naming primitive intellectual traits—shrewdness, cunning, crafty, designing, etc. It also accounts for the large part played by deception in historic social life—military strategy, political diplomacy, and, at present, business shrewdness. It is the legitimate consequence of this stage of mental development. So far as nascent intelligence is directed towards other sentient organisms (as it is where the getting of food or avoiding of enemies is concerned), intelligence is egoistic, living at the expense of other organisms. But a further development takes place when it is directed to inanimate objects. Ingenuity is substituted for cunning, and in so far intelligence becomes objective, impersonal, disinterested. When the savage makes a bow and arrow, his ultimate aim, indeed, is still gratification of appetite; but for the time being his attention must be taken up with a purely objective adjustment—with perception of relations of general utility, not of simple personal profit. In this way intelligence gradually, through the mediation of invention, works free from subjection to the demands of personal desire. It sets up its own interest, its own desire, which is comprehension of relations as they are. Scientific discovery and speculative genius are simply farther steps on this same road.

The ordinary biological theory of society does not see beyond the egoistic, exclusive development of intelligence. Its practical conclusions are, therefore, all in the direction of *laissez-faire*. But a psychological theory must recognize the change in the conditions of evolution wrought by the development of the non-personal, objective power of intelligence. True legislation is simply the application in the sphere of social forces of the principle of invention—of objective co-ordination with a view to increase of efficiency, and preventing needless waste and friction. Given a social science and a psychology as far advanced as present physical science, and *laissez-faire* in society becomes as absurd as would be the refusal to use knowledge of mechanical energy in the direction of steam and electricity. Mr. Ward, however, does not hold that psychology justifies the extreme socialistic conclusion, but rather leaves action a matter of specific conclusion: Let society do as the individual does—do what seems best after detailed study of the relevant facts. This seems good sense, but I doubt if Mr. Ward has duly considered the possibility of this outcome if, as he has previously urged, society has one end, viz., action, and the individual has another, feeling. If this opposition of ends exists, any possible development of intelligence can, it seems to me, only bring the conflict into clearer relief, and bring out definitely the necessity of choosing whichever is considered more important and sacrificing the other. In other words, what is needed is not the substitution of a psychological theory (in terms of individual feeling) for the biological theory (in terms of function), but rather an interpretation of the latter into its psychological equivalents—a theory of consciously organic activity.[3]

[3] Before passing on to the next topic, I wish to remark that Mr. Ward's general theory of the evolution of intelligence seems to me to promise a much more hopeful reconciliation of the *a posteriori* and the

At an early period a differentiation into two main types of intuition occurs: male, whose course we have already followed, and female. Male intuition develops with reference to reaching remote ends; it works out means; it is essentially planning or contriving. It develops new schemes, etc. Female intuition develops with reference to the immediate present; it is a question not of getting food at a distance, against obstacles, but of protecting herself and young against present danger. Female intuition develops, therefore, in the line of ability to "size up" the existing situation; it reads signs: it is essentially interpreting, not projective or contriving. This seems to me the nearest approach yet made to putting the psychology of the sexes on something approaching a scientific basis. When Mr. Ward goes on to argue that the male intelligence is radical, the female conservative, I cannot follow him so unreservedly. It seems to me that both the facts and a legitimate deduction from his own theory justify the conclusion that the male intelligence is radical as to ends, but cautious as to immediate methods to be followed—that is, while entertaining new projects easily, is slow in coming to a conclusion as regards their execution. The peculiar abstractness of the male intelligence results from this combination. The female intelligence, while hesitating in the consideration of radically new ends, is decidedly radical in its adoption of means with reference to ends—its tendency is to take the shortest course, irrespective of precedent. The prevalent theory of the essentially conservative nature of woman's intelligence seems to me a fiction of the male intelligence, maintained in order to keep this inconvenient radicalism of woman in check.

I cannot conclude without adding that Mr. Ward's book is extremely suggestive—as well for what it does not accomplish as for what it does. Its moral (to my mind) is pointing to a step which the book does not itself take. The

---

a priori than Spencer's method. The "raining in" of an external environment upon the organism until its main features are reproduced in the organization of the latter offers more difficulties than it solves. From Mr. Ward's standpoint, the development is always controlled by the organism itself—it occurs in the process by which the latter reaches its own end, and in that sense (probably the only tolerable one) is *a priori*, while the whole process is itself an experimental one.

current theory of mind undoubtedly needs reconstruction from the sociological standpoint; it needs to be interpreted as a fact developing with reference to its social utilities. The biological theory of society needs reconstruction from the standpoint of the recognition of the significance of intellect, emotion, and impulse. Mr. Ward seems to me, when all is said and done, to give a compromise and mixture of the two older standpoints, rather than a re-reading of either of them.

Three ideas run through and through Mr. Kidd's book, repeated and intertwined without much regard to the logic of formal presentation, and yet so put each time as not to convey the effect of wearisome reiteration. These ideas are: 1. Progress is always effected through competition and struggle. There is infinite narrow variation, some variations tending slightly below, others slightly above, the existing average standard. There is in these variations no essential tendency to progress. Progress comes only through selection of favorable differentiations, and there is no selection save where there is rivalry and struggle. This biological law (with regard to which Dr. Kidd follows Weismannism in its extreme form) holds of human as of animal history. Its scene of operation is simply transferred to the rivalry of nations and of industrial life.

On this point Mr. Ward and Mr. Kidd seem to me to provide necessary correctives of each other. The positive evolutionary significance of conflict seems hardly to be recognized by Mr. Ward; he seems to think that intellectual progress can now cut loose from the conditions under which it originated, namely, preferential advantage in the struggle for existence. To me it appears as sure a psychological as biological principle that men go on thinking only because of practical friction or strain somewhere, that thinking is essentially the solution of tension. But Mr. Ward is strong where Mr. Kidd appears defective: in the recognition of the part which coherent, organized science can play in minimizing the struggle, and in rendering effective that residuum necessary to maintain progress. The elimination of conflict is, I believe, a hopeless and self-contradictory ideal. Not so the directing of the struggle to reduce waste and to secure its maximum contribution. It is not the sheer amount of conflict, but the conditions under which it occurs that determine its value. Mr. Kidd seems practically to ignore this possibility of increasing control of conflict, and to leave the individual at its mercy; the individual, according to him, is a tool of the conflict in evolving progress, not the conflict a tool of man.

This brings us to the second point. 2. Progress implies the sacrifice of the individual to the race; the individual has to suffer from the conflict in order that the race may enjoy the benefits of progress. This position of itself offers nothing new; the problem has been felt ever since man became conscious of progress. The contentions between Herder and Kant in Germany, between Malthus and the "perfectionists" in England, represent it. But the use to which Mr. Kidd puts the idea is, so far as I know, original, and marks a mind of scope and daring. As man becomes conscious of the extent to which he is sacrificed to a progress in whose benefits he does not share, and as he gains in rational power, he will squarely propound to himself this problem: Why should I continue to suffer simply for the sake of progress? Go to; let us make the best of the present and eliminate struggle and conflict. And from the standpoint of reason this position is logically justified; there is no *rational* sanction for progress. This is the psychological basis of socialism, for socialism is simply extreme rationalism applied to the existing conditions of life. It proposes to put a stop to the suffering which struggle inflicts on individuals; though this implies a brake on progress.

3. Where then is the sanction for progress, science, or rational method utterly failing to justify it? In feeling subjectively, or religion objectively. The sociological function of religion is to cultivate in the individual passive resignation to or even active co-operation in his sacrifice to the good of future generations. Only in this way can the universality, historical and psychological, of the religious consciousness be explained. The scientific man in his ignoring of, or attack upon, religion fails to notice this sociological, evolutionary meaning, and indirectly plays into the hands of the socialist.

I have given, I think, a fair account of Mr. Kidd's main intentions; what I have not given is his force of statement and his wealth of illustrative material. Any detailed criticism upon such radical and far-reaching propositions is out of the question, but I cannot refrain from two suggestions. If the individual is *continually* sacrificed to the conditions of progress, where is the progress? Mr. Kidd speaks as if sacrifice to progress and sacrifice to welfare of future humanity were the same (see p. 291). But this cannot be; the benefit which will accrue to the future generations must, when their turn comes, be incidental to the sufferings attendant upon conflict as a condition of further progress. The process never amounts to anything, never has any value, *unless it has it both now and then*, *i.e.*, all the time. Mr. Kidd seems to me to have fallen into the old pit of a continual progress *towards* something. This indicates my second suggestion. The antithesis which Mr. Kidd makes between what constitutes the happiness of the individual and the conditions of progress appears to be overdrawn and out of perspective. Overlooking the fact that the sense of contributing to progress is an important, and to many an indispensable, rational ingredient of happiness, what ground is there for the assumption that the individual's rational conception of happiness excludes all suffering arising from struggle? I do not see that the case stands otherwise for the conditions of happiness (individual welfare) than for the conditions of progress (general welfare). A certain intensity and, so to speak, tautness of activity appear requisite to happiness; and rivalry or struggle, for anything we know, is as constantly necessary to keep us strung up to the proper pitch for happiness as it is to afford the conditions which enable preferential selection (progress) to act.

All this is upon the supposition that Mr. Kidd is justified in his extreme Weismannism of premise. If we suppose that consciously acquired activity, and habits formed under the direction of intelligence, are conserved, the case against his point is much strengthened. While struggle and consequent pain are not eliminated, the vibration is so loaded by established habits as to lessen its range. There is even no need to suppose that the conservation of rationalized activity is direct or through the organism; if the environment is so changed as to set up conditions which stimulate and facilitate the formation of like habits on the part of each individual, the same end is reached.

I hope it will not seem an injustice to Professor Adams's lucid and substantial piece of work if, after having called attention to its helpfulness to students of intellectual as well as of political development, I use it to point a moral for psychologists. As giving an adequate and coherent account of the general conditions and movement through the Middle Ages, the book is highly valuable to any one who is trying to understand the philosophy of that period. But from a narrower psychological standpoint the value is, in the main, negative. I mean that it indicates the slight extent to which psychology has as yet penetrated into the sciences which lie nearest to it, the historical. Psychology has not as yet made of itself a generally useful tool; it has not impressed the worker in other fields so that he feels the necessity of keeping his eyes open for the psychical development, the growth in consciousness; nor does it give him much help when he does attempt this. To take one point: Professor Adams recognizes clearly the great significance of the Middle Ages in discovering the individual and bringing him to the light of day (pp. 91, 92). But this is treated mainly as an objective change—a change in political status. The extent to which this depended upon a changed psychical attitude, and the part played by the implicit and explicit psychological theory of mediæval thought—all this does not meet recognition. And yet this seems the key to understanding the outer transformation. Now this, of course, is no reflection upon the historian; he cannot be expected to stop historical investigation in order to make for himself adequate psychological instruments; it is, once more, a warning and a stimulus to the psychologist.

It is hardly necessary to do more than to call attention to Professor Flint's noble beginning of a monumental work. The present volume (of 700 pp.), after an Introduction dealing with Greek and Roman speculation upon history, is devoted to the philosophy of history in France, and we are led to anticipate further volumes upon England, Italy, and Germany. I cannot pretend to have the knowledge required to speak critically of this book; indeed, so wide is its range and so thorough its treatment that I do not see that anybody but Professor Flint himself is competent to speak of it as a whole. It seems, however, to have all, and more, of the solidity, accuracy, and restraint of judgment which marked the older volume upon Germany and France. To risk one more *obiter dictum*, judging from the accounts of authors with whom I have some acquaintance, as Rousseau and Comte, the book is more likely to be serviceable as a statement of the facts of the case than as an account of the underlying *motif* and trend—as interpretation, in short. But this simply means, I suppose, that I should interpret it otherwise myself.

Philosophy and Political Economy in some of their Historical Relations, by James Bonar. London: Swan Sonnenschein and Co.; New York: Macmillan Co., 1893.

It is certainly characteristic of the present condition of philosophy—and I suppose it to be also of political economy—that a book like the present should be produced. Doubtless, the opposition, or at least the gulf, between metaphysics as a speculative science dealing with purely spiritual and transcendental affairs, and hard-headed economics engaged with material and mundane things, has not been as wide or as deep as we sometimes imagine. Philosophy has never entirely lost sight of itself as a social discipline; and the conception, to use Aristotle's phraseology, that men first take thought about living in order then to live worthily, can never have been quite eliminated from the account of man's industrial undertakings and relationships. Yet only at a time when the solution of the economic problem is seen to be bound up with that of the whole human question, and at a time when philosophy is feeling its way to transforming some of its conquests in the transcendental domain into tools for handling present matters, could the attempt to discuss the historic relations of philosophy and political economy have quite its present meaning.

[*First published in* Political Science Quarterly, IX (*Dec. 1894*), 741–44. *Not previously reprinted.*]

I confess that personally I always experience irritation when a book reviewer, instead of giving me an account and estimate of a book from the book's own standpoint, chooses to show what kind of a book the author might have produced, and to criticize the work in hand from this remote vantage-point. Yet I cannot resist the temptation of following that method in this case. At least, in suggesting the hypothetical book which he might have written, I shall not deny or fail to recognize the solid qualities which Mr. Bonar's book has as it is, and it is possible that the contrast will, after all, only serve the better to indicate just what Mr. Bonar has successfully undertaken.

What Mr. Bonar has *not* done is to show how the same fundamental problems and attitudes have underlain philosophic and economic thought from the outset, simply assuming different statements and outward garbs. He has not traced the reflection of philosophic conceptions over into the region of political economy, influencing and even controlling the economic writer without any consciousness on his part of the ideas of which he was the mouthpiece. What Mr. Bonar *has* done is to give a minute and solid account of the economic content to be found in many philosophic writers, *e.g.*, Plato, Aristotle, Hobbes, Kant, Hegel; and of the immediate philosophic connections and leanings of such economists as Adam Smith, the Mills, Karl Marx and Lassalle. In a word, and upon the whole, it is in their more external points of contact and reciprocal reactions, that he has grasped and set forth the relations of political economy and philosophy.

For many reasons, it is better that the task so well performed by Mr. Bonar should have been undertaken first; indeeed, it was probably necessary, as the more intrinsic account which I have suggested would hardly be possible without just such a collection of "materials to serve" as Mr. Bonar has brought together. How precisely it is the latter which is given us, may be easily learned from turning to the last chapter—the summary. Here, even if not explicitly in the body of the book, one might expect to hear something of the persistence of some fundamental problems, common to both philosophy and economics, and differentiating themselves through the various periods of history; might expect to learn what have been the chief crises through which the problem has passed, and the chief types which the solutions have assumed. But no; even here we have the continuous cataloguing: Plato, Aristotle, the Stoics, thought and said this and that; Grotius and Hobbes introduced such and such political concepts; Locke, Hume and the Mercantilists worked on this or that line. As a result, every student of the history of philosophy at least, and I should think most students of economics, will require the book: as a work of reference it is indispensable; it may, with but slight exaggeration, be called encyclopedic in its scope and accuracy. But, for this very reason, few will read it continuously from sheer enjoyment in following the unfolding plot of a continuous history, any more than one would read an encyclopedia in such fashion.

If anywhere there is to be found an exception to this statement, it is in the Fifth Book. Mr. Bonar's human, as distinct from his scholastic, interest seems to be much fresher in dealing with the nineteenth-century socialists, and with the bearing of the doctrine of evolution upon economics —particularly the latter; and as a result his treatment here is much freer, and what he has to say is much more worth reading on its own account, and not simply for consultation purposes.

This encyclopedic character of the book makes reviewing it in one sense out of the question. It is hardly worth while to give a table of contents; and accordingly, after the nature and limitations of the book in general have been indicated, hardly anything remains save to inquire into the accuracy of the particular statements, and the judgment shown in the selection of authors and the proportionate space given them. As far as I have tested Mr. Bonar in these respects, there are but two cases in which I should feel sure that my own judgment marked anything more than the inevitable individual variation. These two cases, however, seem to me almost inexplicable: they are the omission of Rousseau and Comte.[1] Rousseau hardly appears, save as

[1]   Since it has been the French, above all others, who have carried over philosophic ideas into the practical region generally, whether of politics or economics, the attention given French authors seems, in general, disproportionately slight.

an incident in the development of Locke's idea of natural law and rights; Comte as an incident in the evolution of Stuart Mill's ideas. Yet surely it was Rousseau, more than any other writer, who brought to consciousness the position of the economic forces in social organization as such, and the place of the economic problem in the whole social and political problem. It is fashionable to laugh Rousseau to scorn as pre-historic, and even as anti-historic, in his method of dealing with social questions. Yet, however innocent the *Discourse upon the Origin of Inequality* may be of really historic data, its assertions that economic needs and struggles have been the determining force in the evolution of all institutions, set forth (whether the contention be right or wrong) a doctrine too important as theory, and too much *en évidence* in practice to be overlooked. Harrington's *Oceana* is certainly worth notice as an early attempt to state the economic character of history; but it is mere material for the antiquarian compared with Rousseau's doctrine — so much has that been a practically determining force in the social drama of the century. As for Comte, it is true, indeed, that the Germans introduced historic methods and considerations into political economy; but it was the great Frenchman who introduced history bodily.

But the last word must be one of grateful recognition. If Mr. Bonar's book lacks a wide and commanding sweep, it manifests a great sense of the immediate connections and the relevant historical implications of particular writers; its exactness of detail amounts to one of the positive virtues; and it never fails to be suggestive in its discussion of individual authors, — so much so, that a score of monographs could easily be written, developing ideas which are here sketched in outline. In spirit and method, the book is like the best work that we have learned to associate with Germany — save that Mr. Bonar has made his 400 pages suffice, while a German might have filled no one knows how many "handbooks" too big to be handled.

THE STUDY OF ETHICS

———

A SYLLABUS

———

By JOHN DEWEY

ANN ARBOR MICHIGAN
REGISTER PUBLISHING COMPANY
The Inland Press
1894

Prefatory Note

THE EDITION of my *Outlines of Ethics* [*Early Works*, III, 237–388] having been exhausted, I have prepared the following pages, primarily for the use and guidance of my own students. The demand for the former book seems, however, to justify the belief that, amid the prevalence of pathological and moralistic ethics, there is room for a theory which conceives of conduct as the normal and free living of life as it is. The present pages, it may be added, are in no sense a second edition of the previous book. On the contrary, they undertake a thorough psychological examination of the process of active experience, and a derivation from this analysis of the chief ethical types and crises—a task, so far as I know, not previously attempted.

1

Nature of Ethical Theory

1.   Subject-Matter of Ethics

Subject-matter of ethical theory is judgment concerning the *value* of conduct. Three stages. First, practical encouragement and discouragement of certain acts. Reward and punishment primary forms of such judgments. Next stage, urging and restraint through speech. (See Plato, *Protagoras*, 325–26.) Third stage, reflective judgment as to reason for such acts.

Ethical theory is simply (1) a *systematic* judgment of value. The way is prepared for this through the fact that primitive judgments relate not to isolated acts, but to *habits* of action, and to the types of character which are disposed to induce those habits. Necessary spontaneous generalizations. Codes, customary and legislative.

Demand for more systematic generalization arises when, through an extension of the area of life, former habits begin to conflict with each other. Illustrated by Athenian life; by Roman; by modern since the Renascence. Ethical theory is thus (2) a *critical* judgment upon conduct. Not systematic in the sense that it simply catalogues previous judgments, but in the sense that it attempts to reconstruct them on the basis of a deeper principle (see Sec. 11).

It is a matter of indifference whether we say ethical theory attempts to systematize (in the above sense) *judgments* about the value of conduct, or attempts to systematize

conduct itself. Every act (consciously performed) is a judgment of value: the act done is done because it is thought to
be *worth while*, or valuable. Thus a man's real (as distinct
from his nominal or symbolic) theory of conduct can be
told only from his acts. Conversely, every judgment about
conduct is itself an act; it marks a practical and not simply
a theoretical attitude. That is, it does not lie outside of the
matter judged (conduct), but constitutes a part of its
development; conduct is different after, and because of, the
judgment. Illustrated in education, where the main point
is not so much to get certain acts done, as to induce in the
child certain ways of valuing acts, from which the performance of the specific deeds will naturally follow. That
is, the best education aims to train *conscience*. Ethical theory
is only a more conscious and more generalized phase of
conduct. Analogy with place of theory in modern (*experimental*) science. A theory not a fixed or abstract truth, but a
standpoint and method for some activity. It is in this (the
activity as directed by theory) that the value of the theory
comes out and is tested (see Sec. III).

References: Definitions of ethics will be found in Mur-
ray, *Introduction to Ethics*, pp. 1–7; Porter, *Elements of
Moral Science*, Introductory; Muirhead, *Elements of Ethics*,
Chs. 1 and 2; Mackenzie, *Manual of Ethics*, Introduction;
Bowne, *Principles of Ethics*, Introduction.

II.   Rise of Ethical Theory

Origin of reflective morality was in Greece. Other
ethical codes were either customary or else conceived to be
absolute emanations from a divine will. The Greek was in
the habit of discussing questions regarding ends and means
of life. This strengthened by growth of democracy. Also by
methods of education, which (in Athens) relied upon appeal
to individual's own intelligence rather than upon conformity
to fixed rule (Davidson, *Aristotle and Ancient Educational
Ideals*, pp. 11, 70, 86–87). Development of commerce, and
more general social intercourse among the Greeks, with
growth of science and art, resulted in Sophists, who undertook to teach virtue and methods and aims of political in-

fluence; he also discussed the moral standard, some denying any moral criterion whatever, holding it possible to prove arbitrarily an act either right or wrong; others holding the source of moral law to be the superior power of the ruler. Thus they raised the question whether moral distinctions exist in the nature of things, or simply by arbitrary enactment, or for convenience and expediency. While the Sophists themselves tended to answer the question in one of the two latter senses, the dramatists (Æschylus and Sophocles) had, amid the disintegration of the lower religious beliefs, attempted to maintain an eternal and intrinsic moral law and ideal. Socrates took the latter position, and attempted to uphold it by means of the weapons of the Sophists themselves, *i.e.*, by inquiry and reflection. He attacked the ideas that morality is based upon the will of the stronger, that it rests upon custom, and that it is adequately expressed in the more or less haphazard and external conclusions of the poets and ordinary moral teachers of the times. (See Plato, *Republic*, Bks. i–iii.) He insisted that the only adequate and sure basis for morality is knowledge of the Good, *i.e.*, true end of life, and ability to refer the value of particular acts and aims to this supreme end. He thus became the founder of conscious ethical theory.

See Sidgwick, *History of Ethics*, esp. Ch. 2; Grant, *Ethics of Aristotle*, Ch. 2; Paulsen, *Ethik*, Bk. i, Ch. 1; Grote, *History of Greece*, Chs. 57 and 58; Hegel, *History of Philosophy* (trans. by Haldane), Vol. i; Fairbanks, on Sophocles's Ethics, *International Journal of Ethics*, Vol. ii, p. 77; Butcher, *Aspects of Greek Genius*; and *Hellenica*, essays by Myers and Abbott. Consult also histories of philosophy by Erdmann, Windelband, and Ueberweg, portions treating of Sophists and Socrates.

iii. Relation of Moral Theory to Practice

As already said, ethical theory arises from practical needs, and is not simply a judgment about conduct, but a part of conduct, a practical fact. (See Aristotle, *Ethics*, Bk. i, Chs. 2 and 3, Ch. 6, Bk. x, Ch. 9.) The inference sometimes drawn from this is that ethics is not a science but an art. (For two strong statements of this view, see Mill, *Logic*, Bk. vi, Ch. 12, and Martineau, *Essays*, Vol. ii, pp. 6–9; strong statement of contrary view, see Bradley, *Logic*, pp. 247–49.) We have to ask, therefore, whether ethics is practical in value, because it is, or is not, a science. The former position will be taken.

1. Moral value not equivalent to preaching or *moralizing*. Truth has its own moral value, all the greater because not deflected to serve some immediate end of exhortation.

2. Current antithesis between science and art not tenable. Science does not *teach* us to know, it is the knowing; art does not *teach* us to do, it is the doing. Art of morality is practice of it, not rules laid down. Same of art of dyeing, of mensuration, etc. Rules give basis for mechanical routine, not for art. Art is based upon insight into truth, or relations involved.

3. Question whether word "science" or word "art" is to be applied to ethics is of very little account. But question is as to whether ethics is to be regarded as helpful to morals because of scientific insight into truth afforded, or because of its formulation of precepts for action. In the latter case, it "helps" the moral life, only by depriving it of its freedom. Illustrated by physiology and hygiene. In former case, helps by freeing it: by making it more significant and effective — as knowledge of mechanics helps a bridge builder. Importance of distinction illustrated by moral value of teachings of Jesus: Did he lay down rules for life, or did he give insight into nature of life? That is, is "salvation" conformity to some scheme laid down, or is it the freeing of life reached through knowledge of its real nature and relations?

Summary. So far as agent needs rules, or fixed precepts, he does not perform his deeds from full personal preference, and hence is only imperfectly moral: so far as he understands and is personally interested in the acts demanded, he needs no rules. Hence the absurdity of defining ethical theory from the standpoint of rules. Casuistry. Difference between a principle and a rule; former a *method* for action, latter a prescription for it; former experimental, latter fixed; former orders in sense of setting in order, latter in sense of commanding.

Practical value of moral theory is both destructive and constructive. Negative side always visible first. In ideal, destruction is only the reaction of the construction. So far as two are separated, reform becomes merely sentimental, or else mere fault finding.

On practical value of moral theory, see Muirhead, *Elements of Ethics*, Ch. 3; Lotze, *Practical Philosophy*, Introduction. Bradley, *Ethical Studies*, pp. 174–75. Green, *Prolegomena to Ethics*, pp. 338–60; Höffding, *Ethik*, pp. 1–9; *International Journal of Ethics*, Vol. I, No. 2, article by Dewey, on "Moral Theory and Practice" [*Early Works*, III, 93–109]; p. 335, by James on "The Moral Philosopher and the Moral Life" (a very strong statement of the practical character of the moral judgment); Vol. IV, p. 160, by Mackenzie, on "Moral Science and Moral Life."

2

The Factors of Moral Conduct: The Agent and His Sphere of Action

iv.   Conduct as Referred to the Agent

No act is a part of conduct except as it is a part of a system of plans (purposes) and interests. Theory arose (as already seen) when these plans and interests were reflected upon with a view to their unification. Thus (for all European peoples since Socrates) an act must express character if it is to have *moral* meaning; it must be considered as the outcome of some aim and interest on the part of a conscious agent (Spencer, *Data of Ethics*, Ch. 1).

The elements involved in such reference of an act to an agent are: (1) *Some knowledge of what he is about*; that is, some end in view in doing the act. (2) *Some interest in the act*; the act is chosen or preferred. The agent not only knows what he is about as a reasoning automaton might, but the act appeals to him, has value for him.

(3) The insight and the interest must be more than momentary—they must express some stability. *The act must proceed from a disposition, an established tendency, to act thus and so.*

This analysis was begun by Socrates and practically completed by Aristotle. See Xenophon, *Memorabilia*, III, Ch. 9; Plato, *Protagoras*, esp. 352–59; *Apology*, 25; and Aristotle, *Ethics*, Bk. II, Ch. 4. See also Green, *Prolegomena*, pp. 268–72.

The contact of Greek thought with Semitic conceptions (particularly through Christianity) emphasized the necessary reference of conduct to the agent. It made holiness of will (character, dominating idea and interest) the ideal, rather than the performance of certain acts (compare idea of justification by faith) and proclaimed the criterion of moral worth to be in the personal attitude, rather than in the particular act. (See, *e.g.*, 1 Cor., Ch. 13.) In its extreme forms, this emphasis made the act almost indifferent; it was regarded as somehow "external," the ideal and attitude being all-sufficient *per se*.

The contact with the Germanic peoples, with their strong Romanticism, emphasized also the other factor in the analysis—namely the insistence upon the agent's own *interest* in his acts. It asserted the right of the individual to choose his own ends, and the worthlessness (the slavery) of all acts not performed because of this personal preference. In its extreme form, this spirit became the demand for unlimited personal enjoyment—not mere sensuous enjoyment, but the *right* of the individual to realize to the uttermost the emotional value of his own acts.

See Green, *Works*, Vol. iii, p. 92; Carlyle, *Sartor Resartus*, Bk. ii, Ch. 9 (on the happiness of the shoe-black); Royce, *Religious Aspect of Philosophy*, pp. 110–26; Seth, ed., *Essays in Philosophic Criticism*, Kilpatrick, on "Pessimism and the Religious Consciousness."

v.   Reference of Conduct to the Sphere of Action

In analyzing conduct, it is just as important to consider the situation as the agent. While conduct proceeds from an agent, the agent himself acts with reference to the conditions as they present themselves. Conditions (environment) constitute action in the following ways:

1. The agent is moulded through education, unconscious and conscious, into certain habits of thinking and feeling as well as acting. His act, therefore, partakes of the aims and disposition of his race and time. (See Grote, *Plato*, Vol. i, p. 249, for a strong statement of this influence.)

2. Our acts are controlled by the demands made upon us. These demands include not simply the express requirements of other persons, but the customary expectations of the family, social circle, trade or profession; the stimuli of surrounding objects, tools, books, etc.; the range and quality of opportunities afforded.

3. No idea, plan, wish whatever, can pass into action save through the forces of the environment. Unless, then, we mean to confine our definition of conduct entirely to inner states of consciousness, we must include the scene of action within the definition. But the situation does more than execute the plan; through its acceptance or rejection of it, partial or complete, it reacts into consciousness, and strengthens or modifies the plan. All existing ideals of all practical (*i.e.*, non-sentimental) agents are the outcome of such a struggle for realization.

Historic. At the outset of reflection, equal emphasis was put upon the reference both to the agent and to the situation. Ethics, dealing with conduct in its individual reference, and politics, dealing with it in reference to the scene of action, were not separated. Plato, *Republic*, Bk. ii, 368–69, Bk. iv, 427–45; Aristotle, *Ethics*, Bk. x, Ch. 9; *Politics*, Bk. i, Chs. 1 and 2, Bk. iii, Ch. 12. The term ethos meant the disposition or prevailing habit of the community (compare Lat. *mos*, *mores*), and it only gradually shaded over into the idea of individual character. The exclusive reference of conduct to the individual came later, and was due, partly, to the influence of Christianity already referred to, and partly to the general disintegration of local customs and interests, consequent upon the growth of the Roman Empire. (See Renan, Hibbert Lectures, 1880.) The result was that the individual was thrown back into himself, the conditions of action seeming indifferent and even hostile to the realization of moral aims. Stoic, Epicurean, and Sceptic all agreed in setting up as their ideal the individual, self sufficient to himself, independent of everything beyond himself – that is, everything beyond his own consciousness (Sidgwick, *History of Ethics*, pp. 70–73; Windelband, *History of Philosophy*, pp. 164–70). The identification of the highest ideal with a good capable of realization only through supernatural assistance, and, as to content, only in another world, led in the Middle Ages to considering the present conditions of action as indifferent or profane, the state as the realm of force, not moral aims; and there was a corresponding exclusion of objective factors from the theory of conduct. Since the Reformation, however, the tendency has been steadily the other way. It has culminated in the present generation through the development of the idea of evolution and of the historical method, on the scientific side; and through the growth of reforming and philanthropic interest on the practical side. The former have shown the immense part played by historic antecedents and by environment, physical and social, in shaping conduct. The latter has revealed that one of the chief obstacles to general and permanent moral reforms is unfavorable institutions and habits of living.

Herder, *Philosophy of the History of Man*, Bk. IX, and Comte, *Positive Philosophy*, Bk. VI, are important references in the historical development of the present point of view. For various ideas on the social nature of ethics, see Alexander, *Moral Order and Progress*, pp. 5–15, 81–96; *Yale Review*, Vol. I, pp. 301 and 354, Hadley, "Ethics as Political Science"; *Mind*, Vol. II, p. 453, Barratt, "Ethics and Politics"; Vol. VIII, p. 222, Wallace, "Ethics and Sociology"; *International Journal of Ethics*, Vol. III, p. 281, Mackenzie, "Ethics and Economics"; Vol. IV, p. 133, Hibben, "Ethics and Jurisprudence"; *Journal of Speculative Philosophy*, Vol. XXII, p. 322, Patten, "Economics and Morality." The necessity of including social conditions and relations in the idea of conduct is brought out, from different points of view, in Spencer, *Data of Ethics*, Ch. 8; Stephen, *Science of Ethics*, Ch. 3; Green, *Prolegomena*, pp. 191–201; Bradley, *Ethical Studies*, pp. 148–56.

VI. Twofold Formula for Conduct

We may sum up the foregoing, on its practical side, by saying that in order to secure right conduct we find ourselves under the necessity of paying equal attention to the agent and to the conditions with reference to which he acts. No amount of external pressure or influence can secure right conduct of an agent, *except in so far as it ceases to be external*; except, that is, as it is taken up into the purpose and interests of the agent himself. But, on the other hand, there is no way to develop within the individual right plans, and to attach right values to ends, save as these plans reflect the *requirements of the situation* in which he finds himself.

A business situation gives an illustration. The agent, to

be successful, must form his plans with reference to his conditions—state of raw material, transportation facilities, demand in market, and others competing to supply this demand. His purposes, so far as rightly formed, are *a synthesis or co-ordination of the prevailing conditions of his scene of action*. But this situation is not something hard and fixed, outside of the agent. What the situation is to him depends upon his own capacities—his resources, skill, etc. He himself is a part of the conditions to be taken into account. Inferior raw material will yield to an invention which enables him to get more out of it, remoteness from market to his ability to contrive new methods of transportation, etc. In other words, *the situation is nothing but the complete co-ordination of all his powers (abilities) and relations.*

Thus it is with that larger success in conduct, termed morality. From the standpoint of the individual agent,

Conduct is the co-ordinating, or bringing to a unity of aim and interest, the different elements of a complex situation.

From the standpoint of the scene of action,

Conduct is co-ordinating, in an organized way, the concrete powers, the impulses and habits, of an individual agent.

(See Alexander, *Moral Order*, pp. 97–130.)

vii. Moral Functions

Conduct may be considered as the same *consciously* that a biological function is unconsciously. It is the nature of every function to include within itself both organ and environment. The act of respiration is a co-ordination of lungs as organ and air as environment. So digestion, locomotion, etc. We are apt at first to identify function with the organ alone, and conceive of environment as if it bore a more external relation to it. But the reference to environment is absolute and intrinsic. The organ is the point of initiation for the function, and is more permanent than any particular portion of the environment. It is thus of more *immediate* importance. But it is the environment, comprehended in the exercise of the function, that finally fixes the organ (as food builds up the organism), and thus, indirectly or *mediately*, the environment is of the most importance. (Compare the mutual dependence of "apperception" and "retention." *Psychology*, p. 149 [*Early Works*, II, 131].)

It is equally an error then to consider either organ or environment as fixed in itself. Function is not the exercise of a predetermined organ upon an external environment, nor is it the adjustment of an organ to a predetermined environment. The nature of the *function* determines both the organ and the environment. Two animals in whom the function of nutrition is differently performed have, in virtue of that fact, different environments as well as different organs. Spencer (*Biology*, Part One, Ch. 4; *Psychology*, Part Three; *Data of Ethics*, pp. 75–76) has defined life, mind, and conduct as adjustment of inner relations to outer; but the separation involved in calling one "inner" and the other "outer" marks the failure to recognize that function is not a parallelism between organ and environment, but includes and determines both.

VIII. Ethical Postulate

Interpreted in moral terms, the foregoing means that moral conduct cannot be adequately conceived as the property or performance of the agent alone. The agent corresponds to the organ biologically, and is thus, in itself, simply an instrument for exercising certain functions. Its structure, its aims, its interests, are controlled by the ends to be reached, and these ends include the *conditions* of action as well as the *instrument*. In other words, we cannot take the agent as final in defining conduct, because we demand a certain structure of the agent.

Conversely, we require that the conditions of action be modified so as to permit the exercise of functions, so as to become the means of the realization of ends. The exercise of function itself tends to this transformation of environment. (Illustrated by nutrition, by industry, by valor, etc.)

Defining conduct from the standpoint of the action, which includes both agent and his scene of action, we see that

The conduct required truly to express an agent is, at the same time, the conduct required to maintain the situation in which he is placed; while, conversely, the conduct that truly meets the situation is that which furthers the agent.

The word "truly" in this statement means with reference to the exercise of function.

This statement may be termed the *ethical postulate*. Its analogy with the scientific postulate—uniformity of nature, reign of law, etc. That is, we demand order in our experience. The only proof of its existence is in the results reached by making the demand. The postulate is verified by being acted upon. The proof is experimental.

The ethical postulate, in other words, expresses the fact that moral experience continually demands of every agent that he shape his plans and interests so that they meet the needs of the situation, while it also requires that, through the agent, the situation be so modified as to enable the agent to express himself freely.

See Dewey, *Outlines of Ethics*, p. 131 [*Early Works*, III, 322].

The discussion of conduct in relation to the agent constitutes *psychological* ethics: in relation to the conditions of action, *social* ethics. It must be borne in mind, however, that this distinction is one of point of view taken, not of material involved: the agent, that is, is a social fact as well as a psychical fact, and the conditions of action have a psychical as well as a social meaning.

It should also be borne in mind throughout the whole discussion that the aim is not to discover the ideal at which all conduct aims, nor the law which it should follow; the aim, once more, is not to find precepts or rules, but to analyze conduct. The question is concerning the nature of any ideal and the part which it plays in conduct; the conditions which must be met to entitle any fact to the name of law, etc.

PART TWO

PSYCHOLOGICAL ETHICS

3

A General Analysis of Conduct

IX. The Nature of Impulse

All conduct is at first impulsive. It has no end *consciously* in view. The self is constantly performing certain acts more or less determined in results, but without distinct consciousness of their significance. The food impulse; following light with eyes; handling; reaching; locomotion; the talking impulse. All activity is impulsive so far as containing new elements—so far, that is, as it is not purely habitual. Impulse is not used as synonymous with instinct. The latter is a defined or limited impulse; the physical mechanism for the act is pretty definitely prearranged. In man, there are very few instincts pure and simple, but rather the loose beginnings and ends of very many instincts. Hence the range and variety of human, as compared with animal, actions. Hence also the impossibility of a systematic classification of fundamental impulses to action. (Such classifications were frequent in the older psychologies; see also Martineau, *Types of Ethical Theory*, Vol. II, pp. 120–256, esp. p. 246.) While the acts which have proved themselves necessary in the previous life of the race have become so organized into the structure of the individual that they now assert themselves spontaneously as appetites and aversions, each of these is so modified by the experiences and circumstances of the agent that it is meaningless when separated. Such impulses as love of gain, love of fame, etc., are either pure abstractions, there being in the normal man no such thing as love of gain in general (that is, unmodified by the make-up of his entire experience), or else they represent an abstract classification of the various *ends* to which impulses may be directed.

x. The Expression of Impulse and Its Consequences

The various impulses of the individual are not a loose bundle of tendencies existing side by side. Because they have been evolved in relation to the one more inclusive activity of maintaining life, they are interconnected. One impulse in its utterance tends to call up others, and this excitation or stimulation is not wholly dependent upon the circumstances of the moment, but follows (within widely variable limits) certain lines. Thus the movement of the eye in following light and of the hand in grasping an object tend to co-ordinate, etc. The difference again between the lower animals and man is that in the former this co-ordination is predetermined quite specifically, while in man only the very general lines are laid down, thus leaving room for great variation and experimentation—implying possibility of new combinations, and thus the performance of new acts almost without limit. The acts, which to the animals are well defined ends, are, in the human structure, freed from their adjustment to predefined ends and made flexible instruments for a large number of different and much more complex ends. The *definite* coordination of acts is thus, with man, not a *datum* but a *problem*.

Each impulse in its expression tends to call up other impulses; and it brings *into consciousness* other experiences. A child puts forth, by natural impulse, his hand towards a bright color; his hand touches it and he gets new experiences —feelings of contact; these, in turn, are stimulus to a further act; he puts the thing in his mouth, and gets a taste, etc. In other words, *the expression of every impulse stimulates other experiences and these react into the original impulse and modify it. This reaction of the induced experiences into the inducing impulse is the psychological basis of moral conduct.* In the animals, so far as we can judge, the stimulus and the response seem to assume purely serial order, one impulse calling forth its appropriate act, this its proper sequence and so on. The later acts or experiences do not return into the earlier; they are not referred or reflected back. The animal life is one of association, not of thought or reflection.

xi. Will, or the Mediation of Impulse

This back-reference of an experience to the impulse which induces it, we may term the *mediation* of impulse. If we suppose that the series of experiences used in the previous illustration give the experience of an orange, then the next time the same impulse of following light occurs it is modified by all the experiences in which it previously resulted. It is qualitatively different; the image or idea of the pleasant contacts and tastes is now a part of the impulse. A child follows a purely natural impulse in making more or less articulate sounds; these sounds, through the response which others make to them (a response as natural as the sequence of contacts upon the following of light with the eye) set up other experiences of the child, and these induced experiences mediate the original babbling impulses. He finds that, expressing one impulse, he gets attention when he falls down; by another, food when he is hungry, etc. It is not simply that these results *do* follow, but that the child becomes *conscious* that they follow; that is, the results are referred back to the original impulse and enter into its structure in consciousness. It is evident that these mediations, or conscious back-references, constitute the *meaning* of the impulse—they are its *significance*, its *import*. The impulse is *idealized*. The impulse mediated, that is given conscious value through the reference into it of the other experiences which will result from its expression, constitutes *volition* proper.

xii. The Ethical Interpretation of this Process

As the primary point to understand, in ethical psychology, is the return of induced experiences into the stimulating impulse, so the fundamental fallacy to avoid is the *separation* of impulse and induced experiences. It is too common an error to think of the expression of the impulse as an independent act and of the induced experiences as simply certain external consequences which follow upon the act, but which have nothing intrinsically to do with it—which in themselves are indifferent to the act. (See Martineau, *Types of Ethical Theory*, Vol. II, p. 24.) So we hear of the act *and* its consequences. In fact, the consequences, so far as they refer back, *are* the act as a moral or conscious (not simply physical) act. Differences of moral value (as we shall see later) depend simply upon the range and thoroughness of this mediation—the completeness with which the "consequences" of an act are returned into the structure of the natural impulse. We thus see again the mistake of the systems which attempt—like Martineau's—to build up ethical theory on the basis of separate natural impulses. Their moral value is in their interactions, not in themselves as independent. (Bentham, *Principles of Morals and Legislation*, Vol. I of *Works*, pp. 49–55, brings out this truth very clearly; he uses, however, the term "motive" to denote what I call natural impulse, while I shall use the term motive to designate the mediated impulse.)

The mediation of the impulse through the experiences it excites, may be comparatively organic or comparatively external. That is, some "results" are almost entirely conditioned upon the relation of the impulse expressed to other organs of action—as satisfaction from food when hungry, burning hand from putting it in fire, etc., while others are due more to circumstances which accompany the act at the time, but which may be absent as a rule—as poison may be found in a food usually healthy. But this distinction is not rigid (that is, there are no "results" absolutely internal and none absolutely external to the act) and does not afford a natural basis for separation of acts into those truly moral, and those morally indifferent. A large part of our moral discipline consists precisely in learning how to estimate probabilities—to distinguish between relatively necessary and relatively accidental results and to mediate the impulse accordingly.

Psychologically, the mediation of impulse (a) *idealizes*

the impulse, gives it its value, its significance or place in the whole system of action, and (b) *controls*, or directs it. The fundamental ethical categories result from this distinction. The worth of an impulse is, psychologically, the whole set of experiences which, presumably (that is, upon the best judgment available) it will call into being. This, *ethically*, constitutes the *goodness* (or badness) of the impulse—the satisfaction (or dissatisfaction) which it carries. But the thought of the consequences which will follow, their conscious return back into the impulse, modify it—check it, increase it, alter it. The impulse to reach, otherwise immediately expressed, is arrested by the nascent consciousness of the pain of the burn, it is reinforced by the nascent consciousness of the satisfaction of food; the impulse to see is profoundly modified by the response of other experiences when the child learns to read, etc. In this modification, through reaction of anticipated experiences, we have the basis of what, ethically, we term *obligation*—the necessity of modifying any particular expression of impulse by the whole system of which it is one part.

Thus we have, on one side, the moral categories of Satisfaction, Good (Summum Bonum), Value, and, on the other, those of Duty, Law, Control, Standard, etc. Every concrete act unites, of course, the two phases; in its complete character, as affording satisfaction and, at the same time, fulfilling its organic interactions, it is *right* and the agent which it expresses is *free*. Thus we have three main sets of ethical ideas: those centering, respectively, about (a) the *Value*, (b) the *Control*, (c) the *Freedom* of conduct.

4

The Moral Consciousness

XIII.   The Subject of the Moral Judgment

What is the subject, and what the predicate of the moral judgment? That is, to *what* do we attach the ideas of good, bad, right, wrong, etc., and what is the *meaning* of these predicates when attached? We begin by asking what it is that has moral meaning; what conditions must be met in order that ethical notions may be applied to any experience? We may sum up what we have already learned as follows: only an act (and a conscious act) has moral significance; every conscious act, in its lowest terms, is a mediated impulse—"mediation" being the reference back to an impulse of the experiences which it is likely to occasion. In this process, as we have seen, the consequences of the impulse cease to be mere external results and come to form the *content* of the act.

We may recognize three degrees of completeness of this mediation. In the most complete reaction, the original or natural impulse is completely *transformed*; it no longer exists in its first condition; our impulse to locomotion for example is entirely made over when the reaction of other experiences into it is completed—when we learn to walk; the first babbling impulse is wholly transformed when we learn to talk, etc. This also means that the mediating experiences are completely *absorbed* into the initiating impulse; the two sides, the immediate and the mediate, no longer have any separate existence. This complete reaction we call *habit*. When the reaction is less organized into the impulse, and yet is closely connected with it, we have general lines or plans of action; the larger, more continuous and permanent expectations which form the framework, as it were, of our conduct—one's occupation, the daily round of acts which, without being fixed habits, yet form the limits within which one's other acts fall. And finally, we have the particular variable acts, where the experiences which express an impulse are so numerous and complex as to be uncertain. In this case, the "consequences" do not organically react of themselves, but we have to "think it over" and calculate as best we may the probable meaning of an act.

If acts all came under the first principle, we should be slaves of routine; if they all came under the last, our whole time would be taken up with minute and anxious reflection and our deeds would have no effectiveness. As it is, habits are the tools which put at our immediate disposal the results of our former experiences, thus economizing force; our general plans hold us within certain limits and thus keep us from being at the mercy of caprice or the flux of circumstance; while the play of the relatively uncertain elements keeps our life from petrifying and forms an unceasing call to the exercise of the best forethought at command. "Probability is the guide of life." It is the tension between the habitual and the more variable factors that constitutes the significance of our conduct morally. Habits, second nature, give us consistency and force; the reflective element keeps us thoughtful. All of the tendencies to action, taken together, constitute "capacity"—the power of action, whether impulsive, or habitual, or reflective, which an agent has at disposal.

If the view so far presented be correct, we may assert that either *conduct* or *character* is the subject to which we attach moral predicates. The terms "character" and "conduct" do not refer to different subjects, but to slightly different aspects of the same subject. We say character when we are thinking of the mediated impulses as the source from which all particular acts issue. It does not refer to the bald unmediated impulses, nor does it refer to fixed unchangeable habits. It designates the *way* in which impulses (varying, of course, in every person) are directed and controlled—that is, mediated. The impulses are still there, and just so far as, in their expression, they give rise to new experiences, character is modified. There is accordingly no force in the objection sometimes made, that to make character the subject to

which the adjectives, good and bad, apply, does not allow
freedom or the possibility of change. The reaction of the experiences, which the expression of character effects, is sufficient ground for change. Nor is there more force in the
objection that to make character the subject of moral predi-
cation is to afford an excuse for acts which are bad on the
ground of the "good" feeling or disposition from which they
proceeded. Character includes the style and nature of the
ends, the *objects* by which the individual mediates his impulses, and thus affords sufficient basis for taking into account the objective results of acts. We cannot excuse, for
example, an act of unregulated benevolence on the ground
that it proceeds from a good heart or good feeling, when we
judge on the basis of character, any more than when we
judge on the basis of the results of the act. On the contrary
we are only enabled the better to locate the defect; the person's character is such that he does not properly mediate his
impulses; he is defective on the reflective side; or, again, the
nature of the end which that character sets up—the following of the immediate impulse of the moment—is not such
as to be an object of approval.

On the other hand, by conduct we do not mean a mere
aggregate of particular acts. Conduct is the *expression* of the
mediated impulses. Character, according to its definition
(the way of mediating impulses), has no reality apart from
the acts in which such impulses must sooner or later issue.
It is because acts proceed from character that they are not a
mere series of separate things, one after another, but form
the organized whole: conduct. In a word, character is the
unity, the spirit, the idea of conduct, while conduct is the
reality, the realized or objective expression of character. The
objection sometimes made to taking conduct as the subject
of the moral judgment, that conduct is something outward
and therefore indifferent, thus has no place. As character
is a *way* of acting, conduct is the executed way.

We can now deal shortly with a pair of antitheses
which are sometimes set up as the proper object of moral
judgment, viz.: motive on one side, consequences on the
other. Motive is only character in a given instance. Motive
is never a bare natural impulse, but is impulse in the light of

the consequences which may reasonably be supposed to result from acting upon it. A mere impulse to anger is not a motive, and in itself is neither good nor bad. It becomes good or bad according to the nature of the end to which it is attached. Consequences, on the other hand, are no more a part of conduct than they are of character, save as they are foreseen; save, that is, as there is reason to believe that they will follow a given impulse. But, if there is such reason, the consequences become a part of the conditions which enter into the mediation of impulse – a part of character.

For theories denying the necessity of mediation by consequences see reference previously made to Martineau, and Kant, *Theory of Ethics* (translated by Abbott), pp. 28, 44–46, 107–14, 123. For theories holding to consequences see Bentham, *Principles of Morals*, and Mill, *Autobiography*, pp. 49–50, and *Utilitarianism*, Ch. 2 (where, however, the doctrine refers not to the consequences alone, but to the exclusion of motive). For a criticism of Martineau, see Sidgwick, *Methods of Ethics*, Bk. III, Ch. 12. For a discussion of the subject, Muirhead, *Elements of Ethics*, pp. 55–62; Mackenzie, *Manual of Ethics*, pp. 40–46; Alexander, *Moral Order*, pp. 36–46; Green, *Prolegomena*, Bk. IV, Ch. 1.

XIV.   The Predicate of the Moral Judgment

When shall we call the character, or conduct, good or bad? An impulse, it must be remembered, is a native or spontaneous way in which the self acts. The experiences which are referred back to the impulse are experiences which the self undergoes because of its own nature. The mediation of the impulse thus means a process of self-development. It is the process by which the self becomes aware of the meaning, in terms of its own experiences, of one of its own impulses. The impulse, by itself, or in isolation, is a partial or abstract expression of the self. The child who reaches for a light may want the light, but he does not want the burn which is none the less a part of himself, an organic portion of his experience, under the circumstances. So the child may want to talk, but he can hardly be said to want the introduction into new social relations, and into a world of science and literature, which the expression of that impulse brings about. And yet all this is involved in the original impulse. The expression of impulse is thus a process of self-realization. The first meaning of an impulse of anger is simply blind reaction, but this reaction has consequences (relations to others, habits established, etc.), which are, from that time on, part of the impulse. This tendency to act without thought, to set up hostile relations to others, is now the meaning which the impulse has for the self. Or the blind reaction of anger is against some meanness; it serves to do away with that meanness and to brace the self. These relations differentiate the impulse and bring the self to consciousness in this direction. *The completest possible interaction of an impulse with all other experiences, or the completest possible relation of an impulse to the whole self constitutes the predicate, or moral value, of an act.* The predicate is, therefore, identical in kind with the subject.[1] That is, the subject, "this act," in the judgment "this act is right," is an act mediated by reference to the other experiences it occasions—its effect upon the self. The predicate "is right" simply traces out such effects more completely, taking into account, so far as possible, the reaction into the future character of the self, and, in virtue of this reaction, judging the act.

The basis for discriminating between "right" and wrong in the judgment is found in the fact that some acts tend to narrow the self, to introduce friction into it, to weaken its power, and in various ways to *disintegrate* it, while other acts tend to expand, invigorate, harmonize, and in general organize the self. The angry act, for example, in the first case given, is bad, because it brings division, friction, weakness into the self; in the second case, "good," because it unifies the self and gives power.

The first effect of every mediation of an impulse is to check or arrest that impulse. Reflection means postpone-

---

[1]   This has important bearings upon the subject of the *criterion* as we shall see hereafter. Because the predicate and subject are identical in principle, both being the mediation of the impulse, the criterion always lies within, not without, the act. The criterion is nothing but the completest possible view of the act.

ment; it is delayed action. Through this delay the impulse is brought into connection with other impulses, habits and experiences. Now if a due balance is kept, the result is that the original impulse is harmonized with the self, and, when expressed, it realizes not only its own partial nature but that of the whole self; it becomes the organ through which the whole self finds outlet. The moral criterion for an act proceeding from anger or from benevolence is whether only a part of the self or the whole character moves outward in the act. The bad act is partial, the good organic. The good man "eats to live," that is, the satisfaction even of the appetite of hunger is functional to the whole self or life; if we say the man who "lives to eat" is bad, it is because he is sacrificing much of himself to one partial expression of himself.

We see again the impossibility of classifying the impulses into a hierarchy of higher and lower. When an act is right, there is no higher or lower as to the impulse from which it proceeds. The satisfaction of hunger in its place (that is, one which unifies the whole self) is as imperious in its rightness as the noblest act of heroism or the sublimest act of self-devotion.

The good man, in a word, is his whole self in each of his acts; the bad man is a partial (and hence a different) self in his conduct. He is not one person, for he has no unifying principle. (Compare the expressions "dissipated, gone to pieces, shaky, unstable, lacking in integrity, duplicity, devious, indirect, sneaky," etc.)

This conception of the organic mediation of an impulse as equivalent to rightness may be expressed in other ways. Aristotle seems to have meant this by his principle of the "golden mean" (Aristotle, *Ethics*, Bk. ii, Chs. 6–9). While he states it as an arithmetical mean, it is easy to translate what he says into the conception of an active balance in which due regard is had both to the immediate impulse and to the mediating consequences; *e.g.*, courage is the mean between foolhardiness and cowardice, foolhardiness being undue preponderance of impulse, cowardice lack of proper assertion of impulse; moderation is the balance between extravagance (preponderance of immediate impulse) and miserliness (preponderance of reflection), and so on.

Alexander conveys the same idea by calling rightness a "moving equilibrium" (*Moral Order*, pp. 97–111).

The same idea is also expressed in the conception of "self-realization," provided this is understood in the sense of expressing the concrete capacity of an individual agent, and not in the sense of filling in the blank scheme of some undefined, purely general self. (Green, *Prolegomena*, pp. 178–207; Mackenzie, *Manual of Ethics*, pp. 136–38, and Bradley, *Ethical Studies*, Ch. 6, tend to use the idea in the latter sense. For further criticism see *Philosophical Review*, Vol. ii, p. 652, on "Self-Realization as Moral Ideal" [*Early Works*, iv, 42].)

5

Moral Approbation, Value and Standard

xv. Natural Good

The satisfaction which any impulse affords in its expression may be termed its *natural* value. It is equivalent to what the economists term "value in use"—value which is directly enjoyed, but not measured. Such is the satisfaction which accompanies the fulfillment of the appetite of hunger or of thirst, in itself or apart from any consideration of its further bearings. But, as we have seen, the expression of an impulse is always referred back to it, and comes to constitute its meaning or the content of the act. Purely natural good is found therefore only in the original primitive satisfactions of early childhood: it is the state of animal innocence—the state of *knowing* neither good nor evil, but simply enjoying suffering good or suffering evil as they come.

xvi. Moral Good

The mediation of the impulse evidently prevents the immediate satisfaction of the impulse, and thus replaces natural good by a good which is presented to consciousness. This satisfaction mediated in thought, that is, by reflection upon the nature of an impulse in its relation to the self (or the whole system of impulses) is moral satisfaction or *moral value*.

This process of reflection evidently sets up a standard or criterion for the value of the original impulse. It no longer has worth in itself but simply in its relation to the whole set of desirable experiences which it will occasion. And this means, of course, its tendency to further the other impulses in its interaction with them, or to express the self. It may be compared with the measured or defined value of the economists, the measurement here also being through interaction or relation (namely, exchange) creating a tension of various impulses against each other, which makes it necessary to estimate the relative importance of each.

The mediating process evidently has two sides; there are two standpoints from which it may be considered, and in terms of which it may be stated. As in the operation of exchange there is but one reality, one process, and yet that process will be differently described according as it is the buyer or seller who reports it, so in measurement of moral value, or the reference of an impulse to the whole experience of the self. The process of mediation or measurement is one, and yet our mode of stating it will be different according as we look at it from the standpoint of the inducing impulse or of the impulses and experiences induced. The process, as a whole, is one of adjustment, of balancing, of co-ordination. But if we identify ourselves in imagination with the impulse, we have first the checking of the impulse, and then, as dammed up, its gradual transformation and reinforcement—the condition of *desire* and its struggle for fulfillment. The impulse, being the thing which makes itself directly felt in consciousness, is taken to be reality: it is the present factor.

But as the other impulses stimulated (redintegrated) and their results begin to be present in consciousness, we may identify ourselves with them and tell the story from their side. As induced and derivative, not immediately present (present only as results of the original impulse), they are *ideas*; yet, as induced, their reflective character is not equivalent to unreality; they make themselves felt by *checking* the very impulse which aroused them. In this aspect, they are the *law*, the controlling power of that impulse. They determine in what form, under what conditions of time, place, and quality, it may be satisfied. Thus they determine or measure its value; they say to it: You are not what you are alone or in yourself, but your value is what it is in relation to us. In this aspect, the induced experiences (reason, for short) are the *standard* of measurement for the natural impulse.

But the experiences thus reflectively brought forward, while they may transform the original impulse, they also reinforce it. They have their own impulsive quality, or urging for expression. Thus they constitute the *ideal*; what is desired; the *reflective* good. The gradual self-assertion of desire up to choice or preference, and the gradual formation of an ideal up to resolution or decision, are one and the same process of mediation of impulse described from the two standpoints, until they gradually merge in a complete unity —the overt act. The whole process is one of discovering and applying the criterion, a process of estimating value. In other words, it is a process of testing, of proving, until, in the act, there is *ap*-probation.

XVII.   Development of Volition from Side of Idea

We begin with a consideration of the process by which the end becomes developed into an act. This end is at first intellectual—that is, it exists in thought only. It is a *proposed* end, not an actualized one. It is an aim, a plan, an intention, a purpose—all terms expressing its unrealized condition. In its own content it does not differ from any image which may come before the mind. Its relation to the impulse which calls it into being tends, however, to unite its destiny with that of the impulse, and thus confer upon it a practical value. Consider a person who has an artistic impulse—one towards painting. This impulse cannot find its immediate expression; it calls before the mind (by association or redintegration) images of all circumstances which are relevant to it—which seem to be involved in its execution. According to the strength (the insistence and persistence) of the original impulse, the ideas thus aroused will be mere fleeting fancies, vague schemes to be carried out if circumstances favor, or a defined (determined) project. In abnormal cases, hypnotism, "compulsory ideas," etc., we find that every idea suggested to the mind tends to execute itself, or that some idea becomes so dominant that there is no co-ordination between it and others and hence no control. These abnormal cases reveal the normal principle, covered up by complexity of ordinary life—the connection of every idea with an impulse. In childhood we see precisely the same thing, save that here the idea is hardly distinguished in consciousness from the impulse. Attention reveals the same principle in its normal and matured form. Attention is an idea or set of ideas so completely bound up with an impulse that they demand realization. The sole difference from the abnormal "compulsory idea" is that in attention the induced ideas are *organically* connected with the impulse. That is to say, the distinguishing trait of attention is that it arouses the *whole* set of ideas which are relevant to the impulse, and *only* those, other ideas as they arise dying out because of their indifference to the realization of the impulse, while all relevant suggestions are maintained.

The full development of an ideal, an end, is, then, the same thing on the ethical side that we term reflective attention on the psychological side—just as the direct satisfaction of an impulse is equivalent to non-voluntary, or direct, attention. (See Dewey, *Psychology*, pp. 121–29 [*Early Works*, II, 108–14], on natural and acquired value; James, *Psychology*, Vol. I, pp. 416–24, on passive and voluntary attention.) Interest is, by general confession, bound up with attention; we may, therefore, expect to find a similar close connection between ideal and interest in the process of volition.

In the discussion of this development, it is convenient to consider separately two phases which are always, as matters of fact, found together. One of these is the formation of the intellectual content, the end (what is aimed at, the rational structure of the plan); the other, the connection of this intellectual content with the impulse—the *interest* or practical value which attaches to the aim as thought. Before considering them separately, it must again be remarked that while the *content* of the plan is purely intellectual or rational (abstract, or objective to the self), the fact that it is found worth while to develop the plan (that attention remains fixed) shows that this rational content is not, for a moment, freed from its practical or dynamic value—its connection with impulse as the immediately acting self.

XVIII.   Development of Intention or the Rational Content

An intention is what an agent *means* to do. It is thus the primary differentia of a volitional from a purely impulsive act, showing that the impulse is mediated. It constitutes *reflection*, or the control of the impulse by *reason*. The thought, or what one intends, may be a mere image which passes listlessly through the mind—as in the state of building castles in the air; it may be a vague undefined thought of something or other in general—a sentiment, what is sometimes termed "meaning well" or having "good intentions," and yet not meaning the particular *end* which alone is right. When ethically justifiable, it signifies giving attention to all the bearings which could be foreseen by an agent who had a proper interest in knowing what he is about.

So far, we have unduly simplified the account by ignoring the conflict of aims or the difficulty of coming to a conclusion in many cases. The natural satisfaction, that is, the thought of the course which the original impulse would take if left to itself, and the rational, or mediated, satisfaction contend in the mind. This is, as we shall see, the basis of the moral struggle, the conflict of desire and duty. Or, the various suggested *ends* do not harmonize; it is necessary either to bar out some, or else to discover a still more comprehensive aim in which the claims of the conflicting intentions shall be adjusted. Thus we are brought to *deliberation*, the more conscious weighing and balancing of values—consideration. We are apt to describe this process as if it were a coldly intellectual one. As matter of fact, it is a process of tentative action; we "try on" one or other of the ends, imagining ourselves actually doing them, going, indeed, in this make-believe action just as far as we can without actually doing them. In fact, we often find ourselves carried over the line here; the hold which a given impulse gets upon us while we are "trying it on" passes into overt act without our having consciously intended it. Particularly is this the case so far as our character is immature; there is a temporary relapse into a "compulsory idea."

Decision, *resolution*, the definitely formed plan, is the proper outcome of consideration. This expresses the conclusion of the process of conflict among ends, and the emergence of a purpose which, whether through suppression or comprehension of other ends, now expresses the self. It is the completed self under the given circumstances. The appearance of an ideal in the mind and the final selection, or determination, are simply the beginning and the end of one and the same process—there is no thrusting in of an outside power, of will or attention. The process we are describing *is* the process of will or attention. This brings us expressly to a statement of the connection of the intention or aim with the self urging on to action—impulse.

xix. Development of Motive

The reaction of the intended content into impulse renders the former itself an impulse; the original impulse, now enlarged, goes on to express itself. This identification of the aim with impulse is motive, the rational spring to action.

As attention cannot be separated from interest, the formation of a plan cannot be separated from the reaction of that plan into the self. Every end that occurs to the mind awakens a certain amount of interest, or has a *certain value* attached to it. It is this reaction, the extent to which the thought tends to stir the self, to call it out, that measures the motive power of the thought. Abstractly we may distinguish between the conception of the end, which is rational or reflective, and the motive power of this end; actually, we cannot. Whether or not the conceived end remains in consciousness, *even as a conception*, expresses its value to the self. This identity of the evolution of the ideal, on the intellectual side, with the evolution of a determining motive power, on the emotional, *both being forms of self-expression*, is the key to an understanding of the ethics of motive. The ideal, or end, is the abstract, objective expression, of the self; the acting, or real, self temporarily checked as to its overt expression (immediate activity) but deepened and widened in its consciousness of what it is doing—in its appreciation of value. The motive is this abstract self completely related, having its value felt, and thus no longer merely objective but subjective as well, and hence passing into act. (See Dewey, *Psychology*, pp. 15–23 and p. 347 [*Early Works*, 11, 18–24 and 299].)

If we take the reaction of the content into the other impulses of the self, and consider it apart from the reason or purpose of the act, we get the conflict of *emotions*—the stress and strain of feelings, the play of hope and fear, of doubt and expectation, of suspense and adjustment, of tension and growing ease, which is the subjective counterpart of the objective conflict and resolution of ideals already spoken of. (See Dewey, *Psychology*, Ch. 12. The "formal feelings" there described are the consciousness of the *process* of mediation of impulse, apart from its content.) One of these emotions is so important that it is often identified with volition itself; it therefore demands special attention. It is the consciousness of *effort*. Effort is the same process, stated in terms of emotion, that we call consideration, or reflection, when stated in terms of rational content. It is the feeling of the *division* of activity—a necessary accompaniment of the period of suspense within which the original activity is arrested, while the induced impulses which arrest have not yet gained sufficient force to determine the act. It is a period when the impulses are striving towards co-ordination and yet, not having reached it, are in tension against each other —temporarily oppose each other. Such temporary opposition is evidently necessary in order to secure a balance which will utilize each set to the full, or secure the maximum of energy. It is obvious that if the opposition of one set to the other is imperfect, one or the other will get the preponderance too soon. The result will be an undue suppression of the other set, loss of efficiency and ultimate friction. This conflict of impulses *which oppose each other in order to reinforce each other* is reported in consciousness as the feeling of effort, whose distinguishing trait is precisely a peculiar combination of feelings of power and impotence, of activity and resistance to activity.

xx. Nature of Effort or Tension

According to this statement, effort is simply the consciousness of the critical moment in the development of will;

it is not to be identified with the putting forth of will itself. And yet effort is often considered to be will asserting its own power *against* some resistance outside of itself. What is the origin of this fallacy? What are its ethical consequences?

According to the theory given in the text, neither one or the other of the contending forces is to be identified by itself with will; each represents a normal and a necessary phase of will—the mediate and the immediate, the original and the induced, to repeat once more. Moreover their temporary separation and the resistance which one phase of the activity offers to the other is itself a factor of great positive importance in the evolution of a truly rational practical conclusion, or act. Now, if will proper is not this whole process, but is some one distinct power, some force standing outside the other factors, if therefore these other factors are resistance not *in* will, but *to* it, both our psychological statement, and our ethical theory must be radically changed.

It is not difficult to detect the source of the error. We necessarily tend, during the struggle, to identify ourselves especially with that phase of the process which is prominent in consciousness, and to regard the other phase (although equally an expression of ourselves) as indifferent or even as hostile to ourselves. The more interesting, the more important, is, for the time being, the self; it absorbs consciousness. Then we fail to notice that the final act, the complete expression of self, is by no means this side alone, but is colored throughout, and is given value, by the other phase of the self. Take a poor person tempted to steal; suppose he has habits of honesty. Here the self is identified with the thoughts of decency, of self-respect, of reputation, which arise and assert themselves against the direct impulse to take the loaf of bread. The mediating self is *the* self, and the impulse is a mere intruder, something outside the will, outside the self, and yet somehow coming in to tempt it. Yet the very fact that this impulse is presented as an end, that it becomes the *thought* of stealing, shows that that end also, so far as entertained, is self. And if the final determination is not to take the bread, this conclusion, the completed self, has by no means the significance which the same conclusion (the same outwardly) would have when not the outcome of such a struggle; the self has not simply returned to its normal state after having got rid of an intruder. The impulse to steal has become an integral part of the final act —not, of course, in its own isolated state, but in its mediated relationship.[2]

And if the statement as thus formulated seems strange, stated in another way, namely, that the meeting and overcoming of temptation develops character, it seems a mere commonplace.

In other instances, the thought of the original, natural impulse will seem the real self, and the induced experiences the invading force; as, for example, when a man starts to fulfill a natural office of friendliness and then is checked by the thought of the unpopularity of the object as likely to affect him if he does the act. In this case, the very fact that these reasons have weight with the man, that the thought of the obloquy holds his mind, shows that that end expresses himself—in its measure. And yet, the man feels that his "true" self demands the negation of this temptation, and so this end is thought of as external, and the final conclusion (which in reality involves the co-operation of both partial selves) is taken as simply the victory of one over the other. So it may be as to the thing physically done, but in meaning, in its moral (or character) value, it involves both. The same apparent dualism is found in any exhibition of *attention*. In one aspect, the self as attending, the group of impulses and habits, which are endeavoring to assert themselves, seems to be the self, and the content attended to, the object, seems to be outside the self. Yet the fact that the content arouses such interest as to maintain the tendency to assimilate the attending "subject" and the "object" attended to, shows that the integrity of the self, its complete assertion, is neither side separately but the co-ordination of the two phases. Of this co-ordination, the very struggle, or tension, is an integral phase necessary in bringing out the full bearing, or importance of both factors. Every one would admit that we do not get adequate consciousness of the *object* of attention

---

[2]   The bearing of this upon the question of the relation of good and evil, and the possibility of an absorption of evil into good character, or vice-versa (*corruptio optimi, pessima*), will come up later.

until attention has worked itself out; it is just as true that the impulses and habits which press forward to the object have *their* significance and value brought to consciousness at the same time.

The fact that sometimes *the* self seems to be inducing experience and sometimes the induced, shows the absurdity of setting up a *fixed* will or self. When the attraction is *towards* the conceived end, that seems to be self; when that end repels, upon the whole, so that the movement is towards reduction of its value, the self is located in the primary experience. A man's true self in temperance is in the induced experiences; in courage in the inducing, etc.

xxi.   Theories of Abstract Ideals

The ethical consequences of identifying will with a power which puts forth effort against or towards something outside of will flow from the interruption thus abruptly introduced into the moral process.

The existence of the ideal is rendered inexplicable. It is reduced *a*] to a supernatural visitor from a world above that of ordinary experience. The very word "ideal" suggests to a sophisticated mind something which is remote and unattainable—outside of the natural course of life. If not defined as introduced into the mind from without by a divine power, it is thought of after the analogy of this concept. See Martineau, *Types of Ethical Theory*, Vol. ii, pp. 73–74, 97–99, 217–18; and *Study of Religion*, Vol. ii, pp. 26–40, for assertions of the transcendent character of the ideal.

b] Recent moralists have seen the objections which attach to putting the origin and formation of the ideal outside of the self. Yet instead of showing the point, in the normal process of volition (the appearance of the induced experiences which mediate the original tendency to action) at which the distinction arises, they split the self into two selves and attribute the impulses and appetites to one, the actual urgent self, and the ideal to another self, a "higher" or "rational" or "spiritual" self in general.

1. Kant presents one type of this view. According to him, there is a sensuous, "phenomenal" self, constituted by

appetites and impulses; this furnishes the actual material of our volition. Besides this, there is a rational, "noumenal" self, which sets up the ideal or goal of effort (*Theory of Ethics*, pp. 105–24, 144–47).

2. Green recognizes the objection to splitting the self so completely, and falls back on the notion of the moral ideal as meaning the end of the self as a whole, while natural satisfaction means the satisfaction of a particular impulse. This *might* be interpreted in a sense analogous with the theory I have previously advanced, but as matter of fact, Green makes the whole self not the complete definition of the natural impulse, under the conditions, but something quite distinct from any possible development of the particular impulse as such. See Green, *Prolegomena*, pp. 160–62, 178–88, 202–4; *Works*, Vol. ii, pp. 136–48, 308–9, 329, 336–38. Compare with the following criticisms my article in *Philosophical Review*, Vol. i, No. 6 [*Early Works*, iii, 155–73].

Objections to the absolute or separate ideal may be stated as follows:

a] It makes a dualism, practically unbridgeable, between the moral and the scientific phases of our experience. If any account of the ideal can be given meeting the needs of the case, we should certainly hesitate before accepting a mode of statement introducing ideas which not only do not lie within the scope of scientific method as usually presented, but which emphasize their complete *transcendence* of scientific categories and results. All the above theories (any theories which set up an independent, fixed ideal) are necessarily metaphysical in a sense which separates metaphysics from science, instead of making it a more complete recognition of scientific methods and data.

That moral science introduces a set of ideas which are not brought explicitly to the front in the physical or even the biological sciences, there can be no doubt. But the account which I have given recognizes this distinction without changing it into a break. Physical science deals wholly with the rational, abstract or objective content. That is, it leaves out of account (*i*) the fact that every object, or law (relation of objects) *arises*, in actual experience from an inducing impulse, an action of self; (*ii*) the fact that sooner or later it *reacts back* into the impulse, and thus has its *final* meaning in the new significance which it gives to action. In other words, physical science deals simply with the *content* of mediation, leaving one side the whole *process* of mediation. In considering, for example, a flower, it takes account neither of the impulses of seeing, of reaching, touching, smelling, etc., which make the flower into an object in consciousness nor yet the additional value, æsthetic and moral, as well as intellectual, which our activity (our character) will have as result of the study. It omits, in a word, both the *reason* for and the *nature* of the *value* which objects have in our experience—in relation to the self.

While biology is compelled to assume the *fact* of value as possessed by objects in relation to life (most generally their value in either maintaining or hindering the life of the genus in question), it does not consider this value as present to the *consciousness* of the agent. It will describe, for example, the interaction, both favorable and unfavorable, of a race of men and their environment, but it confines itself to results actually accomplished. It puts one side this value as realized in the conscious life of that race, as affording motive and assimilated into character.

Yet science, as science, does not deny the fact of further conscious value. It simply concentrates itself upon other aspects of reality—the *content* which gives value independent of why or how it gives it. Neglect is not denial of value; and recognition of value is not denial of science. Ethics completes the analysis of reality—experience—begun by physical and biological science. It does not introduce a new and opposed set of ideas. (Royce, *Spirit of Modern Philosophy*, Ch. 12, distinguishes between the world of description and the world of appreciation, this distinction being identical in statement with the distinction just made; but he seems to conceive of the "physical" world as a fixed thing, as, indeed, a limitation, due to our "*finite* nature," instead of the intermediate stage in the development of an act: —the definition of the conditions of action.)

The fixed, or absolute ideal, is not only inexplicable, but *is presupposed or ready-made*. Against such ideals, we may urge:

b] No moral value attaches to their working-out, or formation. It may belong to the attitude taken towards them, to their choice or rejection, but nothing more. But, in our actual experience, no such separation exists between forming and choosing an end of action. Our moral discipline consists even more in the responsibility put upon us to develop ideals, than in choosing between them when made. The making of plans, working them out into their bearings, etc., is at once a test of character and a factor in building it up. But this is an impossibility if the ideal is something *given towards* which will is to be directed – if it lies outside the normal process of volition. (Thus, Martineau is logical in holding that only intellectual or prudential value attaches to the consideration of consequences. *Types of Ethical Theory*, Vol. ii, pp. 255–56. With a fixed ideal, they must lie outside, be mere *means*, and moral meaning is found simply in the selection of one or other of the ends given ready-made. *Deliberation* has no intrinsic moral significance. So Green has to draw a decided line between the estimation of acts, and of character, the former being decided by a consideration of consequences, the latter by a consideration of the disposition from which the act proceeds. Moreover the consideration of character, or conscientiousness, he has logically to reduce to a subjective introspection on the part of the agent as to whether "he has been as good as he should have been," not an objective examination of whether his interest, or attention, is rightly distributed. *Prolegomena*, pp. 317–25. On p. 259, Green takes another view of the ideal.)

c] The process of choice, of selection between competing ideals, is rendered arbitrary and meaningless. Why should there be two competing ideals at all, one good, the other bad? And, supposing there are, on what grounds do we prefer one to the other? As to the first question, there appears to be no alternative between saying (with Kant) that there is a fixed dualism in our nature, sense, as inducing to evil, being on one side, reason, as good, on the other; with Green, that the particular impulse is always and fixedly opposed in its realization, to the demand of our entire nature (*Prolegomena*, pp. 180–83, 206–7, 233–34); or (with Martineau) that there is an original fixed scale of higher and lower in our impulses. But experience does not testify to a conflict between ends one labelled, from the start and unalterably, good and the other labelled bad. On the contrary, one *becomes* good, the other bad, *in the process of competition* and deliberation. Moreover our *theory accounts for the presence* of the two competitors and the relative conflict between them; it is the old story of the immediate and the mediating phases of action. It gives positive meaning to the opposition—the deepening of consciousness. (See Alexander, *Moral Order*, pp. 297–316, also *International Journal of Ethics*, Vol. ii, p. 409, for an adequate recognition of the fact that the competing ends are *made* good and bad, by the very process of deliberation and choice; or, as I have previously put it, the process of action is itself one of estimating and constituting value, of proving and approving.)

As to the second question, on what grounds does the self choose between the two fixed ideals, there appears no answer save an appeal to arbitrary free-will, the power of choosing between alternatives without any reason for the choice. The problem of freedom will meet us hereafter; at this point, it is sufficient to note that the sole occasion for bringing in a freedom of the kind just referred to, is that the alternative ends to be chosen are taken as lying outside the development of will. On our theory, the emergence of the ends and the final choice are facts of exactly the same order, being only an earlier and a later stage, in time, of the definition of an impulse in its relation to the self. It may also be noticed, at this point, that the theory opposed to freedom, namely, that of necessitation has its origin in exactly the same assumption that the origin and development of the ends lie outside the self; being conceived as foreign forces, it is natural to draw the inference that the strongest force determines the will—overlooking the fact that ends have motive power, great or small, only so far as they interest, hold attention—that is, express the direction in which the self is already moving.

There is still another difficulty as to choice. If one side comes thus labelled bad from the start, why should it ever be chosen? Why should the bad recognized as such, offering itself as such, have superior value? The doctrine of original sin is the only logical answer, and Kant is perfectly logical in trying to introduce a philosophical statement of that doctrine. *Theory of Ethics*, pp. 339–52 (Abbott's trans., "Religion Within the Bounds Simply of Reason").

d] No basis is afforded for development of moral ideals —for positive progress. The ideal is there once for all and it is only a question of greater or less distance from it. The logical conclusion (not that these writers have been logical enough to draw it) is the Pharisaical one—since there has been progress, how much better morally must we be than savages, or our primitive ancestors, or "the lower classes," or than any one else whose acts do not rank objectively as high as ours! On our theory, it is the ideal, as recognition of the objective meaning of action, which has progressed; so that there is only additional capacity, and thus additional demand, for mediation. One class of persons, as a class, is, then, morally no better than any other; one period no more virtuous than another. Responsibilities not virtues, increase. The increase, that is, of knowledge of the bearings of an impulse makes care in action morally more imperative, we are no nearer a goal of perfection, but action has more intellectual and æsthetic meaning.

e] From this it follows also that progress in character is purely negative;—on the basis of a fixed ideal it consists simply in lessening the gap which separates us from the ideal. The moral life thus becomes a struggle towards something without and beyond, and, in so far, a hopeless and slavish struggle. The ideal never is realized, do what we may. (Kant has to fall back on purely supernatural means to meet this difficulty, *Theory of Ethics*, pp. 218–31.) The ideal has no self-executing, no *moving* power. It is never *of itself a motive*. Upon our theory, the very fact that an ideal is present in consciousness, is, as far as it goes, its realization; it is the self moving that way; in so far as it modifies conduct, it is directive and effective. A *mere* ideal, or unrealized ideal, is a contradiction in terms. The ideal is a very present help in time of trouble.

f] The fixed ideal gives no instruction or information as to the particular thing needing to be done. It does not translate itself into terms of a concrete, individual act—and every *act* is concrete and individual. In other words, it does not and cannot become a *working* principle for what has to

be done. (See Green, again, *Prolegomena*, pp. 317–25, for
the necessity, on his basis, of a double standard.) Such
ideals are pure luxuries; only the sentimentalist and the pure
theorist can afford them. The working man, of busy life,
must have an ideal by which he can go in action, one which
defines specific acts. (Green attempts to meet the need by
reference to the past institutions in which the ideal is embodied; *cf. Prolegomena*, pp. 180, 207–8, 393–94. But, since
such embodiments are, according to him, only apparent, not
real, it is difficult to see how this gives the required instruction. Kant attempts to get to the specific act needed by
reference to the universal, non-self-contradictory character
of the ideal. Of this, more below.) Again, our theory meets
this need, because the ideal is *nothing but* the definition or
mediation of the immediately acting, or impulsive, self.

We conclude then, from our examination of abstract
ideals, that true ideals are the *working hypotheses* of action;
they are the best comprehension we can get of the value of
our acts; their use is that they mark our consciousness of
what we are doing, not that they set up remote goals. Ideals
are like the stars; we steer by them, not towards them.

xxii.   The Hedonistic Theory of Value

According to the theory advanced, value consists in the
realization or expression of impulse, moral value being the
conscious realization of impulse in its relation to the self or
system of active experience. The "ideal" is the consciousness
of the relationship. The function of the ideal is to give content or meaning to the impulse; it is the impulse stated in
objective terms. Abstract idealism was criticized on the
ground that it made the ideal something at which impulse
and activity in general is aimed, and in which therefore it is
exhausted. There is another group of theories which also
sets up an outside goal for activity, although differing as to
the nature of this goal. This group is the hedonistic (from
the Greek, ἡδονή pleasure). It proclaims that pleasure is the
end towards which all action is directed—that pleasurable
feeling (involving the absence of pain) is the Summum
Bonum, the supreme good and thus the standard for measuring value.

Before passing on to its consideration, it may first be contrasted with abstract idealism. Comparatively, hedonism may be termed empirical idealism. It has an ideal—pleasure —but this ideal is a state, a passive experience, something which has already been enjoyed;[3] as against this, the ideal of perfection set up by the other school is attainable only in the remote future—at the end of an infinite time according to Kant and Green. The good of one school is reason, that of the other feeling.[4] The two schools have stood over against each other since the very beginning of ethical speculation. At first, it was the Cynic against the Cyrenaic; then the Stoic against the Epicurean; latterly, the Kantian against the Utilitarian. (See Sidgwick, *History of Ethics*, pp. 32–33 and 71–88.)

Such a continuous opposition is accounted for on the ground not that one is all truth, and the other all error; but on the ground that each school represents the abstraction of one phase of the process of volition. In truth, the process begins and ends in activity; the beginning being impulsive (original or habitual) activity, the end activity whose value has been measured. In this process, reason (the phase selected and set up independently by the abstract idealists) represents the transition from the immediate to the mediated activity—the consciousness of the relations of the impulse, the objectified impulse, while feeling (the phase abstracted by the empiricists) represents the consciousness of value to the agent as an *individual*—the activity in its *subjective* existence. Reason is turning the action inside out, seeing it as part of a general order, independent of the individual's own immediate propensities. Hence the ideas of spectator, disinterested, universal, which associate themselves so easily with reason. Rational content is required to give the individual's feeling substance and *real* worth. Feeling is turning the action outside in; it is the realization of value terms of the agent's own peculiar character.[5]

Hedonism (as compared with rationalism) fails to see

---

[3]   See note to p. 147 of Murray's *Introduction to Ethics*; also Mill, *Utilitarianism*, pp. 348–49; Bain, *Moral Science*, p. 27.

[4]   "Reason is and must be the slave of passion"—Hume. See *Treatise of Human Nature*, Bk. II, Part Three, Secs. 3 and 4.

[5]   Hence Lotze's hedonistic tendencies. See *Practical Philosophy*, pp. 15–20.

that the nature or content of this value (as distinct from the mere fact of some value) depends upon the mediation of reason; while abstract idealism fails to note that the reduction of self to reason or thought leaves the self in the air, with no *individualized* value. Each of them has to disparage the opposite principle, or reduce it to a mere means to its own end. The theory of experimental idealism (as we term the position here taken), because of its recognition of activity as the primary reality is enabled to give both thought and feeling their due. It does not attempt the impossible task of setting up for activity some end, whether a state of feeling or one of perfect reason, outside itself. It is content to note that activity, moving according to its own law and principle, becomes objectively conscious of its value in the ends which its projects (ideals) and subjectively conscious of its value in the emotions which accompany the realizing of these ends.

As compared with the facts, then, both ethical rationalism and empiricism take a derived and secondary phase for the whole truth. As compared with each other, rationalism is right in so far as it asserts that feelings (or pleasure and pain) are mere abstractions apart from the objects (or rational contents) which give them their quality, while empiricism is right in asserting that an end which is not *felt* (that is, appreciated as part of the agent's own being) has no moral validity or claims.

XXIII.   Feeling as End or Ideal

We shall consider pleasure-pain, (1) as end or ideal of action, (2) as motive, and (3) as criterion or measure of value.

The contradiction in hedonism meets us at the outset. Pleasure and pain as feelings exist only as they are actually felt, and to the one who feels them. Because we have one word, we are apt to suppose that there is some one fact or entity corresponding. There are, indeed, pleasures and pains, but no such thing as pleasure in general. Hence we cannot aim at pleasure. It is a pure abstraction.

We may aim, however, it will be said, at some particular pleasure, the pleasure of eating an apple, of performing a

charitable act, of deceiving an enemy, etc. Even here, however, there is ambiguity, and even self-contradiction in the
theory as ordinarily stated. There is confusion of an *ideal of
pleasure*—the conception of what constitutes pleasure—with
pleasure as an ideal. Since pleasure exists only while it is
felt, to say that it is aimed at must mean that there is a
thought of it formed. Now this thought will either be an
image so distinct that it is itself pleasurable, or it will be a
conception of the objects or ends which afford pleasure, or
yield satisfaction. Take any of the instances above given and
it will be seen that these two alternatives exhaust the possibilities. Neither of them is equivalent to pleasure as an
ideal. In the former case, a pleasure is actually felt and no
action is called forth aimed at it. In the latter case there is a
presentation of the ends whose attainment is regarded as
affording satisfaction, and (through redintegration) of a
certain amount of accompanying pleasure. But neither actually experienced pleasure, nor a consideration of the objects which afford enjoyment is pleasurable feeling as an
aim of action. This latter is a psychological impossibility.
But since the idea has prevailed, not only that pleasure is a
possible end of action, but that it is the only end, it must be
examined in more detail. The idea is usually presented in
connection with a theory of desire. (For the notion that
pleasure is the object of desire see: Mill, *Utilitarianism*, pp.
354–55; Bain, *Emotions and Will*, Part Two, Ch. 8, *Senses
and Intellect*, pp. 338–44; Spencer, *Data of Ethics*, pp. 26–
44; Sully, *Outlines of Psychology*, pp. 574–89, *Human Mind*,
Vol. ii, pp. 196–207; Thompson, *System of Psychology*, Part
Nine; Lotze, *Microcosmus*, Vol. i, pp. 678–706. Most of
these cover other points in the hedonistic theory besides the
relation of pleasure and desire. Stephen, *Science of Ethics*,
pp. 42–57 and 246–63, is noteworthy for the clearness with
which he shows the confusion in ordinary hedonism as to
the end, while still himself holding that pleasure is *motive*.)

xxiv.   Happiness and Desire

It is generally held by hedonists to be self-evident that
we desire pleasure, and avoid pain. The doctrine is even

tautology, according to them. Good, pleasure, the desirable are synonomous terms; evil, pain, that to which we are averse, mean the same experience. Substituting "happiness" for "pleasure," "misery" for "pain," we agree unreservedly to this statement, and yet insist that it does not mean that pleasure is the object of desire, or aim of action. It is true that good (happiness) is the satisfaction, evil the thwarting of desire. This measures, or defines, happiness in terms of desire; desire is the primary fact, happiness its fulfilling, its completion. Hedonism sees the connection, but reverses its direction. It takes happiness as a fixed fact, and then tries to define desire in terms of happiness—as that which aims at it. It is true that happiness is found in the satisfaction of any desire, particularly in the degree of its dominance; happiness *is* this satisfaction of desire. But hedonism transforms this fact into the notion that somehow pleasure is there as an ideal, and its contemplation arouses desire. As Green says (*Prolegomena*, p. 168) the hedonists make the "mistake of supposing that a desire can be excited by the anticipation of its own satisfaction."

This identity of happiness with satisfaction of desire is the reason for substituting "happiness" for "pleasure." Pleasure and pain are often passive and accidental (pathological, Kant terms it, *Theory of Ethics*, p. 106). A child goes on the street and hears pleasant music; he runs and has a painful fall; a man inherits money and finds himself in the possession of new resources; he invests money safely, as he supposes, and finds it swept away by a sudden panic. It is absurd to deny that satisfaction and dissatisfaction, in the way of pleasure and pain, result in all these instances; yet common speech agrees with sound theory in holding that any one or all of them may become parts of either happiness or misery, weal or woe, *according to the relation assumed towards them by the dominant desires (that is character) of the individual.*[6] (See Alexander, *Moral Order*, pp. 212–18.)

---

[6]   I do not mean that the words "pleasure" and "happiness" are marked off to denote exclusively these two kinds of satisfaction, one comparatively extraneous to character, the other measured by it, but only to insist that there are these two types of satisfaction, and that common speech is quite aware of their difference.

xxv. The Nature of Desire

The hedonist, then, gives the following account of desire: Admitting that the original, or impulsive, activity does not occur for the sake of pleasure, it is held that when pleasure or pain is experienced as a result of action, the image of memory of the feeling occurring afterwards arouses a desire for its renewal (if pleasure), or aversion, a movement to escape it (if pain).

Concerning this account a question arises. How does this image of memory happen to occur to the mind? No image or memory can come into the mind directly or of itself; there must be some suggestion, association or exciting stimulus. We may suppose (*i*) that the object which gave the satisfaction before is seen (as a child, having eaten sugar once, sees it again), and this redintegrates the pleasure image. Now (a) this, at most, is an accidental and, morally, unimportant way for desire to originate. A character whose desires were habitually aroused in this style would be immature; it would be the sport of caprice and circumstance, with no settled lines of action. This theory presupposes that the mind is, like Micawber, passively waiting for experiences to "turn up." In the child, or in any character so far as morally immature, the relatively accidental recognition of an object may arouse its own isolated line of action. But moral training consists not in perpetuating this mode of action, but in eliminating it. As a matter of fact, even a child is actually engaged from the outset and all the time in activity. He has his own impulses, or lines of discharge, representing the selected outcome of generations of activity. The child's immaturity chiefly consists not in the fact that it is passively dependent upon external excitations, but in the lack of continuity in the activities set up by the organs themselves. One way of action gives way to another without reference to a general or comprehensive plan. In other words, the impulse is not mediated or rationalized. (b) Even in the child, therefore, the object arouses the desire because *of the activity already going on.* The child's primary impulse is already there—that of eating. The presentation of the object, and the representation of the satisfaction previously had in connection with it, simply deflects, or mediates, this activity.

This suggests the fundamental fallacy in the old case of the ass evenly balanced between two bundles of hay. It supposes that the desirable quality, the power of inciting activity, resides in the *object* entirely independent of the activity of the organism. As matter of fact, the animal (and so with man) is already doing something, looking, or moving, this way or that, and so the hypothesis of a purely indeterminate equilibrium is absurd—it assumes impossible conditions.

Pleasure, in other words, is *not suggested immediately by the object*, sugar, but by the activity of tasting, which constitutes the practical meaning of that object.

This brings us (*ii*) to the normal case. The pleasure is aroused because the activity already asserting itself, as a habit more or less organized, *hits in idea upon the object (that is, the conditions) which will afford it fulfillment.* The recognition of the congruity of the object to the activity arouses the pleasure. A hungry child, seeing or thinking of something to eat, experiences gratification in the thought; an engineer, trying to express his engineering capacity, thinks of a new machine and experiences pleasure, etc. Instead of the image of pleasure exciting the action, the activity already going on sets up a pleasure by calling into consciousness the conditions (the object) of its satisfaction. There is *no image* of a past pleasure once experienced or of a future pleasure to be attained; there is a *present* pleasurable experience. This brings out the fact that desire, instead of being the beginning of activity caused by a state of feeling, is a stage in its development arising when both the original and the induced activity are in consciousness but have not yet come to a complete agreement, or co-ordination. (It is the same condition as that already noticed as effort.) Desire is not excited or aroused by any end, whether pleasure or anything else. It is a phase in the growth of valued, or rationalized, action.

At this stage of development there is more than pleasure felt; there is also pain. Pleasure is felt so far as the object (the mediating or induced experience) is present *in idea*, thus promising future satisfaction. Pain is felt so far as it is present *only* in idea, not in act.

The actual perception of the sugar is still, in part, merely ideal, so far as the activity is concerned: the activity which is striving to assert itself is not seeing the sugar, but *tasting* it. So far as the sight promises success, by redintegrating further acts (reaching, etc.), it is pleasurable, the draft the organs of tasting make upon it being honored. But so far as the *full* activity is still non-existent, there is pain.

The very essence of desire is tension, *divided* activity. The self is divided against itself; activity is partial. So far as it goes, it is *action*, and hence pleasurable; but as *partial*, it is painful. Desire is neither complete activity aiming at a state outside itself, nor a condition of sheer emptiness.[7] It is conflicting activity. The man who desires an education in so far as he can "objectify" his desire (that is, present to himself the conditions which will further his self-assertion in that direction), is *in so far* already acting in the desired direction, and there is satisfaction; but in so far as he is at present acting in ways which must be mediated, or transformed, there is conflict and dissatisfaction. The pleasure-pain condition of desire *reports*, in other words, the existing state of action; it does not initiate it.

In any account of desire, there are three elements to be dealt with – activity, object of desire (end thought of as satisfying), and feeling. According to hedonism, the object awakens feeling, and the feeling arouses active desire. I have tried to show above that the feeling *is* the activity subjectively appreciated; it is equally true, on our theory, that the object is no independent thing, but is the activity presented to intelligence – is the content of action, the statement of the conditions involved. The thought of food *is* the definition, in objective terms, of hunger; a complex set of commercial relations (a plan of business) is the objective definition of the impulse to assert one's self in nature; the conception of conditions of political power the objectifying of its special impulse, etc. "Object" and pleasure-pain feeling

---

[7]   The double sense of words here is suggestive. Want means both *lack* and *demand*; it is dynamic, and still partial. Capacity means both power (actuality) and possibility (ideality).

are thus the correlative phases, objective and subjective, of activity.

The fundamental fallacy of both perfectionism and hedonism is thus the same. Both assume value as something presented to the self, and awakening and measuring activity. In truth, value is constituted by activity. (An interesting form of the assumption of a fixed system of goods or values [not hedonistic] towards which activity should be directed will be found in the *International Journal of Ethics*, Vol. III, in an article by Mr. Davidson, entitled "The Ethics of an Eternal Being." All formulæ like the one there given [p. 306] reverse the real state of the case. They assume the existence of valuable ends towards which interest, attention, affection are to be directed, forgetting that such ends *are simply the objective expression of interest and attention.*)

Arguments against the idea that pleasure is the object of desire will be found in James, *Psychology*, Vol. II, pp. 549–59; Green, *Prolegomena*, pp. 163–77; Bradley, *Ethical Studies*, pp. 226–35, and *Mind*, Vol. XIII, p. 1; Sidgwick, *Methods of Ethics*, pp. 34–47, *Mind*, Vol. II, p. 27, and *Contemporary Review*, 1872, p. 671; Alexander, *Moral Order*, pp. 186–225; Dewey, *Outlines of Ethics*, pp. 17–30 [*Early Works*, III, 252–59]; Muirhead, *Elements of Ethics*, pp. 92–111; Murray, *Introduction to Ethics*, pp. 160–73; Mackenzie, *Manual of Ethics*, pp. 89–116. Most of these references deal with the question of motive as well as of end. The criticisms of hedonism advanced above are practically identical with many of those contained in the references. The positive doctrine of desire is, perhaps, more nearly allied to that of Spinoza, according to which desire is a form of fundamental self-assertion. It is not aroused by some "end," but the "end" or "object" is the consciousness of the nature, or content, of self-assertion. See Spinoza, *Ethics*, Part Three, Props. 6–9 and Def. 1 of the affects. In Part Four, Props. 14–37, desire seems at times to be defined in terms of "Good," and good at other times in terms of desire—as the content of self-realization. The latter is the characteristic doctrine, in any case. See Three, 9, Schol., and 39, Schol.

XXVI. Pleasure and Motive

As already stated, most hedonists confuse the idea of pleasure as object of desire with pleasure as motive. This confusion testifies to a right psychological instinct: that which is an aim of action must also move to action. There must be an identification of the real concrete ideal with the impelling spring to action. Unless the aim or ideal itself becomes a moving force, it is barren and helpless. Unless the moving force becomes itself idealized, unless it is permeated with the object aimed at, it remains *mere* impulse, blind and irrational. According to hedonism, the ideal and motive may be confused with each other, but they cannot be identified. The thought of pleasure is either simply an abstract conception, coldly intellectual, of the means to getting pleasure, or it is a concrete image of pleasure—that is, itself a pleasure. In neither case is it a motive. In the former case, it is simply an abstract idea, without practical efficiency; in the latter case, the pleasure is already enjoyed or experienced, and there is no cause for action.[8]

We are in this dilemma in hedonism. If the motive is feeling, it can suggest no intention whatever, and thus cannot move to anything in particular. There is a certain state being experienced, and that ends the story. Or, if there is a definite aim or intention in view, that end will arouse feeling only in the degree in which it expresses activity—tendency towards or away. The feeling excited will not be the moving spring, but will indicate or register the extent to which the *self is moved*. There is no connecting link, on its theory, between aim and motive.

We may freely admit, with the hedonist, that bare thought does not induce, is not motive. But before we can infer from this that an ideal is not motive, we must be able to show that an ideal, or aim, is *mere* thought. On the con-

---

[8]   Stephen, *Science of Ethics*, p. 51, holds that pleasure means persistence in given state, pain change. So also Ward, *Psychic Factors of Civilization*, p. 54, who goes to the extreme of holding that all desire is pain, while still defining it as representation of pleasure as well as pain (p. 52).

trary, it is the induced or mediating *activity*. The ideal, indeed, is a conception or thought; but as such, as intellectual, it simply gives definiteness and coherency to the content of the induced self. The concrete ideal is always activity asserting itself in another direction from the present, natural, activity.

Physiology has, indeed, afforded a complete disproof of any theory which makes a gap between the ideal (or intellect) and overt action. From the side of the expenditure of energy, the sole difference between thought and action is in the external, or gross, visibility of the discharge. Thinking involves molecular motion, and continued discharge to the muscles and glands. The question of the final passage of idea into act is simply the question of the concentration (unification) of this organic activity in some definite direction. Physiologically, the entire function of thought consists in transforming the vague, diffuse and non-valued (valuable, but not defined or measured as to value) activity of infancy into definite, co-ordinated and intentional (measured) activity.

Upon our view, then, the ideal and motive are both names for self in certain phases of action. If a man kills another intentionally, his ideal, the thought of the removal of the other man, is not something beyond himself — there is no way for the thought, even as thought, to come into his mind, save as a projection of himself. That the thought dwells there and becomes an impelling force to action (a motive) is simply the realization, the definite recognition, of the extent to which the self is involved in that ideal, of the extent to which that ideal *is* the self. The act of reflection is a phase of the act of fulfillment.

We thus come to the question of intention and motive. The hedonist asserts that the motive is always a feeling of pleasure-pain, the intention is the consequences aimed at.[9]

We assert that both intention and motive are the self in action, and the sole difference is that motive is intention completely developed, the *concrete* or unified self.

A man wills to kill another. Roughly speaking, inten-

---

[9]   Mill, "The intention is what the agent wills to do, the motive is the feeling that makes him so will to do."

tion corresponds to what he wills, motive to why he wills it. His intention is the "foreseen consequences," his motive, that which makes him desire them. His intention is the death of another man; his motive varies according as he is seeking revenge, is a soldier in war, or is engaged in defending himself from an assault. So far all agree. Does the complete separation of intention and motive follow from this account?

Intention, as above illustrated, is an abstraction of intellectual analysis. No man ever intends *merely* to kill another. He intends to save his own life, to defend his country, to "get even" with another, to get money, or, maybe, to exhibit his own marksmanship. The "killing another" is simply *part* of the intent, of the whole aim. It is necessary to discover intention in the narrower sense in order to determine *that* one acts in the moral sphere at all, but it is necessary to discover the whole concrete aim before we can find *what* a man really wills. Now the moment we have the whole aim, we have motive also. To defend self, to get revenge, is what *impels* a man to act. Or, if on the other hand, we say revenge, ambition, avarice, patriotism is the motive to murder, this sense of motive is a *mere* sentiment, an abstraction (and hence incapable of inducing action), or it means *an active attitude towards certain ideals*—and this is simply the concrete aim. Suppose Napoleon's motive was ambition. Many men are ambitious; why do they not do what he did? If ambition is a *mere* feeling, it will never induce action at all; it will not define or suggest any particular act to be performed. It will remain stuck in its own sentimental, self-absorbed dreaming. A working ambition must translate itself into thought, into the idea of objects, and must be interest in these definite ends or objects; it must be *a demand for the reality of certain ideas*. It thus *includes* intention, in the abstract sense of that word, and *is* intention in its full sense—that at which a man really, and not simply incidentally, aims.

An objection sometimes made will bring out the point. Suppose a man shoots at game, knowing that a man is near the line of fire; he kills the man. Now, it is urged, his motive clearly implies lack of regard for life, but it cannot be said that he intended to kill the man.

Or, from the other side, it may be said that Brutus

intended to kill Cæsar, and yet the killing of Cæsar was not part of his motive (Mackenzie, *Manual of Ethics*, p. 40). As to the first, the agent did not intend, *by itself*, to kill the man; yet neither did he intend, merely by itself, to kill the deer. He intended, as a result, a form of satisfaction of which the *possible* death of a man, as well as of a deer, was a part— and this aim, as self-expression, was the impelling force. As to the second instance, Brutus did not intend simply to kill Cæsar; he intended a certain deliverance of his country, or a certain self-advancement, the death of Cæsar forming a constituent part of this aim; and in just this same sense the thought of the death of Cæsar (which is what I take Mackenzie to mean by the loose phrase "the killing of Cæsar") was a part of his motive; he took a positive interest in the thought of Cæsar out of the way, an interest which was sufficient to induce him to do the deed. His whole ideal, of which the removal of Cæsar was a part, was what moved him.

The identity of the complete intention and the motive may also be gathered from a consideration of the circumstances under which we give credit to a man for a good intention even when no act is obvious. We do so only when the agent can point to effort on his part, and to obstacles which prevented execution. If a man says he really intended to do a certain duty but forgot it, we may indeed recognize the intention so far as entertaining the thought is, psychologically, action, but at the same time must recognize that the possibility of forgetting shows that the matter was not really "on his mind." That is, we infer from the fact that it did not move him to the fact that it was only half-formed intention. We always, practically, judge intention from act, provided we have sufficient data to enable us to judge intelligibly concerning the *act*. Sound psychology justifies our condemnation of the man who has "good intentions" but no deeds to show; his action, in revealing himself, reveals his true intent and gives the lie to his profession.

The impossibility of really judging the conduct of others, as maintained by Kant (*Theory of Ethics*, pp. 23–24) and by Green (*Prolegomena*, p. 318), is a fiction resulting from separation of motive and intention. There is, of course, always difficulty in deciding what the *act* is, but so far as we can tell this, we can tell the *intention*, and knowing the intention executed, can tell *in what kind of ends the man is sufficiently interested to be moved by them to act* — can estimate his character.

This brings us again to the question: Is feeling motive? Yes, and no. Decidedly no, in the sense in which the consistent hedonist must use the term feeling—a state of experienced pain—or pleasure. Yes, in the sense in which practical life uses the term: *An active interest in certain ends*, that interest expressing the controlling lines of activity.[10]

The distinctions of interest from *mere* feeling, or passive affections are:

1. Interest is active, projective. We *take* interest. Interest is demand, insistence. Whenever we have an interest in any thought, we cherish it, cling to it, endeavor in all ways to realize or fulfill it.

2. Interest implies an object—the end, or thought, which claims attention. We are interested in *something*, while *mere* feeling begins and ends in itself. In common speech an "interest" means the end which dominates activity.

3. Interest (*inter-esse*) implies the relation which the interesting end bears to the controlling lines of action, to *character*. It expresses the *identification* of the object with the subject. Mere feeling does not involve this complete interaction with character. Because of this difference, mere feeling is of value only while felt, as actually experienced; an interest has value on its own account (as the outworking of character) whether the objective aim included within it is ever *externally* experienced or not. "It is better to have loved and lost than never to have loved at all." It is better to aim at anything which calls forth the powers of the self than to get the passive enjoyment of any object whatever; the true satisfaction of interest lies in the assertion of its activity

---

10   Common speech often uses feeling to denote impulse. Höffding, *Psychology*, seems to use feeling in a dynamic sense which brings it close to impulse, and yet pp. 235–36, he makes impulse a derivation from feeling.

and not in the mere results attained. That is, the assertion of self *is* the result, in comparison with which all other results are insignificant. This is that independence of the moral agent of all the contingencies of life, of which the Stoics made so much.

We conclude, then, by saying that the term "motive" simply expresses the moving force or interest of a given end or aim, this interest indicating the extent to which the self finds its own character involved in the realization of that end. Confirmation, if any further is necessary, is found in the fact that all hedonists, since James Mill, have used their theory of motives to furnish the machinery by which certain ends are made active interests of the individual agent. The subject with which they have really dealt is not the psychology of motive as such, but rather this problem: Given certain ends which are requisite to the welfare of society, how can these ends be rendered motives to the individual? Their answer has been: We must so connect, through the instrumentalities of pleasure and pain, these ends with the individual's own welfare that they shall become identified with his conception of himself. In other words, their practical assumption is not that feeling as such is motive, but that feeling may be so *used* as to make certain aims, otherwise lying outside of the agent and hence indifferent, *interests* to him.

The following references will give the status of the discussion of intention and motive from the time of James Mill to the present. James Mill, *Analysis of Human Mind*, Vol. ii, Chs. 22 and 25; Bentham, *Principles of Morals*, Chs. 8 and 10, pp. 71, 92–95, 97–103; Austin, *Jurisprudence*, Vol. i, Chs. 18–20; Mill, *Utilitarianism*, p. 27, note (English ed., not in American, but quoted in next reference); Green, *Prolegomena*, pp. 315–25; [Alexander, Mackenzie, Muirhead, and Ritchie], *International Journal of Ethics*, Vol. iv, pp. 89–94 and 229–38, and references there given.

XXVII.   Pleasure as Criterion

We saw that pleasure as feeling could not be ideal, because every ideal is present as thought, not as feeling; we saw, however, that the ideal, or thought, might awaken present pleasure, and so the question arose whether this present pleasure might not be impelling motive. We were obliged to deny it, on the ground that mere feeling ends in itself, or has no dynamic power, and because concrete feeling, as actually experienced, (a) depends upon the activity already going on (instead of exciting it), and (b) is colored throughout by the character of the end or idea which defines the activity. We concluded, then, that the pleasure-pain condition is not motive; but registers the interest which a given individual takes at the given time in a given act.

This brings us to the question of pleasure as criterion or standard of the worth of action. Giving up the thought that it is either aim or motive, have we not arrived at the conception that it indicates, registers, reports the worth of action, and is thus its test? In the following sense, yes. The satisfaction (interest) which a given individual takes in an act measures the worth which that end, as a matter of fact, has to him at that particular moment. But this does *not* mean that pleasure or pain is the moral criterion. It means that if we know the kind of ends and acts in which a certain agent *takes* pleasure (instead of passively enjoying it), we know how to estimate his moral character. If he rejoices in temperance, he *is* temperate; if he grieves at it as an enforced thing, or as merely useful to some further end, he is still partial in that virtue, etc. Pleasure does not determine the worth of an act, but the kind of act which affords pleasure determines the worth of an agent. That is, *we measure the worth of a given experience of pain or pleasure by reference to a standard of character, by reference to the moving ideal which calls it forth.*[11]

But the hedonist himself contends that it is not the present felt pleasure which measures the value of the act, but the *results* of the act in the way of pleasures and pains —

[11]   See Plato, *Laws*, Bk. ii, 653–54, Aristotle, *Ethics*, Bk. ii, Ch. 3; Plato, *Laws*, Bk. ii, 659–61, and Aristotle, *Ethics*, Bk. x, Ch. 5. I am not able to see that much advance has since been made as to the ethical psychology of pleasure and pain. The artistic sense of the Greek who understood that it was a mark alone of a true gentleman to know how to take (as to when, where and how much) his pleasures and pains, divined the truth.

an act is good according as it effects a net balance of pleasure over pain, bad when painful results predominate over pleasures. It is this doctrine which we must discuss. We note that it makes a break between criterion and ideal and motive. Not the same pleasure, or pleasure in the same sense, is criterion that (on their theory) impels to action or that is the desirable end. (a) The motive must be present and individual; the results are distant and, according at least to one school of hedonists,[12] general, consisting in pleasure or pain to all men, or to all sentient creation. (b) According to the hedonist, no one would ever *aim* at anything but pleasure, but the *act* may result in pain as well as in pleasure, may bring other pleasures than those aimed at, or may bring none at all. If the criterion and the ideal were the same, every act whatsoever must be right – because an unadulterated pleasure.

1. Thus to dissever criterion from ideal is to reduce moral experience to a chaos. A person may aim at anything whatsoever, may have any end we please to suggest and the character of that end has nothing whatever to do with the morality of his act. The whole process of forming intentions, of defining ideals, of discussing aims, has absolutely no moral value. It is true that Mill (*Utilitarianism*, p. 27, note, English ed.) says "the morality of the action depends entirely upon the intention," but this seems a complete reversal of hedonism. It proclaims that the test of an act is not the pleasures and pains which, as matter of fact, result from it, but whether, in doing the act, the agent *aims* at bringing pleasure or pain to himself and others (Mill being a "universal" hedonist). By no conceivable stretch of language can this be interpreted as meaning that pleasure is the test of morality; it makes the *character* of the agent, the sort of result he aims at, the kind of end that moves him, the criterion.

Only extended quotation can show how typical this reversal is of all modern utilitarianism, though it seems, in the main, to have escaped the critics. The only hedonistic view is that which measures an act, after it has been performed, by its results in pleasures and pains. Every utilitar-

---

[12]   Termed by Sidgwick, universalistic hedonism, as distinct from individualistic, but commonly called utilitarianism.

ian has substituted a criterion for the formation of right ideals. It says to an agent: Before you act, consider as thoroughly as possible the results of your actions, the pains and pleasures that are likely to result to all people and animals from them; then, if you decide upon the act which promises to bring a balance of pleasure, your act is right. See, for example, the "hedonistic calculus" as explained by Bentham, *Principles of Morals* (p. 16), noting such expressions in the memoriter verses as "*such* pleasures *seek*," "*such* pains *avoid*," which clearly indicate that he is setting up a standard for the kind of ideals at which men ought to aim. We do not here need to discuss this criterion of morality; whether correct or incorrect, it is not hedonistic. *It measures conduct not by pleasure and pain, but by the character of the agent as manifested in the end which he attempts to realize or bring into being.* It virtually says that the act performed by an agent in a spirit of benevolence (defined as that which aims at giving pleasure to sentient beings) is right. The utilitarian confuses results which do happen with *foreseen results moving to action.* Yet if he does not make this confusion, he has no alternative but to say that intention, aim, etc., have nothing to do with the morality of an act. As matter of fact, our criterion and ideal must have a common denominator: the worth of an act must be measured by the worth of its intention, or the experiences aimed at.

2. Similar confusion results from the divorce of criterion and motive. The test for the morality of the agent is made one thing, and the test for the act another, *and both conceptions contradict the view just stated.* The *motive*, being pleasure, is, according to the hedonist, always good (Bentham, *Principles of Morals*, p. 48). "A motive is substantially nothing more than pleasure or pain operating in a certain manner. Now pleasure is in itself a good. . . . It follows, therefore, immediately and incontestably, that there is no such thing as any sort of motive that is in itself a bad one.[13] If motives are good or bad, it is only on ac-

---

[13]   It would seem as if "pain operating in a certain manner" ought logically to be bad. But if Bentham admitted this, being obliged to hold also that pain impels away from further evil, he would be in an obvious dilemma: the motive would be at once bad and good. The same contradiction, of course, is involved in holding, at one and the same time, that pleasure as motive is good, and yet that motive is good only by its effects.

count of their effects." Here the criterion is distinctly stated
to reside in the *effects* of the act. Hence the separation of
the morality of the act from that of an agent. The agent, as
expressed in motive, may be "good," his act "bad," or the
contrary. Two entirely different sets of considerations decide
the respective cases. The rightness of the act is decided by
its actual effects; of the agent by his predominating feelings.

It is quite true that other systems beside the hedonistic
make such a separation, generally under the names of the
"formal" and "material" rightness of an act. (For the historical origin of this distinction, see Sidgwick, *History of
Ethics*, p. 200; its meaning to those who accept it will be
found well stated in Bowne, *Principles of Ethics*, pp. 39–40.
The best assertion known to me of the doctrine of the text
[the identity of agent and act] is found, of all places, in
Brown, *Philosophy of Mind*, Vol. III, pp. 489 and 499–502.)
According to this distinction, formal rightness pertains to
the motive of the agent; it is his will to do the right. But
with the best will in the world, the agent may still act
contrary to the conditions of well-being, and do something
whose consequences are evil (materially wrong). The distinction seems to avoid a real difficulty in our judgment of
conduct. But this very avoidance is the chief objection to it.
It restates the difficulty in generalized form instead of solv-
ing it. It introduces a fundamental dualism into moral experience by making it possible for a good man to be continually doing bad acts, and for a bad man to express
himself constantly in good acts. No amount of criticism can
say more than the mere statement of the doctrine says. It
tends to reduce good character to mere sentimental well-
wishing in general, eliminating the objective factor, the kind
of ends aimed at, and to reduce good action to mere conduciveness to external results, eliminating the factor of self-
reference, of spontaneous vital self-assertion.

As the outcome, we are left with no working criterion
for acts. There is no way in which the individual can convince himself in advance of the right thing to be done. The
pleasures and pains which may result from any act depend so much upon circumstances lying outside both the
ken and the character of the agent, that it is impossible to

foresee them, or to get any guidance from their consideration. If we already have a belief that certain lines of action
are, upon the whole, right, we may act in the faith (never
with the proof) that such lines of conduct will, upon the
whole, result in more pleasure than pain; but if we are
dependent upon calculation of the painful and pleasurable
consequences, in each instance, we shall have an infinite
task. On the reference of an act to the self, to the immediate
and to the secondary impulses, there is a defining principle,
something which sets the minimum and maximum limits.
But the pleasures and pains which may proceed from an
act are so remote from the intrinsic nature of the act that
there are no assignable values in the problem; it is indeterminate throughout. A wholly consistent hedonist would be
in the position of one having the "mania of doubt"; the
condition of an agent who cannot start to do anything
without thinking that if he does the act, this, that or the
other painful consequence may follow, and who, conse-
quently, passes his life in self-absorbed, futile worry.[14] From
the standpoint of *possible* consequences, the position is legitimate; however improbable, such possibilities cannot, with
reference to external results, be disproved. Only the force of
inner impulse and the demand of the occasion, the power of
self-assertion, carry the normal individual out of such endless reflections into act. The limit must be self-contained.

   Criticisms upon the hedonistic standard will be found
in the following references, some of which duplicate criticisms upon the subject of ideal and motive, but, so far as
possible, confined to the subject of criterion: Bradley, *Ethical Studies*, Essay III; Green, *Prolegomena*, pp. 233–55,
361–88 and 399–415; Martineau, *Types of Ethical Theory*,
Vol. II, pp. 308–34; Lecky, *History of European Morals*,
pp. 1–75; Grote, *Examination of the Utilitarian Philosophy*;
Birks, *Utilitarianism*, Chs. 1–4; Alexander, *Moral Order*,
pp. 204–11; Murray, *Introduction to Ethics*, pp. 167–205;
Dewey, *Outlines*, pp. 31–51 [*Early Works*, III, 260–73].

---

[14]   See, for example, Cowles, *American Journal of Psychology*, Vol. I,
pp. 222 and ff., especially p. 238.

xxviii.   The Standard of Happiness

In spite of all said concerning the unworkable character of the hedonistic ideal, motive and criterion, there is little doubt that, in its modern or utilitarian form, it has been the chief theoretic instrument of practical reform. Such a paradox demands attention. Its explanation is found, I think, in the fact that while nominally the utilitarian has been insisting upon happiness as an ideal and standard, *really* he has (*i*) been engaged in working out an ideal and standard of happiness of a wide, free, and often lofty nature; has (*ii*) insisted that every individual, without respect of birth or accident of fortune, have the freest chance to realize this happiness for himself, and has, (*iii*) identified happiness with general welfare, or common good, demanding that all the machinery of law and education be employed to make reference to the general interest a controlling motive with the individual. In all these respects, utilitarianism has been in the forefront of modern political and industrial development. But none of these demands is, in itself, hedonistic; indeed, all are signs of a more organic view of the individual and of society than is logically possible to hedonism. It is the advance beyond hedonism which has constituted the power of the doctrines, while their entanglement in the individualistic psychology of the 18th century (which gave them their hedonistic character) has, in so far, reduced their effectiveness. A brief sketch of the development of modern utilitarianism will at once complete our criticism by showing how hedonism has abandoned its own ground of happiness *as standard* and has set up *a standard for happiness*, and will enable the criticism to take a more appreciative attitude toward the practical spring and worth of the chief modern writers.

In Bentham (1748–1832), utilitarianism was made the instrument of legal reform in the interest of the whole people and a weapon of attack upon class interest. Great abuses had deflected law and its administration from equal regard to the community interest, and made of it a device by which a few profited at the expense of the many. The abuses were protected in the name of custom and precedent, and these, in turn, were consecrated, it seemed to Bentham, by an ethical philosophy which held that right and wrong were inherent characteristics of things, without regard to the end to which they contribute, or their practical serviceableness. Now as against this view, Bentham testified that every idea and institution must be cross-questioned, and if not able to justify itself by showing its contribution to the happiness of the world, be condemned to pass out of existence. Bentham equally insisted that this justifying end of happiness was public or common, not individual or belonging to a class. Hence the two war-cries of utilitarianism, "the greatest happiness of the greatest number," and, in its computation, "everyone to count for one and for only one." Here we have the standard, which is, in practical substance, the well-being of the community as a whole, with equal and impartial reference to the well-being of each member of the community. To a period when the democratic spirit was rising against the survivals, finally become useless, of an aristocratic civilization, such a theory proved a most useful standard and rallying point.

In such a standard, there is nothing of necessity hedonistic. Happiness is the common name for welfare, well-being, a generally satisfactory condition of life. It conveys, of itself, no suggestion concerning what constitutes happiness, and is far enough from identifying itself with the hedonistic notion of a series of states of agreeable sensation.

The other side of utilitarianism developed through the need political reformers have, at least practically, of framing a theory of motives. Bentham differed from earlier utilitarians largely in his appreciation of the necessity of inducing the individual to take sufficient interest in the general welfare to direct his conduct in accordance with its requirements. Pain and pleasure seemed to him just the instruments needed. Especially interested in criminal procedure and prison administration, pain, in the form of punishment, seemed to him to have great possibilities as a motive power when brought to bear, under the direction of a scientific psychological analysis, upon the individual. On the other hand, the growth of commercial life, as reflected in current political economy, had brought to consciousness the ties of interest which hold men together in modern society; it had revealed, in the language of the day, how far the self-interest of one coincides with the self-interest of others. Here, pleasure, as personal profit, seemed to be a powerful inducement to men to seek the common welfare.

As happiness, under the influence of the dominant individualistic psychology, was translated into agreeable sensation, so social interest, under the same influences, was interpreted as sheer personal pains and pleasures, abstracted from the objective conditions which, in their relation to the activity of the individual, really determine and measure them.

James Mill (1773–1836), who had a knowledge both of current psychology and current political economy denied to Bentham, completed the fusion of these various elements; and bound, seemingly irretrievably, the new standard and ideal of industrial democracy to the analyses of an individualistic psychology. John Stuart Mill (1806–1873), his son, while continuing the tradition, yet even more than Bentham changed the idea of happiness as a standard into a standard of happiness, defining it still *nominally* as agreeable sensation, but in reality in terms of the objective conditions which determine it.

1. Bentham and James Mill had dwelt only upon the *quantity* of pleasure, in the various forms of its intensity, duration, fruitfulness (as to further pleasures) and purity (or freedom from pain).[15] John Stuart Mill insisted that the *quality* of pleasure must also be taken into account, and that a small amount of a higher quality might, or should, take precedence of a much larger bulk of a lower quality. Now differences of quality in pleasure as to higher and lower evidently imply a standard of measurement. What is it? Mill gives (or at least suggests) two answers: (*i*) The standard is the preference of those who have experienced both. Now of this it may be said that such preference only

[15]   Criticisms of the conception of greatest sum of pleasures, showing the implied presence of an objective standard, will be found in Green, *Prolegomena*, pp. 235–40; Alexander, *Moral Order*, pp. 207–10; Watson, *Journal of Speculative Philosophy*, Vol. X, p. 271.

proves that it is preferable to that person or body of persons; but, even if they were unanimous in their judgment, this would not mean that one was higher for me unless I found it so. But a more serious objection is that this puts the standard of pleasure in the character of the person enjoying it, instead of making pleasure the standard of character, and thus contradicts hedonism. This aspect comes explicit when we find (*ii*) Mill saying that a "sense of dignity," presumably a sense of the kind of pleasure that is appropriate to a human being to enjoy, comes in to decide as to higher and lower (Mill, *Utilitarianism*, pp. 309–13).

Now when we define a higher pleasure as that (a) which any person, or (b) a person of higher character, *prefers*, we have obviously referred pleasure to that in the person's character which makes it preferable—we have an objective standard.

2. As to motive, the question again arises how an individual agent may be induced to prefer the general well-being to his own private profit. The previous answer had been: through the influence of punishment, of reward, of education, etc., setting up *associations* in the mind of the agent between his own happiness and that of others. Mill saw clearly that an identification resting only upon association is artificial, and likely to dissolve through the force of intellectual analysis (which happened in his own case, leaving him with a feeling of isolation, *Autobiography*, p. 136), and that there must be some intrinsic connection. This is the social unity of mankind; the nature of the individual is so thoroughly social that he cannot conceive himself "otherwise than as a member of a body." He, therefore, comes to identify happiness with harmony with his fellows (Mill, *Utilitarianism*, pp. 343–47). Here the social value of the individual is made the criterion of the moral worth of happiness. *This thoroughly socialized ideal of happiness* is the most characteristic feature of Mill's ethics. It is noble, but it is not hedonism.

Spencer marks the final stage in the transformation of happiness as pleasurable sensation over into the accompaniment of certain objective conditions. As John Stuart Mill is signalized by recognition of the dependence of pleasure upon

social law and unity, Spencer is signalized by recognition of
the dependence of pleasure upon the laws not of society
alone, but of the universe which conditions the life of society
and of the individual. (See his criticisms of the older utilitarianism, *Data of Ethics*, pp. 56–63, with which compare
Stephen's *Science of Ethics*, pp. 353–79.)

According to Spencer, we must "*deduce, from the laws
of life and the conditions of existence, what kinds of action
necessarily tend to produce happiness*." And to derive perfect
moral laws, we must postulate the case of a "completely
adapted man in a completely evolved society," defining,
therefore, man "in terms of the conditions which his nature
fulfills." (See pp. 57, 275, 279 of *Data of Ethics*.) Under
present conditions, pleasure is not an adequate test of morality; we make it so only by reference to the thought of the
complete relation of individual to environment. At present,
pleasure and rightness conflict in at least three respects. (1)
We have to do things through sense of obligation only, with
constraint, dislike and pain. (2) We have to compromise,
and surrender present to future pleasure, while in a "right"
state we would enjoy both. (3) We have often to sacrifice
our own pleasure to that of others. (See Dewey, *Outlines of
Ethics*, pp. 75–78 and references there given [*Early Works*,
III, 288–90].)

Now we do not have to ask concerning the adequacy of
Spencer's analysis here. In any case, it is all but the most
explicit recognition that pleasure is not of itself a standard,
but that certain activities and conditions, defined in objective
terms, measure, or are a standard for, pleasure.

In a similar manner, Stephen practically sets aside
happiness as a criterion, and substitutes for it conduciveness
to the vitality and development of the social organism. The
objective conditions have finally encroached more and more
upon the "agreeable feeling," and have made it only a very
thin shell upon a very solid core.

Höffding, *Ethik*, compare also *Monist*, Vol. I, p. 529,
on "Principle of Welfare," represents the best contemporary
effort to develop utilitarianism along the lines of John Stuart
Mill, but distinguishing frankly between welfare as social
criterion, the motive which actually impels the individual,

and the pedagogical problem of so influencing his motives as to make him interested in the social end. Gizycki, *Manual of Ethical Philosophy* (trans. by Coit) occupies much the same position, but with less clear and thorough analysis. Compare, *Mind*, Vol. xi, p. 324, article by Coit on Ultimate Moral Aim, and *International Journal of Ethics*, Vol. i, p. 311, by Gizycki on Final Moral End. A good statement of the best side of utilitarianism is found in the last named *Journal*, Vol. iii, p. 90, by Hodder.

xxix. Standard, Ideal and Motive

We conclude this phase of the subject by stating what seems to be the true relation of the three. At first, in the life of the child and of the race, the ideal or aim is comparatively particular—it is to do this or that thing. As the ideal is formed before, and with reference to, a given act so the criterion is applied to a given act after it has been performed. The act is judged at first by its outcome; primitive people carry this to the point of making no distinction between intentional and accidental acts. Even inanimate things, axes, trees, as well as animals, are tried and condemned.[16] At this stage, intention or ideal is also undefined, acts resulting from custom or instilled habit rather than from tension of habit and intent. But with further development, there is recognized the need of a criterion not simply for acts after they are performed, but for the process of forming ends and purposes. As we have seen, the utilitarian, while nominally dealing with the former, really concerns himself with the latter. Now the act is judged beforehand as well as afterward; the agent asks not simply whether the act is *good*, *i.e.*, satisfies impulse, but also whether it is *right*, *i.e.*, whether the impulse itself meets the requirements of a certain standard. This change is at the same time obviously a change in the char-

---

[16] Curious survivals of the early point of view are still found in the procedure of admiralty law, relating to libelling of ships. O. W. Holmes, Jr., *Common Law*. The same book contains a careful analysis of the legal view of motive, showing that law, in its practice, identifies motive not with feeling, but with foreseen consequences as inducing to action, and that "malice" is inferred wherever the consequences aimed at or assumed are not of a kind a standard character would aim at.

acter of the ideal; the ideal is no longer this or that particular act, its generality being simply in the unconscious, underlying habit, but is the *relation* of this or that act to a more general aim. The aim becomes comprehensive, and the particular act simply one form which the permanent aim assumes.

The criterion thus comes to be only the generalized ideal, while the ideal is a specific definition of the more general standard. They are related as a foot-rule in the abstract, and this rule translated into the defined length of some portion of space. The original mediation of impulse is through the special consequences related to that special impulse. But as consequences develop, it is seen that they are not one lot of experience isolated from the whole system. It is seen that the consequence chief in importance is that upon the agent's own habits of action, his capacities, tastes, attitude toward life, ways of forming ends, etc.; in short, *the* consequence is the mediation, not of this or that impulse, but of the entire actual self. The mediation of the particular impulse has meaning only in relation to the placing or function of that impulse in the system of activity. The generic standard and ultimate aim—expression of self—are thus one (see Sec. XIII). The act is the subject; but *what* the act is—the predicate—is known only by placing the act, in its obvious features, in its right position in the whole activity. If we look at this whole activity as that which the agent is urging towards in every "act," it is Ideal; if we look at it as really deciding the nature and value of the "act," it is Criterion.

The practical application of this conception of criterion may be briefly stated.

1. Such a criterion is workable. The individual always has his criterion with him, because it is himself. It is nothing more nor less than the thought of the consequences of the act with reference to his own efficiency as an agent in the scene in which he participates. The formulation here is abstract; it must be, because it is not a criterion for action at large, but a criterion for some agent, this or that or the other particular individual, with his own experiences and part to play. Just because it is so absolutely concrete for

him, the criterion can be stated at large only in abstract terms. The criterion and its application both exist in terms of the individual's own moral life; it is always putting two and two together; doing the best possible with the material available. Its terms are the given impulse and its bearing in the agent's own life; it is simply a complete view, or judgment, of the intrinsic nature of the act. Only a criterion which does lie within the range of the self is workable; an outside criterion, just in the degree of its externality, will never translate into terms of the individual's own needs and powers; it will not connect. The hedonistic criterion of consequences in the way of pleasure and pain has no intimate intrinsic connection with the individual's own habits and aims, and while the rationalistic criterion is the self in name, it is only in name. The self is a blank all-engulfing whole which does not define itself in terms of definite experience.

2. Such a criterion is absolute, yet relative. It is permanent, yet flexible. It is absolute in the sense of containing all its conditions and terms within itself, it is self as a living actuality. It is relative, in that it is not an abstract rule excluding all difference of circumstance, but applies to the concrete relations of the case. It is permanent or identical, because self is one in its life and movement; but flexible and variable since the self is one in and through activity and not by its mere static subsistence.

3. Such a criterion excludes all taint of casuistry and Pharisaism. In any standard save the efficiency, the expression, of the agent himself, the criterion is one thing, its application another. The standard is a rigid something, external to that to which it is applied. As a result, questions always arise as to rules of application, as to possible exceptions, as to variation according to circumstance. The fatal weakness of encouraging the agent to consider how far the rule may or may not apply to this special case comes in. With complete, or organic, mediation as criterion, the case and the standard are really one; it is always a question of what the case really is, when looked at not partially, but in the light of the agent as a concrete, effective agent in his vital relationships. Moreover, fixed, external criterion encourages fixity of condemnation. A man is condemned

because he does not come up to this abstract standard, entirely independently of his own instinctive tendencies, and his own situation. Only when the criterion is defined as we have above defined it, can we judge the agent on his own ground according to the meaning the act has for him. The external standard means always a false complacency, a fixed self-congratulation whenever we conform to the rule. A criterion which is nothing but the act completely viewed imposes action by its very nature; it leaves no time nor opportunity for self-directed complacency. The joy is in the action, not in the thought of the self as good enough to do it. Such a criterion, finally, requires acute and objective examination of the conditions of action, as the external criterion demands continued subjective introspection to see how far along we have got. The latter makes the agent keep his eye on his subjective attitude *towards* action, instead of simply finding his attitude *in the act*.

So much for the connection between ideal and criterion, and the identity of each with the act organically viewed, or referred to self as self. How as to motive? That again names the organic act from a certain side—the side of the interest as the act because expressing the self. It names the extent to which the ideal and criterion are such in deed, and not in name: the extent, that is, to which they are one with action. An ideal which does not move is no part of the self and hence not an ideal, or guide to action. A criterion which is not an application of character, an individualized, habitual view of considering conduct, is mere knowledge that other persons think well of an act; it is second handed information. A man's ways of judging acts—his standard—are just as much a part of himself as are the performance of the acts. The judging is one way of acting. The real criterion is the way of estimating action; the value which the self puts upon it, the interest it takes—*i.e.*, motive.

We have now finished our study of approbation, or the conscious value attached to action, on the sides both of the good (ideal) and its standard. We have seen that action is itself the process of measuring and defining goods, and that ideal and standard both come into existence as phases of action. We have seen that conscious action *is* the process

of approbation involving the development of a general standard of reference and its translation into definite terms. In all
this it is implied that the act measures the agent, and that
the act tests the standard as well as the standard the act.
It is this implication to which we now pass.

6

xxx. Reflective Approbation, or Conscience

The identity of agent and act has been our guiding principle. Because of this identity, we have insisted that impulse, ideal, motive and standard, all express various phases of character. But so far we have overtly considered this identity only on the side of the passing forth of the agent into act, showing that the act is the conclusion of the process of estimating value entered upon whenever any impulse is referred to its probable consequences. This also means, as just said, that the act in manifesting character, reveals it — makes *it* a subject of judgment. This reaction of a deed back into the estimation of character, the reflective weighing of character and motive in the light of the acts which express it, constitutes conscience. We measure the act by our controlling standard — *direct* approbation; we must equally measure our standard by the act as seen in its expression — *reflective* approbation and reprobation, with the involved ideas of merit and guilt.

The act from the standpoint of intention, that is the act in consciousness before performance, is an abstraction. The act as done, the deed with its import brought home, the act in consciousness completed, is concrete or individual. The abstraction, in intention, comes from the fact that character, the organized habits, the relatively permanent ideas, are taken for granted. The agent is *consciously* concerned only with the objective conditions under which the permanent, assumed ends take their particular shape. A man will measure land well only when he keeps his thought concentrated upon that one fact of measuring, abstracting both from his larger end (selling it, building a house, etc.), and from his largest end — self-expression. But this act done, its meaning in terms of his own life, as realized self, must to some degree, appear. Before, the act was defined, or measured, in terms of the objective conditions involved in its performance; now, it is measured, or appreciated, in terms of its significance for the self, one's own individuality. It is this fuller value, in its relation to the partial value, that constitutes *conscience*. It is the return of the ideal, the motive, the standard, back out of its abstraction into terms of character, of living self. We have first to notice the different sense which attaches to this return in the cases of the good and the bad act respectively.

The good man's ideal is the next thing to be done, the step which requires taking. But in so far as the agent is good, the act, no matter how specific, utters his whole self. The definite act and the generic end are one. It harmonizes his powers, reducing his impulses, both primary and induced, to unity. His whole self being in the act, the deed is solid and substantial, no matter how trivial the outer occasion. As Aristotle says (*Ethics*, Bk. I, Chs. 10, 12), the nobility of the good man shines through ignoble circumstance. The good man *always* builds better than he knows. Furthermore, the very aim of the good man is itself a unification in thought, as the deed is in act, of the realities of the situation (see Sec. VI). His intent lines up, focuses the demands of life. In doing the deed, then, the universe of Reality moves through him as its conscious organ. Hence the sense of the dignity and validity of the act – the essence of the religious consciousness. Hence the joy, the feeling of full life, and the peace, the feeling of harmonized force, which accompany the good act. The "moral sense," on the part of the good man, is this realization of himself in his deed, the consciousness of the deed in its organic significance.

The moral consciousness is thus one with the consciousness of the act. The joy is in the act itself, not in the goodness of the agent as distinct from the act; the peace is found in doing the deed; it is not an end to be reached by the deed as a means. The moral consciousness is not a distinct thing, apart from the act: *it is the act realized in its full meaning*. We instinctively recognize that there is something unhealthy in over-conscious morality. There is a Pharisaic paradox, as well as a hedonistic one. As pleasure can be got only by aiming at something else, so the consciousness of moral worth, the sense of right doing, can be had only when it is not sought for. And there is a necessary reason for this: the consciousness of goodness is the consciousness of a completely unified self. If the agent is thinking of his own glory, or credit, or moral worth, or improvement, he is, by that fact, *divided*; there is the deed to be performed, *and* the reflex of it into himself. In so far as the latter is the real motive for action, the interest is not in the act as self (or in the acting self), but in the act as means to a state of enjoyment (in the mere getting a certain experience). Attention to the act is, of necessity, partial, for it does not absorb interest. Hence the moral emotion which is the internalizing of complete activity, or attention, is missed.

Mackenzie (*Manual of Ethics*, p. 164) takes the ground that conscience refers only to wrong doing; that good action is unconscious of itself. That there is no *separate* consciousness of good action follows, indeed, from the above. But when Mackenzie says (p. 338, 2d ed.) that there is probably *no* pleasure of conscience proper, since (*i*) the moral ideal can hardly be attained, and (*ii*) "if any individual did attain it, he would attain it only by a devotion to objective ends, which would exclude the possibility of any feeling of self-satisfaction," he seems to me to make the moral life absolutely meaningless. (*i*) The first assertion sets up our old friend, the "abstract ideal" (Sec. XXI), not a working ideal, and brings out a further objection to it. The continual non-attainment must mean continual dissatisfaction. Healthy interest in work for its own sake, the only genuine and self-persisting form of morality, is rendered impossible. Instead, we must have an anxious craving for a remote future and a restless irritation with the present. (Humility means not that what we have done is worthless, but that its *present* worth is the *use* we can make of it; humility is willingness to throw the past achievement into the stream of life, instead of clinging to it as a life preserver. And so aspiration is not a striving for a vaguely higher ideal, but the tense muscle, the full interest in the present deed. It is humility on its positive side, or utilized for the future.) (*ii*) The second assertion brings out the contradiction in the doctrine of self-realization when self is conceived as remote, or is presupposed as in any way existing outside the definite act. There is no alternative apparently save choice of a self-satisfaction which is exclusive and, really, hedonistic, or a devotion to objective ends which does not mean self-satisfaction—in reality, asceticism or self-sacrifice. All this, because it is not seen that devotion to objective ends (*i.e.*, the mediation of impulse) *is* self-satisfaction. No theory which sets up a self at large can recognize that the only satisfaction which really satisfies is the interest, the value of the act itself. Only a doctrine which sees self to be specific, defined activity can admit the consciousness of satisfaction, or good, as a normal fact, and yet not set it up as a separate (and therefore hedonistic) aim. To it, there is no self save in the conscious act; no consciousness of satisfaction save the interest, the value, of the act itself.

This disposes of the "disguised selfishness" theory concerning virtue, the argument that the good man gets his satisfaction out of the good act as much as the bad man out of the evil act. Of course he does, and more. But it is a misunderstanding, already dealt with, to suppose this means that he does the act *for* his satisfaction; he does it *as* his satisfaction. What makes him a good man is precisely the fact that such acts *are* his interest, his satisfaction. In the good man, the act measures or exhibits the interest; the self is only in the moving act; in the bad man, the act is done for the sake of a self, an interest, outside the act; it is measured by a fixed self. (A good ethical statement here is Mackenzie, *Manual of Ethics*, App. B, IV; a good psychological statement, James, *Psychology*, Vol. I, Ch. 10.)

XXXI. Moral Condemnation

The recognition that an act is evil (moral condemnation or consciousness of guilt) takes quite a different form, though based on the same principle. Were all our acts approved, we should have no moral consciousness *distinct* in any way from our consciousness of action; but reprobation means a distinct, a reflex, consciousness. We are morally glad *in*, not for, our deed; but we are sorry *for* it. The condemning judgment is one which stands, in a sense, outside of the act as well as within it. It holds the act out; looks back upon it, and feels its unworthiness as measured by a standard self, up to which the act has not come. This consciousness of division, of act *and* self, value *and* standard, is the very essence of the troubled conscience. Yet, in principle, the consciousness of evil is the same as consciousness of good; *i.e.*, it is the realization of an act in its full meaning, as brought out through doing the deed. But the *meaning* of the bad act *is* division; the agent has intended an unreality; his aim, his ideal, has been severed from the conditions of the situation, from the realities of the universe; he has set up a *merely* subjective end, and thus isolated himself. In so far as the performance of the act reveals the true nature of the act, there is recoil, rebound; the deed kicks. The agent feels his separation. The dissatisfaction of the act performed reveals the unreality, the split of self.

Hence the peculiar dualism in all remorse. The agent at once feels the extremest repugnance at the very thought of the act, would repel it as far from himself as possible, and yet feels that that act was his very self—knows, indeed, that he feels this repulsion just because the act was himself. As *his*, the act holds him, fascinates him, perhaps to the point of morbidness; literature is filled with accounts of this binding, gnawing, insistent character of evil done. As not *truly* himself, because unreal and false in its very nature, the agent is repelled, he attempts to thrust out the memory, to drown remorse, and deaden conscience; to have "the damned spot *out*." The contradiction of these two sides of remorse marks the emergence in consciousness of the contradiction in the act itself. No one intends an act save as good; but the completed act stands forth as most thoroughly not good.

The moral condemnation, in other words, is directed essentially at the ideal and standard of the act. Not because the agent consciously aimed at evil does he have the guilty conscience, but because the good (ideal) aimed at was of such a kind as to show a character which takes for good that which in the light of enlarged character is seen as evil. Again, guilt is imputed not because the agent already had a standard of good and then fell short of it. On the contrary, the remorse is, for the first time, the experience of shortcoming. The guilt is imputed because it reveals the previous standard of good. How unworthy my character must have been, how defective myself to have such a conception of value! The evil was radical, not simply in the act; it was in the way the self determined, or measured good, in the way it set up ends as approved. Prior to the act, the agent measures by his existing standard of good, and does the deed as good; afterward, the deed, in its full content, reveals his own character, and thus measures the standard.

It is implied that the very condemnation, the consciousness of evil, means the consciousness of a new standard of a higher good. If the agent is still on the same level as that in which he performed the act, no compunctions arise. The act is still good to him, and he is still good as exhibited in that act. Only because the bad act brings to light a new good is its own badness manifested. The reaction of the deed into character, in other words, brings that character to consciousness; it shows character its own powers and requirements, and thus enables it to pass judgment upon, *i.e*, to appreciate, its own unworthiness. Moral condemnation, in fine, if really moral, if itself approvable, is of itself always *repentance* or the beginning of better things. Only because to some extent the self is moving more organically does it realize the disorganic character of its past efforts. Only the man becoming good recognizes evil as evil.

From this appears the duty of the agent with reference to his experiences of guilt, or unworthiness. It is *not* to experience them for themselves, but to get their reaction into character. One is to dwell on his mistakes and shortcomings just enough to get the meaning, the instruction, the mediation of impulse and habit, which is in them. The more the attention is turned upon the bad act *in itself*, the more that act becomes a fixed, external thing, a finality; the dwelling upon the fact that one *has* done a bad act is positively demoralizing save as one gets from it correction and stimulus for the future. It simply widens the very division, hardens the very isolation, which is the badness, while the true function of *consciousness* of division is to enable one to heal the gap. In other words, one has the same duty regarding his experiences of guilt that he has regarding every other experience, viz., to use them, to make them functional in activity, instead of merely experiencing them.[17] It is a common

17   The doctrine of "salvation by grace," as expressed in the writings of St. Paul, with the immense meaning attached to it, seems to have for its ethical content the first historical consciousness, on the part of humanity, that sin, when it becomes a *consciousness* of sin organically referred back to character, means also a consciousness of a good which can take that evil up into itself and so conquer it, which, in fact, has already begun so to do.

fallacy to suppose that the mere experiencing of painful consequences from bad action has of itself any remedial power. As we noted (Sec. xxiv), pleasures do not mean satisfaction; here we note that pains do not, of necessity, mean dissatisfaction. The "wicked" man may experience an indefinite mass of pain from his badness, and yet get none the better for it, if it is not reflected back into his character, is not used as a standpoint whence to measure his previous standard of good. And the professionally "good" man may get nothing out of his compunctions, his pangs of conscience. He may even, as a dilettante, come to enjoy them, relishing them as indications of his sensitive moral nature. This happens when he isolates them, instead of using them as symptoms by which to locate, and correct, his unworthiness of character.

If the foregoing is correct, then ethical writers have tended immensely to exaggerate the distinction between regret and remorse, in holding that the former applies simply to consequences, having no moral meaning, while the latter refers to motive and is essentially moral. The true difference is simply one of perspective, of proportion; both relate to a *reaction of consequences into motive* as used to guide the latter. It is regret when duty demands that we do not dwell much upon the past bad act; when we can get the good of it without much reflection upon the unworthiness of a character which could assume such consequences. It is remorse (normal, not morbid) when in order to get the change of attitude for the future, it is necessary to realize, more radically, how unworthy was the self displayed in an act of such consequences. Regret and remorse stand on the same basis so far as the implication of character is concerned. One no more regrets the death of a friend, caused by himself without shadow of intent or carelessness, than he regrets the earthquake of Lisbon. He may do infinitely more than regret it; he may be stunned and haunted by it; but "regret" is as futile in one case as in the other.

It is impossible to give many references to distinctly ethical writers in agreement with the foregoing position. It is the view, in substance, of Emerson, expressed perhaps most definitely in his essay on "Compensation." The view regarding the essential defect of the Puritanic morality, viz., that it aimed at the moral consciousness by itself, has been very forcibly expressed in the various writings of James Hinton, and of William James, Sr.

XXXII. Various Aspects of Conscience

Conscience, as used in common speech, is a term as wide as the entire moral consciousness of man. It is absurd, accordingly, for theory to attempt to narrow the word to some technical or special meaning. But common speech indicates by the word, at different times, certain typical phases of the moral consciousness, and theory may follow with a description of these typical phases.

1. We hear of a tender, a hardened conscience, the pangs, pricks, compunctions, pains and joys of conscience. This evidently refers to conscience as an *emotional fact*; the interest of the act as brought home to the agent in terms of his own feelings.

2. We hear of the voice of conscience, conscience telling us to do this and that, of an enlightened conscience, of educating conscience, etc. Here we are thinking of the *intellectual* content of the moral consciousness; moral judgments as a system of truth, of ideals and standards.

3. We also hear of the commands of conscience, of its majesty, its inviolability, that aspect which Kant terms "categorical imperative." Here is clearly indicated the *authoritativeness* of any act recognized as moral.

XXXIII. Conscience as the Moral Sentiments

The intellectual aspect of conscience is most conveniently discussed in connection with the question of intuitionalism and empiricism; that of the authority of conscience in connection with obligation.

Concerning the emotional side of conscience, it is hardly necessary to do more than gather together the scattered threads of what has already been said. The purport of the theory, as already developed, is that the valuation of an act assumes an objective and a subjective form. The objective is the analysis of the act into its various conditions, its definition or limitation—the ideal, intention, etc. The subjective is

the feeling excited in the individual, by either the contemplation of the act in thought or by its actual execution in deed.
The thought, the intention, is not colorless; it represents a
projection of the self, and the moral emotion is simply the
realization by an individual of the value of the projected act
for himself as an individual. The thought of every act must
have, therefore, its own peculiar, qualitative, emotional accompaniment. We are somehow *affected* towards every
plan. Hope, fear, disgust, tedium, love. hate, etc., etc., so
far as excited not directly by some object, but the *thought of
an object as an end to be reached* (so far as mediated by
ideas of acts) are thus all forms of moral consciousness, on
the emotional side. Such feelings are evidently no adequate
criterion of the act. On the contrary, they depend upon that
which needs judgment—individual character—and vary with
it (see Sec. xxvii).

The emotions which are usually picked out as pecu-
liarly ethical, correspond to the generalized ideals already
spoken of (Sec. xxix). When the feared or hoped for end is
itself brought into relation with the self as a whole, with
organized character, an emotional response appears which
is "moral" in a definite sense. A person who is susceptible to
such reactions is the one with tender or acute conscience; it is
natural for him to feel the indwelling reference of character
as a whole to any special act; if a child, we say his moral nature is easily appealed to.

To a considerable extent, this sensitiveness to given
acts as expressions of the whole character is a natural gift,
a temperamental quality; one person always differs in kind
and range of it from every other. This consideration shows
how little we can rest in this emotional response as an ultimate fact, or regard it as an adequate criterion for the distinction between right and wrong.[18] It is, psychologically,
simply one phase of æsthetic susceptibility in general. Like
all the other phases, its moral value lies not in itself but in
the use to which it is put, the ends to which it is made subservient. A "sensitive" conscience may become an ingredient
of a bad character, and a somewhat inert one a factor of a

[18]   As some writers, naming it "moral sense," have considered it.

good character. The former happens when the sensitiveness leads the individual to taking the easiest way out of moral difficulties, as relieving a beggar simply to quiet the clamor of his own "conscience," or hiding scenes of sin and misery from himself because they pain him so grievously. The latter happens whenever the inertness is changed into the habit of looking every situation squarely in the face as it comes, and deciding it on its own merits, without regard to the merely personal feeling awakened by it. Over-pietistic training has almost always tended to make the emotional response of conscience a criterion in itself, instead of recognizing that it is a part of conduct to which the same responsibility for right use attaches, as to the passion of anger, or the desire for food.

So far as responsibility for the emotional side of conscience is concerned, the great need is to insure that emotion take the form of *interest*—that is, satisfaction in the working out of an idea into deed,—and not the form of *mere feeling*, even though it be called "moral feeling." In the main, this is secured just in so far as there is interest in the deed *on its own account*—just as the artist is interested in painting his picture, the chess-player in his game, the engineer in the execution of his drainage project, etc. It must be remembered that every deflection or defect of interest as to the deed itself, means lack of attention to it, and means diversion of thought in some other direction, and hence, of necessity, something slighted, scrimped or distorted in the act itself. Completeness of action and complete possession of consciousness (full interest) by the thought of the act are synonymous terms.

In this sense, the moral emotion, or interest, and the artistic interest, are identical.[19] Both, to be genuine, are in-

---

[19]   I say "artistic," not "æsthetic." Artistic interest is interest in the *execution* of an idea; in its assumption of that concrete fullness of detail which is realization. Æsthetic interest is interest rather in the contemplation of some idea *already* executed. It is the difference between art as a process to the *artist* and a *work* of art to the spectator. The latter *may* free activity in the beholder and so be artistic in turn; but it may stop in itself, in the mere self-absorbed feeling awakened. All the attacks, worth considering, of moralists upon art as meaning self-indulgence, effeminateness, corruption, etc., seem to me to rest on the confusion of artistic with æsthetic.

terests in adequate, non-slighted execution of ideas; a phrase
which, after all, means only undivided, organic, pure interest in the act itself. The artist whose chief interest is in
his product, *qua* product,[20] and not as fulfillment of a process
(who separates, that is, the thought of the completed house
from the steps necessary on his part to complete it, who looks
at the making of a statue as a *mere means* to the objective
statue) is, by that very fact, so far short as an artist. He has
not sufficient interest in his performance to give it the care
and attention it demands. *A fortiori*, any interest which looks
beyond the objective result to the reflex of that result into
personal profit or credit is partial and must manifest itself in
a partial—that is, inartistic—execution.

It is necessary, however, not to be too rigid in our conception of the act; not to attempt to draw lines too narrowly
as to just where the act itself begins or leaves off and external considerations come in. A man who should write a
book for the mere sake of fame would not be, relatively,
much of a writer; his aim would not direct him; yet the
thought of fame may become fused with the thought of the
book and add a deepened touch of interest to his work. A
man who should carry on a profession simply for the sake
of supporting his family would be partial in his morality,
and would reveal his moral disintegration by carelessness
at some critical juncture. But the *identification* of his
family's welfare with the pursuit of his calling reinforces,
by so much, his attention to his business, the fullness with
which he gives his whole mind to his duties.

In the same way, appeals to personal profit or loss often
do not have the selfish (in the bad sense) meaning, which, at
first sight, attaches to them. A man's indignation at some
cruelty to humanity is often first stirred by some bitter experience of his own. A cynic may contend that all his efforts
are now put forth simply because of the personal injury he
himself has suffered; as matter of fact, the appeal to his own
interest may mean simply an enlargement of himself. The
shock has acted as a stimulus to call his attention to matters

[20]   "You look to the result, you want to see some profit of your
endeavors: that is why you would never learn to paint, if you lived to be
Methusalem." Stevenson, in *The Wrecker.*

previously ignored; it has revealed to him his own implication in that which had previously seemed external. So a man
may first be awakened to the public's need of improvement
of transit facilities, or sanitation, by coming himself to own
property in the needy region; but it is, psychologically, poor
taste to assume that of necessity such an one is moved simply
by his own advantage. It may again be that his own personal
interest serves as a connecting link in giving a stimulus to
attention.

This principle gives a basis[21] for judging concerning
the moral value of rewards and punishments; of appeals to
do a deed because of the profit it will bring self, or because it
will please parent or friend or God to have the act done. So
far as these ends tend to become distinct ends, *substituted*
for the act itself, the latter being reduced to a *means*, the
tendency is thoroughly immoral. If these appeals are used
as stimuli to bring *the self to consciousness of itself*, to *bring
home to self* the real intrinsic nature of the deed needing
to be done, in so far the effect is moral—provided always
these instrumentalities are the most efficient ones, under the
circumstances, in effecting this end.

Our general principle enables us to deal with the assertion that a pure conscience always is attached to the right
"for the sake of the right." Correctly interpreted, this statement is true to the point of truism, but many who insist upon
it appear to interpret it so as to make it false theoretically,
and dangerously sentimental practically. In reality, to do a
thing for the sake of its rightness means to do it for its *own*
sake; the rightness is not an *end beyond* with reference to
which the act is a means; it simply names that phase of the
end or aim which confers upon it a claim to pass into act.
Rightness names the quality of the deed in itself as the
fully mediated activity, or expressed self. We may say that

---

[21]   See again, James, *Psychology*, Vol. I, pp. 317–29, especially pp.
325–27. Alexander, *Moral Order*, pp. 317–23 is helpful, though he seems
to give too personal a definition to interest. The statement "when it is
worth a man's while to do wrong, the guilt lies as often with others as
with himself," may be safely changed, I think, into the statement that
whenever there is opposition between principle and interest, there is
always a responsibility upon others to change the conditions which make
the individual conceive of himself in the narrow way.

"right" is primarily and fundamentally an *adverb*; we are to act *rightly*, in a certain way or fashion. It then becomes an adjective; the deed is "right" when performed in this way. Finally, it is a noun. Rightness simply denominates this quality wherever found. To make it an end in itself is to set up a sheer abstraction for the moral ideal. The result is the same as when moral approbation, or a satisfied conscience, is made the end (see p. 274). The end lying beyond the act, attention to the latter is partial and diverted; the act is only partially, that is, *wrongly*, done.[22] The theory avenges itself.

Yet there can be no doubt that conflicts arise, times when interest in the act itself and interest in right as such do not immediately coincide. In times of great temptation, or at periods of change, when it is necessary to do some act so novel that as yet it does not present interest for its own sake, such conflicts occur. We feel that the right in general demands that the act be done, and yet the act, in itself, is decidedly a bore or even repulsive. Or we feel that an act which has all the argument of attractiveness on its side must be foregone simply for the sake of right. Moreover, it is precisely at such junctures that moral fibre is made. Only through such discipline is character other than wishy-washy. Only at such periods is morality freed from extraneous recommendations, and the self thrown back naked upon itself in its own innate vigor. Do not these facts contradict the theory laid down?

The apparent contradiction vanishes the moment we subject the meaning of "Right" in general to analysis. The conflict then turns out to be not between interest or self, and moral law or principle, but between two selves, between an interest in the act narrowly viewed, and an interest in the act more fully realized. My interest as a momentary being, with capacities for enjoyment, may be in some self-indulgence; my interest in myself as a member of a family is

[22]   When Green says (*Works*, Vol. II, pp. 335–36), "The highest moral goodness . . . issues in acts done for the sake of their goodness. . . . But it is impossible that an act should be done for the sake of its goodness, unless it has been previously contemplated as good for some other reason than that which consists in its being done for the sake of its goodness," he seems to fall into this error. Of course, acts done earlier as good are done later with a deeper consciousness of what their goodness consists in, but this is quite a different matter. Upon the whole subject, see Bradley, *Ethical Studies*, Essay II.

in abstinence; my interest in myself as, abstractly, a person who can procure enjoyment out of possession is in getting the better of my customer in a bargain; my interest in my self as actively participating in the interchanges of life is in honor and good faith. In other words, the Right which demands loyalty to itself in spite of the inducements of immediate interest, is not some Rightness at large; it is a view of the particular act as expressing the self wholly and not partially. And in general, whenever there is talk of a conflict between a lower and a higher self, a material and a spiritual self, and of the necessity of sacrificing one to the other, as identical with sacrificing self-interest to the demands of Law and Right, it will be found that the lower self, the interest, is a partial, passive, possessing self; the higher self, the Right, is not some abstraction, but is the self *performing some concrete function*, as father, neighbor or citizen.

We conclude, then, with the statement that the emotional side of conscience expresses the interest which every working ideal and act have for the self—have by their very nature psychologically.[23]

xxxiv.   Nature of Conscience as Moral Knowledge[24]

The intuitional theory holds that conscience is a peculiar faculty which gives man, directly and immediately, knowledge of principles, or rules, of right. In attacking the opposed theory of empiricism, it is quite customary, how-

---

[23]   While not in all cases discussing the same questions, the standpoint of Alexander seems to be close to that of the previous pages. In addition to references already given, see *Moral Order*, pp. 148–60, 181–93, 324–32. See Stephen, *Science of Ethics*, pp. 311–39, and 396–417. On "moral sense," Mackenzie, *Manual of Ethics*, pp. 49–52 and references there given. Also references in next section. An interesting though (it appears to me) somewhat abstract view of moral emotions will be found in Laurie, *Ethica*, Chs. 8, 23, 26 and 27. Schmidt, *Das Gewissen*, contains an interesting account of the historical development of ideas about conscience, from the early Greek and Hebrew period to the present. It includes much more than the emotional side. A further statement of the doctrines of "higher" and "lower" selves will be found in Dewey, *Outlines of Ethics*, pp. 216–20 [*Early Works*, III, 374–77]. A discussion of a point barely alluded to in the foregoing will be found in Sharp, *Æsthetic Element in Morality*.

[24]   This is to be interpreted as knowledge of right and wrong, not of obligation. To that, a further section is devoted.

ever, for the intuitionalists to shift their ground, and substitute a doctrine of the *intrinsic nature* of rightness for a
doctrine of *immediate knowledge* of it. There is no necessary connection between these two standpoints; rightness
may be a quality which belongs to acts in themselves (and
not because of any considerations or results extraneous to
the acts) and yet it not be known, except through experience, in what this rightness consists. Any relation made
known by physical science certainly belongs to mass and
energy in their own intrinsic character (if true, at all), but
it does not follow that we perceive these relations upon bare
inspection of the facts. It takes experience, often long and
painful, to bring home to us these "intrinsic" qualities; there
is every reason to believe the same is the case with the
quality of rightness. It is no more a matter of direct perception, than is the law of gravitation. It will be found upon
careful reading of most modern intuitionalists that they are
really concerned to uphold the real and necessary character
of the moral distinctions in themselves, rather than any
special theory regarding the way in which these distinctions
are made known.

A good historical sketch of intuitionalism will be found in
Sidgwick, *History of Ethics*, pp. 167–200, 213–24. The same author
gives a theoretical analysis in *Methods of Ethics*, Bk. I, Chs. 8 and 9,
and Bk. III. The following will indicate the positions of some of the
modern intuitionalists. Martineau, *Types of Ethical Theory*, Vol. II,
Part Two, Bk. I, especially pp. 17–64; Calderwood, *Moral Philosophy*; Maurice, *Conscience*; Rickaby, *Moral Philosophy*; Janet, *Theory
of Morals*.

A good criticism of ordinary intuitionalism will be found in
Porter, *Elements of Moral Science*, Ch. 10; while in Ch. 8 will be
found a theory of reflective intuitionalism.

In general, the intuitional theory in its older form has
been shattered by a series of objections which may be
summed up as follows: The intuitional theory, instead of
saving the necessary and objective character of moral
distinctions, swamps them all in the merely subjective consciousness. An appeal to "intuition" as final means in reality
an appeal to purely individual opinion, to the dogmatic
deliverance, or the unproved sentiment of this or that man.
If we go outside the "intuitions" of the individual, there is

left only an appeal to a vague common-sense, which is often unenlightened, the product of mere custom and prejudice. In general, intuitionalism leads to the consecration of established opinion. It allows every existing creed and institution to resist challenge and reform by the assertion, "I represent an eternal and necessary intuition."[25]

The development of historical and comparative science and of the doctrine of evolution have dealt the theory hard blows. The former has revealed the great variety of ideas conscientiously maintained upon matters of right and wrong in different ages and in different peoples, and also largely accounted for this variety of ideas by showing their relativity to types of social life. The latter theory, as it gains in acceptance, leaves no room for belief in any faculty of moral knowledge separate from the whole process of experience, and cuts the ground out from under any store of information given directly and immediately.[26] The modern standpoint and method in psychology also make it almost impossible to attach any intelligent meaning to the thought of a special faculty of knowledge.

On strictly ethical ground, the value of such moral intuitions, if we had them, would be open to grave question. Intuitionalism would take the form of knowledge either (a) that this or that *particular* act is right, or (b) that certain *kinds* of action (honesty, chastity, etc.) are right. The former alternative would be useful if the essence of morality were a short-cut to doing the exact things which are right. But if we abandon this materialistic ethics, and recognize that the heart of morality is development of character, a certain spirit and method in all conduct, such intuitions would

[25]   These are, in substance, the trenchant objections of Bentham, *Principles of Morals*, Chs. 1 and 2. The objection to intuitions as always inuring practically to the conservative party is as old as Locke, see *Essay*, Bk. I. It largely determined John Stuart Mill's standpoint. See *Autobiography*, pp. 273–74.
[26]   The first objection is generally met by intuitionalists by holding that certain ultimate principles are alike, though their "application" varies. This transfers the ground entirely from a question of mode of knowledge to a question of validity of content. In connection with the theory of evolution, Spencer's contention that it restores a modified intuitionalism (empirical for the race, intuitional, by inheritance of consolidated experience, for the individual) is to be noted. *Data of Ethics*, pp. 123–24.

much lessen the range of self-expression, and render hard and mechanical what little remains. It would shut out all that growth of character, all that opening up of consciousness and experience of values that comes in the search for and testing of right and wrong; it would leave the individual simply with the sheer, arbitrary decision to abide or not to abide by the right once for all revealed.

If intuition reveals general principles, then the responsibility of the individual is limited simply to their application. More than this, moral principles once for all made known go necessarily with an *external* ideal and standard. Casuistry—the consideration of an act from the standpoint of different rules, in order to see *under* which one it is to be brought—is a necessary outcome.

The term "intuition" has a popular as well as a philosophic sense. Examination indicates that the popular sense is really much more philosophical than the one professedly so. In practical life, we mean by intuition the power to seize as a whole, in a single and almost instantaneous survey, a complete group of circumstances. It is the power to read off at a glance the meaning of a given situation. It is opposed *not* to experience, but to abstract logical reflection. It is the outcome, on the theoretic side, of habit on the practical side. A custom of dealing with a certain sort of facts and conditions often gives an almost incredible facility in coming to an immediate conclusion. When the quality is largely temperamental, we term it (or rather the response in action based upon it) "tact"; developed through experience, it constitutes the "expert." The architect sizes up a plan at once, and is prepared to act. The landscape gardener takes in at a look the possibilities of a certain "lie" of ground, and sketches its future development, etc.

In this practical sense, much of our moral knowledge is constantly assuming the form of intuitions. The demand for quick appreciation of conditions for action in general is much greater than it can be in any one special direction, like carpentry, or treatment of guests. Thus every individual comes to have ways of judging action which are practically instinctive.[27] It must also be remembered that the whole

---

[27]   See Dewey, *Psychology*, pp. 344–46 [*Early Works*, II, 271–80].

experience goes on in terms of the individual self. Both initiating impulse and mediating idea are acts of self. This reference to self always limits the field for reflection, and also makes this field a whole, a self-contained unity. That a man should get intimate practical acquaintance with self, should come to appreciate quickly his own deepest concerns, that he should form habits so fundamental that they at once take up a given set of facts into themselves and thus judge its value—all this is matter for no surprise.[28] Two qualifications are to be noted. First, such intuitions are not an ultimate criterion. They test individual character, because they are functions of it; that is, the kind of judgments immediately passed shows the kind of character engaged in making the judgment. No *moral* judgment is ever *merely* intellectual, because it reflects the aims and interests of the judge. These intuitions must, therefore, upon occasion submit themselves to wider judgment, must become conditions of a fuller character. Secondly, strength of moral character demands a continued tension between the reflective and intuitive sides, as between conscious aim and habit (see pp. 240–41). The intuitive side means quickness, certainty, and, above all, concreteness and solidity; the reflective side is the demand for continued mediation, for continued reaction of the whole into the part, for enlargement of scope. It means delay, but a delay which permits a wider field to be surveyed; uncertainty, but an uncertainty which makes the final making up of one's mind more reasonable.

The empirical theory of conscience is that the individual has no immediate knowledge of right and wrong, either as to particular acts or general principles, but that such knowledge is the outgrowth of continued experience. Logically, this is all the empirical theory is required to mean; and in this strict sense, empiricism seems to be true. The theory, however, has no special meaning, until there is a further analysis of what experience is. In general, the saying that "knowledge results from experience" is a meaningless one; the point of interest is always in the question *how* experience gives birth to knowledge.

[28]   Emerson has stated the intuitive character of moral knowledge as a result of the individual's own activity more clearly than any moralist. See, for example, his essay on "Self-Reliance."

The force of this general statement is apparent when we note that historically the ethical empiricist has gone far beyond the harmless statement above made, and insisted that moral knowledge comes from a calculation of the consequences of the act, those consequences lying outside the content of the act itself. In other words, the empiricists have, as a rule, been hedonists, and have interpreted their empiricism as meaning that moral quality is *extrinsic* to the act, lying in the results of the act in the way of pleasure and pain, not intrinsic to the act itself.

Thus the *negative* side of both intuitionalism and empiricism has been their strength. The empiricist has kept up his side by denying that we have immediate knowledge of right; the intuitionalist has sustained his by denying that moral quality is found in considerations alien to the act's own structure. Both have failed in interpreting the positive significance of their own contentions. The failure of empiricism need hardly be re-argued here. The force of the objections already brought against pleasure as standard finally comes back to the idea that pleasure as a result, lies outside the act itself, outside the character of the person willing the act, and, therefore, is accidental, externally variable, incapable of being foreseen, tending to produce either undue laxity or undue anxiety—in general, unusable.

On the ground of the principles hitherto advanced, experience *is* precisely the mediation of impulse; the execution of impulse brings it to consciousness, shows the meaning for life as a whole of that impulse in particular. By reaching in a certain way (that is, in connection with other impulses of ear or eye) we find out what this impulse means, its value, in terms both of the content of the impulse, the object (ball, or hot iron or whatever) and in terms of the place which that object occupies in our own sentient experience—pleasure or pain. Experience is the revelation of the meaning of our impulses, of our acting selves. As such, there must be all the regard to consequences in forming aims, and using standards, which the most extreme empiricist could urge. But these consequences are not extrinsic to the act—they are the act unfolded, defined. (See Sec. XII. A most suggestive illustration and formulation of this principle will be found in Vol. I, No. 6, of *Philosophical Review*, article by James.)

7

Obligation

xxxv. The Psychology of Obligation

A typical phase of conscience is indicated by such phrases as "I ought, am bound," "it is my duty," to act thus and so. There is here a consciousness of a double relation. "I ought to go to my business today" means there is an agent on one side, and a certain idea on the other; that the former owes something to the latter, while the latter imposes a certain necessity (a *bounden* somewhat) on the former (duty, due, debt; ought, owe). What is the meaning of this peculiar relation between agent and ideal? This problem becomes clearer when we compare it with the question of the good. In that also, there is a distinction between immediate agent and ideal; the one being in a condition of lack and effort, and the other expressing satisfaction, and a completed act. But both terms of the relation are in the same line of movement. The immediate self is striving to attain the good; the good is this striving satisfied. But in duty, the distinction between present self and ideal seems pushed to the point of dualism. The present self does not want, of itself, it would seem, to realize the ideal; the latter rather presents itself as a demand, an exaction, if not a coercion. It stands over against the agent and utters the "categorical imperative" (Kant), "thou shalt," "thou oughtst," instead of drawing the agent on by its own intrinsic attractiveness.

Were the relation one of sheer compulsion or coercion, however, the problem, in some respects, would be easier to deal with. We could, at least, class it with other exhibitions of brute force; the relation would be simply one case of a superior energy overcoming a lesser. But, on the contrary, in spite of all the apparent opposition and resistance between agent and ideal, the consciousness of duty carries with it the sense of a fundamental underlying identity. The sense of obligation is not the sense of a stronger alien force bearing down; it is rather the sense that the obligatory act is somehow more truly and definitely one's self than the present self upon which the obligation is imposed. "I ought to do this act," implies that "this act" is really "I"; in so far as the idea of the act is felt as merely alien to self, it is felt as irritating, as something to be got rid of, not as authoritatively binding.

We thus have before us, in a descriptive way, the main features of the consciousness of duty. It is a consciousness of the present self in relation to an idea of action, this relation involving (a) a certain opposition and conflict between the two, based on the reluctance of the immediate self to identify itself in action with the idea, and thus realize it, and (b) a consciousness that in reality the ideal is a more adequate expression of the self than is the present agent.

The psychology of this relation may be most easily approached by a return to the distinction of self as immediate and mediate. At a given time, there is always a certain body of positive impulse and habit urging forward for complete expression. But this very structure, in its expression, stimulates certain other tendencies and activities which are not, on their face, compatible with the prior activities which induced them. It is, for example, upon the basis of certain present activities that a person marries, or, again, engages in a certain profession. The activities corresponding to these latter engagements are stimulated by the former, and are, indeed, necessary to their normal psychological completion. Nevertheless, the person has now, as we say, "assumed the obligations" of a new condition or occupation. He cannot possibly continue his former habits unchanged; they must, moreover, not only be modified here and there, in pieces, but must be subordinated, readjusted to the new aims. Here we have the psychical conditions for the feeling of obligation. The old habits tend to assert themselves; they maintain themselves by their own inertia and momentum. Moreover, it is highly important, from the moral standpoint (as well as necessary from the psychical) that they should do so. If the habits are entirely resolved, or disintegrated, there is no efficient instrumentality by which the new aims may realize themselves. The person relapses into a moral pulp. What is wanted is not the destruction of the old habits and desires, but their utilization in new directions. Now, just in the degree in which the habit is definite and efficient, it will resist an immediate and speedy assumption of a new direction. It is, upon the whole, safe to say that only in matters of slight importance, or of weak and unformed character, will the habit slip easily and naturally into new channels, and become, through its co-ordinations with other habits, a subordinate factor in a more comprehensive habit. It is of its very nature to continue its self-assertion.

And yet the newly aroused tendencies and ideas are organically connected with this habit. They are included within its self-assertion. The expression of the old habit carries *within itself* the making over of the old habit. The responsibilities of the new profession which demand a surrender of old acts and enjoyments, which require a redistribution of time, which impose changes in the direction of attention and interest—all this is not a visitor from an outside sphere, but arises from the former acts and impulses, the former interests and lines of attention. The new which requires the readjustment of the old is necessary to the integrity of the old. Hence the sense of finding *self* in the duty, the sense of unity, as well as of conflict and difference. The two sides in their tension give that consciousness of authority and subjection which is the marked phase of the sense of duty.

The sense of duty is thus a phenomenon of moral *progress*, appearing in so far as an intention or ideal demands the transformation of impulse and habit, by adapting them to instruments of its own realization. Without the new ideal, the habit becomes monotonous and dead, sheer routine. Not being in tension with an aim, it falls entirely below consciousness, and thus loses all value and significance. It is the essence of habit to be *instrumental*, a means for accomplishing ends. If the end *has* been accomplished, the unmodified repetition of the habit is useless, and is paid for by disintegration; the habit sets up in business for itself, runs on its own account, and its action becomes at odds with the activity of the organism as a whole. The habit of eating, for example, has been initiated and developed with reference to the end of maintaining life; it is relative, as habit, to an organic function, and must, to be efficient, be controlled constantly (held in check, be made to operate as to when, where and how much) by reference to the function.

Biologically and psychologically, it is a division of labor; yet, as such, it gets a certain independence and tends to isolation; to become the act of eating for the mere sake of eating.[29] This *tendency* is involved in its becoming a division of labor, with its own specific, defined structure and modes of operation. To do away with the *tendency* would be to destroy the specialization of structure, and relapse into a relatively unorganized life, one homogeneous as to parts and organs.

The problem here arises, in other words, from the very nature of progress. Progress demands *definite* individualization, *specific* organization. It requires effective instruments, and no instrument is effective save as its structure is individualized with reference to the special service to be performed by it. As long as the movement to be accomplished is rough and bulky, one and the same physical lever will serve for a multitude of ends; let the ends to be reached become refined and valuable, the idea of leverage has to be differentiated into thousands of physical shapes, sizes and materials. Every instrument then, as instrument, must assert its own specific, differentiated character, or relapse into uselessness. But, on the other hand, it is the nature of progress to require that instruments be truly instrumental, that they *serve* for ideas, for ends. The instrument must be flexible, must be continually readjusted to meet new needs and requirements. This antithesis between differentiation, definition (stability) and co-ordination, interaction (flexibility) gives, once more, the conditions involved in the consciousness of obligation.

The progressive action of any organism illustrates the same relationship. The eye represents in its structure defi-

[29]   To recur to the ethics of hedonism, we thus get a criterion for the moral value of pleasures and pains. Any pleasure or pain is normal (moral) in so far as it accompanies the working of an organ which is stimulated into action by the demands of the organism as a whole; is pathological (immoral) in so far as the organ assumes to work *per se*, or on its own credit.

nite habits of action; it represents a specialization of the whole organism for a certain purpose. It is effective and orderly just in the degree of its specialization. It must assert itself, assert *seeing*, and not attempt, upon occasion, to hear or to reach. There is, therefore, a continued tendency to isolation, a continued tendency *merely* to see. The healthy organism keeps this differentiated action in tension by rendering the habit of seeing adapted to the needs of other organs. The eye sees and only sees, but not for itself merely. It sees to help the hand reach, to help the legs walk, etc., etc. In short, there is a continued relative distinction and continued reconciliation, on basis of organic unity, of *structure* (organ) and *function*. The individual agent, as present self, is so much immediate impulse and habit, so much structure, a definite organ; while the ideal which demands a certain quality, a certain direction of the agent, stands for function, for organic service. In this process, "organ" evidently stands for the self as distinguished, as partial; function for self as unified, as whole.

Here, as everywhere, both the conservative and the radical factors are required for progressive action, nay, for each other. An ideal, without existing habits and impulses which represent the past (impulses, the history of the race, habits, of the individual) has no machinery, no instrument of realization. It is in the air, impotent, sentimental, dreamy. The reform must always be a re-form, a readjustment of the existing habits giving them new value. But the existing habits, save as they become subordinate factors in a larger value, lose their power. The past can be maintained only by being used, and that means readjusted. Left to itself, it decays, introducing friction. Power is lost, not conserved.

To sum up: The consciousness of obligation arises whenever there is felt the necessity of employing an existent habit or impulse to realize an end with which it is connected on the basis of present need, though not of past history. Its peculiar double relationship arises from the fact that it is the nature of habit and impulse *in themselves*, or abstractly, to demand immediate discharge on the basis of their own past; thus they tend to resist readjustment, and go their own way. But habits and impulses are, after all, developed with reference to the needs of the organism; the habit is not isolated, but connected, and the consciousness of this functional connection comes out in the recognition that the required thing is somehow bound up with our own being, and not imposed from without.

This connection of duty with critical periods, periods of a greater or less readjustment, of adaptation of old habits to new needs, determines the extent to which the *consciousness* of duty should, normally, enter into conduct. Practical common-sense recognizes two extremes equally repugnant to it. On one side is the character which professes to bring every act, from small to great, in connection with duty; which professes to perform every act under the guidance of a stern sense of duty—which never lets itself go, never plays morally. Our repulsion to this standpoint as pedantic, narrow, as indicating an ungenerous disposition, making us suspect hypocrisy, is justified by the previous analysis. It is true that every act of the moral man should, objectively viewed, be a dutiful act; it should always be possible to say of it (that is, when it is reflected upon) that it was the act which, under the given conditions, ought to have been performed. But it by no means follows that because every moral act is dutiful (*i.e.*, right) that it should be accompanied with a distinct sense of obligation. On the contrary, since the larger number of the acts of a decent man are covered by some general plan in pursuance with which they occur, the normal attitude in these cases is that of unconsciousness of duty. The act is taken care of by the general line of attention, by the comprehensive interest. It falls, in so far, within the habit of action; the tension between habit and plan or ideal is slight. The reflection or tension, between immediate act and mediating idea, necessary for value, is maintained simply by reflection upon means, upon the best expedients or instrumentalities for realizing the end. Think of the moral futility of a mother caring for her child, a business man following his calling, by accompanying all acts with consciousness of duty! There is not sufficient reconstruction of ends to demand any such consciousness, and if it enters in, it is forced and unreal.

But there is another moral tendency which insists that

duty must be swallowed up in inclination and love—that so
far as one is moral, he performs all his acts with no consciousness of authority and subjection, no sense of bounden
duty, but from the overflowing spontaneity of his own affection. Practical sense, without being able to give its reasons,
is as suspicious of this view as of the other. Analysis reveals
the reasons. The steady affection, the direct outflow of
interest, will cover all actions which lie within the scope of
any one end, less or greater. But when the acts appropriate
to that end are exhausted, when the end has become realized,
a readjustment of attention is required. A new end comes in,
and demands a rearrangement, a reform, of older habits and
interests. This means suspense, resistance, conflict, the
sense of subjection and of authority in some form. Were
there no critical periods, no times of readjustment, the absorption of duty in direct inclination would occur, but so
long as they come—so long in other words, as progress
through *relative* discontinuity or nodal points is the law of
life—a character without sense of obligation is inadequate,
slippery and wishy-washy. The practical point is that there
is no occasion to be continually stirring up the feeling of
obligation, to be reminding one's self of it *ab extra.* Interest
in work is the normal condition, and the open-minded man,
with broad and flexible interest, will find that very interest,
at critical periods of his work, forces the problems of obligation upon him, without his hunting them up afield.

This connection of obligation with the periods of reconstruction in moral progress also accounts for the relativity, or better, the individuality,[30] of duty. Let theorists
deal with the facts as they may, the fact remains that no two
persons have or can have the same duties. It is only when we
are dealing with abstractions that they appear the same.
Truth-telling is a duty for all, but it is not the duty of all to

[30]   The theories which have made so much of "relativity" in ethics
seem to me, without exception, to stop half way. The very idea of
relativity implies that there is still somehow a single, absolute standard
and duty for all, but that owing to circumstances or "finitude" or some
other unanalyzed category, we aren't up to it yet, and have to make a shift
with our relative morality. Assume frankly once the standpoint of the
individuality of conduct, and the whole relativity industry is outlawed,
while all the facts brought out in its maintenance are amply preserved.
The standard and process are absolute, but (and because) individual.

tell the same truth, because they have not the same truth to tell. Any other conception is like the pedagogical theory which has mechanized our schools—that all the children are to recite the history, the geography, the arithmetic lesson in the same way. It is only the abstraction, the text-book, which is the same. The truth to each child is this abstract fact assimilated into his own interests and habits, and proceeding from them vitalized—free. The great underlying contradiction, the lie, in modern moral methods, is the assertion of individuality in name, and the denial of it in fact. Duty always expresses a relation between the impulses and habits, the existing structures of a concrete agent, and the ideal, intention, purpose which demands a new service of that structure. By the necessities of the case, it is only the general form of duty, the relationship between habit and demand, which is alike in different individuals, or in the same individual at different times. A man of real self-control is no more conscious (save at critical junctures) of the duty of temperance than the thief is conscious of the duty of regard for property. In the former case, there is no impulse or habit to fall into tension with the demand for control, and hence no sense of duty—save again at the times when new circumstances flood in, arousing dormant impulses. In the latter case there is no ideal to create the tension. For consciousness of obligation to arise in the former case (save in conditions mentioned) indicates degeneration; in the latter case, it is the potency of reformation. Let this extreme instance serve to indicate the dependence of consciousness of duty upon individuality.

Other mooted questions with reference to obligation, the conflict of desire and duty, of interest and reason, of the "ought" and the "is," will best be discussed in connection with the two types of one-sided theories of duty next to be considered. Each of these theories abstracts one phase of the relationship between immediate acting and mediate ideal, and by exaggerating it to cover the entire field, by denying or minimizing the other phase, presents a distorted view of moral experience. Here again we may consider the Stoic and Kantian ethics as the abstraction of the ideal side, and the hedonistic ethics as the abstraction of the direct side.

xxxvi.   The Kantian Theory of Obligation

Kant's starting point is the unconditional character of morality. It admits of no exceptions; allows of no parleyings, of no ifs and buts. It says without compromise, "Thou oughtst." It does not follow, but precedes and commands inclination. It does not depend for its authority upon any desire or tendency towards itself; it rather requires of desire a certain quality and of tendency a certain direction. It proposes not a dependent, but an absolute end—it is a *categorical*, not a hypothetical imperative. Some commands read, "Do thus and so *if* you would reach a certain end"; but morality says, you *must* do this, you must have a certain kind of end in view.[31] Thus duty imposes laws, while hypothetical aims, ends which presuppose a further end, can give rise only to either rules of skill—the most suitable ways of reaching that end—or to counsels of prudence—provisions for securing happiness.

Beside the universal, independent authoritative character of duty, its important feature is its relative opposition to immediate inclination. The notion of duty, says Kant (*Theory of Ethics*, p. 13), implies certain subjective restrictions and hindrances. In other words, it is *imperative*, as well as categorical. The very fact that it takes the form of command, of law, of authority, implies a subject who may, if left to himself, resist.[32] As thus stated, the doctrine seems practically identical with that already laid down. This apparent identity is reinforced when we find that the source from which the "categorical imperative" proceeds is not external to self or will, but is the self or will in its universal nature. Obligation is a relation holding between will in one

---

[31]   "There is an imperative which commands a certain conduct immediately, without having as its condition any other purpose to be attained by it. This imperative is categorical. . . . This imperative may be called that of morality." *Theory of Ethics*, p. 33; see whole passage, pp. 30–39; also pp. 112–44, 119–21, 125–27, 153.

[32]   This aspect comes out most clearly in the case Kant takes to distinguish the *dutiful* from the *holy* will. (See *Theory of Ethics*, pp. 58, 121, 174–78.) The latter will is so identified with the ideal that the ideal presents itself not as law or duty, but simply as good. This is a condition to be always striven for, but never attained by "finite" beings, like man.

aspect, that of universal rationality and validity, and will
in another aspect, individual preference (*Willkühr*), not
between will and any external end or power. Kant insists
strenuously upon this point, terming true obligation "*au-
tonomous*," while false theories make it "*heteronomous*."
(See *Theory of Ethics*, pp. 50–54, 57–59, 72, 180–81.)

The identity disappears when we study in detail the
meaning which Kant attaches to the conception of self as
unconditional (authoritative) law-giver, and the relative
opposition of this law-giving self to the subject-self. We
shall find that Kant interprets these ideas negatively—by
abstraction. By the universality of self he means something
which *excludes* all specific material of experience; by the
opposition of the duty-imposing self to the immediate agent
something which *excludes* any natural underlying identity
of the two.

The course of the argument runs as follows: Since the
authority of moral law, or duty, is unconditional and absolute, it cannot rest upon anything given in experience (see
references given at end of Sec. xiii). Everything which
rests upon experience is contingent and variable; experience
at most can determine that a thing has been so and so in the
past, not that it is so without qualification. Much less can it
establish that a certain duty *ought* to be done, for the duty
may refer to an ideal which has *never* been realized—which
(Kant would sometimes seem to say) *can* never be realized,
and which it is none the less our duty to strive to realize.
Now if we remove all content of experience from the law
thus imposed there remains nothing but the mere form of
will, or practical reason, nothing but the bare idea of law
universal.

The same kind of considerations determine the nature
of the opposition between duty and the immediate agent.
The immediate agent may be reduced to an impulsive, desiring being; all ends posited by man in this capacity are
matters of experience and have, therefore, to be neglected in
considering the end involved in doing one's duty, the end
imposed by the rational will. Furthermore, those ends which
the impulses and desires propose for themselves are not only
to be *excluded* as empirical, but they must be suppressed (in

forming the moral motive) as anti-moral. For all these natural inclinations reduce themselves to a desire for happiness,
to self-love. And while this is not evil *per se*, yet *as suggesting itself to the will as its motive*, its controlling power, it is
the great antagonist which duty has always to meet. So far
as anything is done from inclination as motive, it is still non-
moral; nay, immoral, as representing the victory of inclination over duty. It is not enough even that the right thing (the
thing *conformable to duty*) be done; it must be done
out of respect for law as motive. The consciousness of law,
of authoritative obligation (while furnishing no concrete
material) is thus necessary to give to all material, to every
special act, its motivation, if the act is to be done morally.
This conflict of inclination and law, and the use of the idea
of law as motive, occur not simply at critical reconstructive
points, but with each and every act. The ideal moral character would be he whom the practical judgment of men un-
hesitatingly terms a moral pedant.[33] (For this account see
Theory of Ethics, pp. 9–20, 54–56, 105–16.)

Kant's position evidently involves two questions, questions which are the analogue of what we have previously
considered as "ideal" or "intention," and as "motive" respectively; the rational content of the moral will, and the propulsive, dynamic quality of this content. Or, putting the first
problem in terms of Kant's own position, how can a consciousness of will in general, a consciousness of law universal, be transformed into consciousness of specific volition,
of particular acts required; how can the "form" get concrete
filling? This is a question which must be met. However
universal the law may be, all acts are specific, individual;
there must be something in the law that gives instruction as
to the special duty which the general law imposes in the

[33]   The extent to which Kant carries this may be well seen by this
account of the good man in distress (*Theory of Ethics*, p. 182). "He
still lives only because it is his duty, not because he finds anything
pleasant in life." For my own part it seems less an exaggeration to say
that a man who consciously lives simply because it is his duty to live is a
self-absorbed egotist or a moral pedant and valetudinarian. There can be
no doubt that upon occasion of wreckage of hopes and habits, failure of
concrete interest in life may arise. But surely, upon such occasion, it is
one's "duty" to bestir one's self to find something worth while in life—
not merely to live from a sense of duty.

given act. How do we get from the mere consciousness that duty *is* duty, to the consciousness that truth-telling, that purity, etc., are duties? How do we get to the consciousness that my duty, in the present situation, is *just* thus and so? The second question is: how can the consciousness of duty get sufficient hold upon the agent to interest him, to move him to act for its realization? This problem is particularly acute in the Kantian ethics, because it is *through* the agent as instrument, in any case, that the law must be executed, and Kant has reduced the agent, *qua* agent, to a mere seeker for happiness as already given in experience.

According to Kant, instruction as to concrete acts proceeds from the very *universality* of the law. Universality, even in its most formal interpretation, means self-identity, non-contradiction. Morality requires consciousness of a universal law, but a universal law, by its very nature, must be one which can maintain itself without contradiction. Hence the general consciousness of duty may be thus translated. "Act only on that motive which can become a universal law" or act upon the same basis on which you would act, if you were an omnipotent Being, so that your principle of action were made a law of nature (*Theory of Ethics*, pp. 38–42, 115, 55–56, 119, 133, 161–62).

The way in which the universal imperative "Do thy duty," thus becomes transformed into the particular imperatives "do this, that and the other specific thing" may be illustrated as follows:

a] Some one, wearied by what he conceives to be the entire misery of life proposes to commit suicide, but he asks himself whether this maxim based on the principle of self-love could become a universal law of nature; and "we see at once that a system of nature in which the very feeling, whose office is to compel men to the preservation of life, should lead men by a universal law to death, cannot be conceived without contradiction." That is to say, the principle of the motive which would lead a man to suicide cannot be generalized without becoming contradictory—it cannot be made a law universal.

b] An individual wishes to borrow money which he knows that he cannot repay. Can the maxim of this act be universalized? Evidently not: "a system of nature in which it should be a universal law to promise without performing, for the sake of private good, would contradict itself, for then no one would believe the promise—the promise itself would become impossible as well as the end it had in view."

c] A man finds that he has certain powers, but is disinclined to develop them. Can he make the maxim of such conduct a universal law? He cannot *will* that it should become universal. "As a rational being, he must will that faculties be developed."

d] A prosperous individual is disinclined to relieve the misery of others. Can his maxim be generalized? "It is impossible to *will* that such a principle should have the universal validity of a law of nature. For a will which resolved this would contradict itself, inasmuch as many cases might occur in which one would have need of the love and sympathy of others, and in which, by such a law of nature, sprung from his own will, he would deprive himself of all hope of the aid he desires."

See *Theory of Ethics*, pp. 9–46. Caird's *Critical Philosophy of Kant*, Vol. ii, pp. 171–81, 209–12.

Criticism. That a valid moral motive is capable of generalization may be admitted without question. But what is the nature of this generalization, and what is implied as to its relation to inclination—to desire? Is generalization possible only on the basis of reason standing over against desire. Nay, is it possible at all on such a basis? Let it be admitted that truly moral action involves rationality or generalized validity, does this rationality proceed from a faculty outside the natural impulses and desires, is it attained only by abstraction from them? or (to state the alternative theory definitely) is not rationality, universality, found in the co-ordination, the reduction to a harmonious unity of the impulses and desires? Admitting that the moral life involves, as one of its features, a certain relative opposition of sensuous material and rational form, are form and content separate in origin and purpose? or is the "form" simply the movement of the "material" to its own organic unity? Or, again, admitting that it is often helpful to test a proposed line of conduct by reference to the capacity of its motive to be universal law, are we to understand universal law in the sense of uniformity, of bare likeness among different circumstances, or is the universal law found in the organization of the different conditions? To sum all these questions up in one: Are we to do an act *in* its universality, or *because of* its universality?

These points may be tested by Kant's own illustrations. In every case we find the question raised is not whether universality is the motive, but whether a *specific* motive can be generalized. In every case, also, we find the answer to the question turning not upon formal, but upon material identity. The question is treated as if it were one concerning the character of the content involved. There is nothing formally self-contradictory in the idea that every one should, from self-love, shorten life when its continuance promises a balance of harm. Contradiction enters only when there is postulated a *system of nature*, in which the impulse of self-love has a certain *definite quality*—tending toward "improvement of life." Grant this, and there is no difficulty in showing that the general system contradicts itself if the impulse is turned against itself. It is the character of the system of nature, or of the impulse, which affords the real criterion—material, not formal considerations. So in the other cases. A social system and the impulse to better one's self through the assistance of others would both contradict themselves when promises were made not to be kept. It is as a "rational being," that is, as a person with a certain definite constitution, that one wills that faculties be developed, and self-indulgence contradicts that organization of things which man conceives to be truly rational. And so again a social system in which men are interdependent would go to pieces if men never assisted one another. In every case, the contradiction is within a certain assumed structure or system. Presuppose such a system, and it is simply a matter of adequate *detailed* knowledge to discover whether a given line of action will tend to reinforce or to disintegrate it. The criterion is workable and often helpful, but it is in no way formal. Universal is interpreted as falling in line with the maintenance of the system as a whole. A self-integrity, material self-consistency is the real standard. In this sense, every good act must be legislative; it must execute principles which tend to the maintenance of the system of which it is a member.

Not only do Kant's examples all go against a formal rationality and point to a rationality which is none other than the organization of content, but a formal universality would absolutely break down. If I kill a man in defence of my family or country, I cannot will that everybody should always kill; if I will to aid a man by charity, I cannot will that everybody at all times should try to relieve all the distress that comes before him. My moral imperative is to kill or to give, but I cannot will that it be *formally* universalized, that is, be made a uniform principle of action. I can only be willing that where *all relevant circumstances are the same* the same principle be followed. In other words, I could wish my motive to become general law only in so far as the particular material conditions have been—not excluded from, but— *taken into the motive.*

Reason, then, not mere sense, must constitute the law of the moral will; it alone can substantiate the ideal. But this "practical reason" is not a faculty separate from desire; were it thus separate it could furnish no directions whatever to the desire. It could but demand its obliteration; not its functioning in a specific direction. The reason that consciousness of duty always involves specification into some definite requirement is precisely because we cannot separate the consciousness of self as a whole from the consciousness of a particular desire of the self. Take the former in its adequate differentiation and it becomes the latter, just as the consciousness of a particular desire conceived in its relations, not abstractly, is the consciousness of the whole moving self.

Duty as Motive. We turn now to the other aspect of the question. How is it, upon Kant's theory, that the consciousness of law universal becomes an *interest*—a conception which takes hold practically and moves to execution; how does it become a motor, become dynamic?

Kant's solution may be summarized as follows: The moral law must of itself be the spring to action; if it make use of some feeling already in existence to become the motive, then an act will be performed which has legality (*i.e.*, outward conformity to duty) but not morality, because not springing from a purely moral motive. "The essential point is that the agent be determined simply by the moral law, not only without the co-operation of sensible impulses, but even to the rejection of all such" (*Theory of Ethics*, p. 165). Thus the moral law snubs the impulses, and in so far gives rise to the feeling of *humiliation*; the pretension of the agent to worth in himself (self-conceit) is struck down, and his effort to be happy (self-love) is deprived of all valid claim to control. Here then we have one feeling, humility, which tho' itself sensuous (or pathological) is yet originated by reason. Moreover, this negative feeling of humility gets the obstacles (self-conceit and self-love) to the moral law out of the way, and thus is the same as so much positive impetus added to the law. It is equivalent to "a feeling of respect, reverence for law." "Humiliation on the sensuous side is an elevation of the moral esteem for the law itself on the rational side" (p. 171). Reverence is thus not simply a motive *to* morality, "it is morality itself viewed subjectively as a motive; for our practical reason, by rejecting the rival claims of self-love, gives authority to the law which now alone has influence" (p. 168; see the whole of Ch. 3, on the Analytic of Practical Reason).

Criticism. Criticism turns here upon the relation assumed to exist between reason and sensibility as the system of impulses. It may be urged that Kant's position is in unstable equilibrium. If the relation between reason and sense is as external and mechanical as he makes it, the operations which he describes cannot occur; or, if these operations do take place, the relation must be conceived as so organic and intrinsic as to make necessary an entire reconstruction of the theory of desire.

In the first place, it is sheer assumption that the sensuous impulses may be adequately described under the heading of self-love, in any sense in which self-love is equivalent to seeking for pleasures. Kant retains the whole substructure of the hedonistic psychology of desire; sees the evils which result ethically from it, and then adds on the top story of reason as an offset. If the discussion already had (pp. 267–70) is of weight, the true course is to make over the theory of desire.

If, however, impulse and desire are as self-absorbed as Kant declares them to be, we must question the adequacy of the machinery by which Kant makes law a motor. If there is no *intrinsic* connection between desire and reason, how can the former, even when checked and held in by reason, give rise to the feeling of moral humiliation? This presupposes some moral capacity already *in* the desires; something capable of recognizing the authority and value of law—which is not only the thing to be explained, but also impossible if desire has the purely low and selfish character Kant attributes to it. At most, the desire would simply feel restraint, coercion, and would be correspondingly impatient and desirous of breaking away—the reverse of humility.[34] When Kant changes the negative feeling of humiliation into a positive one of reverence, it simply attributes even more frankly some kind of positive moral capacity to impulse. That the feeling is supposed to *originate* from reason, emphasizes rather than avoids the difficulty. If the moral law can transform itself into feeling; if reason can become an impulse, then feeling and impulse cannot be so depraved as Kant has already defined them to be. When Kant says (*Theory of Ethics*, p. 170), the agent "can never get enough, when he has laid aside self-conceit, of contemplation of the majesty of law, and the soul believes *itself* elevated in proportion as it sees the moral law elevated above it and its frail nature" there is something intrinsically akin to law ascribed to the "frail nature" of the soul. It is simply a roundabout way of saying that the "soul" is not so frail after all, if only it be given a chance.

Moreover the whole question is begged from the start. It is only in so far as the reason is already itself impulsive or moving that it can check and restrain the sense-nature and thus occasion humility. To hold that "whatever diminishes the obstacles to an activity, furthers this activity itself" (p. 171) is to admit that reason already possesses an active, self-realizing power, *i.e.*, is impulsive.

The further difficulty in the separation of sense and reason may be seen in the utter inability to answer, from

[34] It is worth notice that Plato, who has substantially the same dualism between reason and appetite, is obliged to bring in a third and mediating power, the *active* impulses (spiritedness), to bridge the gulf.

Kant's standpoint, the question as to why, in a given case, the moral law does or does not become a motive. I do not mean simply that it cannot give a detailed account—perhaps no theory can do that. But it cannot point to any method of approaching the question. Failure cannot be due to lack of authoritative presence of the moral reason—that is always there. It cannot be due to the mere presence or agency of the sensuous impulses—they are always present and always self-ishly urgent. There is absolutely no connecting link by which to indicate any explanation of why the machinery of humiliation and reverence should get itself adequately into operation in some cases and fail in others. We are thrown back on bare chance. The ideas of approval, blame, responsi-bility are made meaningless. All this because the actual concrete unity of individual character is surrendered and the two abstractions of sense and reason substituted.

Thus far we have taken Kant purely on his own ground. It may be added that, historically, reverence seems to have no special priority or moral pre-eminence over mo-tives like patriotism, manliness, desire for community esteem and recognition; that when it did appear it took, until the development of specialized technical reflection (like Kant's own), the form not of recognition of superiority of moral law as such over sensuous impulse, but the recognition that the community welfare is higher in its claims than the im-mediate pleasures and pains of the agent. (See for example, Plato, *Laws*, Bk. I, 647, 649; Bk. II, 671, on reverence as fear of pain attached to right objects.) If we turn from theoreti-cal analysis to actual life, it is at once evident that to make reverence for duty the sole motive would lead to a Pharisa-ism which must deny morality to the vast masses of man-kind, and permit it only to a few who have attained a certain stage of intellectual abstraction.

Upon the whole question, positively, it may be said: (1) The truth in Kant's main contention is adequately rec-ognized in the statement that an action is to be done *as* duty, that is, for its own intrinsic meaning independent of any reflex advantage, but not *for* duty. The latter makes an ab-straction of duty, reduces the act to a mere means, and thus introduces division and lessens interest (see pp. 85–87).

(2) The consciousness of the opposition between desire and duty, with the correlative feelings of humility and reverence, arises not *essentially*, by the nature of each, but *historically* —that is, when the appearance of a more comprehensive and organic end demands a readjustment of desires, demands that they attach themselves to the new end, instead of following their past course.

Kant's account, therefore, strengthens our original analysis. The sense of the majesty and inviolability of duty is the consciousness of the moving, the functioning self as against a partial habit, which in its narrow self-assertion, tends to become isolated and static, instead of connected and instrumental. The moral feeling of humility is in its essence the continued attitude of not hanging on to attainment for its own sake—of recognizing that it has no worth save as changed into power. Reverence is the correlative continued openness of will and interest to new and larger demands (p. 75). They require not the absolute opposition of a higher and lower nature to explain them, but the relative opposition between differentiation and inter-connection of impulses and habits.

Convenient accounts and criticisms of Kant's Ethics will be found in Caird, *Critical Philosophy of Kant*, Vol. II; Muirhead, *Elements of Ethics*, pp. 112–24; Mackenzie, *Manual of Ethics*, pp. 55–70.

XXXVII. Hedonistic Theory of Obligation

The problem of duty for the hedonist assumes the converse aspect from that presented to the Kantian. For the latter, the main difficulty is in showing how the consciousness of law, proclaimed by reason, should come into working relations, intellectual and motor, with desire, so great is the assumed opposition. For the hedonist, the difficulty lies in getting enough opposition to desire to subject the latter to authority[35]—or in getting that *kind* of opposition which should give rise to a feeling of duty rather than of coercion.

---

[35]   Bentham felt this difficulty; he wished to banish the very term "duty" from ethical discussion.

Upon the basis of hedonism, it may be said that it is to an
agent's profit or advantage or superior interest to take such
and such a course, but how can it be said to be his duty?
Pleasure is the good, and man's natural desire is for pleasure. How can there be any checking of desire, save as another desire, promising more pleasure, presents itself? Such
a checking as this has none of the elements of the consciousness of duty.

The traditional hedonistic answer has been through the
idea of *sanction*, some foreseen evil attached to the satisfaction of a desire which, in itself, would give pleasure.[36]

The essence of Bain's theory is the transfer within the
mind of the agent of a relation, now existing between elements of his own conduct, which originally existed between
the agent's conduct and the behavior of others. The ideas of
authority (command) and obedience are correlative. The
lesson of obedience is taught from the outset of life to every
agent. "The child's susceptibility to pleasure and pain is
made use of to bring about this obedience, and a mental
association is rapidly formed between disobedience and apprehended pain, more or less magnified by fear." The knowledge that punishment may be continued until the act is
discontinued "leaves on the mind a certain dread and awful
impression as connected with forbidden actions." This
"dread of offending" is the germ of the consciousness of
duty. It is reinforced, first, by the sentiment of love or respect for the person imposing the command—which brings
in a new dread, "that of giving pain to a beloved object."
Then a tertiary factor comes in: "When the young mind is
able to take notice of the use and meaning of the prohibitions
imposed upon it, and to approve of the end intended by them,
a new motive is added on and begirds the action with a

[36]   Besides the authors considered below, this conception has been
developed by Paley, *Moral Philosophy*, in a theological form (virtue is
"doing good to mankind, in obedience to the will of God, and for the sake
of everlasting happiness"); by Austin, *Jurisprudence*, in jural form; by
Bentham, in jural and social form, in his *Principles of Morals*; and by
J. S. Mill, notes on his father's *Analysis of Human Mind*, Vol. II, pp.
324–26, and *Utilitarianism*, Ch. 5. It should be remarked, however, that
Mill's account only touches the question why we judge the conduct of
others from the standpoint of duty; it does not answer the question why
a man conceives something as obligatory upon himself.

threefold fear." This latter fear is more definitely stated as follows: "If the duty prescribed has been approved of by the mind as protective of the general interests of persons engaging our sympathies, the violation of this on our part affects us with all the pain that we feel from the inflicting an injury upon those interests." (See Bain, *Emotions and Will*, pp. 285–87.)

Now this sentiment of fear or reverence attached to superior power, "at first formed and cultivated by the relations of actual command and obedience, may come at last to stand upon an independent foundation." The third factor mentioned above seems, from Bain's further account, to be not so much a factor as a revolution. When the child appreciates the "reasons for the command, the character of conscience is entirely transformed" (*Emotions and Will*, p. 288). The form of authority and subjection remains, although the authority is no longer imposed from without. Conscience becomes an "ideal resemblance of public authority" (*Emotions and Will*, p. 264; the references are all to the 3d ed., London, 1888); "it is an imitation within ourselves of the government without us" (p. 285). When the thing which a person regards as obligatory is so far from being enforced by social pressure, that it contradicts received moral ideas, "even then the notion, sentiment or *form* of duty is derived from what society imposes, although the particular matter is quite different. Social obedience develops in the mind originally the feeling and habit of obligation, and this remains when the individual articles are changed. . . . The person has so assimilated in his mind the laws of his own coining to the imperative requirements of society, that he reckons them as of equal force as duty" (p. 289 note; see also pp. 467–73, and his *Moral Science*, pp. 20–21 and 41–43).

Criticism. Now just as we did not question the principle of generalization, but simply the way in which Kant interprets it, so here the question is not as to the account given by Bain, but rather as to its real meaning, especially as to its consistency with hedonism. (1) Admitting that a consciousness of duty arises historically in connection with commands and fear of punishment, does it follow that the sense of duty is, even at the outset, equivalent to fear of pain? (2) And how can this whole content of fear drop out at the proper moment and leave the pure sense of duty—the man a moral law to himself?

1. In so far as there is any moral consciousness at all, any sense of *authority*, we must say that from the start there is a sense of the reasonableness of the command, and not a mere dread of the pain to result from its infringement. The latter alone gives rise, even at a very early age, to a sense not of duty and authority, but of wrong and smarting injustice, or else to apparent acquiescence while the one commanding is at hand, and to great cleverness in evading whenever the pressure is removed. Any careful observation will reveal three cases: (a) that in which it is necessary to prevent, and at once, a given line of conduct—as a child's going into a fire. Here the motive of sheer fright may be appealed to, but not with any moral end, or with reference to developing a sense of duty or as punishment; but simply as the necessary way of preventing, under the circumstances, the occurrence of a given overt act. Every sensible parent appeals to this motive when necessary, but does not assume too easily that it is necessary; and tries to replace it by more rational means as soon as possible. (b) Second, there is the case already referred to of using the dread of *punishment per se* as motive. This, as suggested, is so far from calling into being the sense of duty, that it arouses irritation and anger, duplicity and slyness. (c) There is the use of punishment to draw positive attention to a content otherwise ignored—punishment as a means of enforcing an idea not strong enough to make its own way in an immature mind. The first case is non-moral, the second immoral, the third alone moral. Here again careful observation will reveal that punishment, in the case say of a lie, is morally effective just in the degree in which fear of it does not operate as an isolated motive, but is the emphasis required to bring out the undesirable quality of the act itself. It is a means of revealing the hatefulness, the repulsiveness of the lie. Bain himself speaks of the "fear of offending," and this is quite other than the fear of punishment.

2. Only in so far as punishment is a means of calling

attention to the intrinsic quality of the act, does it afford a
transition to the third stage—the independent conscience, or
one which recognizes the act as obligatory because of its own
significance. The more we use punishment to effect simply a
dread of itself the more surely we prevent the growth of the
conscience which can recognize acts as valuable "in themselves." Logically and practically (so far as the theory is
acted upon), there is not only no bridge from the first of
Bain's stages to the last, but the two are exclusive. (For
some practical phases of this discussion, see the August 1894
number of the *Popular Science Monthly*, article on "Chaos
in Moral Training" [*Early Works*, iv, 106–18].)

The point of these criticisms is that Bain unconsciously
begs the whole question. The authority somehow resides
already in the idea (the act proposed) and the agent in
recognizing the idea purely, must recognize its authoritative
quality. The punishment simply serves to bring the idea
adequately into consciousness (compare what is said pp.
302–3). Punishment may provide the psychological conditions (put the mind into shape) for recognizing authority,
but cannot possibly constitute it. Unless the positive value,
capable of being seen, already reside in the idea, punishment causes either rebellion or servility or trickiness—or a
mixture of all three. The question is still untouched: What
is that which constitutes the value of the proposed idea so
supreme that it is authoritative, and gives some rational
assurance that punishment, judiciously used, will assist the
growth of conscience?[37] In lack of a better, our previous
answer must still stand; because the act proposed stands
for the active, the functioning and thus the *whole* self, while
the agent to whom it appears obligatory, or authoritative, is
the static, the instrumental (and thus if isolated, the partial)
self.

Spencer's Theory of Obligation. Spencer, like Bain,
holds that the sense of duty originates from social pressure.

---

[37]   In strict logic, the term "judiciously used" cannot be employed in
Bain's theory. Everything falls back upon the mere punishment, apart
from its relations and attachments; there is no duty as respects the use of
punishment, because it is the source of duty, just as in Hobbes's political
philosophy the sovereign, being the source of law, cannot be subject to it.

He emphasizes, perhaps, the element of fear less than that of restraint—the checking of the immediate impulse or desire. The chief inhibitory agencies in the history of the race have been the "visible ruler, the invisible ruler, and public opinion"—the policeman, the priest, and public opinion, as someone has alliteratively summed it up. These restraining agencies operate mainly through fear—the dread awakened of, respectively, "legal penalty, supernatural punishment and social reprobation." As in Bain's theory, the sense of restraint thus originated gradually works itself free from the incidents of its birth and growth, and asserts itself as an independent factor in consciousness. The favorite hedonistic analogy is the love of gold on the part of the miser—a love which can have arisen only in connection with the special benefits derived from the gold, but which finally sets itself free from these accompaniments, and attaches to the gold *per se*. The individual learns to connect the foreseen evil effects resulting intrinsically from the satisfaction of a given present impulse or desire with the feeling of compulsion, and this representative association suffices to restrain the urgency of the desire.

The "essential trait in the moral consciousness is the control of some feeling or feelings by some other feeling or feelings" (*Principles of Ethics; Data of Ethics*, p. 113). In general, and upon the average, the feelings which control are related to those controlled as the compound to the simple, the remote to the proximate, the representative to the presentative (*Data of Ethics*, pp. 103–9).

The connecting link with the element of social coerciveness is thus found by Spencer: "Since the political, religious, and social restraining motives, are mainly formed of represented future results; it happens that the representatives, having much in common, and being often aroused at the same time, the fear joined with three sets of them becomes, by association, joined with the fourth. Thinking of the extrinsic effects of a forbidden act, excites a dread which continues present while the intrinsic effects are thought of; and being thus linked with these intrinsic effects causes a vague sense of moral compulsion." And from this Spencer draws the logical conclusion (logical because true morality refers *only* to the *intrinsic* effects of an act, *Data of Ethics*, p. 120) that the "sense of duty or moral obligation is transitory, and will diminish as fast as moralization increases." The duty comes to have interest of itself, becomes itself pleasurable if persisted in, and the aspect of coerciveness dies out (pp. 127–28).

Criticism. Insofar as Spencer's theory resembles Bain's, the same criticism, of course, holds. External compulsion (which generates, by association, the feeling of self-compulsion) is positively anti-moral, because bringing into play the motive of sheer fear; if it have moral potentiality at all, even in furthering the transitional sense of obligation at a certain imperfect stage of moral development, it is because it does *not* operate as coercion, but as bringing to light, or reinforcing against opposition, the intrinsic authoritativeness of the acts proposed. Spencer's contention that with moralization the sense of duty tends to disappear is a recognition of the immoral character of the sense of coercion. But the contention, after all, only emphasizes the difficulty. Is it not the logical conclusion, from Spencer's premises, that we should *never* use or appeal to the sense of obligation; that, from the outset, we should strive to prevent the growth of this feeling, instead of encouraging it through punishment, blame, etc.? Or, otherwise stated, if Spencer's *conclusion* is correct, we must condemn all the social agencies which develop in the child the sense of compulsion (whether external or self) and leave the child to the expression of his own impulses, till he learns, by intrinsic reflection, to control some of them.[38]

In the other factor of Spencer's theory, the doctrine of intrinsic control as connected with increasing complexity, remoteness and representativeness of ends, we have, I think, an approximation to the true doctrine. It is, indeed, impossible to see why these facts should of themselves confer

[38]   The difficulty is only increased when we remember that, upon Spencer's theory, the postponement or checking of a desire involves pain and the sacrifice of pleasure, and thus, *absolutely* is bad, even if relatively right (*Data of Ethics*, pp. 183–84, 260–61). The reader may be reminded that, upon the theory already stated, the sense of duty ever disappears with respect to certain ends as these become absorbed into a habit, but not absolutely. It reconnects itself with those other ends, which, for any reason, demand readjustment of habits.

any claims to control. Carlyle's "do the thing that lies near-est" is just as valuable as Spencer's remote end. Indeed, Spencer himself calls attention to the fact that cases often arise where the simple and present desire has moral supre-macy on its side. He gives, however, no explanation of why one or other has this claim, this supremacy. An analysis of his biological accounts, will reveal however, that the real criterion in each is the self in its wholeness. And if we translate complexity, remoteness, etc., into terms of stand-ing for the self as a whole, the moving, functioning self, all the mystery vanishes. It is not *qua* remote, or *qua* proxi-mate, that an end exercises authority, but as comprehending within itself the self as functional unity. On the other hand, the criterion of complexity, it seems to me, will *always* work, because the complex, by its very definition, represents the self as organic activity. In the conflict, say of hunger impulse with the impulse to give food to children to keep them alive (the example given by Spencer, *Data of Ethics*, p. 110), the former may be more, not less, complex than the latter, and *is* more complex whenever its fulfillment is a condition of fulfilling the latter. In this case, to feed one's self is an act which, psychologically, includes within itself the feeding of others. The same may be said of the claims of health as respects the claims of meeting obligations to others; in so far as the former is supreme it is also more complex, carrying the other within itself—representative, in other words, of the whole self. We repeat, then, the original statement—the sense of duty, with its correlative phases of authority and subjection, is a sense of the supreme value of the functional self and the relative, or instrumental value of the structural self. Authority is not to be identified with coercion, any more than with the action of self conceived as a blank metaphysical form.

8

Freedom and Responsibility

xxxviii.   The Psychology of Freedom

The volitional has been defined and developed as the mediation of activity, at first impulsive or direct. It has been shown that the ideal (intention), with the deliberative process, is the growth of the mediation; that this finds its completion in the standard or generalized ideal. But the end and law react by their very natures into the direct impulses, and present another phase of moral experience: desire and consciousness of good, so far as the end and standard reinforce the immediate tendencies of impulse and habit; effort and consciousness of duty, so far as this reaction checks and reconstructs.

It must be remembered that the process of reaction is not one which follows in time after that of projection of ends and recognition of law. The origin and growth of the mediate, the rational content, proceed contemporaneously with its use in reinforcing and in checking the impulse or habits. Whatever completes the development of the ideal, the concrete recognition of the end and principle of action, completes the habit urging forward for expression. It is this completion with which we now have to deal.

The completely mediated activity is what we term a *deed*. The deed cannot be distinguished as act in contrast with mere getting ready to act. The whole process of working out ends, of selecting means, of estimating moral values, of recognizing duty, is, as we have seen, one of activity at every point; it is dynamic and propulsive throughout. The deed is simply this activity focused, brought to a head. The deed is the activity, concluded; it is the "round up," and in this conclusion at once (1) defined, marked out, and (2) unified.

1. The overt act or deed is the *definition of self*. Up to this time all is tentative; it is the experimenting of self in this direction or that, seeking outlet, forming and revising possible ends, trying on this satisfaction and that. In the deed, this movement of the self culminates; the activity is no longer tentative, but definitive. Up to this time, the self has been exploring, trying to find self and to come to consciousness. The deed is the net result of the exploration, of the learning; it exhibits or shows what the self, at the time, is. The voyage of discovery is summed up in the map which shows the limit, external and internal, of the activity.

2. This culmination of activity is complete *co-ordination* or unification. Starting from the immediate, impulsive activity, the whole intervening development may be regarded as one of increasing range of stimulation, bringing this and that further habit or impulse into play. This increasing range or scope of action is not merely quantitative, as just said, it finds a limit, an end. Now this limiting principle prevents the increasing waves of activity from being mere diffusive, expansive outgoing agitation without meaning. This principle, confining and determining the range and distribution of intervening activity, is, in biological terms, the function of the organism; in psychological terms, the unity of the self. The increase of activity, the continued suggestion of new ends and tentative adoption of new means, does not go on *ad indefinitum*, but with reference to a *whole*—the self. The deed expresses the attainment of this whole.

In this connection we must recall the fact that a moral struggle means, psychologically, not the sacrifice or exclusion of one value by another, but its inclusion, comprehension (pp. 252–53); the process of control is not one of suppression of desire or habit, but one of directing, using it—making it a tributary factor. Physically, outwardly, the deed is a selection of one impulse or ideal, and a rejection of the other. A man takes either the right or left hand road; steals or remains true to his trust; is self-indulgent, or puts his passions to the service of others. But morally the meaning, the value, of this defined, or one-sided deed, has the competing of ends and habits absorbed into it; the process of completion determines the significance of the deed in and to the agent's own consciousness.[39]

We have various words to designate the completion, the finality of the process; some naming it from the side of the impulsive, others of its intellectual phase. Preference[40] brings out the definiteness, the individuality of the conclusion. So also does determination, with the added shade of wholeness in its idea of firmness and certainty; decision and resolution name it considered both as the outcome of a complex, tangled intellectual process and as indicating the single volitional attitude assumed for the future. All these various implications are pretty well blended in the term "choice," and thus that is the most characteristic moral term.

The essence of this account of choice is obviously the conception of it as the normal outcome of the process of will, the conclusion of a process which in its primary stage is named impulse, and at a later stage deliberation (intellectual) and effort (emotional). It is thus opposed to those conceptions which regard all that goes on before as non-voluntary, and regards choice alone as act of will. The latter makes will, self, personality, an entity existing outside of the operations of impulse, habit, desire, reflection, etc., and coming in *ab extra* to settle a process which in itself is endless, and to import an ethical element into a process otherwise mechanical. Upon the basis of psychological analysis, there is no more a dualism between non-volitional

[39]   This gives another point of view for criticizing Martineau's theory of preferential selection of one of two impulses in the scale of values. It fails to note how the *value* of the impulse chosen (that is, its moral character) includes the rejected impulses. It also shows why an agent who is continually conscious that he has done an act of self-sacrifice is still immoral; he has not succeeded in comprehending the "sacrificed" end within the act performed. It is still there, asserting itself on its own isolated account. Paradoxical as the phrase may sound, the fact that it is felt *as* sacrifice shows that the sacrifice is not yet made. On any basis save that of the text, the moral life reduces itself, as Emerson says, to mere expiation for something else; it never asserts itself as of *positive* value. See Emerson's essay on "Self-Reliance," p. 54.

[40]   Preference seems sometimes to be opposed to choice, as when one says, "I should prefer that, but I choose to do this." But this is only an abstract preference; it says, under other circumstances, with changed conditions, I should prefer otherwise. But with things as they are, the agent prefers what he chooses. Preference, however, undoubtedly has more reference to the natural, unmoralized (unmediated) aspect. We prefer *things*; we choose acts or lines of action.

data on one side, and will, on the other, than there is in the process of intellectual judgment. We do not have, in the latter, two separate faculties, one, that of gathering data, weighing, rejecting and accepting evidence, the other, an outside power, reason, to draw the inference. The whole process is rational in form, and is determined by rational considerations as to its content; the drawing of the inference is the conclusion arrived at when the data assume coherency and completeness—that is, exhibit neither such mutual contradictions as to stimulate the mind to make them over, nor such gaps as to set the mind hunting up more facts.

Self-made problems incapable of solution, result from the identification of volitional action with choice alone, difficulties which are not existent upon the other theory. Such questions as these arise only to be unanswerable: What induces the will to interfere? how does it know the proper time at which to do so? is it unerring in its selection of time, or may it operate too soon or too late? are the sources of error in the will or in the outside soliciting elements? upon what basis does the will select this side rather than that? etc., etc.,—all the interminable discussions, in fact, which since the time of the scholastics have haunted the problem of freedom of will. No justification in the psychology of will can be found for the view which gives rise to these insoluble difficulties; whether the explanation of moral freedom and responsibility demands them will be considered later.

The foregoing account implies that choice and doing (the deed) are morally identical. This appears to run against the conviction of practical sense that we can choose to do a thing at a future time, make up our mind to act in a certain way, at a distant period—that choice is not doing but getting ready to do. Cannot a man choose to eat without beginning to eat, choose to go to Europe without at once starting? The consideration of this difficulty will serve to bring out more clearly the identity.

A more appropriate name than choice for conclusions of the sort indicated is decision. The question is not a merely verbal one; in some cases only the intellectual phase of the process is developed, and, accordingly, the conclusion is still abstract, hypothetical. To say that I have decided to act in a certain way if attacked by a burglar, or to go to Europe, etc., means that intellectually I present a certain hypothetical case to myself and draw the appropriate conclusion. It is an anticipation or prior rehearsal which gets the various relevant conditions before one and thus shortens and facilitates the actual choice when that is necessary. We decide to do so and so, if something happens. We decide not to act, but how to act. The categorical, concrete implication of the whole self does not occur, hence no deed and no true choice.

In cases which are not intellectual preparations, choice is really a beginning to act on the spot. If I really choose to eat an apple, I at once bend all my energies to getting it; if I do not begin on the spot, choice is still hypothetical; I choose to when I get a good chance. If I really choose to go to Europe, while outwardly a spectator may not see the action commence, psychologically the deed at once begins. I *now*, at once, act differently than I would otherwise, and this different way of acting is an actual part, under the circumstances, of going to Europe.

The moral meaning of this identity of choice and act comes out in such an illustration as this: A person virtually says, "I decide, I will to reform, but circumstances are such that I must do this one evil act; to-morrow I positively will do better." Such a person is simply deceiving himself. He still wills the evil thing and that only; the supposition that he has chosen another line, and that this is an exception which doesn't count, is one of the best (and commonest) devices imaginable for keeping one's self from squarely facing things as they are. The person who wills merely to do something in the future is in an impossible state psychologically and a dangerous one morally. The identity of choice, deed and will is the culmination of psychology, as well as the supreme moral lesson.

xxxix.   The Ethics of Freedom and Responsibility

The ethical conception of freedom is the recognition of the meaning for conduct of the identity of self and act, of will and deed. There is no factor in the act foreign or alien to the agent's self; it is himself through and through. No action is moral (that is, falling in the moral sphere) save as voluntary, and every voluntary act, as the entire foregoing analysis indicates, is the self operating, and hence is free. Impulse is self, the developing ideal is self; the reaction of the ideal as measuring and controlling impulse is self. The entire voluntary process is one of self-expression, of coming to consciousness of self. This intimate and thorough-going *selfness* of the deed constitutes freedom.

Ethical writers have distinguished "formal" and "substantial" freedom; and have claimed that only *right* acts are really free. This claim involves this truth: Every conscious act is free in the sense that it expresses the self; it is psychologically free. But is the intention, the purpose, of self, one "really possible"? Does it square with the conditions of things, with the laws of the universe? Is it possible for the self to be what it would be? No intention guarantees its own execution. Its execution depends upon the co-operation of reality; it must fit into the forces which really make up the course of events. Now if the self has a solid intention, one which reality itself reinforces, one whose execution is guaranteed by the conditions of the case, the agent is said to be really, as well as formally, free. But if his intention is *merely* subjective, if it involves objective impossibilities, the attempt at execution involves friction, loss, a negative, or destructive, reaction of deed into self. In such cases, the agent is really (ethically) in bondage. He is self-contradictory. He cannot express the self he aims to express. It is not so much a paradox as it seems, to say that only the good can be *really* willed; that we only *seem* to will, only go through the motions or form of willing, the bad.

This same identity of self and deed is, of course, the basis of responsibility. We are responsible for our deeds because they are ourselves. Responsibility is a name for the fact that we are, and are something definite and concrete — specific individuals. I am myself, I am conscious of myself in my deeds (self-conscious), I am responsible, name not three facts, but one fact.

There is a formal and a substantial responsibility. One is liable, accountable, *held* responsible *for* his acts, because they are himself. This is formal responsibility, and may coincide with moral irresponsibility. Every bad man is (in the substantial sense) irresponsible; he cannot be counted upon in action, he is not certain, reliable, trustworthy. He does not respond to his duties, to his functions. His impulses and habits are not co-ordinated, and hence do not answer properly to the stimuli, to the demands made. The vicious man is not socially responsible, and one part of his nature does not respond to the whole. Irresponsibility is but another name for his lack of unity, of integrity; being divided within himself, he is unstable, we can never be sure of him, he is not sure of himself. Yet this is consistent with formal responsibility. He is capable of foreseeing consequences, and of having these foreseen consequences influence or modify his conduct. The person who fails in one respect or other of these factors is insane, imbecile or morally immature and is not responsible.

One's conduct calls forth certain reactions from others — reactions as natural as those called forth when one comes in contact with a physical force. The individual lives as truly in a social as in a physical environment, and the reaction of the one to his deed is as much an intrinsic organic consequence of the deed as that of the other. If the individual has not properly mediated his habit or impulse, if he acts upon intention which is one-sided, the reaction brings out that factor of the deed. In one case, it may be the burn from putting his hand in the fire, the other case the rebuke or punishment for violating or coming short of social functioning. This is no external consequence (see pp. 236–38); it is an organic factor of his deed, formerly hidden, but brought to light through the action. The deed executed brings the agent to a more definite consciousness of himself; the reactions of others in the way of praise or blame are simply phases of the return of the deed into the agent, arousing him to consciousness of certain features hitherto obscure. A person who is not capable of such experiences, of having the consequences of his action react back into himself, and become motives or modify character, is not (even formally) responsible; one who has this capacity is responsible. This capacity for mediation is not the cause, and responsibility the effect; this capacity for mediation *is* responsibility.

But if this *power* of being influenced by the foreseen consequences is a *habit* we have *substantial* responsibility. This is an attainment, a conquest, not an original possession; it is a name for virtue or rightness of will. Such a man is responsible *in* his acts, not simply liable *for* them. He does not try to escape himself in his deeds; when they are bad, he does not "lay it off" on circumstances, but stands up to the reckoning, and in the very identification of himself with the evil deed in its consequences gets beyond it. He meets the demands of the situation. He is sufficiently interested in his function adequately to translate it into its rational detail of specific aims, and to carry out these aims to overt conclusion in deeds. Just as to say that a man is truly free is to recognize his realization of moral good, so to say that one is truly responsible is to give him the highest commendation for actual faithfulness to duty.

XL. Determinist and Indeterminist Theories

We are, however, told that man cannot be responsible unless he is free in another sense; that a man cannot be responsible unless at the time when he acted he could equally well have acted otherwise than as he did act, and this without any change of character and motive. We are told that self-blame, remorse, etc., are inexplicable without this freedom of indifference; and that rebuke and punishment from others become meaningless and unjust without such freedom. All arguments to this effect seem to rest upon an ambiguity. Just so far as a man believes that he was *forced* to act as he did act, he excuses himself – and rightly; the act was not himself at all, it was the external compulsory force that really acted. The condition of responsibility, that the deed be the concrete will or unified self, is absent. The confusion comes in when absence of adequate self-motivation is substituted for absence of external compulsion. "I might have done otherwise" – that consciousness *is* itself my miserable condition, my blame or remorse, and not simply a condition of it (pp. 295–97); but what it means is not that I might arbitrarily or with no different self have done otherwise, but that the sole reason for my acting as I did lies in myself, is attributable to no external cause. I might have done otherwise had I been a better self, had I been a worthy person—had I been one to whom this right end adequately appealed, but I was not such an one; I was just such an one as would do this sort of deed, which I now see in all its badness; this *is* my blame.

The whole problem arises because the objector insists upon carrying the dualism between agent and deed which he himself makes over into the doctrine of his opponent. He continually says: "Ah, then, according to your doctrine, the agent at the time he acted could not have done otherwise than as he did; this I call not freedom but necessity." He has simply imported here his own separation of agent and act. Upon the basis of the theory against which the objection is brought, this sentence must be rendered as follows: "The man was himself and did act precisely as he acted."[41]

The entire sting of the proposition vanishes and it becomes a harmless truism. But the content of this truism gives the only basis of responsibility. Everything which lessens or loosens the concrete, specific organic connection of the agent with his act, in just so much relieves the agent from responsibility for his act. If the abstract, metaphysical will or self intervenes between the concrete self, the impulses, habits, ends, and the deed, then it and not this concrete individuality must assume the responsibility for the act; it is none of my doing. In the desire to magnify the self, the indeterminists deny the specific, real self, which is in and through action, and erect an abstract, outside self, reducing freedom to an irrationality, and responsibility to a myth.

Only a few of the indeterminists carry the argument beyond an expansion, generally rhetorical and hortatory, of the dependence of self-blame and just punishment upon ability to have acted otherwise. Martineau has attempted a more detailed statement (*Study of Religion*, Vol. ii, Bk. iii, Ch. 2, esp. pp. 210–27). An analysis of this shows that the real

[41] The "determinism," in other words is a logical determinateness, and not an external predeterminism. See an article in the *Monist*, Vol. iii, p. 362, "The Superstition of Necessity" [*Early Works*, iv, 19].

origin of the doctrine of indifference is not the need of justifying moral responsibility, but a defective psychological analysis of will, making of it an impossible abstraction.

Mr. Martineau gives the following case (pp. 213–15). You suffer from calumny admitting disproof; to make the exculpation would cast a shadow on some one else, or embitter some precious friendship. The impulse to exculpate self is arrested by another impulse, equally natural. Now in the decision of this conflict Martineau claims that the following factors are involved:

(1) "The two incompatible springs of action; (2) Your own past, *i.e.*, a certain formed system of habits and dispositions brought from your own previous use of life. The former head comprises the *motives* that are offered; the latter the *character* that has come to be. Do these settle the matter between them? . . . Or, is our account of what is there still incomplete, and must we admit that, besides the motives felt, and besides our formed habit or past self, there is also a *present self* that has a part to perform in reference to both? . . . In all cases of self-consciousness and self-action there is necessarily this duplication of the ego into the *objective*, that contains the felt and predicated phenomena at which we look, or may look, and the *subjective*, that apprehends and uses them. It is with the latter that the preferential power and personal causality reside." And further (p. 216):

"I submit that no one can sincerely deem himself incapable by nature of controlling his impulses and modifying his acquired character. That he is able to make them the objects of examination, comparison and estimate, places him in a judicial and authoritative attitude towards them, and would have no meaning if he were not to decide what influence they should have. The casting vote and verdict upon the offered motives is with him, and not with themselves; he is 'free' to say 'yes' or 'no' to any of their suggestions; they are the conditions of the act; he is its agent. . . . You do not let yourself sway to and fro with varying fling of the motives upon your character, like a floating log on an advancing and retreating wave; but address yourself to an active handling of their pretensions. . . . You yourself, as a personal centre of intelligence and causality are at the head of the transaction and determine how it shall go."

The passage has been quoted at length because it clearly reveals the process which leads to the fiction of a distinct, deciding self, a self separate from the material estimated, the impulses competing. That process is an unreal abstraction of motive on one side, and of character on the other. These abstractions being erected into fixed things, some other power has to be brought in to make up for the omitted elements and to bridge the gulf: —Martineau's third factor, or self in which alone selecting power resides. If motive and if character were what Martineau assumes them to be, certainly something else would be required to get a moral action under way.

1. Consider the matter from the side of "motive," and see what an impossible abstraction Mr. Martineau has made. Here is the impulse to clear one's repute; there the impulse not to hurt the friend's reputation or affection. And these set over *against* character, and supposed to be acting upon it or acted on by it! A very moderate amount of reflection will reveal that each impulse is what it is, in intensity,[42] in intellectual significance and in moral weight, *as a function of character*. The desire to clear my standing cannot even occur to me save as I have certain habits and dispositions. Its very existence is the expression of a certain tendency of character; *what* it is, whether a mere dislike to be thought ill of, a love of popularity for its own sake, a recognition of the commercial or professional value of good standing, or the need of having everything that concerns one squared and true—all this is constituted wholly by character; finally, the weight which it has with respect to other "motives," the relative value attached to it, the whole process of estimation, etc., is a process of *internal* development, of revelation of the extent to which character is bound up with, is *present in the motive*. The mere appearance of the "impulse" is the immediate, hasty, possibly superficial moving of character in a given direction; the constitution of its intellectual significance and moral import is the mediated, persistent assertion of self, developing itself in this defined direction. And the completion of the motive *is* the volition, the deed.

2. Equally fictitious is the assumption of the character as fixed, given or presupposed. One would imagine from Mr. Martineau's account that habit means only mechanical routine, formation is equivalent to fossilization and organiza-

<hr>

[42]   Martineau afterwards recognizes this much (*Study of Religion*, p. 229), but without reconstructing his theory of motives at all. They still remain objective, phenomenal, etc., etc.

tion to a static arrest of development. When one reflects that the difference in the *dynamic* efficiency of amœba and man is the difference in habits, in structure, in organization, one sees how much truth is likely to be arrived at from this assumption. Habit is no final, rigid attainment—were it only for the reason that every habit is a dependent function of the whole organism, is a member of a system of habits, and *must* co-ordinate, must stimulate and be stimulated by others—must, in a word, be flexible, continually readjusting itself. The development of volition is a continued exhibition, self-revelation of character, just as the formation of motive is one with passage of self into unified activity or deed. We know what we are and what we can be only through what we do. If character were this solid, inert lump that Martineau conceives it, undoubtedly it could not originate an act which is free and responsible. But in reality the whole process of initiating impulse, considering, deliberating, choosing is a movement of character aiming at adequate discovery and exhibition of self.

3. The necessity of the third factor, the deciding self, is a necessity originated wholly through the failure to recognize the present moving self in "motive" and "character." The defect comes out clearly when we find the problem stated as if it were an alternative between determination of the volition *by* character and motive, or *by* the Self, the free will. It is in reality simply a question of the resolution of a volition into its definite factors. There is no third thing, a volition, determined by motive; the volition *is* the completed motive; and just so it *is* the exhibited character, the fulfilled self. The introduction of self as a third factor (instead of the recognition that the whole process is one of self-movement) marks the break, due to defective psychological analysis, between character and deed. It is the flagrant symbol of the failure to recognize that the deed *is* the concrete agent, the self in functional (that is, definitive and co-ordinated) activity.

The truth of the matter is that Martineau (and so with all the other indeterminists) simply accepts the adequacy of the necessitarian psychology of volition up to a certain point, accepts its dualistic separation of impulse and motive from self, and then, seeing the ethical insufficiency, help themselves out by bringing in the *Deus ex Machina*, a Free Will. This is the reason the contests between indeterminists and determinists (in the causational, not logical sense) are so futile and unending. *Both have the same premises*, the product of inadequate psychological analysis. The only way to "rescue" freedom from the attack of the determinist is not to bring it in as a "third factor," but to reconstruct the theory of motive and character to bring out the functional presence of the self in them, and their consequent flexible, dynamic structure.

The criticism of the indeterminist holds equally, therefore, against the determinist, that is, the predeterminist. He makes the same abstraction of motive, erecting hunger, love of praise, modesty, etc., into little entities which pull and haul on a self outside of them. Or, going into a wider field, he talks of the determination of self *by* heredity and environment. He has the two things, set over against each other, and with only a mechanical connection between them, one of force, just as the indeterminist can get only an arbitrary relation. They both argue then as if it were a question between mechanical causation on one side, and arbitrary interference on the other, forgetting that *both* alternatives arise from the unexamined assumption of the dualism of self and ideal and motive. The whole controversy vanishes in thin air when we substitute for the determination of volition *by* circumstances or *by* Free Will, the determination of Self *in* volition, *in* deed — its passage into definite, unified activity.

The best statement of the determinist position will be found in Bain, *Emotions and Will*, Ch. 11. For indeterminism, see, besides the above reference to Martineau, his *Types of Ethical Theory*, Vol. II, pp. 34–38; Lotze, *Practical Philosophy*; and James, *Unitarian Review*, Vol. XXII, p. 193, "Dilemma of Determinism" (James's refutation of *Pre*determinism is convincing; but I see nothing in his positive argument for indeterminism which does not fall in with the determinateness of action argued for above); Calderwood, *Moral Philosophy*, Part Two, Chs. 3 and 4. Stephen's *Science of Ethics*, pp. 274–93, seems to be in unstable equilibrium between predeterminism and determinateness. Much the same may be said for Gizycki, *Introduction to the Study of Ethics*, Ch. 6. Green, *Prolegomena*, Bk. II, Ch. 1, would be in substantial agreement with the view above

stated were it not for his abstract view of the Self, which compels
him to separate self as ideal (future) from character, making the
latter fixed, or past only, and thus bringing him to the determination
of deed *by* character and circumstance. Alexander, *Moral Order*, pp.
336–41, does not seem to me wholly free from the idea of character
as static, but brings out more clearly than any other writer that
choice, preference *is* freedom, and that it is irrational to try to get
back of choice as both indeterminist and predeterminist attempt to
do. Dr. Ritchie, "Ethical Implications of Determinism," *Philosophical Review*, Vol. II, p. 529, turns the tables neatly against the indeterminist's usual assertion that he alone can "rescue" responsibility.
(Gizycki is strong here also; Hodgson's statement, quoted in Martineau, *Study of Religion*, Vol. II, p. 224, is also excellent). Bradley's
Ethical Studies, Essay I, is a thorough-going statement of the identity of freedom and responsibility, as they are valued by the popular
consciousness, with concrete Selfhood. Muirhead, *Elements of Ethics*,
pp. 50–54; and Mackenzie, *Manual of Ethics*, pp. 140–50, are in ac-
cord with the text, but hardly adequate upon the psychological side.

9

Virtue and the Virtues

XLI. The Twofold Statement of Virtue

It is implied in what has already been said that virtue, the active good will, or unified self, may be stated from either of two standpoints; that of freedom or of responsibility. Virtue may be considered either as a case of substantial freedom, of solid, thoroughly unified action, or as a case of substantial responsibility, of flexible, properly adjusted, interaction—the adequate intellectual recognition of, and adequate emotional interest in, the demands of the situation. We have, here, the emphasis, first upon one side, then upon another, of the idea of co-ordination. Co-ordination implies the attained order, organization—freedom. But as co-ordination, it implies the reciprocal adjustment of the various *sub*ordinate activities involved—responsibility.

It is because the unity of will is a functional, a dynamic unity, because deed is simply self in full activity, that freedom and responsibility are the correlative phases of virtue. Every organic function is maintained through the co-operation, the working together of a number of organs, and the higher the specialization of the function (the definiteness of the deed), the more comprehensive the number and scope of reinforcing organs.

Freedom, again, names virtue from the standpoint of good, of value; responsibility from the standpoint of duty. To be a free and responsible self at every point, and in every act, is at once the sole *law* and the sole *end* of conduct.[43]

This gives the solution of the apparent paradox of virtue. Some writers insist that virtue is not virtue until it is

---

[43] The principle, it may be observed, is formal *in statement*, just because it is so full of *detailed content in actuality*.

wholly free, or one's very nature, until it is spontaneous self-movement from sheer inclination; that every sign of struggle, of effort, of constraint, must be eliminated.[44] Others hold that it is the essence of virtue to express effort, resistance and conquest; it is, in Kant's expressive words, "the moral disposition warring," in Laurie's, "it is mediation through pain" (*Ethica*, p. 145). Now a case can be made out for either of these positions; and this fact would seem to indicate some common ground. This is found, I think, in the fact that both contentions have in view in their conception of virtue the wholeness of the self in the deed, but approach it from different points of view. The first view thinks of the relation of the whole to the part, reinforcing, completing it; the self so present in the deed that there is no resistance, so that we, as Emerson says, "do by knowledge what the stones do by structure." It is the fullness of the mediation that is in mind. The second view thinks of the readjustment of the original, or isolated, tendency, of the part, involved in its membership in the whole. It thinks of the re-construction, the readjustment involved in mediation. It is not because there has been no struggle that we identify virtue with full, easy nature, nor is it merely because of struggle that we identify virtue with conquest. It is, in both cases, because conquest means struggle *brought to an issue*. We know well enough that the man to whom virtue is natural has had his own fights, and we reverence him the more that he has subdued his own enemies, and not inflicted part of the burden upon us, nor distracted our own efforts by continually calling attention to his. We reverence him because he has turned even his struggle into power.

We may assume that the position of maximum ease and æsthetic freedom in the human body is not one of impotence or flabbiness, or even of being asleep; but the maximum exertion of all the muscles, the limit being found in the principle of balance. In looking at such a poise, one might praise it as indicating the power of doing maximum work, another as indicating that it is not work but play. So,

----

[44]   See Aristotle, *Ethics*, Bk. II, Ch. 3, and still more expressly, Emerson, "Spiritual Laws."

after all, there is no inconsistency in the statement that it is not easy to be virtuous, and that yet we are not virtuous till it is easy.

XLII. The Classification of Virtues

Virtue being the wholeness of self, the full and definite manifestation of agent in act (the adequate mediation of impulse), the various virtues will naturally name various phases of this act. The main phases were first hit upon by Plato (*Republic*) and have since been named the "cardinal virtues." These are wisdom (practical judgment), temperance (self-control), courage and justice. After the psychological analysis now completed, the derivation and significance of the virtues should be obvious. Wisdom, as a virtue, is evidently the habit of considering the bearings and relations of a given act; it is the habit of interpreting and appreciating it in terms of the self, of taking it concretely and seriously, instead of abstractly; whether the abstraction be of brute irrationality, or of that sentimentality which sometimes constitutes an over-refined culture and sometimes a crude flippancy. It is, in short, the habit of defining impulse in terms of its objective content, a preparation for giving its due function, of attaching it to its proper use.

The over-subjective ethics of one-sided individualism, fostered by evangelical phases of Protestantism, need a reconstruction upon the basis of Hellenic thought as regards this virtue. The modern "I have to follow my conviction" finds substantiality only in the ancient "wisdom is the guarantee of all virtues." There is and can be no duty of living up to conviction till we have some surety as to the rationality of conviction; no duty of "obeying conscience" till we have taken pains to have an instructed conscience. Moral education requires a shifting of the centre of obligation, locating it less in the mere doing of what seems to be right and more as the habit of searching for what is really right. As mediæval Catholicism, in its consciousness of the superiority of spirit over matter, is accused of confusing dirt with piety, so modern Evangelicalism, in its emphasis upon moral emotion and attitude, is open to the charge of encouraging an ignorant sentimentalism at the expense of a truthfulness which is not simply formal truth-telling, but which insists upon knowing what the truth is.

The tendency to derogate from the ethical claims of knowledge on the ground that knowledge is merely intellectual, is entirely aside from the point. As long as an idea (an aim, purpose, reason) is essentially involved in voluntary conduct, so long responsibility will attach to the formation of the idea, and attention to this need will be a virtue. While the idea itself, in its content, is "merely intellectual," that factor determining *what* this content shall be, is not "intellectual" at all; it is *character*: which may be stated, in emotional terms as the *interest* in the adequate recognition of what one is doing; in volitional terms, as the *habit* of attending to the bearing and value of acts. In short, it is that phase of virtue ordinarily termed conscientiousness. The Socratic identification of wisdom and virtue is much nearer the truth than the modern view which, holding to knowing the good and still doing the evil, substitutes a conventional state of being informed, a second-hand, representative or symbolic set of opinions, for vital intelligence.

So much for the mediate side. But we have also the relation of the mediate and immediate—the tension due to their interaction. Now because this is a process of mediation, not of suppression or substitution, each phase of the process must duly assert itself. If the process be looked at from the side of the necessity of self-assertion of impulse, we have courage. Courage, as a virtue, is the habit of adequate persistence on the part of impulse, in the face of external resistance or obstacles, such as, when transformed into self-experience, give rise to fear.

But mediation involves change of direction, and this involves the adequate assertion of the *mediating* activity. As the present felt pleasure is apt to be connected with the immediate impulse, representing as that does some assured satisfaction of the past, we seem here to have a struggle against pleasure, as, in the case of courage, one against pain. The virtue of adequate assertion of the mediating activity is self-control, temperance, in the Greek sense of whole-mindedness.

The man under self-control does not go off at a tangent, he does not act partially; he has himself in hand, at command, and hence acts as a whole. Unfortunately, the virtue has become associated mainly with the negative aspect of this virtue, with the immorality of false asceticism and false Puritanism. Self-denial has flourished upon the perversion. The rational injunction, deny yourself *this* or *that* satisfaction, has been changed into the impossible and immoral injunction, Deny *Yourself*—without qualification. That is, the need of checking the primary tendency of a desire, the need of transforming it by attaching it to a more functional end has been perverted into a need for suppressing, or, if that is impossible, minimizing, desire itself. The continual assumption has been that appetite itself is evil. In reality, the negative phase of temperance is but the partial development of the positive, arrested in its incompleteness. It is but a step, a means; as an end it is meaningless. The positive phase, clearly embodied in the term "control," is power; efficiency as an agent or instrument. To abstain, to mortify, —this, taken absolutely, is immoral; to attain mastery, to live, undergoing whatever sacrifice and refusal of particulars may be involved in the attainment of full power, is the law of self.[45]

There is need for a return to the Greek standpoint from which many traits now regarded as gifts of fortune, or as happy acquirements, as talents or mere accomplishments, were considered as virtues. The very term "intellectual virtue" sounds strangely to our ears, so given up are we to the habit of considering knowledge as the choice possession of a few. Yet continuity of thought, power of concentration, clear-sightedness, sincerity, all these are but particular forms which the one virtue of conscientiousness assumes, and there can be no concrete conscientiousness save when these specific powers are developed according to the measure of the agent. So persistence, patience, honor, good humor are but

---

[45]   So far as "egoism" and "altruism" is a psychological problem, this principle applies there also. To say that altruism is a *definition* of the ego, indicating its essential outgoing character, is one thing; to suppose that besides the self there is another end is to affirm a psychological impossibility. The sole value of the idea of altruism, in other words, is in forming a demand for a wide and flexible conception of self.

the varied manifestations of courage, while readiness, alertness, flexibility, industry, balance, decorum are as much forms of self-control as are chastity, and moderation in eating and drinking. All the so-called minor morals, or manners, in fact, are but the detailed contents of the great or cardinal virtues, their translation into the daily detail without which conduct is a barren ideality, an iridescent dream. If it be said that concentration of attention, good humor, presence of mind, equable temperament are gifts of nature, the answer is "Yes," as *capacities*, "No," as habits. And precisely the same is to be said of truthfulness, modesty, honesty, charity, or any virtue which has a secured place in the catalogue of the Moral Pantheon. In every case there is a natural impulse in the given direction, which becomes virtue when transformed into a rational habit—that is, into an impulse attached to the realizing of a certain end or idea. Our failure to recognize these traits as true virtues does not mark, as we are apt to flatter ourselves, an advance over the Greeks in distinguishing between the gifts of nature and the attainments of will; it marks rather a falling off in the standards of responsibility, a more abstract idea of will.

The conception that Justice is a term applied to the process in its entirety, designating its organic character, the adequate and completed unification of impulse and reason, may be approached by reflection upon the mutual dependencies existing between wisdom, temperance and courage. Wisdom is impossible without courage; what makes our intentions, our ideals, imperfect is our unwillingness to face the thought of consequences of a given habit or desire; our tendency to shy when the first unpleasant thought comes to view. There is no courage in the world like the courage of holding ourselves fairly and squarely to the import of our own deeds. From this point of view, all vice is letting things drift, waiting to see what will turn up, hoping for a turn of luck, a miraculous intervention which shall come between our deed and its legitimate fruit. (See James, *Psychology*, Vol. II, pp. 563–64, for an excellent statement.) Wisdom is equally dependent upon temperance. To follow the lead of appetite, of passion, is the same thing as not to think. The checked impulse, the arrested habit, *is* reflection commenced. The self-denial of prejudice, of hasty assumption, of one-sided opinion, of cherished tradition is as real and as virtuous as the conquest of any lust of the flesh. The interdependence of courage and temperance stands out on the face of things when we give the latter its positive name, self-control. Self-control is ever passing into self-assertion; the fruit of the spirit into second nature. On the other side, there is no rejection of the solicitations of pleasure, of the allurements of the Siren, that is not equally ability to bear the infliction of pain. All these mutual dependencies are inexplicable, if, making an entity of each virtue, we suppose them to be causal. They are inevitable if courage, temperance and wisdom denote simply phases of every moral act; and the name is given according to the phase which, in a given case, happens to be uppermost.

Justice, then, is the name for the deed in its entirety; it names as a whole what we name in aspects when we use the other virtues. It is not another virtue; it is the system of virtue, the organized doing: whose organic members are wisdom, the will to know; courage, the impulse to reach, control, the acquired power to do.

Justice is the habit of maintaining function, concrete individuality, in its supremacy and of giving every impulse, desire, habit its value according to its factorship in this function. Justice conveys so fully, in the very term, its meaning of regard for the whole, but for the whole maintained by the positive maintenance of its parts as organs, instead of by their suppression, that it is hardly possible to bring out the idea more closely with any number of words.

Aristotle (*Ethics*, Bk. v, Ch. 1), points out a supposed ambiguity of meaning in the term justice; in one sense, it is equivalent to obedience to law, and equals complete virtue; in this sense the just man is the man who fulfills all requirements, the good man. In the other sense, it means fairness, equity; the just man being he who demands simply his share in an apportionment. The first sense is the whole of virtue; the second simply a part, according to Aristotle.

There can be no doubt of these two senses, and yet I think practical sense is wiser in fusing them than Aristotle in separating them. It seems, again, to be a case of considering the organization of self in action, the co-ordination of impulse and habit, from the standpoint first of the co-ordination as such, of the whole, and then of the process of co-ordering the constituent factors. The just man (in the first sense), is after all simply the man who is fair, impartial in meeting demands; he is the man who adequately distributes his attention, giving to each impulse and habit precisely its place, neither more nor less, in the whole function. Because the unity of a good act is a unity of function, that is of content, an organization (not simply a formal unity), it must have the aspect of the adjustment, the fitting in of one part to another. But co-ordination both as effective organization, and as mutual adjustment of parts according to the claims of each (equity), is goodness as a whole; the difference is simply one of emphasis. If justice as obedience to moral law is severed from justice as equity, as due attention to every aspect of one's nature, it becomes external, the law is no one knows what, and obedience is mere conformity. If justice, as due sharing in the distribution of a whole, is severed from justice as law-obeying, it loses all standard; there is no measure by which to tell what the due share of each is.

And this suggests Aristotle's other division of justice into corrective and distributive (*Ethics*, Bk. v, Chs. 3 and 4). The former is sharing in the distribution of an evil (*i.e.*, punishment), and its rule is arithmetical; *i.e.*, make the individual suffer according to his deed—simple *re-quital*, redress. The latter is sharing in the distribution of honor, wealth, etc., positive goods; and its law is not arithmetical equality, but geometrical (that is, proportion, not simply equality of sums). It is fair (equal), that the better citizen should receive more, not the same honor as another; the workman of skill more, not the same return as another. It seems obvious that when we deal with this positive, distributive equity, we have nothing save justice as full virtue. Certainly the man who gives *value* to every impulse and habit according to its *service* in the constitution of his function is precisely the good man, the man of fully mediated impulse, of adequate concrete interests in life.

And this suggests that the current distinction between justice as penal, and justice as concrete recognition of positive merit by the share awarded an agent in the conferring of praise, honor or wealth, is far too rigid. Justice, in this distributive aspect, involves the whole question of merit and blame, and of rendering a man his due. If we ask what *is* his due, we are told his deserts; his merits according to his service. Then into this answer, not so much true as tautological, is unconsciously inserted an assumption of the most momentous character. The question, *what is* a man's due, his desert, his merit; that is, what estimate is to be set upon him remains wholly unanswered; but unconsciously there is smuggled in the assumption that worth is static, that it is to be measured by what the man *has* done; that what the man *has* done is somehow complete in itself, and serves to indicate his merit, and, therefore, the way in which he should be treated. Service is taken as some *thing* rendered, not as function.

Re-tribution, re-quital is, indeed, just; it is the good, and the only good; but, after all, what is retribution? And the assumption that it is an arithmetical measuring out to the individual of pain similar to that which he has inflicted, the restoring of an algebraic equation, is monstrous as an assumption, even if it should turn out to be justified by examination. The whole subject of a *standard* of measurement is ignored, and yet that is the all-determining question.

What is due the self is that it be treated *as* self; what is due a man is that he be regarded in his manhood. Nothing less than this is "fair." But a *given* deed taken as something which *has* been performed is not the self, it is an isolation, an arrest, an abstraction. The deed in its living concrete character is *activity*; it has the whole self implicit in it, and that self is an urgent, on-going power, not a finished performance, or a settled accomplishment. What is due the self is that it be made aware of itself in its deed, be brought to full consciousness of itself through the mediation of the deed. In other words, its due is that its deed in fact and not merely in name be the self manifested, and that there follow the re-action, the re-flection of the "consequences" of the deed back into impulse and habit; that character be transformed and developed through this continual mediation.

Now this reaction may be of a kind to inhibit, and require modification of dominant habits. In that case there is pain, punishment. The return of the deed into the agent's consciousness is painful, negative, *i.e.*, destructive. It tends to disturb, to uproot existing tendencies or directions of action. But this, of course, is but the first phase in re-construction, in the re-adjustment; it is new habit beginning. That is, so far as the pain is normal, and not pathological, it is reform. Stated in the abused antithesis of current language, all punishment is re-tribution, but the only genuine retribution is reform. The conception that the desert of the self is anything other than to be self is as monstrous in its content as it is as an assumption. No man can concretely realize the definition of the self involved in any other idea, without indignation at the degradation, the meanness of character involved in the harboring of such an idea about manhood and life. The worst pessimism is not that which flaunts itself as such, but that which damns human nature at its very heart.

But the very fact that it is necessary to spend so much time upon justice as penal, shows how almost completely, under the influence of one-sided aspects of Christianity, ethical theory has come to be dominated by pathological, rather than by healthy, physiological considerations. The normal case, that to which punishment is incident, is the reaction of the whole into the part, of function into habit, stimulating, reinforcing, expanding – setting free. Justice is thus self-realization.

The contention that the "Platonic" classification of cardinal virtues is incomplete, and needs to be supplemented by the distinctively Christian virtues of faith, humility, aspiration (reverence) and love is due simply to retaining narrow conceptions of wisdom, courage, temperance and justice. Aspiration, hope, if other than sentimental longing, is self-assertion, courage in its pure form; and the same may be said of the relation of temperance to humility, if the latter is other than artificial self-effacement. Faith, as virtue, is but the adequate consciousness of the practical character, the volitional stamp of all knowledge: the staking one's *self* upon the reality of the idea, affirming it absolutely as identical with self, instead of resting content with the easy acknowledgment of it as mere object.

When it was said that the ordinary conception of desert concealed a momentous assumption, it was meant that the whole dualism of justice and love is involved. If justice be conceived as mere return to an individual of the equivalent of what he *has* done; if his deeds, in other words, be separated from his vital, developing self, and, if therefore, the "equivalent return" ignore the profound and persistent presence of self-hood in the deed, then it is true that justice is narrow in its sphere, harsh in form, requiring to be supplemented by another virtue of larger outlook and freer play —Grace. But if justice be the returning to a man of the equivalent of his deed, and if, in truth, the sole thing which equates the deed is self, then quite otherwise. Love is justice brought to self-consciousness; justice with a full, instead of partial, standard of value; justice with a dynamic, instead of static, scale of equivalency.

Psychologically, then, love as justice is not simply the supreme virtue; it is virtue. It is the fulfilling of the law — the law of self. Love is the complete identification of subject and object, of agent and function, and, therefore, is complete in every phase. It is complete interest in, full attention to, the objects, the aims of life, and thus insures responsibility. It provides the channel which gives the fullest outlet to self, which stirs up the powers and keeps them at their fullest tension, and thus guarantees, or *is*, freedom, adequate self-expression. It alone is wisdom, for anything but love fails to penetrate to the reality, the individuality of self, in every act, and thus comes short in its estimate of values. It alone is courage, for, in its complete identification with its object, obstacles exist only as stimuli to renewed action. It alone is temperance, for it alone provides an object of devotion adequate to keep the agent in balance and power. It alone is justice, dealing with every object, aim and circumstance according to its rights as a constituent, a member, an organ of self — the sole ultimate and absolute.

In many respects the discussions of virtue by Plato and Aristotle are still unequaled. The Platonic dialogues are so permeated with the idea of virtue throughout that it is impossible to give specific adequate references. The *Republic*, Bk. IV, 427–34, suggests the main principle. See Aristotle, *Ethics*, Bk. III, Chs. 6–12; Bks. IV, V, VI. Modern ethics has been so occupied with the problem of duty in its metaphysical and practical aspects as to be very defective in its treatment of virtue. For the most part, the question is ignored or else there is given an empirical cataloguing of virtues, with no attempt to discover any principle. Again, the writings which do use a principle of classification generally use that of individual and social virtues, failing to see that no matter how social a virtue may be in its content and object, it must, as a quality of character, or attitude and disposition of will, be capable of a thorough-going psychological statement. Since a certain type of character, since the right activity of will, is confessedly the goal of all practical endeavor, the slighting of this goal in the theoretical treatments, as if it were a mere incident or corollary, is the more fatal. The following references will serve to indicate the various methods of treatment: Sidgwick, *Methods of Ethics*, Bk. III, Chs. 2–5, 9–10; Bk. IV, Ch. 3; Spencer, *Principles of Ethics*, Vol. II, especially, pp. 3–34 and 263–76 (justice is public; beneficence private, and either negative or positive); Stephen, *Science of Ethics*, Ch. 5, courage, temperance, truthfulness—individual, efficiency of the agent; justice and benevolence,—social vitality. In spite of this (to me) false disjunction, Stephen's treatment is exceedingly real and faithful in detail; Alexander, *Moral Order*, pp. 242–53 (denies the value of psychological classification, holding they refer to social institutions—has the advantage of sticking to a single, instead of a cross, principle of classification).

The question of "natural ability" *vs.* "virtue" is suggestively handled by Hume, *Treatise*, Part Two, Bk. III, Sec. 4, and *Enquiry*, Appendix IV. See also Bonar, *Intellectual Virtues*.

The literature upon penal justice or punishment is almost endless. Emerson's essay on "Compensation" has the advantage of being written from the normal instead of the pathological point of view— and is a good substitute for a large quantity of other discussions.

APPENDIXES

1

The Relation of Philosophy to Theology

In the latter part of the last college year Professor Dewey addressed the Ministerial Band on the above subject. It was expected that a stenographic report would be made, but as this has not been done, the readers of the *Bulletin* may find of value the following summary from notes:

In discussing this question I wish you to remember that I take the standpoint of philosophy. The theologians will be able to take care of their end. What is philosophy? The value of philosophy lies in its method, not in what it arrives at. Philosophy as a method means interpretation of experience, or the full life of the race in all times and ages as far as we can get at it. Interpretation involves criticism and reconstruction, mental readjustment. Criticism is testing, investigation, not simple fault-finding. Philosophy is the standpoint of science extended to all life. Inquiry proves that a man has already had something which he believed to be true, and also some doubt or dissatisfaction. When any one has put himself into this attitude of inquiry, he is a scientist. Philosophy is to go beneath the surface and inquire. It does not create anything, but remakes what *seem* to be facts. It remakes the facts *for us*. Any set of facts, in that sense, are never what they were before, after they have been subjected to the tests of philosophy, to scientific or philosophic investigation. But still we may find that our old beliefs were true.

[*First published in the* Monthly Bulletin *of the Students' Christian Association of the University of Michigan*, XVI (*Jan. 1893*), 66–68. *Not previously reprinted.*]

Religion is one phase of all our human experience, and hence is in the region of philosophic investigation. As soon as any fact of life is said to be outside scientific investigation, philosophy is no more and dogmatism has begun. Religion is the subject-matter of philosophy the same as anything else is. Either theology and philosophy have no relation, or theology is philosophy. It is the business of philosophy to go on till it has got to the radical, living unity, which it calls God. From the standpoint of philosophy no two things can do the same work. So far as any one sets out to be a philosopher, and sets aside any portion of life which he says is entirely beyond further interpretation and knowledge, he fails to accomplish his end. He may be much better than a philosopher; I do not wish to argue that question. Philosophy acknowledges nothing outside or above it.

There are two dispositions in interpreting philosophy to common, intelligent men. By the first, philosophy is good, but doesn't go far enough; there is something entirely beyond it. The second patronizes philosophy as far as it strengthens already accepted ideas, but denies *in toto* the philosophic method. In other words, it makes apologetics out of philosophy. If theology has the same method as philosophy, it is philosophy; if it does not have the same method, it has no relation to philosophy whatever.

[After this many questions were asked by persons present, some of which with their answers are given below:]

Q. What is the test of truth?

Not a foot-rule. It is found in this philosophic process itself. The ultimate test of truth is truth itself. The human mind could never doubt the whole body of truth at once, but one thing at a time by which the whole is changed. The test is the unity, the harmonizing principle.

Q. How do we know when it harmonizes?

There is no standard of harmony outside of harmony itself. How can you tell harmony on the piano? But you must not stop with the sense and feeling of harmony,—you must go on.

Q. What does philosophy say in regard to future life?

In so far as future life has nothing to do with experience, philosophy can have nothing to do with it. The man who denies what cannot be proved, goes by faith as much as the one who accepts it.

Q. What about immortality?

In one sense no man ever fully lives while he is alive. He is hemmed in by local bearings. Death is the condition of the removal of local and temporal bearings. After death any man's thought has its full force. This is what Jesus meant in saying that it was better that he should go away. So as the truth for which a man stands becomes more strong and true after death, why should it not also be purer and truer to him? Any consciousness that is not self-consciousness, is not true consciousness. Self-consciousness cannot become, for all becoming is in terms of it.

Q. What is the meaning of the atonement?

Atonement is the coming to consciousness of what has always been there, — man's true relation with God. It is nothing but a change in consciousness. Any man that accepts in good faith and loyalty the conditions which he finds is reconciled to God. "Be ye perfect," points to a willingness to accept the conditions of life. A man's relations to God are his relations to life when he takes his life the most seriously and earnestly possible. As far as we have any evidence, Jesus was the first character in history to bring man to a realization of his unity with God, and do it consciously. And he did it the best any man ever did. The function of the church is to universalize itself, and thus pass out of existence. What Jesus taught and the fourth Gospel and Paul interpreted him to mean was that man *is* saved, not to add another burden to seek out his own salvation.

The next religious prophet who will have a permanent and real influence on men's lives will be the man who succeeds in pointing out the religious meaning of democracy, the ultimate religious value to be found in the normal flow of life itself. It is the question of doing what Jesus did for his time. "The kingdom of God is among you," was a protest against Judaism.

Q. But how are we going to believe the things that are necessary?

There is no reason from an intellectual standpoint why

anyone should be in a hurry to believe anything. If theology is an intellectual system, it can arrive at truth by no shorter road than philosophy. If it is a practical attitude, then it is not what we commonly understand by theology; it may be religion.

Q. What is prayer?

Prayer is the "seek and ye shall find," the inquiry of science. If you put yourself in that attitude, you will get light. It is both subjective and objective. The scientist seeks and finds something,—results. "Pray always," must have meant that the essence of prayer is in a certain attitude.

2

Comments on Cheating

One day in the early part of last month Professor Dewey made a few remarks on cheating to his largest class in the University. He spoke about as follows:—

During the last year the fact was brought to my attention that a great deal of cheating had been going on in my classes. I have known the course of events more or less thoroughly for the past ten years, and I am aware that practice and public sentiment in the matter of cheating has been continually on the down grade in this University. I acknowledge my share of the responsibility for leaving in the faculty code until recently a rule that treated the matter as a light offence. I admit that the members of the faculty are largely to blame for the low tone of public sentiment on the question, even among good students. But the blame lies most largely with the respectable and upright students who connive at the evil by silence or merry-making. With them primarily rests the responsibility for the present condition of public sentiment. I don't know that I shall change the policy I have so far pursued to any great extent. I shall endeavor not to go to sleep in class, but shall not act as a spy. In any large body of persons, like that in this University, there is always a presupposition by the balance of probabilities that some tricksters and shysters will be found. If there are any such in my classes,—I am glad to say that I do not know that there are,—but *if* there are such, any who pursue disreputable methods outside of the class room, I have no objection to their doing the same inside, and I will write them out

[*Reported in the* Monthly Bulletin *of the Students' Christian Association*, xv (*Dec. 1893*), 38.]

their credit to get rid of them. But I do object to decent and respectable students, who are upright in other things, resorting to underhand and dishonest methods in the class room. I wish it understood that any who may come to the class room and cheat, I regard with the utmost contempt, not simply officially, but *personally*.

3

Ethics and Politics

In December Professor Dewey presented [to the Philosophical
Society] a paper entitled "Ethics and Politics."

The paper presented was an attempt to show that ethics
and politics, as sciences, do not differ in the main from each
other as to their intellectual content or subject-matter, but in
the standpoint from which, and the interest with which, this
content is approached—politics being taken not in the narrower
sense of a theory of government, but in the wider (or Aristotelian) sense of the social relations and forms. This result was
reached from an analysis of conduct. Conduct involves two correlative factors: the agent and the sphere (or conditions) of
action. The definition of conduct from the standpoint of the
agent alone, and the consequent identification of morality with
a purely inner state of mind, is relative to a certain stage in the
historical development of conduct, and results in emptying it
of all meaning.

In at least three particulars an intrinsic and organic
constitution of conduct through the scene of action occurs.
(1) The moulding of habits, beliefs, predispositions and dominant ideas through the process of education, conscious and unconscious, makes the individual agent reflect his practical
situation. (2) The demands which the conditions of action
make, the requirements made of the individual in the family,
the neighborhood, the vocation or occupation adopted, etc.,
intrinsically affect conduct. (3) The action of the environment
is required to carry an idea into execution. If we eliminate the
conditions of actions from our definition of conduct, there remains in it nothing but merely internal intention, with no manifestation or expression whatever. Moreover the relations which
the environing forces have to the idea—their acceptance of it,
or their refusal to execute it—react into the idea itself. Existing

[*First published in the* University (*of Michigan*) Record, III
(*Feb. 1894*), *101–2. Not previously reprinted.*]

ideals always are the outcome of a long struggle for existence, *i.e.*, realization. They are in continual modification in order to meet the situation.

There thus exists a two-fold formula for conduct. While conduct involves both agent and scene of action, we may define it from the standpoint of either one or the other; when interested in some individual agent, we bring in the condition of action simply as affecting him; from the standpoint of the permanent and structural conditions of action, we bring in the agent simply as a maintainer and developer of these conditions. The two-fold formula would read about as follows: Conduct (defined with reference to an *agent*) is the process of bringing to a unity of aim or ideal the diverse and otherwise scattered elements of a practical situation or scene of action. Conduct (from the standpoint of the *situation*) is the process of securing organized harmony among the needs and acts of a group of agents.

Working from the former formula, we get psychological ethics or, more briefly, Ethics; from the standpoint of the latter, social ethics or Politics. Both have ultimately the same subject-matter, but the latter carries on its investigations in terms of the institutional relations which harmonize individual agents; the former deals with this material in terms of the psychical processes by which the individual maintains and develops the organized situation of which he is a member. The one important difference, on the side of the subject-matter, is found in the fact that the individual in realizing his environment develops it; politics would thus be a statement of ethical statics, the conditions making up the moral order; ethics would give an account of the functioning of these conditions, dealing with social dynamics and progress.

The remainder of the paper was concerned with a rapid sketch of the historical development of the relations of ethics and politics, from the period of their practical identification (Plato and Aristotle) through the gradual withdrawal of ethics into an inner purely individual region, with the consequent shoving of politics into a morally indifferent or "profane" sphere, up to the present tendency to reunite them by recognizing the necessary social character of all morality, and the moral factors involved in all political organization. This latter tendency, so marked a feature of the present century, was held to be the legitimate outcome of the individualistic period, and not a mere reaction from it. The very emphasis upon the necessity for personal insight and preference, as essential conditions of morality, requires (to save it from practical absurdity) an equal emphasis upon securing such conditions of action as will bring personal insight and choice really and not simply nominally within the power of the individual. It is self-contradictory to say there is no true morality without personal insight and choice, and yet practically endure conditions of social life which shut most men out from the possibility of meeting these requirements. Hence (among other reasons) the growing emphasis upon ethics as a political science, and politics as an ethical science.

Checklist of references

Checklist of references

Titles of works and authors' names in Dewey's references have been corrected and expanded silently and conform to those in the original works. Corresponding corrections necessary in the texts appear in the List of Emendations in the Copy-Texts.

Following each Checklist entry are symbol references to the works in which Dewey mentions or quotes from that entry in the present volume. When Dewey's reference included page numbers, it was possible to identify the edition he used. In other references, among the various editions possibly available to him, the one listed is the most likely source by reason of place or date of publication, or on the evidence from correspondence and other materials and its general accessibility during the period.

Abbott, Evelyn. "The Theology and Ethics of Sophocles," in *Hellenica*, ed. Evelyn Abbott, pp. 33–66. London: Riverton, 1880. (SE)

Abbott, Thomas Kingsmill, trans. *Kant's Critique of Practical Reason and Other Works on the Theory of Ethics*. 3d ed. London: Longmans, Green, Reader, and Dyer, 1883. [Part Four, pp. 325–60, is the first part of *Die Religion innerhalb der Grenzen der blossen Vernunft*, first published separately by Kant in 1792.] (JM, SE)

Adams, George B. *Civilization During the Middle Ages*. New York: Charles Scribner's Sons, 1894. (PF)

Alexander, Samuel. *Moral Order and Progress: An Analysis of Ethical Conceptions*. London: Trübner and Co., 1889. (SE)

——. "Natural Selection in Morals," *International Journal of Ethics*, II (July 1892), 409–39. (SE)

——. "On the Meaning of 'Motive'," *International Journal of Ethics*, IV (Jan. 1894), 233–36. (SE)

Aristotle. *The Nicomachean Ethics of Aristotle*. 2d ed. Trans. F. H. Peters. London: Kegan Paul, Trench and Co., 1884. (SE)

——. *The Politics of Aristotle*. Trans. J. E. C. Welldon. London: Macmillan and Co., 1883. (SE)

Austin, John. *Lectures on Jurisprudence; or, the Philosophy of Positive Law*. 2 vols. London: John Murray, 1869. (AT, JM, SE)

Bain, Alexander. *The Emotions and the Will.* 3d ed. New York: D. Appleton and Co., 1876. [Reprinted, 1888.] (JM, SE)

———. *Moral Science: A Compendium of Ethics.* New York: D. Appleton and Co., 1869. (JM, SE)

———. *The Senses and the Intellect.* 3d ed. New York: D. Appleton and Co., 1874. (SE)

Baldwin, J. Mark. "The Origin of Emotional Expression," *Psychological Review*, I (Nov. 1894), 610–23. (TE)

———. "Utilitarianism," in *Johnson's Universal Cyclopædia*, VIII, 415–16. New York: D. Appleton and Co., 1894. (JI)

Barratt, Alfred. "Ethics and Politics," *Mind*, II (Oct. 1877), 453–76. (SE)

Bentham, Jeremy. *An Introduction to the Principles of Morals and Legislation.* Oxford: Clarendon Press, 1879. (JM)

———. *The Works of Jeremy Bentham.* Ed. John Bowring. 11 vols. Edinburgh: William Tait, 1838–43. (JM, SE)

Birks, Thomas Rawson. *Modern Utilitarianism; or, the Systems of Paley, Bentham, and Mill Examined and Compared.* London: Macmillan and Co., 1874. (SE)

Bonar, James. *Philosophy and Political Economy in Some of Their Historical Relations.* London: Swan Sonnenschein and Co.; New York: Macmillan Co., 1893. (JM, PP)

———. *The Intellectual Virtues.* New York: Macmillan Co., 1894. (SE)

Bosanquet, Bernard. *A History of Æsthetic.* London: Swan Sonnenschein and Co.; New York: Macmillan Co., 1892. (H)

Bowne, Borden Parker. *The Principles of Ethics.* New York: Harper and Bros., 1892. (SE)

Bradley, Francis Herbert. *Appearance and Reality: A Metaphysical Essay.* London: Swan Sonnenschein and Co., 1893. (WS)

———. *Ethical Studies.* London: H. S. King and Co., 1876. (JM, SE)

———. *The Principles of Logic.* London: Kegan Paul, Trench and Co., 1883. (SE)

———. "On Pleasure, Pain, Desire and Volition," *Mind*, XIII (Jan. 1888), 1–36. (SE)

Brown, Thomas. *Lectures on the Philosophy of the Human Mind.* 20th ed. London: William Tegg, 1860. (SE)

Burgess, John William. *Political Science and Comparative Constitutional Law.* 2 vols. Boston: Ginn and Co., 1890–91. (AT)

Butcher, Samuel Henry. *Some Aspects of Greek Genius.* New York: Macmillan Co., 1891. (SE)

Caird, Edward. *The Critical Philosophy of Immanuel Kant.* 2 vols. Glasgow: James Maclehose and Sons, 1889. (JM, SE)

————. *The Social Philosophy and Religion of Comte.* 2d ed. New York: Macmillan Co., 1893. (JM)

————. "Metaphysic," *Encyclopædia Britannica* (9th ed.), XVI, 79–102. [Reprinted in *Essays on Literature and Philosophy*, II, 384–539. Glasgow: James Maclehose and Sons, 1892.] (S)

Calderwood, Henry. *Handbook of Moral Philosophy.* 14th ed. London: Macmillan and Co., 1888. (JI, SE)

Carlyle, Thomas. *Sartor Resartus.* 2d ed. 3 vols. Boston: J. Munroe and Co., 1837. (SE)

Cicero, Marcus Tullius. *Oratio Pro T. Annio Milone*, in *Select Orations of M. Tullius Cicero, with Notes*, by E. A. Johnson, pp. 107–36. New York: D. Appleton and Co., 1873. (JI)

Clarke, Samuel. *A Demonstration of the Being and Attributes of God.* 5th ed. 3 Pts. London: James Knapton, 1725. (JI)

Coit, Stanton. "The Final Aim of Moral Action," *Mind*, XI (July 1886), 324–52. (SE)

Comte, Auguste. *The Positive Philosophy of Auguste Comte.* Trans. Harriet Martineau. New York: W. Gowans, 1868. (SE)

Cooley, Thomas McIntyre. *A Treatise on the Law of Torts, or the Wrongs Which Arise Independent of Contracts.* 2d ed. Chicago: Callaghan and Co., 1888. (AT)

Cowles, Edward. "Insistent and Fixed Ideas," *American Journal of Psychology*, I (Feb. 1888), 222–70. (SE)

Cudworth, Ralph. *A Treatise Concerning Eternal and Immutable Morality.* London: James and John Knapton, 1731. (JI)

Darwin, Charles Robert. *The Descent of Man, and Selection in Relation to Sex.* 2 vols. New York: D. Appleton and Co., 1871. (JM, TE)

————. *The Expression of the Emotions in Man and Animals.* New York: D. Appleton and Co., 1873. (TE)

Davidson, Thomas. *Aristotle and Ancient Educational Ideals.* New York: Charles Scribner's Sons, 1892. (SE)

————. "The Ethics of an Eternal Being," *International Journal of Ethics*, III (Apr. 1893), 336–51. (SE)

Dewey, John. *Outlines of a Critical Theory of Ethics*, in *The Early Works of John Dewey, 1882–1898*, III, 237–388. Carbondale: Southern Illinois University Press, 1969. (S-R, SE)

————. *Psychology, Early Works*, II. (TE, SE)

————. "The Chaos in Moral Training," in *Early Works*, IV, 106–18. (SE)

————. "Green's Theory of the Moral Motive," in *Early Works*, III, 155–73. (S-R, SE)

————. "Intuitionalism," in *Early Works*, IV, 123–31. (JM)

————. "Moral Philosophy," in *Early Works*, IV, 132–51. (JI)

———. "Moral Theory and Practice," in *Early Works*, III, 93–109. (SE)

———. "Self-Realization as the Moral Ideal," in *Early Works*, IV, 42–53. (SE)

———. "The Superstition of Necessity," in *Early Works*, IV, 19–36. (SE)

Emerson, Ralph Waldo. *Essays*. First Series. New and rev. ed. Boston: Houghton, Mifflin and Co., 1883. ["Self-Reliance," pp. 45–87; "Compensation," pp. 91–122; "Spiritual Laws," pp. 125–57; "Art," pp. 327–43.] (H, SE)

Erdmann, J. E. *A History of Philosophy*. Ed. N. S. Hough. 3 vols. New York: Macmillan Co., 1890. (SE)

Essays in Philosophical Criticism. Eds. R. B. Haldane and Andrew Seth. Preface by Edward Caird. London: Longmans, Green, Reader, and Dyer, 1883. (SE)

Ewald, Paul. *Der Einfluss der Stoisch-Ciceronianischen Moral auf die Darstellung der Ethik bei Ambrosius*. Leipzig: Bredt, 1881. (JI)

Fairbanks, Arthur. "The Ethical Teaching of Sophokles," *International Journal of Ethics*, II (Oct. 1891), 77–92. (SE)

Flint, Robert. *History of the Philosophy of History*. New York: Charles Scribner's Sons, 1894. (PF)

Fowler, Thomas, and Wilson, John Matthias. *The Principles of Morals*. 2 vols. Oxford: Clarendon Press, 1886–87. (JM)

Gizycki, Georg von. *An Introduction to the Study of Ethics*. Adapted from the German by Stanton Coit. London: Swan Sonnenschein and Co., 1891. (SE)

———. *A Students' Manual of Ethical Philosophy*. Trans. Stanton Coit. London: Swan Sonnenschein and Co., 1889. (SE)

———. "The Right Final Aim of Life," *International Journal of Ethics*, I (Apr. 1891), 311–30. (SE)

Grant, Sir Alexander. *Two Essays on the Ethics of Aristotle*. Oxford: Privately Printed, 1856. (SE)

Green, Thomas Hill. *Prolegomena to Ethics*. Ed. A. C. Bradley. Oxford: Clarendon Press, 1883. (S-R, JI, JM, SE)

———. *Works of Thomas Hill Green*. 2d ed. 3 vols. Ed. R. L. Nettleship. New York: Longmans, Green, and Co., 1889–90. (AT, JM, SE)

Grote, George. *A History of Greece*. 12 vols. London: J. Murray, 1846–56. (SE)

———. *Plato, and Other Companions of Sokrates*. 3 vols. London: J. Murray, 1865. (SE)

Grote, John. *An Examination of the Utilitarian Philosophy*. Cambridge: Deighton, Bell, and Co., 1870. (SE)

Grotius, Hugo. *Hugonis Grotii de jure et belli pacis libri tres.* Paris: Nicolaus Buon, 1625. (JM)

Gulliver, Julia H. "The Ethical Implications of Determinism," *Philosophical Review*, III (Jan. 1894), 62–67. (E)

Hadley, Arthur T. "Ethics as a Political Science," Part One, *Yale Review*, I (Nov. 1892), 301–15; Part Two, *ibid.*, I (Feb. 1893), 354–67. (SE)

Harrington, James. *The Commonwealth of Oceana.* London: G. Routledge and Sons, 1887. (PP)

Hegel, Georg Wilhelm Friedrich. *Grundlinien der Philosophie des Rechts. Werke*, Vol. VIII. Ed. Eduard Gans. Berlin: Duncker und Humblot, 1833. (JM)

———. *Lectures on the History of Philosophy.* Trans. Elizabeth S. Haldane. Vol. I. London: Kegan Paul, Trench, Trübner and Co., 1892. (SE)

———. *Die Philosophie des Geistes. Werke*, Vol. VII, Bk. 2. Ed. Ludwig Boumann. Berlin: Duncker und Humblot, 1845. (TE)

Herder, Johann Gottfried. *Outlines of a Philosophy of the History of Man.* Trans. T. Churchill. London: J. Johnson, 1800. (SE)

Hibben, John Grier. "The Relation of Ethics to Jurisprudence," *International Journal of Ethics*, IV (Jan. 1894), 133–60. (SE)

Hildenbrand, Karl. *Geschichte und System der Rechts- und Staatsphilosophie.* Leipzig: Engelmann, 1860. (JI)

Hobbes, Thomas. *Leviathan; or, the Matter, Form and Power of a Commonwealth, Ecclesiastical and Civil.* 3d ed. Intro. by Henry Morley. London: G. Routledge and Sons, 1887. (JM)

Hodder, A. L. "Utilitarianism," *International Journal of Ethics*, III (Oct. 1892), 90–112. (SE)

Höffding, Harald. *Ethik.* Leipzig: Reisland, 1888. (JM, SE)

———. *Outlines of Psychology.* Trans. Mary E. Lowndes. London: Macmillan and Co., 1891. (SE)

———. "The Principle of Welfare," *Monist*, I (July 1891), 525–51. (SE)

Holland, Thomas Erskine. *The Elements of Jurisprudence.* Oxford: Clarendon Press, 1880. (AT)

Holmes, Oliver Wendell, Jr. *The Common Law.* Boston: Little, Brown and Co., 1881. (A, SE)

Hudson, Richard. "The Formation of the North German Confederation," *Political Science Quarterly*, VI (Sept. 1891), 424–38. (AT)

Hume, David. *A Treatise of Human Nature.* Ed. L. A. Selby-Bigge. Oxford: Clarendon Press, 1888. (SE)

———. *An Enquiry Concerning the Principles of Morals,* in *Essays: Moral, Political, and Literary,* eds. T. H. Green and T. H.

Grose, ii, 169–287. London: Longmans, Green, and Co., 1889. (SE)

Ihering, Rudolph von. *Der Zweck im Recht.* 2 vols. Leipzig: Breitkopf und Härtel, 1877–83. (JM)

Irons, David. "Prof. James' Theory of Emotion," *Mind,* n.s. iii (Jan. 1894), 77–97. (TE)

James, William. *The Principles of Psychology.* 2 vols. New York: Henry Holt and Co., 1890. (S-R, SE)

———. "The Dilemma of Determinism," *Unitarian Review,* xxii (Sept. 1884), 193–224. (SE)

———. "The Moral Philosopher and the Moral Life," *International Journal of Ethics,* i (Apr. 1891), 330–54. (SE)

———. "The Physical Basis of Emotion," *Psychological Review,* i (Sept. 1894), 516–29. (TE)

———. "Thought Before Language: A Deaf-Mute's Recollections," *Philosophical Review,* i (Nov. 1892), 613–24. (SE)

Jameson, John A. "National Sovereignty," *Political Science Quarterly,* v (June 1890), 193–213. (AT)

Janet, Paul Alexandre René. *Histoire de la philosophie morale et politique.* 2 vols. Paris: Ladrange, 1858. (JM)

———. *The Theory of Morals.* Trans. Mary Chapman. New York: Charles Scribner's Sons, 1883. (SE)

Jodl, Friedrich. *Geschichte der Ethik in der neueren Philosophie.* Stuttgart: J. G. Cotta, 1889. (JM)

Kant, Immanuel. *Kant's Critique of Practical Reason and Other Works on the Theory of Ethics.* Trans. Thomas Kingsmill Abbott. 3d ed. London: Longmans, Green, Reader, and Dyer, 1883. [Part Four, pp. 325–60, is the first part of *Die Religion innerhalb der Grenzen der blossen Vernunft,* first published separately by Kant in 1792.] (JM, SE)

———. *Kritik der praktischen Vernunft. Immanuel Kants sämmtliche Werke,* Vol. v, Part One. Ed. Gustav Hartenstein. Berlin: L. Voss, 1867. (JM)

———. *Kritik der Urtheilskraft. Immanuel Kants sämmtliche Werke,* Vol. v, Part Two. Ed. Gustav Hartenstein. Berlin: L. Voss, 1867. (H)

Kidd, Benjamin. *Social Evolution.* New York: Macmillan Co., 1894. (PF)

Kilpatrick, Thomas Buchanan. "Pessimism and the Religious Consciousness," in *Essays in Philosophical Criticism,* eds. R. B. Haldane and Andrew Seth, pp. 246–77. London: Longmans, Green, Reader, and Dyer, 1883. (SE)

Köstlin, Karl Reinhold. *Geschichte der Ethik.* Tübingen: H. Laupp, 1887. (JM)

Laurie, Simon Somerville [Scotus Novanticus]. *Ethica; or, the Ethics of Reason.* London: Williams and Norgate, 1885. (SE)

Lecky, William Hartpole. *History of European Morals from Augustus to Charlemagne.* 2 vols. London: Longmans, Green, Reader, and Dyer, 1870. (JM, SE)

Lewis, George Cornewall. *Remarks on the Use and Abuse of Some Political Terms.* London: B. Fellowes, 1832. (AT)

Locke, John. *An Essay Concerning Human Understanding.* New rev. ed. [Ed. Thaddeus O'Mahoney]. London: Ward, Lock, and Co., 1881. (SE)

Lotze, Hermann. *Microcosmus: An Essay Concerning Man and His Relations to the World.* Trans. Elizabeth Hamilton and E. E. Constance Jones. 2 vols. Edinburgh: T. and T. Clark, 1885. (SE)

————. *Outlines of Practical Philosophy.* Trans. George T. Ladd. Boston: Ginn and Co., 1885. (SE)

McCosh, James. *The Intuitions of the Human Mind.* New York: Macmillan Co., 1865. (JI)

Mackenzie, John Stuart. *A Manual of Ethics.* 2d ed. London: University Correspondence College Press, 1894. (SE)

————. "Moral Science and the Moral Life," *International Journal of Ethics,* IV (Jan. 1894), 160–73. (SE)

————. "On the Meaning of 'Motive'," *International Journal of Ethics,* IV (Jan. 1894), 231–33. (SE)

————. "The Relation Between Ethics and Economics," *International Journal of Ethics,* III (Apr. 1893), 281–308. (SE)

Mackintosh, Sir James. *Dissertation on the Progress of Ethical Philosophy, Chiefly During the Seventeenth and Eighteenth Centuries.* 4th ed. Edinburgh: Privately Printed, 1872. (JM)

Maine, Sir Henry Sumner. *Ancient Law: Its Connection with the Early History of Society, and Its Relation to Modern Ideas.* Intro. by Theodore W. Dwight. 1st American ed. from 2d London ed. New York: Charles Scribner, 1864. (JI)

————. *Lectures on the Early History of Institutions.* New York: Henry Holt and Co., 1888. (AT)

Martineau, James. *Essays, Reviews, and Addresses.* 4 vols. New York: Longmans, Green, and Co., 1890–91. (SE)

————. *A Study of Religion.* 2d ed. rev. 2 vols. Oxford: Clarendon Press, 1889. (SE)

————. *Types of Ethical Theory.* 2 vols. Oxford: Clarendon Press, 1885. (JM, SE)

Maurice, John Frederick Denison. *Ancient Philosophy: A Treatise of Moral and Metaphysical Philosophy Anterior to the Christian Era.* 4th ed. London: Griffin, Bohn and Co., 1861. (JM)

————. *The Conscience*. London: Macmillan and Co., 1868. (SE)

Mill, James. *Analysis of the Phenomena of the Human Mind*. Ed. with additional notes by John Stuart Mill. 2 vols. London: Longmans, Green, Reader, and Dyer, 1869. (SE)

Mill, John Stuart. *Autobiography*. London: Longmans, Green, Reader, and Dyer, 1873. (SE)

————. *Dissertations and Discussions, Political, Philosophical and Historical*. 4 vols. Boston: W. V. Spencer, 1865–68. [*Utilitarianism* is printed in Vol. III.] (JM, SE)

————. *A System of Logic, Ratiocinative and Inductive*. 8th ed. New York: Harper and Bros., 1874. (SE)

————. *Utilitarianism*. Boston: W. Small, 1887. (JM)

————. *Utilitarianism*. 2d ed. London: Longman, Green, Longman, Roberts, and Green, 1864. (SE)

Mohl, Robert von. *Die Geschichte und Literatur der Staatswissenschaften*. 3 vols. Erlangen: F. Enke, 1855–58. (JM)

More, Henry. *Enchiridion Ethicum*. London: Benj. Tooke, 1690. (JI)

Morris, George Sylvester. *Hegel's Philosophy of the State and of History* (German Philosophical Classics for English Readers and Students, ed. George S. Morris). Chicago: S. C. Griggs and Co., 1887. (JM)

Muirhead, John Henry. *The Elements of Ethics: An Introduction to Moral Philosophy*. New York: Charles Scribner's Sons, 1892. (SE)

————. "On the Meaning of 'Motive'," *International Journal of Ethics*, IV (Jan. 1894), 229–31. (SE)

Mulford, Elisha. *The Republic of God*. Boston: Houghton, Mifflin and Co., 1881. (CD)

Murray, John Clark. *An Introduction to Ethics*. Boston: De Wolfe Fiske and Co., 1891. (SE)

Myers, Frederic William Henry. "Greek Oracles," in *Hellenica*, ed. Evelyn Abbott, pp. 425–92. London: Riverton, 1880. (SE)

Paley, William. *The Principles of Moral and Political Philosophy*. 2 vols. London: Longman, Hurst, Rees, Orme, and Brown, 1814. (SE)

Palmer, George Herbert. "Can Morals Be Taught in Schools?" *Forum*, XIV (Jan. 1893), 673–85. (T)

Patten, Simon N. "Can Economics Furnish an Objective Standard for Morality?" *Journal of Speculative Philosophy*, XXII (Sept. 1892), 322–32. (SE)

Paulsen, Friedrich. *System der Ethik*. 3d ed. 2 vols. Berlin: Besser, 1894. (JM, SE)

Peirce, Charles S. "The Doctrine of Necessity Examined," *Monist*, II (Apr. 1892), 321–37. (S)

Checklist of references

Plato. *The Dialogues of Plato.* Trans. B. Jowett. 4 vols. Boston: Jefferson Press, 1871. [*Protagoras*, I, 97–162; *Apology*, I, 303–39; *The Republic*, II, 1–452; *Laws*, IV, 1–480.] (A, JM, SE)

Porter, Noah. *The Elements of Moral Science, Theoretical and Practical.* New York: Charles Scribner's Sons, 1885. (JI, SE)

Price, Richard. *A Review of the Principal Questions and Difficulties in Morals.* London: A. Millar, 1758. (JI)

Raumer, Friedrich Ludwig Georg von. *Über die geschichtliche Entwickelung der Begriffe von Recht, Staat und Politik.* 3d ed. Leipzig: Brokhaus, 1861. (JM)

Renan, Ernest. *The Future of Science.* Trans. [?]. Boston: Roberts Bros., 1891. (RL)

———. *Lectures on the Influence of the Institutions, Thought and Culture of Rome on Christianity and the Development of the Catholic Church* (The Hibbert Lectures, 1880). London: Williams and Norgate, 1880. (SE)

———. *La réforme intellectuelle et morale.* Paris: Michel-Lévy frères, 1871. (RL)

Rickaby, Joseph John. *Moral Philosophy; or Ethics and Natural Law.* New York: Longmans, Green, Reader, and Dyer, 1888. (SE)

Ritchie, David George. *Darwin and Hegel.* London: Swan Sonnenschein and Co., 1893. (JM)

———. "On the Meaning of 'Motive'," *International Journal of Ethics*, IV (Jan. 1894), 236–38. (SE)

———. "On the Meaning of the Term 'Motive,' and on the Ethical Significance of Motives," *International Journal of Ethics*, IV (Oct. 1893), 89–94. (SE)

Ritchie, Eliza. "The Ethical Implications of Determinism," *Philosophical Review*, II (Sept. 1893), 529–43. (SE)

Rousseau, Jean Jacques. *A Discourse upon the Origin and Foundation of the Inequality Among Mankind.* Trans. [?]. London: R. and J. Dodsley, 1761. (PP)

Royce, Josiah. *The Religious Aspect of Philosophy.* New York: Houghton, Mifflin and Co., 1885. (SE)

———. *The Spirit of Modern Philosophy.* New York: Houghton, Mifflin and Co., 1892. (SE)

———. "The Knowledge of Good and Evil," *International Journal of Ethics*, IV (Oct. 1893), 48–80. (CP)

———. "On Certain Psychological Aspects of Moral Training," *International Journal of Ethics*, III (July 1893), 413–36. (CP)

Schleiermacher, Friedrich. *Grundlinien einer Kritik der bisherigen Sittenlehre.* 2d ed. Berlin: G. Reimer, 1834. (JM)

Schmidt, Wilhelm. *Das Gewissen.* Leipzig: Hinrichs Verlag, 1889. (SE)

Schurman, Jacob Gould. *The Ethical Import of Darwinism.* New York: Charles Scribner's Sons, 1887. (JM)

——. *Kantian Ethics and the Ethics of Evolution.* London: Williams and Norgate, 1881. (JM)

Scott, Fred Newton. *Æsthetics: Its Problems and Literature.* Ann Arbor: Inland Press, 1890. (F)

——. *The Principles of Style.* Ann Arbor: Register Publishing Co., 1890. (F)

——. "Boccaccio's 'De Genealogia Deorum' and Sidney's 'Apologie'," *Modern Language Notes,* vi (Apr. 1891), 97–101. (F)

——, and Denny, Joseph V. *Paragraph-Writing.* Ann Arbor: Register Publishing Co., 1891. (F)

——, and Gayley, Charles Mills. *A Guide to the Literature of Æsthetics.* Berkeley: [State Printing Office, Sacramento], 1890. (F)

——, Gayley, Charles Mills, and Stanley, A. A. *Songs of the Yellow and Blue.* Ann Arbor: Sheehan and Co., 1889. (F)

Sharp, Frank Chapman. *The Æsthetic Element in Morality and Its Place in a Utilitarian Theory of Morals.* New York: Macmillan Co., 1893. (SE)

Sidgwick, Henry. *The Methods of Ethics.* London: Macmillan and Co., 1874; 2d ed., 1877; 3d ed., 1884; 4th ed., 1890. (JI, JM, SE)

——. *Outlines of the History of Ethics, for English Readers.* London: Macmillan and Co., 1886; 3d ed., 1892. (JM, SE)

——. "Hedonism and Ultimate Good," *Mind,* ii (Jan. 1877), 27–38. (SE)

——. "Pleasure and Desire," *Contemporary Review,* xix (Apr. 1872), 662–72. (SE)

Simmel, Georg. "Moral Deficiencies as Determining Intellectual Functions," *International Journal of Ethics,* iii (July 1893), 490–507. (CP)

Sorley, William Richie. *On the Ethics of Naturalism.* London: William Blackwood and Sons, 1885. (JM)

Spencer, Herbert. *The Data of Ethics.* New York: D. Appleton and Co., 1882. (JM, SE)

——. *The Principles of Biology.* 2 vols. London: Williams and Norgate, 1864–67. (SE)

——. *The Principles of Ethics.* 2 vols. New York: D. Appleton and Co., 1892–93. (JM, SE)

——. *The Principles of Psychology.* 2d ed. 2 vols. New York: D. Appleton and Co., 1870–72. (SE)

Spinoza, Benedictus de. *Ethics*. Trans. William Hale White. New York: Macmillan Co., 1883. (SE)

Stahl, Friedrich Julius. *Geschichte der Rechtsphilosophie. Die Philosophie des Rechts*, Vol. I. 5th ed. Tübingen: J. C. B. Mohr, 1878. (JI, JM)

Steinthal, Heymann. *Allgemeine Ethik*. Berlin: G. Reimer, 1885. (JM)

Stephen, Leslie. *History of English Thought in the Eighteenth Century*. 2 vols. London: Smith, Elder and Co., 1876. (JM)

———. *The Science of Ethics*. London: Smith, Elder and Co., 1882. (JM, SE)

Sterrett, James MacBride. *The Ethics of Hegel*. Boston: Ginn and Co., 1893. (JM)

Stevenson, Robert Louis, and Osbourne, Lloyd. *The Wrecker*. New York: Charles Scribner's Sons, 1892. (SE)

Sully, James. *The Human Mind: A Text-Book of Psychology*. 2 vols. London: Longmans, Green, and Co., 1892. (SE)

———. *Outlines of Psychology, with Special Reference to the Theory of Education*. London: Longmans, Green, Reader, and Dyer, 1884. (SE)

Télfy, Iván. *Corpus juris Attici*. Greek and Latin. Leipzig: G. Laufferi, 1868. (A)

Thompson, Daniel Greenleaf. *A System of Psychology*. 2 vols. London: Longmans, Green, Reader, and Dyer, 1884. (SE)

Tracy, Frederick. *The Psychology of Childhood*. Boston: D. C. Heath and Co., 1893. (P)

———. "The Language of Childhood," *American Journal of Psychology*, VI (Oct. 1893), 107–38. (P)

Ueberweg, Friedrich. *A History of Philosophy from Thales to the Present Time*. Trans. George S. Morris. 2 vols. New York: Charles Scribner, 1871–73. (SE)

Venn, John. *The Principles of Empirical or Deductive Logic*. New York: Macmillan Co., 1889. (S)

Voigt, Moritz. *Die Lehre vom jus naturale, aequum et bonum und jus gentium der Römer*. Leipzig: Voigt und Günther, 1856. (JI)

Wallace, William. "Ethics and Sociology," *Mind*, VIII (Apr. 1883), 222–50. (SE)

Ward, Lester F. *The Psychic Factors of Civilization*. Boston: Ginn and Co., 1893. (PF, SE)

Watson, John. "Hedonism and Utilitarianism," *Journal of Speculative Philosophy*, X (July 1876), 271–90. (SE)

Whewell, William. *Lectures on the History of Moral Philosophy in England*. Cambridge: Deighton, Bell, and Co., 1862. (JM)

Williams, Cora May. *A Review of the Systems of Ethics Founded on the Theory of Evolution.* New York: Macmillan Co., 1893. (JM)

Wilson, John Matthias, and Fowler, Thomas. *The Principles of Morals.* 2 vols. Oxford: Clarendon Press, 1886–87. (JM)

Windelband, Wilhelm. *A History of Philosophy.* Trans. James H. Tufts. New York: Macmillan Co., 1893. (SE)

Wundt, Wilhelm Max. *Ethik: Eine Untersuchung der Thatsachen und Gesetze des sittlichen Lebens.* 2d ed. Stuttgart: F. Enke, 1892. (JM)

Xenophon. *Xenophon's Memorabilia of Socrates.* Notes and Intro. by R. D. C. Robbins. New York: D. Appleton and Co., 1868. (SE)

Ziegler, Theobald. *Geschichte der Ethik.* Vols. I–II. Strasbourg: Trübner, 1881–86. (JM)